AMY BIEHL'S LAST HOME

AMY BIEHL'S LAST HOME

A Bright Life, a Tragic Death, and a Journey
of Reconciliation in South Africa

Steven D. Gish

OHIO UNIVERSITY PRESS / ATHENS

Ohio University Press, Athens, Ohio 45701
ohioswallow.com
© 2018 by Ohio University Press
All rights reserved

Printed in the United States of America
The books in the Ohio University Research in International Studies Series
are printed on acid-free paper ⊗ ™

28 27 26 25 24 23 22 21 20 19 18   5 4 3 2 1

Library of Congress Cataloging in Publication Control Number: 2018015586

To the Cawdrys—

Dave, Anne, Clive, Gary, and Andrew—

for their warm welcome so many years ago

Instead of hatred and revenge we chose reconciliation and nation-building.

—Nelson Mandela speaking at Nobel Square,
Cape Town, South Africa, December 14, 2003

Saw a number of postings about 'true reconciliation.' Just for the record, there is no such thing as 'true reconciliation.' Reconciliation is always difficult, messy and unpredictable. Sometimes it works, and then it is a gift to humanity and to those involved. It is not a legal or political process; it is, in all its frailty, a very human process.

—Jonathan Jansen (rector of the University of the
Free State), Facebook post, December 16, 2015

Contents

Illustrations

Abbreviations

ABC	American Broadcasting Company
ABFT	Amy Biehl Foundation Trust
AIDS	Acquired Immune Deficiency Syndrome
ANC	African National Congress
AP	Associated Press
APLA	Azanian Peoples' Liberation Army
AWB	Afrikaner Resistance Movement (Afrikaner Weerstandsbeweging)
AZAPO	Azanian Peoples' Organization
BFP	Biehl family papers
CA	California
CBS	Columbia Broadcasting System
CDS	Centre for Development Studies
CEO	Chief Executive Officer
CIA	Central Intelligence Agency
CNN	Cable News Network
CODESA	Convention for a Democratic South Africa
COSAG	Concerned South Africans Group
COSAS	Congress of South African Students
COSATU	Congress of South African Trade Unions
CSU	California State University

c.v.	curriculum vitae
D.C.	District of Columbia
DNC	Democratic National Committee
GDP	Gross Domestic Product
GPA	Grade point average
IDASA	Institute for a Democratic Alternative for South Africa
KS	Kansas
LA Times	*Los Angeles Times*
LAX	Los Angeles International Airport
M.A.	Master of Arts
MA	Massachusetts
MBA	Master of Business Administration
MESAB	Medical Education for South African Blacks
MP	Member of Parliament
NAACP	National Association for the Advancement of Colored People
NADEL	National Association of Democratic Lawyers
NASA	National Aeronautics and Space Administration
NBC	National Broadcasting Company
NCAA	National Collegiate Athletic Association
NDI	National Democratic Institute for International Affairs
NGO	Non-governmental organization
NPR	National Public Radio
NY	Native Yard
NY	New York
NYT	*New York Times*
OCR	*Orange County Register*
PAC	Pan Africanist Congress

PASO	Pan Africanist Students' Organization
PhD	Doctor of Philosophy
Rev.	Reverend
SABC	South African Broadcasting Corporation
SADF	South African Defence Force
SADTU	South African Democratic Teachers' Union
SAIRR	South African Institute of Race Relations
SAP	South African Police
SWAPO	South West Africa People's Organization
TRC	Truth and Reconciliation Commission
UCLA	University of California at Los Angeles
UCT	University of Cape Town
UDF	United Democratic Front
UK	United Kingdom
UN	United Nations
UNESCO	United Nations Educational, Scientific and Cultural Organization
US	United States
USAID	United States Agency for International Development
USIS	United States Information Service
USSR	Union of Soviet Socialist Republics
UWC	University of the Western Cape
WNC	Women's National Coalition
YMCA	Young Men's Christian Association

1   Southern Africa in the early 1990s. (Map by Brian Edward Balsley, GISP)

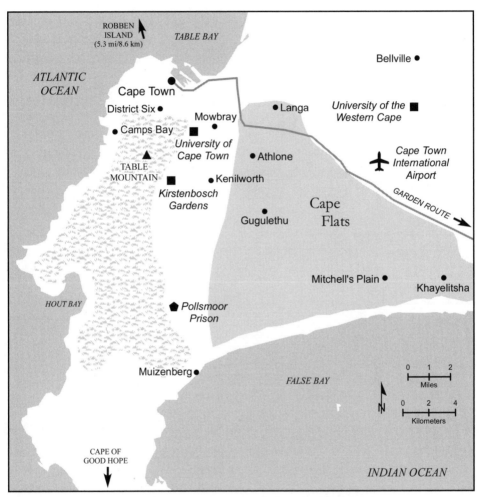

2   Cape Town and its environs. (Map by Brian Edward Balsley, GISP)

Introduction

OF THE approximately 18,000 people killed in South Africa's political violence during the last decade of apartheid (1984–94), a handful of victims received disproportionate publicity. One was Amy Biehl, a 26-year-old American Fulbright scholar based in Cape Town in 1992–93 who was studying the role of women in South Africa's transition to democracy. Biehl's commitment to democracy and women's rights was widely hailed by South Africans of all races who worked with her during her 10-month stay in South Africa. On August 25, 1993, two days before her scheduled return to the United States, Biehl was attacked and killed by a group of militant black youths chanting antiwhite slogans as she was giving some black friends a ride home. She was the only American killed in the political violence that accompanied apartheid's demise.

Biehl's death made headlines all over the world. So did the magnanimity of her parents, who established a foundation in Amy's name to conduct humanitarian work in Cape Town's black townships. Not only did Peter and Linda Biehl accept amnesty for their daughter's killers, but they eventually reconciled with two of the young men and hired them to work for the Amy Biehl Foundation. Today there is a monument in Gugulethu marking the spot where their daughter Amy was killed. Years before this monument was unveiled, Gugulethu residents put up a simple banner memorializing the fallen American with the words "Amy Biehl's Last Home."

Few Americans—apart from political leaders and entertainers—penetrated South Africans' consciousness as much as the Biehls did in the 1990s. Amy captured people's attention because of the supreme irony of her death. She had worked closely with black South Africans and supported the transition to majority rule, but she was killed by a group of young blacks who regarded her as a "settler" because of her white skin. After her death, Amy was widely regarded as one of the many foot soldiers in South Africa's struggle for democracy and human rights. In the years that followed, her parents became icons of forgiveness and reconciliation.

Amy Biehl and her parents personified South Africa's hopes and fears during the transition from apartheid to democracy. Amy's death sparked an unprecedented wave of national soul-searching about whether racial hatred in South Africa had escalated beyond the point of no return, just as the country was advancing toward democracy. Her parents' generosity of spirit symbolized South Africa's greatest hopes as democracy dawned—that South Africans of all races could emerge from apartheid, forgive each other, and move forward toward a better future. The reality, of course, was never this simple.

In August 1993, I was a graduate student at Stanford, Amy's alma mater, writing my dissertation on South African history. Two days after Amy was killed, I saw her photo in the *San Jose Mercury News* and recognized her. I had been in a class with Amy six years earlier. It was a course on African politics open to both graduate students and undergraduates. Amy had been a junior majoring in international relations; I was working toward my doctorate in African history. I hadn't known Amy personally, but I remembered her. I had been following South Africa's political struggles for years, sharing the world's joy at Nelson Mandela's release from prison and despairing as the country's political violence escalated. Amy's death felt like a punch in the gut. At a visceral level, I identified with her. I too was a young white American student at Stanford interested in South Africa, supportive of the antiapartheid struggle and an admirer of Mandela. I had been to South Africa for extended periods and had witnessed protest marches and visited black townships. But now South Africa's violence seemed personal. I followed news about Amy and her parents for years. The publicity surrounding the family came in waves and covered Amy's death, her family's visit to South Africa two months later, the trials of her killers, the Truth and Reconciliation Commission's amnesty hearings, the establishment of the Amy Biehl Foundation, and Linda and Peter Biehl's relationship with two of the young men convicted of Amy's murder. While following news about the Biehls, I pursued my research interests in the antiapartheid movement and focused on the historical contributions of two black South African leaders—Dr. Alfred B. Xuma, the president of the African National Congress in the 1940s, and the Nobel Peace Prize laureate Archbishop Desmond Tutu. As I did so, I came to believe that Amy Biehl's story should also be woven into the narrative of South Africa's freedom struggle.

This book looks at how Amy Biehl and her family became part of South African history. Part I focuses on Amy's life and death. The rough outline of her story is well known, but her activities in South Africa are not. The simplified narrative—that Amy was an exchange student working on voter education in South Africa when she was killed—was not technically correct. Her previous work in Africa was unknown to most journalists, as were the range of her activities and contacts in South Africa in 1992–93. Amy witnessed South Africa's transition to democracy up close, especially women's efforts to participate in this transition and enshrine their rights in new ways. Amy sometimes found it difficult to balance her role as a scholar and an activist, but as she attempted to do so, she experienced parts of South African life that were usually unknown to outsiders. Documenting her range of contacts in antiapartheid groups and women's organizations also helps explain the extraordinary outcry over her death. Appalled and embarrassed by her murder, many in South Africa's liberation movement eulogized her as "a comrade" and "a sister."

Amy often criticized the South African press for focusing on the relatively few white victims of political violence when the majority of victims were black. Ironically, her death received enormous international publicity. It provoked wide-ranging discussions about South Africa's past, present, and future. It also highlighted many of South Africa's fault lines, especially those of race, politics, generation, and gender. In the United States, some compared Amy with American civil rights icons who had sacrificed their lives for racial justice. Others feared that the undue focus on her death would obscure the sacrifices made by many more black South Africans.

Part II focuses on Amy's parents—their establishment of the Amy Biehl Foundation, their participation in South Africa's Truth Commission, and their eventual reconciliation with some of the young men involved in Amy's death. Peter and Linda Biehl's forgiveness and their establishment of the Amy Biehl Foundation were among South Africa's most heralded stories of reconciliation. To many observers, the couple personified the values promoted by Nelson Mandela and Archbishop Tutu as they tried to unite a long-divided nation. The Biehls seemed to symbolize the triumph of the human spirit after the tragedy of apartheid, which was part of the narrative of the "rainbow nation" that Mandela, Tutu, and others were trying to construct. Despite the accolades and attention, the Biehls faced constant challenges and controversies. Just as Amy's murder had caused South Africans to reflect on the state of their nation, the amnesty hearings for Amy's killers sparked a national conversation about the Truth and Reconciliation Commission. Was the commission helping or harming the country's future prospects? What was the difference between "retributive" justice and "restorative" justice, and which was preferable? While praised by many observers, the Biehls' statements and actions generated heated debate. Some South Africans were uncomfortable or even offended by their attitude toward amnesty. While Peter and Linda embraced the amnesty process, many South Africans rejected it. Some black and white South Africans opposed amnesty in the Biehl case in particular, believing that Amy's murder was an inexcusable hate crime. The enormous controversy that erupted after the convicted men received amnesty reflected the wider controversies surrounding the Truth and Reconciliation Commission and showed that South Africa's wounds were still raw.

Just as in Amy's case, the narrative surrounding the Biehls has been simplified over the years. Initially, Peter and Linda never dreamed of befriending Amy's killers. They did not even support amnesty at first. Their reconciliation was a journey, not an immediate reaction, a fact that often got lost in the blizzard of media coverage. When the Biehls eventually hired two of the amnestied men to work at the Amy Biehl Foundation, it challenged both Americans and South Africans to envision forgiveness in new ways. Some disapproved of the Biehls' relationship with the two men, finding it inexplicable and even perverse. But despite the controversies, the Biehls' legacy as international role models of forgiveness and reconciliation would inspire others for decades to come.

In the years since her death, Amy Biehl has been memorialized in numerous ways—by the monument in Gugulethu, in a novel and play by Sindiwe Magona (*Mother to Mother*), in a documentary film on the Truth and Reconciliation Commission (*Long Night's Journey into Day*), and through the continuing work of the Amy Biehl Foundation. In 2016, production began for a dramatic film about Amy, her parents, and the Truth and Reconciliation Commission. In the minds of many South Africans and Americans, the Biehls' story lives on. This book seeks to explain why.

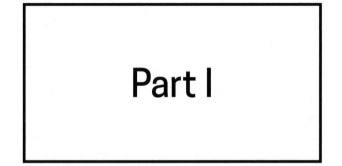

Part I

Part 1

1

Complete Determination

"YOU WANT to raise your children so you can enjoy them as adults," the child psychology professor told the class. Linda Shewalter had been listening intently. She and her boyfriend Peter Biehl intended to marry and start a family together as soon as they could. Born in 1943, both Linda and Peter had grown up in Geneva, Illinois, a small town about an hour west of Chicago. They met each other at the local Congregational Church and became high-school sweethearts. Peter, the son of a prominent businessman, played football in high school, and Linda did some modeling. The two remained close even after Peter's parents sent him to Choate, the famous New England prep school. Later Peter entered Whittier College in California; Linda enrolled at Stephens College in Missouri and then Lake Forest College in Illinois. After the two were married in 1964, Linda transferred to Whittier so that she and Peter could be together. Peter's two passions in college were acting and playing football, while Linda's was art history. Both graduated from Whittier with BAs in history in 1965. Then they moved back to the Midwest, this time to Chicago, where Peter began working for his father at Fry Consultants, Inc. Peter's 32-year career in consulting and corporate management was about to take off.

Children arrived in short order. Kim was the first, born in Chicago in late 1965. The next spring, Peter transferred to Fry's Los Angeles office, and so he, Linda, and the baby moved to Santa Monica, where two more daughters were born in the next few years. Amy Elizabeth Biehl was born at Saint John's Hospital in Santa Monica on April 26, 1967; Molly came along in 1970. Peter's job required frequent travel. Linda was equally busy raising the children, though she did find time to volunteer in a local art museum. In the child psychology lingo of the day, the Biehls' parenting style was neither authoritarian nor permissive. Linda consciously tried to raise the girls with a balance of openness, responsibility, and respect. "The children were curious, verbal, and responsive," Linda recalled. "I had fun with them. We loved taking them out to help them see the world. We expected them to behave and they did."

Linda remembers Amy as "extra-challenging—highly motivated almost from birth. Even in the womb, Amy kicked and rolled constantly." So began a high-energy life. When she was barely able to walk, Amy would climb to the top of the high slide at the beach. When she was one and a half, she fell climbing out of her crib and broke her collarbone. When older sister Kim was learning to read at age four, Amy taught herself to read at age three. When the family moved to Palo Alto for a year in 1970, Amy went to preschool on the campus of Stanford University and played with the professors' children. Three-year-old Amy made up her mind that when it was time to go to college, she would attend Stanford. She was her parents' most demanding child. "Amy was very much a tomboy—challenging and active. She had a competitive spirit," Linda recalled. At age four, Amy met the Lone Ranger during an event at a California restaurant. She then became obsessed with cowboys and insisted on going to preschool dressed as the Lone Ranger for four months straight, with a mask as part of the ensemble. It became "a battle of wills" between Amy and her mother. Exasperated, Linda finally made a deal with Amy— she could dress as a cowboy on most days as long she wore a dress (and no mask) on Wednesdays. Amy agreed. As Kim put it, "Amy was completely determined to do what she wanted to do. Complete determination, from the youngest age."

In 1971, the family moved again, this time to Tucson, Arizona. Peter eventually became president and CEO of AAC Corporation, an electronics manufacturer. He also became active in Arizona's Republican Party. He became the party's state financial chairman and chaired the "Trunk 'n Tusk Club," the party's organization in Tucson. In this capacity he met George H. W. Bush and Barry Goldwater, and he and Linda hosted cocktail parties for Gerald Ford and Bob Dole. The Biehls were moderate Republicans and considered themselves "middle of the road" po- litically. They believed in civic engagement. Besides being a board member of the Arizona Chamber of Commerce, Peter was also on the board of the Tucson branches of the NAACP and the Urban League. The family attended the Casas Adobes (Congregational) Church in Tucson, where the girls participated in Sun- day school and performed in the bell choir. Although not unduly religious, Peter and Linda were people of faith who believed in an ethical life. Linda led the life of a busy housewife, helping with a Brownie troop, carpooling the girls and their friends to their swimming and ballet lessons, and volunteering at church, the Tucson Museum of Art, and the Junior League. She became even busier when their son, Zach, was born in 1977.

Although all of the Biehl children were active, Amy embodied "human energy in its purest form," her uncle Dale Shewalter observed. Her parents couldn't simply tell her to go out and play; she demanded much more than that. Years later, Amy even admitted that during her childhood, she was "hell on wheels." Athletics became an outlet for some of Amy's excess energy. She and her sisters began swimming, gymnastics, and ballet in elementary school, and Amy began to accumulate a roomful of first- and second-place ribbons and trophies for her abilities. When Kim and Amy swam together in Tucson, they had to switch teams after Amy had an argument with the coach. "Amy always kind of ran the family," Kim later admitted with a smile. Unlike her sisters, Amy insisted that her parents get her the best coaches, buy her the best sports clothing and equipment, and take her to the clubs with the best facilities. She was determined to excel in more than just sports. In fifth grade Amy started playing the flute seriously and would always be among the best in her school; she also received recognition for her skills in ballet. And she had not forgotten her dream of attending Stanford. She worked hard academically, earned all As during elementary school, and was often chosen as class president. But she had higher aspirations. In a speech contest in sixth grade, Amy announced her intention of becoming the first female president of the United States.

In 1979, when Amy was 12, the Biehls moved to Santa Fe, New Mexico. There Peter and Linda opened the Los Llanos Gallery of Contemporary Art, which showcased works by Native American artists. While Linda ran the gallery, Peter worked with several different industries as an independent consultant. The family attended the First Presbyterian Church in Santa Fe, where they made many close friends.

Amy loved the natural beauty of Santa Fe, with its unique adobe houses, surrounding mountains, and deep blue skies. Adjusting to a new school proved to be difficult, however. The majority of students were Hispanic, and white students—sometimes labeled "Anglos"—felt greatly outnumbered. Amy was determined to win the acceptance of her Hispanic classmates, but such acceptance was not automatic. As challenging as the school environment was for Amy initially, it prompted her to think about issues of race and ethnicity that would so interest her in the future.

In the fall of her junior year, Amy wrote something in her journal that her mother later found significant. Amy commented that in class discussions, some of her fellow students paid lip service to helping the less fortunate but had no real intention of doing so. Amy was troubled by what she perceived as a lack of sincerity. There was nothing wrong with making such virtuous statements, Amy wrote, but only if people really meant what they said. She admitted that while helping others made her feel good, it wasn't always her first priority. To 16-year-old Amy, honesty was more important than false idealism. "There is nothing wrong with having such wonderful intentions," she wrote, "but our class needs to have a little more honesty—I think. From now on I'm going to do my best to be myself. I want to let other people know who I really am, a normal kid, not some phony overly mature adult."

Amy's drive to be the best was on full display in high school. She originally planned to become a doctor, and so she took the most challenging courses the school offered—chemistry, trigonometry, calculus, French, advanced English—and would accept nothing less than As. Her younger brother Zach remembers Amy as "driven, demanding, and difficult. She was determined. She would freak out if she got a B on a test." Often Amy wouldn't start her homework until nine in the evening because of all the extracurricular activities she was involved in. But she would stay up all night if it meant getting an A for a chemistry test. Her work ethic paid dividends. She earned all As in high school and was inducted into the national honor society of secondary students when she was 16. As Linda saw it, Amy earned the stellar GPA not because she was the smartest, but because she worked the hardest.

Amy played flute in the high school concert band, but when it came to marching band, she opted for a different role. She became the drum majorette for the Santa Fe High School Demons marching band in the fall of 1982, her sophomore year. "It is far more fun than being a lowly flute player following some line of people during performance," Amy wrote in her journal. "As drum majorette I am in command. I get to do a couple of special things, and I really get to perform!" Clearly Amy enjoyed being in the spotlight and preferred to lead, not follow. She was still intent on being an outstanding flute player, but she could not always hold onto first chair. Lamenting the fact that she didn't have enough time to practice, Amy wrote, "My problem is that I want to be the best at everything, but I do too many things!"

Amy craved challenges and liked to push herself to do what others couldn't. When she was fourteen or fifteen, she wrote about the high she felt when she transcended her "pain barrier."

> During a particularly hard swim practice the other day, I broke my pain barrier. It is an incredible feeling, one that is very difficult to explain . . .

In order to reach my pain barrier, I have to swim so long and so hard that it feels like I am trying to pull a brick wall behind me. Each time I bring an arm out of the water it feels like lead and each breath I take is a monumental strain on my lungs. I have to keep pushing myself far past the point when I feel like I have reached my limit to where my body starts trembling and I feel nauseous. . . . And then just when I think I am going to drown, a sudden burst of energy works its way from my heart to the tips of my fingers and toes. My lungs loosen up as though I have released a tremendous burden, and my arms feel feather-light. My stroke quickens and I develop a comfortable rhythm that continues until the end of the set.

So many people won't even try to reach such a point, but I try as often as I can to do so. Ever since I experienced that first broken barrier, I've had to reach it again and again. I can't get enough.

Being so competitive did have a downside. Amy put so much pressure on herself to succeed in academics and sports that she began to have migraine headaches. Some parents quietly dubbed her "Saint Amy" because she was such a high achiever. But younger sister Molly was full of admiration. "Amy was my beacon," she said. "I wanted to be like her. She motivated me. I didn't have the natural drive she had. She pushed me, she pushed everybody."

But Amy was far from being a joyless, single-minded high achiever. She had more admirers than detractors among her peers. She had a busy social life, making friends with her swim teammates and some of the Hispanic girls who had first hassled her. She loved to party and go out dancing with her friends. One of her classmates described Amy as "consistently the happiest, most positive, most enthusiastic person in the room." He admired her not just because she was so talented in music, sports, and academics, but because she earned the friendship of so many of her fellow students. As her brother Zach observed, "Whatever she did, she did to the nth degree"—including having a good time.

Kim was the first in the family to become interested in Africa. While in high school, she read *The Struggle Is My Life,* a collection of Nelson Mandela's speeches and writings, and began listening to African music. She shared the book with Amy, who hadn't known anything about apartheid in South Africa before. Around the same time, Amy heard the song "Free Nelson Mandela" on the radio, and Mandela became one of her heroes. As the girls got older, they identified with the Democratic Party rather than the Republican Party of their parents, with Kim leading the way. These developments didn't concern Peter or Linda, however. On the contrary, they welcomed their children's political awakening. They had always encouraged their kids to be interested in other cultures and peoples. In Linda's words, "When you raise your kids, you raise them to be free."

Amy's real passion in high school was diving. Her swim team needed a diver, and she volunteered, despite—or perhaps because of—her fear of heights. As she wrote in her journal, "I love diving because it is an individual sport that requires the ultimate control and timing. It also contains that element of danger which makes it such a thrill. A diver's highest goal is to achieve perfection, not just beat everyone else, and I really like that. It is graceful, but exciting—so controlled and yet on the brink of disaster." Amy would sometimes tremble with fear when climbing the platform to dive, but she felt exhilarated when she would make her dive. "There is a high in meeting a challenge and succeeding," her mother Linda said, describing Amy's mindset. Amy trained at the University of New Mexico in Albuquerque, both because it had better facilities than Santa Fe and because the university's diving coach, Ann Jones, offered to work with her. During swim season, Amy's day began at 5:30 a.m., when she would wake up and prepare for an hour of swim practice before school (she was both a swimmer and a diver for her team). After school she would drive 60 miles to Albuquerque to practice diving at the University of New Mexico pool. Upon returning home at around 9:00 p.m., she would start her homework. "I would often hear her cursing or crying at midnight when she was exhausted yet determined to get a problem right. Then she'd wake up the next day and start all over," Molly recalled.

Diving brought Amy more recognition. She won many competitions, including the first-place trophy at the Rio Grande Invitational in 1985. That year, the National Interscholastic Swimming Coaches Association of America ranked Amy as one of the top high-school divers in the country. Amy was pleased, but disappointed that she didn't make All-American honors in swimming as well. Her drive to excel was as strong as ever: "I kind of am addicted to exercise and get very bored if I'm not constantly busy. School is very important to me, but being active and well-rounded are necessary for me to be happy. I want to have a 4.0, but I also want to be an award winning drum major, first chair flute, and a state champion diver. As far as I'm concerned, why can't I?"

Amy's work ethic continued to pay dividends. Her list of awards went on and on: participant in New Mexico Girls' State; honors society president; 1984–85 New Mexico Scholar; certificate of outstanding academic achievement; and 1984–85 Presidential Fitness award. She was one of 21 seniors to be recognized as "super scholars" by the Santa Fe superintendent of schools in 1985. She even won an oratorical award from the Optimist organization. Amy graduated with a perfect 4.0 grade point average and was co-valedictorian of her class.

With such a stellar academic record, Amy was a college admissions officer's dream. In the summer of 1984, after her junior year in high school, Amy and her father visited Stanford, Northwestern, Amherst, Harvard, and Indiana, where they met with admissions counselors and swimming and diving coaches. She was offered diving scholarships at Northwestern and Princeton, but not Stanford, which she had wanted to attend since preschool. Seeing that Stanford was still her top choice, her parents agreed to pay the steep tuition fees there so that Amy could realize her lifelong dream. Whether she would make Stanford's diving team remained to be seen.

Just about the time Amy headed to Stanford, her family moved again, this time to Newport Beach, California, a wealthy coastal community in Orange County. Peter and Linda were concerned that their art business wasn't providing enough of an income, especially as they thought about paying their four children's college expenses. Peter became president of McCormick & Co., a New York–based consulting firm, while Linda worked as a manager at high-end retailers I. Magnin, Saks Fifth Avenue, and Neiman Marcus. As of fall 1985, the family's livelihood would no longer depend on the vagaries of the art world. They settled into a house right across from Newport Harbor High School, less than a mile from the Pacific, in one of the most desirable areas of Orange County. Although newspapers would later refer to Amy as being from Newport Beach, she had spent her formative years elsewhere.

Now she was headed back to Palo Alto, halfway between San Francisco and San Jose, where as a preschooler she had played with the children of Stanford professors and dreamed of attending college. The "Farm," as Stanford was colloquially known, was one of the most prestigious universities in the country. If Amy had "a fullness of life, a vitality," as a family friend later remarked, then so did Stanford. While a student there, Amy thrived. She put even more energy into her academics, athletics, and social life than she ever had before and somehow managed to balance all three.

As a freshman, Amy's first priority was to make the Stanford diving team. Even though diving coach Rick Schavone hadn't offered her a scholarship, she was determined to earn a spot on the team. During the first week of practice in September 1985, Schavone didn't view Amy as one of his top prospects, but he believed she did have some talent. "What stood out was how timid she was—a quality not useful in diving and one she worked very hard to overcome," he said. Sensing Amy's fear, Schavone initially discouraged Amy from attempting dives from the 10-meter platform, but she insisted on proving she could do it, even though she would be trembling before she dove. Schavone was known as "a yeller" and "grinded on" his divers continuously. The practices were clearly hard on Amy psychologically, but she and her teammates realized that Schavone cared about his divers and wanted to make them better competitors. As Amy became used to Schavone's gut-wrenching practices, she toughened up and became an indispensable part of the team.

In order to succeed in the pool and the classroom, Amy had to be ultra-organized. Her friends noticed her habit of making lists of things to do and then crossing items off one by one. She eventually got a moped so that she could speed across Stanford's campus and zip from her dorm to class to diving practice. To the amazement of her friends, Amy could dance all night at one of her favorite clubs and then get up early the next morning to run or go to the library. She studied with as much intensity as she practiced diving. As her freshman humanities instructor remarked, "I remember the big smile, the freckles, the blond hair (short when she was a freshman, longer later), and her ebullient personality. She seemed like an archetypal California girl. I remember her hair was often wet from diving practice. She was an excellent student, always in the A range with her papers, always ready to pitch in to a class discussion, never less than enthusiastic."

Even before she arrived at Stanford, Amy had decided against preparing for medical school. Instead she initially planned to study political science and prepare for a career in law or business. Her interest in Africa resurfaced when she took David Abernethy's course The Politics of Race and Class in Southern Africa during her freshman year. The antiapartheid movement was highly visible at Stanford in 1985–86, and Amy heard Archbishop Desmond Tutu speak on campus during the winter quarter. Her sense of moral outrage over apartheid deepened as she took Professor Abernethy's class, and she even began signing her letters "Free Mandela." She decided to major in international relations after taking history professor Kennell Jackson's course Africa since 1945 during her sophomore year. Jackson, an African American who had taught at Stanford since the early 1970s, was impressed with his new student's commitment to Africa. But at first he worried about the dynamics in his Africa seminar.

> [The class] had a large share of black students in it, mostly from the ranks of the black student leadership on campus, and greatly militant. Amy was one of two white students in the class, and at first, I wondered how the mixture of a majority of black militant students and a very few white students would work out. Amy swam through it all with the greatest of ease, and made friends with people and made other people become friends with one another. In addition to her devotion to learning, she was already a social agent of rare mobility.

By the end of her second year at Stanford, Amy was thinking about a career in the Foreign Service or international law. She was interested in third world development, particularly in Africa. In her proposal to major in international relations, which she submitted in June 1987, she discussed her interest in African nationalism and her desire to travel to Africa or the Caribbean so she could conduct research for an honors thesis, although she did not yet have an exact topic in mind. She took as many Africa-related courses as she could during the next two years, including Africa: Development and Dependence, South Africa and the British Empire, and Education and Radical Change in South Africa. Amy made her presence known in the classes she took. As an undergraduate, she was the most outspoken person in her class on African politics, even though a number of her classmates were graduate students, had been to Africa, or were from Africa. Hardly a class went by in which Amy didn't speak out boldly and substantively about some issue regarding contemporary Africa, whether it was Chinua Achebe's novel *Things Fall Apart*, American attitudes toward Africa, or the way Africa had been portrayed in film.

Stanford was an ideal place to focus on sub-Saharan Africa in the late 1980s. It had a federally funded African studies center with high-profile speakers, special course offerings, conferences, and language instruction. Faculty with special expertise on Africa included political scientists, historians, economists, anthropologists, and drama and literature specialists. These professors usually sympathized with the antiapartheid movement, while some scholars from the Hoover Institution, a conservative think tank on campus, supported white rule in southern Africa. Besides Archbishop Tutu, a host of well-known Africans and Africa experts spoke on campus during Amy's years at Stanford, including Chinua Achebe, Chester Crocker, Nadine Gordimer, Pallo Jordan, and Donald Woods. There were many African students at Stanford of different backgrounds and nationalities, both graduate students and undergraduates, who contributed to campus life, both inside and outside the classroom. The university was also home to a talented group of American students interested in Africa, many of whom were on campus while Amy was enrolled. Jendayi Frazer, a graduate student in international development, would eventually become US ambassador to South Africa in 2004 and assistant secretary of state for Africa in 2005. Michael McFaul, a graduate student studying Soviet foreign policy in Africa, would become US ambassador to Russia under President Barack Obama. Susan Rice, an undergraduate history major, would become Bill Clinton's assistant secretary of state for Africa and ambassador to the United Nations and national security advisor during the Obama administration. Stephen Stedman, a graduate student in political science, would become assistant secretary of the United Nations under Secretary General Kofi Annan. For someone as curious and as motivated as Amy, Stanford's faculty and students, campus speakers, and active antiapartheid movement combined to create a superlative learning environment.

Amy's social life also took off at Stanford. She eventually joined the Pi Beta Phi sorority along with her close friends Mimi Ballard, Katie Connors, Carole Sams, and Miruni Soosaipillai. Amy developed a passion for reggae music and dance clubs. She often invited her friends to go dancing with her at Club Afrique in East Palo Alto, a poor, mostly black and Hispanic neighborhood across Highway 101 from leafy, affluent Palo Alto. At Club Afrique, she and Katie would sometimes get up, take over the stage, and start singing until they collapsed in a fit of laughter.

Amy met Scott Meinert during her sophomore year. Meinert, a political science major from Salem, Oregon, was a six-foot-two point guard on the Stanford basketball team. After the two athletes met in the weight room, their friends "actually forced us to go out on our first date," Meinert recalled. The two went to a formal together and began a relationship that would last for seven years, from 1987 until 1993. Scott was Amy's first and only serious boyfriend and would become her best friend and confidant. When he met Amy, she had already developed a strong interest in Africa and was committed to the antiapartheid movement, which had inspired students on many American campuses in the 1980s.

By her second year at Stanford, Amy was beginning to come into her own as a collegiate diver. Coach Schavone believed she had improved "tremendously" and called her "one of the most improved divers on the team." The pair's initial wariness toward each other had eased considerably. They became closer, Schavone recalled, "mainly because I found her so interesting and dynamic. We have what we call 'mat chats' when the divers stretch before practice and we discuss issues. She was the most informed and extremely intelligent." Amy was determined to please her coach and earn his respect. Divers would lift weights in the morning, go to class, and then go to practice. This constant training meant that Amy, five foot five, never weighed more than about 100 pounds in college. For an athlete, she may have been physically small, but she had a "depth and a discipline" that struck her teammates.

As an upperclassman, Amy was an indispensable part of the Stanford diving team. In 1988, she placed second in the Pac-10 championship in the dive from the 10-meter tower. She was then named co-captain of the team in her senior year. This was an opportunity that was made for Amy. "Amy knew she wasn't the best diver at Stanford," Scott remembered, "so she figured out how to make it the best team." She motivated her teammates and encouraged them when they were struggling. Her efforts paid off. In 1989, the Stanford women's swimming and diving team won the National Collegiate Athletic Association championship, and Amy scored points that helped the team clinch the title. She felt justifiably proud that as a walk-on, she contributed to the victory.

There was still an academic hurdle ahead. Amy decided to apply for an honors degree in international relations, which required students to do an independent research project with a faculty advisor. As Stanford's course catalog stated, "Such a project requires a high degree of initiative and dedication, significant amounts of time and energy, and skills in research and writing." This would be a colossal understatement in Amy's case.

Amy decided to do her honors thesis on Assistant Secretary of State Chester Crocker's role in the negotiations for Namibian independence. Crocker was instrumental in forging the key agreements, the Brazzaville Protocol and the Tripartite Agreement, which were signed at the UN in December 1988, Amy's senior year. These agreements paved the way for Namibian independence—South Africa agreed to leave Namibia, which it had administered illegally for decades; Cuba agreed to withdraw its troops from Angola; and free elections would be held in Namibia. The timing for Amy's thesis was perfect. The negotiations had just been completed, and some of the participants were available at Stanford. Kennell Jackson agreed to serve as Amy's advisor for the project, which dominated Amy's attention for much of her senior year.

Amy secured interviews with the key people involved. She interviewed Crocker at the State Department in Washington, D.C., on December 16, 1988; Edward Perkins, US ambassador to South Africa, at Stanford on March 13, 1989; and the recently retired secretary of state, George Shultz, at Stanford the next day. Amy's substantive questions revealed her knowledge and thorough preparation. Reflecting on her interviews, Jackson recalled, "Amy definitely had in mind what she wanted to get out of these people." When questioning Secretary Shultz, Amy coaxed him, and if he responded too briefly, she would say, "And?" During his meeting with Amy, Shultz praised Crocker's commitment to Africa and made a comment that foreshadowed Amy's future approach to Africa. He said, "Africans look for people especially who are willing to take an interest and try to understand Africa—be friends with Africa . . . they respond very much to genuine friendship and they reciprocate on a personal level." During the next few years, Amy would take Shultz's words to heart.

Unfortunately, Amy's tape recorder hadn't worked during her interviews with Crocker and Shultz, but she chalked it up to bad luck and consoled herself with the fact that she had taken detailed notes. But that was only the beginning of her bad luck that year. In April 1989, a wall socket short-circuited in the off-campus house Amy shared with friends Carole and Miruni and started an electrical fire, seriously damaging the house, gutting Amy's room, and destroying her possessions. Everything was gone, including all the material for her thesis, which was due in a matter of weeks. Amy was devastated. After the fire, she went to Professor Jackson's office in tears and told him that all of her work had gone up in smoke. "She felt sorry for herself for about a day," Scott recalled. "She'd invested so much in it, it was too important to abandon." So she started over, working every day between 2 and 9 p.m. in Meyer Library to redo her thesis. Jackson was amazed that Amy could find the resolve to recover from such a misfortune. "She reconstituted the whole dang thing," he said.

Amy completed her thesis in May 1989, not long after the fire. Titled "Chester Crocker and the Negotiations for Namibian Independence: The Role of the Individual in Recent American Foreign Policy," her thesis was comprehensive, well written, and multidimensional. She didn't just report what Crocker thought and did but revealed the problems and controversies that his approach sometimes generated. She was sensitive to how events beyond Crocker's control forced him to shift his approach at critical times. She criticized him for being too tolerant of South Africa's slow pace of internal reform and its regional destabilization campaign, but she praised his "persistence and tenacity" that led to the eventual breakthrough. In her judgment, Crocker's role in forging an agreement among such disparate and hostile parties (South Africa, Angola, Cuba, and the USSR) was a considerable achievement.

Reading the thesis, one would never suspect that it had been started again from scratch in the spring of Amy's senior year after fire destroyed her notes. Jackson thought the thesis was outstanding. In fact, he would later get requests from other scholars and UN officials for the work, because it was the first to so fully analyze the negotiations leading to Namibian independence. Crocker's own discussion of his role would only be published three years later, in 1992.

With the thesis finished and submitted just in time, Amy participated in Stanford's ninety-eighth annual commencement in June 1989. Before the ceremony, held outdoors in the Stanford stadium, Scott helped tape the words "Free Mandela" on Amy's cap. The clear and sunny skies of that late spring California day mirrored Amy's mood. But her work was not quite done.

International relations majors were required to have an overseas studies experience in order to receive their degrees. Amy had postponed this in order to continue her diving training in the off-season. Now, fresh from her final championship season, Amy could begin planning her overseas studies program. In May 1989, she had been awarded an International Student Identity Card scholarship to support a 10-week trip to southern Africa. Out of 102 applicants, Amy was one of only 17 to be awarded the scholarship, whose recipients were known as Bowman scholars. She proposed to observe Namibia's transition to independence and then write up her observations as a kind of epilogue to her thesis. Armed with the travel guide *Africa on a Shoestring* and a book on staying healthy in the third world, Amy prepared for her first trip to Africa.

She arrived in Johannesburg on July 5, 1989. South Africa was still under a state of emergency after nearly five years of ongoing political unrest. Now Amy would get to see firsthand the region that she had studied so intensively from a distance. While in Johannesburg, Amy met with professors of African studies at the University of the Witwatersrand and visited a teacher training center in Soweto, the largest black township in South Africa with well over a million residents. She and a student from Columbia University were shown around Soweto by an African guide. He took the two Americans to see the illegal shacks, the upscale areas, and everything in between, including the homes of Nelson and Winnie Mandela and Walter and Albertina Sisulu. At one point, Amy and her companions saw some African women at a well filling up jugs of water and carrying the jugs on their heads. The Americans asked if they could take photos and the women agreed, even giving Amy a jug to balance on her head. The photo of a smiling Amy getting her first "water-balancing lesson" might seem like a typical tourist pose, but it foreshadowed the genuine kinship Amy would develop with African women in the years ahead.

Next Amy headed to Namibia to observe that country's transition to democracy. During her six weeks there, Amy was in overdrive. She attended political rallies and protests, spoke to a wide range of Namibians and foreigners on conditions in the country, visited the headquarters of the UN peacekeeping force, and spoke with an official from the United States Information Service. She also met a German reporter who took her to press conferences and shared his information on Namibia's election preparations. The press conferences Amy attended gave her the opportunity to hear from many different groups, including a black student organization that held a press conference in Katutura township near Windhoek. Already Amy was comfortable going into black townships, something few white Namibians ever did. She found Windhoek a hive of political activity and was energized by the opportunity to convert her academic interests into real-life experience. For her thesis she had studied Namibia from the perspective of American foreign policy, but now she could observe Namibian perspectives firsthand. She was excited to see a democratic transition unfolding before her eyes. While she was in Namibia, voters were registering for the November election and exiles were returning to the country. Amy believed that the scheduled election was irreversible, but she worried about the contentiousness of the preelection process.

Amy's stay in Namibia was not all work. She lived with a German-speaking family in Windhoek who took her on a memorable four-day camping trip in the vast Namib Desert. Amy had a marvelous time, traveling with her companions in huge Land Rovers, seeing the wildlife and unique desert vegetation, sampling Namibian beer at sunset, and sleeping outside. Far from being intimidated by being alone halfway around the world in an unfamiliar country, Amy was exhilarated. She had gathered information, made contacts, traveled extensively, and sought new experiences. She was clearly in her element. "So far, this trip has been very good for me," she told Scott. "I've had a chance to see things the way they really are, to test myself out on my own, and to think about what I really want to do." As stimulating—even life changing—as the trip had been for Amy, she also realized how much she missed Scott and wanted to be near him.

But Amy's journey was not quite finished. She returned to South Africa for two more weeks in mid-August 1989 and traveled around the country. She frequently caught rides in minivans—often called "kombis" in South Africa—which were the most affordable mass transit option for the country's black citizens. Amy could easily have flown to her destinations, but she wanted to understand what conditions were like for the majority of South Africans. As Scott later recalled, "She told me about a conversation she had with a woman on a kombi about that woman's journey and life, and I remember she marveled at the woman's matter-of-factness and spirit in talking about a really challenging life." After two weeks of traveling within South Africa, Amy spent early September in Zimbabwe and returned to Johannesburg on September 7, the day after a South African general election. F. W. de Klerk's National Party had been reelected on the promise of a reformist agenda, giving Amy much to talk about with the South Africans she met.

Amy returned to her family's home in southern California on September 11, 1989, after a brief stopover in Paris. She wrote a short report on her trip for Stanford's International Relations Department and a longer analysis discussing the status of Namibia's independence process. Kennell Jackson was so impressed with her longer paper that he assigned it to his modern African history class at Stanford. Most revealing was Amy's journal, in which she recorded her experiences during her southern African trip that summer. Searching for a way to end the journal—she didn't expect to begin another until her next trip and already wanted to return—Amy wrote,

I guess what I want to express is how lucky I feel to have had this opportunity to make this trip. This is a great time in my life—I feel young, independent, fairly attractive, and now worldly! It's kind of scary to think of what lies ahead. I just hope I can keep building on these great experiences and find a life in which I can do something meaningful and stay as happy as I am right now. I am so fortunate to have had the great family, friends and education that I've been given—I really hope that I can give some of that back to the world (I'm not trying to be some kind of idealist, but I do believe this) . . . And here I go!

2

To Washington and Beyond

DURING AMY'S last year at Stanford, Margaret Jones, one of her best friends from Santa Fe, came up to the Bay Area for a visit. The two had known each other since seventh grade, and now, on the verge of college graduation, both were trying to figure out what to do with the rest of their lives. Over margaritas in San Francisco, Amy and Margaret decided to move to Washington, D.C., after they graduated, find a place to live together, and look for work. Neither one had a job lined up, but that was all part of the adventure. After spending time with her family in Newport Beach following her trip to southern Africa, Amy flew to Santa Fe, helped Margaret load her car, and set out for Washington with a few suitcases, a road atlas, and her childhood friend.

The pair arrived in Washington in early October 1989. Eager to shake off the confinement of their cross-country drive, Amy and Margaret participated in a 10-kilometer run in Georgetown the next day. The run would be an apt metaphor for Amy's years in Washington—she was constantly on the go. Amy was ready to "dive in and live in the city," according to Margaret. She wanted to live in an interesting, eclectic area, close to the action, not a dull suburb in an outlying part. She and Margaret found an apartment on the 1700 block of U Street in the capital's Adams-Morgan district, an ethnically diverse neighborhood populated by a mixture of whites, blacks, and Hispanics. In Margaret's words, it was a "pretty fringy" area that some D.C. residents considered unsafe, but Amy was attracted to its diversity and nightlife. The neighborhood was home to inexpensive Ethiopian, Caribbean, and Salvadorean restaurants and to bars and stores that stayed open late. The blue townhouse that Amy and Margaret moved into was near the center of the action. The pair would share the two-bedroom apartment for the next three years.

Hoping to find work in international relations, Amy contacted think tanks and foundations but was unable to land a job in her field. As a stopgap measure she got a job as a waitress at the Brickskeller, a legendary bar in Washington that served beers from all over the world. That Amy could find a job only as a waitress was hard on her ego at first, but at least she enjoyed the atmosphere at the Brickskeller and earned good tips on weekends. Amy and Margaret managed to have fun together, despite the fact that neither had much money. They ran, went to sporting events, and partied together. Amy especially liked going to Kilimanjaro, an African-themed dance club near her apartment. "It reminds me so much of the discos in the African townships that I went to—everyone gets all decked out and everyone is a hot dancer!" she wrote to a friend. Amy "was very interested in getting to know people who weren't entitled Caucasian, wealthy people," Margaret recalled. She marveled at her friend's spirit. "[Amy] wasn't necessarily interested in going to the trendy, expensive places. She wanted to go to places with character and fun people that might be a little more edgy," she said.

Margaret wasn't Amy's only friend in D.C.—her boyfriend Scott moved to the city around the same time she did. His job at the national office of the Republican Party provided plenty of opportunities for good-natured debate, since Amy was a committed Democrat. The two continued their relationship in Washington, although their future plans were still uncertain. Miruni Soosaipillai, another Stanford friend, was also in D.C., having started law school at Georgetown just when Amy arrived in town. The group was very social, going out to eat, drink, and dance, sometimes formally, sometimes informally. Amy had a wardrobe to suit every occasion, thanks in part to her mother Linda, who worked as a couture manager at Neiman Marcus. As Amy's friend Gina Giere remembered,

> She was very pretty and she knew it. She loved to look good. She loved clothes. She wasn't a frumpy do-gooder. She was a really fun, fun, beautiful, interesting person. She wasn't perfect. She could be a little too focused sometimes. She was definitely a leader and a motivator. She liked to plan fun stuff. She would have great parties. . . . She took us places that no white women would ever go. But she was just like, "They have great blues, we gotta go there!" So we'd go to lounges in the worst parts of town and we'd be there dancin' and singin' and laughin.' She just felt at home everywhere.

Amy was determined to stay in shape while in Washington and turned to running now that her collegiate diving career was over. She ran in the city's Marine Corps Marathon in November 1990 and finished 478th out of almost 11,000 runners, despite the fact that this was her first full marathon. She would continue to enter other races in the years ahead.

Sometimes Linda Biehl worried about Amy's safety as she ran through the streets of Washington, but when she questioned her daughter, Amy would say, "Well, Mom, the crack dealers all know who I am. They protect me as I go." Scott remembers this as well. He also worried about Amy, but once while he and Amy were walking through her neighborhood, a homeless person told him, "We're watching out for her, brother, we're watching out for her." There was no denying that crime was a problem in Washington. Amy and Margaret's apartment was broken into in 1992, and Amy's bike was stolen at a local YMCA. But Amy wanted to engage with the less fortunate in D.C., not shun them. On Sundays, she and Margaret volunteered at Mount Carmel House, a shelter for homeless women, bringing popcorn and candy to the women, playing bingo, or bringing a movie to watch. She and Margaret volunteered at the shelter for eight or nine months, until Amy starting traveling more frequently.

Amy hadn't given up the search for more satisfying work. In late 1989, she was hired as a paid intern for Bart Gordon, a Democratic congressman from Tennessee. She continued to work at the Brickskeller at night while interning on Capitol Hill during the day. Her hours were punishing—often she would arrive at the office at 7:30 a.m. after working until 2 a.m. waitressing—but she considered it a worthwhile challenge. As she pondered her future, she thought about getting a master's degree in international relations or business. She took the Graduate Management Admission Test in 1990 and requested that her scores be sent to the Harvard Institute for International Development, the American Graduate School of International Management, and the business schools at Stanford, Berkeley, and UCLA. As of February 1990, she still didn't have what she considered a "real" job. But she was convinced that greater things lay ahead. "She always told me she was going to be famous," Margaret later recalled. "It wasn't until we moved to D.C. that I realized it could happen." Amy did find short-term work with "Democrats 2000," a political action committee, but she still wanted a job in international relations, particularly one that involved Africa. She also talked about Africa-related job opportunities with Chester Crocker, then retired from government service and based at Georgetown, and she interviewed at the Brookings Institution.

Finally the job Amy wanted materialized. In September 1990, she was hired as a program assistant at the National Democratic Institute for International Affairs

(NDI). NDI was a nonprofit organization established in the mid-1980s to promote democracy in the world. Funded by Congress through the National Endowment for Democracy and affiliated with the Democratic Party, it was particularly dedicated to encouraging democratic transitions and strengthening young democracies. Its work involved election monitoring, training for political parties and legislators, and civic education. When Amy came on board, NDI was expanding rapidly. The fall of the Berlin Wall in 1989 triggered a wave of democratization in the world, which some analysts called "a new world order." Political commentators hoped that democracy would not only spread but become dominant in the world, replacing tyrannical regimes and one-party states in quick succession. As communism collapsed in the Soviet Union and Eastern Europe, fears of nuclear conflict lessened and Cold War tensions eased. As these changes reshaped the world's political landscape, NDI grew dramatically in terms of both staff and funding. It developed programs to promote democracy in Eastern Europe and the independent states of the former Soviet Union and expanded its work in Africa.

The fall of 1990 was a perfect time for Amy to join NDI. By the late 1980s and early 1990s, the movement toward multiparty democracy was steadily gaining momentum in Africa. Namibia held its first free elections in 1989; formal negotiations to end apartheid began in South Africa in 1990 with the unbanning of liberation movements and Nelson Mandela's release from prison; Benin held multiparty elections in 1990; Zambia would do so the following year; and pressure for multiparty elections surfaced in other parts of Africa around the same time. NDI was well placed to contribute to these trends.

Amy started working at NDI on the same day as another recent college graduate, Gina Giere. The pair moved into an office together and joined an organization that was hiring more young interns and program assistants than ever before. "It was all these young, idealistic, totally committed smart kids," Gina said, "and it was really fun at the same time. We were all there because we believed in what we were doing. None of us was making a nickel. We were making next to nothing. You bonded very quickly in that kind of environment."

Amy fit the bill perfectly. She quickly made friends among her new coworkers, many of whom were drawn to her sense of humor, energy, and commitment to Africa. Gina found Amy "fun, super enthusiastic about everything, [and] confident. She was a little idealistic, so passionate about what she believed in and what she struggled for." Even though Amy had apparently found her dream job, she did become frustrated at times. Not content to be merely a "gofer," she wanted to be actively engaged in NDI's programs. But she found that some people on the job didn't take her seriously at first, partly because she was an attractive young woman.

One senior NDI official who did take Amy seriously was Sean Carroll, but even he recognized the qualities in her that sometimes misled others. "It's hard to put into words," he said, "but there aren't too many academics who have the personality and appearance she does. She's bright, attractive, exuberant, friendly, and at the same time she is a serious academic who has done a lot of work." Sometimes Amy had problems getting African men to take her seriously. As her roommate Margaret observed, "People would regularly underestimate Amy, because she's so gorgeous and so sporty and blonde and blue-eyed. She's tiny, she's very petite. And easy to underestimate in a way. She was fighting those impressions as well. She was very eager to convince people what a cool white person she was. That she knew what they were talking about and that she knew the politics and that she loved the food and the language and the people and the country. . . . She wasn't shy."

Patricia Keefer was NDI's senior associate for southern African programs in the early 1990s and thus supervised many of the projects on which Amy worked. She was not an Africanist by training but had years of experience as a political organizer, much of it with Common Cause. She immediately recognized Amy's potential to contribute to NDI: "She was very bright, she was very together, she was very self-confident. Her trip through Africa on kombi buses was amazing to me. It said to me here's a young woman with spirit and adventure and she doesn't have boundaries. She really wanted to work in South Africa and Namibia and she knew a lot about it. She probably knew more than I did in terms of all the policy and background. . . . I saw this as, 'My God, how could I be so fortunate to have somebody who knows all this?'"

But Pat had a reputation for being a tough boss, admitting years later that she pushed her team to their limits. "When you went to work on my team at NDI, you did things in a way that was pretty extraordinary," she said. Pat realized that some Africans viewed Americans with suspicion, and so she wanted to earn their trust by putting together exceptionally well-planned programs that ran without a hitch. She would sometimes ask her staff to work weekends and over holidays to prepare for upcoming conferences. Pat's demands didn't always sit well with Amy, and tension eventually developed between the two. "She was brilliant and the more brilliant she was, I think the more I asked of her, and I think she didn't want to acknowledge her limits," Pat remembered. One friend noticed that Amy had become far more confident and outspoken after having graduated from Stanford, and perhaps the tension she felt with Pat was the inevitable result of two strong-willed people working on the same team. Despite the personality clash, Amy admired Pat's abilities and commitment to democracy in Africa. As her friend and coworker Gina observed, "[Amy] came in really wide-eyed and idealistic and ready to do amazing things in the world. She always knew she was going to be an amazing person—I don't think she ever doubted that for one second. She just knew she was going to be someone to reckon with and she would tell you. But at NDI she met reality a little bit. It wasn't all a bed of roses. It was really hard at times. And she worked for some really strong personalities and she had a really strong personality." Amy was given more responsibility at NDI as time progressed, and eventually she became a key player in running the organization's programs in Africa. In her two years at the Institute, she traveled to Namibia, Zambia, South Africa, Ivory Coast, Republic of Congo, Burundi, and Ethiopia, returning to some locations multiple times.

Amy's greatest wish was to return to Namibia, and in March 1991 she got her chance. NDI planned a conference titled "Namibia: The Parliament and Democracy Symposium" for March 18–20, 1991. The Institute had been interested in Namibia for several years, and when the country became independent in 1990, NDI hoped to assist its young democracy. "Namibia wasn't just one more country for NDI," Pat Keefer explained. "It was the first country to welcome NDI to be part of its democratic development." She and Amy agreed that Namibia could be a showcase for what NDI stood for and how it could work with liberation movements. For Amy, her March 1991 trip to Namibia was the first in a series of trips she would take with NDI to organize seminars for Namibia's new legislators. The March 1991 conference enabled her to return to a country she had written about and visited in 1989, just before independence, and observe Namibia's new democracy in action.

The symposium, held in Windhoek and cosponsored by the National Assembly of Namibia, featured a series of seminars on parliamentary procedures for Namibian legislators. The Namibian cochairman of the conference was the Speaker of the National Assembly, Mosé Tjitendero, who had developed close ties to the United States as a student at the University of Massachusetts. He admired NDI and welcomed the international delegation it brought from Africa, the Caribbean, Europe, and the United States. The visitors discussed the inner workings of their own parliaments, interactions between various branches of government, the role of party leaders, and ways of holding government ministers accountable. Most of the members of Namibia's National Assembly attended the seminars, including the prime minister and foreign minister, and the conference was full of optimism, encouragement, and stirring words about Namibia's young new democracy.

Amy was excited to return to Namibia as a professional. The atmosphere had clearly changed since her last visit, when the talk was all about the country's upcoming elections. Now it was the first anniversary of independence. "The funny thing is that the personalities are all the same, just switched around in the power structure. I guess that includes me too!" she wrote Scott. She worked with Pat and Sean on the logistics of the conference and was part of the NDI delegation that met President Sam Nujoma at the statehouse. She and the president smiled broadly while their photograph was taken as they stood next to the Namibian flag. Amy also met Speaker Tjitendero and two South African delegates: Brigitte Mabandla of the African National Congress's constitutional committee and Bushy Molefe of the ANC's working group on international relations. After the conference ended, Amy spoke at greater length with Molefe, who had been a prisoner on Robben Island. "Amy was impressed that this victim of apartheid could be so willing to forgive his oppressors," the NDI president, Brian Attwood, remembered. "He wanted to vote, she said, but he didn't want to exclude the people who had excluded him. He wanted to see South Africa become a full-fledged democracy. This experience left a deep impression on Amy; she wanted to sign up for the cause." Amy also developed a friendship with Brigitte Mabandla at the conference. Mabandla, a lawyer who had worked for years at the ANC's headquarters in Lusaka, Zambia, encouraged NDI to come to South Africa and work with the ANC. NDI's work in Namibia thus paved the way for its later engagement with South Africa. Before they returned to the United States, Pat and Amy stopped briefly in Cape Town, where Mabandla introduced them to Zola Skweyiya, chairman of the ANC's constitutional committee. They discussed the possibility of NDI sponsoring a series of seminars on electoral systems later that year in South Africa. The door to South Africa had been opened—both for NDI and for Amy.

Amy's next trip with NDI took her to Zambia. NDI and the Carter Center in Atlanta had formed the Zambian Voter Observation Project—known as "Z-Vote" for short—in order to develop a monitoring plan for upcoming Zambian elections. Zambia had been a one-party state since independence in 1964, and President Kenneth Kaunda had not allowed opposition parties to form until December 1990. Even though he had bowed to pressure and agreed to hold national elections in 1991, he initially rejected calls for international observers to monitor the voting. He then changed his mind and joined with opposition leaders in inviting former US president Jimmy Carter to observe the elections. Carter and NDI officials organized a voting observation team in order to support free and fair elections in Zambia and to encourage the consolidation of multiparty democracy there. The program involved sending three preelection missions to Zambia between August and October 1991, plus a delegation of election observers to monitor the voting.

Amy was asked to staff NDI's September mission and headed toward a country on the cusp of major political change. She arrived in Lusaka on September

19, a few days before the preelection mission officially began. "The weather in Lusaka is gorgeous," Amy wrote her roommate Margaret. "I got to ride around in a motorcade with President Carter and carry a walkie talkie. I also went running with the secret service men who promised me I could run with Pres. Carter if I slowed down! He only went one time, but I missed it!" The program assistants' main responsibility was to make sure that everything ran smoothly; they could sit in on policy sessions as long as they had taken care of the logistics first. NDI didn't escape controversy in Zambia. The media and the ruling party occasionally criticized the organization for allegedly favoring the opposition or meddling in Zambia's internal affairs, but President Kaunda urged Zambians to respect the mission. All this gave Amy a taste of working in an uncertain, high-stakes political environment. Just two years out of college, she was doing substantive preelection work in southern Africa, clearly on the fast-track to a high-level career in diplomacy and African studies.

On October 31, 1991, Zambians voted in the first multiparty elections in more than two decades. Despite noticing some irregularities, international monitors deemed the election free and fair and certified that Frederick Chiluba's Movement for Multi-Party Democracy had won 75 percent of the vote. Kaunda stepped aside after 27 years in power. NDI's final report reflected a sense of optimism over prospects for democracy in Africa. Zambia's election was hailed as evidence of a great wave of democracy washing across Africa at the time. Amy was thrilled not just to witness this tide, but to have supported it. It was a heady time for Amy and her colleagues to work on the continent, when openness and democracy seemed to be gaining the upper hand after years of tyranny and struggle.

Amy's commitment to Africa continued to grow. In the fall of 1991, she decided to apply for a Fulbright scholarship to conduct research on the role of women in South Africa's transition to democracy. Her interest in women in Africa was relatively new and stemmed in part from her own experiences. In her Fulbright proposal, she wrote, "As a young woman in Washington I have recently been made aware of gender discrimination with men at work—both in Washington and in other countries. I have also observed women from around the world strive to eliminate gender discrimination in the new democratic societies they have helped fight for, most recently in South Africa." She observed that in the transitions to majority rule in Botswana, Namibia, and Zimbabwe, women's rights were not sufficiently enshrined in the new legal frameworks in those countries. Because African women played an important role in the struggle against white domination, they wanted to be liberated from gender discrimination as well. She was encouraged that the ANC's constitutional committee was discussing the need to protect women's rights, but she believed the prospects for success depended on women's role in the negotiation process.

Amy's proposal to study the role of women in South Africa's transition came at an opportune time, as South Africa's constitutional negotiations were just getting under way. Amy proposed to spend a year at the University of the Western Cape (UWC) near Cape Town because its Centre for Development Studies was affiliated with the ANC's constitutional committee, and she believed that the ANC had the most progressive agenda on gender of South Africa's political parties. She had made connections with key people at UWC, such as Brigitte Mabandla, who was based at the University's Community Law Centre and was the only woman on the ANC's constitutional committee. She had also gained the backing of Randi Erentzen at UWC's Centre for Development Studies, whom she met during a short stay in South Africa in early 1991. He wrote her a letter of recommendation for the proposal, as did NDI senior program officer Lionel Johnson and NDI president Brian Attwood. Amy hoped to interview women from all over South Africa, at all levels, from as many different parties and organizations as possible. The timeliness of her topic, combined with her academic background, relevant work experience in Africa, and links with ANC scholar-activists, made for a strong proposal, but she would have to wait until spring for the Fulbright committee's verdict.

Around the time Amy was preparing her Fulbright application, she headed to South Africa again—this time for her longest stay to date. She was going to participate in a series of voter education workshops cosponsored by NDI and UWC's Centre for Development Studies (CDS). The planning for the workshops took months, involving Pat and Amy from NDI, Mabandla and Skweyiya of the ANC, and Erentzen at CDS, who would become the South African coordinator of the project. As in NDI's past workshops, an international delegation would be flown into the country to lead the seminars. Amy wrote the briefing paper for the delegation, which was scheduled to arrive in South Africa in November 1991. Her 44-page paper was authoritative, comprehensive, and well written. She provided political background on South Africa, reviewed the main issues and political organizations, provided a chronological overview of negotiations, and discussed the violence racking the country. In her view, many obstacles still hindered the transition to democracy in South Africa, and she correctly predicted that tensions would grow until a settlement was reached. "The scenario of chaos which threatens to occur should the talks fail and the violence continue serves as a continual reminder to the majority of South Africans that a peaceful, democratic solution is the most desirable outcome for all," she wrote.

NDI's series of seminars, called "Towards a National Election," took place over 10 days in six different locations in South Africa. Instead of focusing on the major urban centers, the program based itself in less densely populated regions and was designed for people representing "disenfranchised political organizations" such as the ANC, PAC, the Congress of South African Trade Unions (COSATU), the Azanian People's Organization (AZAPO), and Inkatha.

Amy arrived in South Africa with NDI coworker Mary Hill on October 27, 1991, to lay the groundwork for the program. "It's an interesting time to be here," Amy wrote Margaret back in D.C. "Negotiations are getting closer, violence is increasing. I think the program will be very useful." She marveled at the beauty of Cape Town and wrote on a postcard to Scott, "This is really what Cape Town looks like—it's gorgeous! Unfortunately the view from the townships isn't this nice! We'll fix that!" Amy was assigned to be Randi Erentzen's "teammate" during the voter education seminars, beginning what was to become a warm friendship. They and their colleagues traveled together throughout South Africa, eager to prepare the people for the country's first democratic elections. Amy's colleague Mary likened their work to "a traveling road show on elections and how to vote." They both realized how meaningful the seminars were to South Africans who had never voted before. "We witnessed black South Africans vote for the first time in a mock polling station. Their gratitude was overwhelming," Mary observed. Some of the participants even wept as they cast their sample ballots, moving Amy and Mary deeply. As Amy recorded in her journal,

> The things I will remember most are the singing of liberation songs and the toyi-toyi dance that happened at each workshop. It was absolutely chilling to hear these beautiful songs which mean so much to the people and see their passion as they toyi-toyi.
>
> I will also remember the close attention paid by each participant, from the 14-year old die-hard communist to the 71-year old local chief who "voted" in a mock election for the first time.
>
> I will remember the personal relationships I established with some of the top level people of the ANC. . . . I will remember going to a tavern in a township and receiving the warmest response from everyone. I will remember staying out all night at the Cotton Pub in Jo'burg and having my picture taken with Hugh Masekela.

But as uplifting as many of Amy's experiences were, she was troubled that apartheid attitudes still existed in South Africa. Her journal continues,

Then I will remember the [illegible] of apartheid who treat violence and the loss of family as an everyday occurrence. I will remember the Afrikaner woman who refused to give a key to the bathroom to one of our faculty from Zimbabwe. I will remember the racist hotels and the uncomfortable looks we received from hotel managers and restaurant owners when we were accompanied by the ANC.

Out of these troubling incidents I have developed the greatest appreciation for the discipline, patience and tolerance exhibited by the anti-apartheid organizations in the country. Where I grew angry, they were patient and where I was intolerant, they were tolerant. It gives me a great deal of confidence in the eventual outcome of the transfer of power.

Soon it was time to return to Namibia. Foreign Minister Theo-Ben Gurirab invited NDI to convene a conference titled "Advancing and Strengthening Democracy in Southern Africa" in mid-January 1992. The conference would be held at Mount Etjo, 150 miles north of Windhoek, at one of Namibia's most famous game lodges. From January 18 to 22, 1992, approximately 60 delegates from nine countries in southern Africa converged on the resort to discuss multiparty democracy with an international delegation of political and labor leaders, legal experts, and scholars. *Washington Post* reporter David Ottaway was impressed with what he saw and aptly called the conference "a long-distance reverberation from the democratic earthquake that has struck the Soviet Union, Eastern Europe and Third World countries." As proof that the recent elections in Zambia had energized prodemocracy movements in southern Africa, elections were scheduled in Angola, Mozambique, Lesotho, Namibia, and Botswana over the next two years, and South Africa was moving toward majority rule as well. Several African delegates noted that despite having elections, their countries were not yet fully democratic. But in Namibia, the atmosphere was still positive as the second anniversary of independence approached. Multiparty democracy was intact, though Speaker Tjitendero admitted that his country still had a long way to go: "After you have acquired a constitution, which may be praised worldwide, and achieved the goal of political independence and liberty, we have learned that votes in the ballot box are not edible." Governments like his still faced the overwhelming challenge of alleviating poverty and meeting the needs of their people.

As she hinted on her postcards to her friends back home, Amy's trips for NDI were exhilarating, but they could be stressful at times. Even NDI president Brian Attwood recognized the pressure that Amy was under. Years later, he described Amy as "young and eager to take on the most difficult jobs. So we gave them to her. She had the energy to work all night or to party all night—whatever was needed! She was also very idealistic. She knew she could make a difference and it showed. She didn't have the most glamorous of jobs. She planned training conferences. She helped out with logistics. But she made more African friends than anyone else. She was fascinated to learn about their lives, their hardships, their pleasures, and their dreams for the future."

Not all of Amy's projects with NDI involved southern Africa. Her work also took her to west and central Africa. In mid-1992, she traveled to the Ivory Coast and the Republic of Congo, giving her the opportunity to see new parts of Africa and practice her French. But Amy's real interest had shifted to South Africa by this point. As she awaited word on her Fulbright application, she sharpened her focus on that country's shifting political landscape. Nelson Mandela had been free for more than two years, but negotiations for a new government seemed stalled. All the while, political violence there was about to intensify. Shortly after returning from Brazzaville (Republic of Congo), Amy attended a conference on South Africa's transition sponsored by the School of Advanced International Studies at Johns Hopkins University. There she heard the latest perspectives from some of the world's leading South Africa experts, including Steven Mufson (*Wall Street Journal* correspondent and author), Bill Gould (Stanford law professor), Jacklyn Cock (South African feminist scholar), Colin Bundy (prominent South African historian), Robert Price (Berkeley political scientist), Anthony Marx (Columbia political scientist), and Lindiwe Mabuza (the ANC's representative to the United States). Even Chester Crocker was there, the former assistant secretary of state and subject of Amy's honors thesis.

After having worked extensively in South Africa herself during the transition process, Amy had become an astute and perceptive observer in her own right. She had long admired Mandela, but her perspectives had become much more sophisticated than ever before. She shared her insights with her 15-year-old younger brother Zach, who was writing a school report on Mandela in the spring of 1992 and had asked for his older sister's help. Although she was about to leave for another trip—this time to Burundi—she sent Zach her thoughts.

> I think that Nelson Mandela is uniquely qualified to lead black South Africans during this critical time of transition in South Africa.
>
> Many former prisoners from Robben Island and elsewhere whom I have talked to tell me that prison was the best education they could have ever received in South Africa. At a time when most South Africans were refusing to attend school because they didn't want to learn in Afrikaans,

etc., those who were in prison read every book and newspaper they could get their hands on. They developed codes in order to get information from outside. They gained a sense of purpose in terms of what they had to do when they were released from prison. They developed a better understanding of those who were keeping them in prison, as well as a special compassion that often causes former prisoners to be more conciliatory with the white government than those ANC members who had been in exile or working with the UDF.

Nelson Mandela never lost his sense of purpose while he was in prison. In fact he came out with a very clear understanding of what he had to do. He did everything he could to learn what was behind the motives of the white government. He began a dialogue with former President Botha and de Klerk while he was still in prison to lay the groundwork for his release and establish a working relationship. During all those years in prison he was preparing himself to lead.

Nearly everyone I have met in South Africa has a favorable opinion of Mandela. The old white people still think he is a communist. The radical black youth in the townships believe he has "sold out" by negotiating with the current government, but nearly all of them respect him. My impression is that this massive responsibility weighs heavily on Mandela, but that he knows that he is the one who must see the transition through. However, I do not believe that he is self-aggrandizing, or that he plans to consolidate his personal power if and when the ANC comes to power. Instead I believe that he is old and tired. He actively seeks new young leaders.

Amy's judgments proved to be remarkably accurate. Her reflections are all the more significant when one considers that she wrote them well before such perspectives were widely known, before the publication of Mandela's autobiography and before the publication of other insiders' accounts of Robben Island, the secret negotiations that preceded Mandela's release, and the transition process in general. When it came to writing reports about South Africa, younger brother Zach was a fortunate student indeed.

As if to confirm Amy's potential as a scholar of South Africa, she received some good news that spring—she would be a Fulbright scholar in the fall. But her work at NDI was far from over. In fact, her last few months at the Institute were among her busiest yet. For several of her remaining projects, she worked with Lionel Johnson, a senior program officer who managed NDI programs in Haiti, Eastern Europe, Southeast Asia, and East and Central Africa. Amy worked with

Johnson on programs for Burundi, Rwanda, and Kenya. Johnson was impressed with Amy's energy and skill at networking, noting that "she interacted at a pretty young age with a lot of senior people." Many of these senior people were drawn to Amy's magnetic personality, including Johnson himself.

As a program assistant for NDI's Central Africa division, Amy monitored developments in the region, recruited individuals to participate in NDI conferences, managed the logistical aspects of these conferences, wrote briefing materials for participants, and helped develop the program for the conferences. Amy also accompanied her NDI colleagues to Burundi in mid-May 1992 on a mission to promote multiparty democracy.

Back home in the United States, Amy spent part of the summer hosting South African visitors for NDI. The Institute organized a study tour for South African legal experts, and among the delegates were Brigitte Mabandla, Kader Asmal, and Albie Sachs, all members of the ANC's constitutional committee. They spent three weeks traveling in the United States to study the American government. "Amy did a lot to set up that study tour," Pat Keefer recalled. "It's about moving people, it's about scheduling, and she was very proficient and efficient at it. Great briefing book, materials they could take. And it gave her an opportunity to meet people like Dullah Omar and Albie Sachs and Kader Asmal." NDI also sent Amy and Gina to the 1992 Democratic Convention in New York to assist with the Institute's international visitors program. Every four years, NDI brought people from all over the world to see American political conventions, and the program assistants set up panels on American elections, political parties, and US foreign policy and invited American speakers to address the guests. Amy and Gina took their visitors onto the floor of the convention so that they could hear the speeches and see the voting. To Amy's delight, one of those visitors was Namibian president Sam Nujoma. Stepping into the spectacle of the political convention was exciting work for the program assistants, Amy included. One of the people Amy befriended in New York was Gill Noero, who was part of a South African delegation to the United Nations at the time. Amy would later work with Noero on women's projects in South Africa in 1992–93.

Amy's last overseas trip for NDI took her to Ethiopia between September 8 and 19, 1992. She participated in a training seminar on election monitoring for the Organization of African Unity in Addis Ababa, an event NDI cosponsored with the African-American Institute. Few of Amy's experiences there were documented, other than the fact that she enjoyed being in Addis Ababa despite the "freezing" temperatures (although in the tropics, the city is approximately 8,000 feet above sea level).

Another country in Africa increasingly interested Amy, one that she never visited—Malawi. Hastings Kamuzu Banda had led the small southern African nation since its independence in 1964 and declared himself "life president" in 1971. But a prodemocracy movement began to gain support in the early 1990s, partly the result of multiparty elections in neighboring countries. Amy took an interest in these developments and began to push NDI to "do something about Malawi," as Sean Carroll remembered. She met some Malawian opposition figures in Washington and invited them to her office to talk to her. She befriended Thoko Banda, the son of the important opposition figure Aleke Banda (no relation to President Hastings Banda), who appreciated her help in publicizing human rights abuses in Malawi. The two discussed how Malawi could become part of the democratic change that was happening in other parts of Africa. Thoko viewed Amy as a key ally in the struggle for multiparty democracy in Malawi and later told a journalist that she was "the only American I trusted." He put Amy in touch with his father Aleke, who spoke to Amy twice by telephone. In September 1992, just before Amy left Washington, NDI held a forum on Malawi, thanks largely to Amy's and Thoko's initiatives.

Change came to Malawi in 1993–94. In June 1993, Malawian voters approved a referendum calling for multiparty elections, and in the May 1994 vote Hastings Banda and his party lost power. After the old regime's ouster, Aleke Banda was appointed to the cabinet in the new government. Tim Johnston, a contact of Amy's at the Washington-based Overseas Development Council, appreciated Amy's efforts on behalf of Malawi's prodemocracy movement and later made a worthwhile point. "Amy proved to be an important ally to those of us concerned with the fate of that country," he wrote. "Although she was clearly dedicated to the freedom struggle in South Africa, she believed in freeing all Africans from oppression, not just that perpetrated by whites."

Probably the most significant initiative that Amy launched during her last few months at NDI involved gender. Both Margaret and Scott noticed that Amy's interests had shifted since her arrival in Washington three years earlier. When she first moved to D.C., she was interested in promoting democracy in Africa, but she then began to focus on promoting women's rights in Africa's prodemocracy movements. Her growing interest in women's rights manifested itself not only in her Fulbright proposal, but in her work at NDI as well.

She was motivated by both her personal and her professional experiences. While representing NDI, she sometimes felt that men regarded her more as a pretty young blonde than as a professional colleague. She noticed that men in dance clubs started making advances toward her, both in Africa and the United

States. Her friend and coworker Gina told a revealing story about one of Amy's trips to southern Africa. She was staffing a conference at which one of the attendees was a former freedom fighter. Everyone had a couple of drinks with dinner, the activist got tipsy, and when they were dancing and having fun, "he hits on her." Amy's illusions were suddenly shattered. As Gina remembers it, Amy told colleagues, "'I've admired this man my whole academic life, but I can't kiss him!' That was the first time she saw the messy side of people, of men. That was harder for her to process than other people. She was so pure and convinced in her motives and ideas and beliefs and she never wavered from it."

Amy also observed that in Namibia, although women had fought for liberation alongside men, they didn't play a prominent role in Namibia's new government. She once told Thoko Banda that women had a great deal to contribute to Africa's emerging democracies, but they weren't given enough opportunities to do so. She wanted to help women get involved. Impressed by the role women played at the 1992 Democratic convention in New York, Amy concluded that the rights of women needed to be promoted more vigorously in emerging democracies. Having just been awarded a Fulbright to study the role of women in South Africa, Amy was ready to speak out.

In August 1992, Amy wrote a detailed memorandum on gender issues to the NDI staff. "I would like to initiate a discussion on how we can institutionalize a policy of gender equality," she wrote. She recognized that NDI had sought to increase women's participation in its programs, but she wanted the organization to go further. She believed NDI should actively promote women's rights in societies that were making the transition to democracy, and she drafted a set of gender guidelines that she wanted coworkers to consider and discuss at a meeting. In her words, NDI needed to "make gender equality an institutional priority."

Around the same time that Amy circulated her memo on gender, she drafted a statement discussing how election monitors should address gender issues. She noted that in countries undergoing democratic transitions, women's issues tended to be downplayed or ignored, even though women had also struggled to achieve democracy. Amy was careful not to advocate a single model for gender equality; she believed that how gender issues were addressed should depend on the country involved. Following Amy's initiative, NDI developed a program to strengthen the participation of women in politics. The program was directly inspired by Amy's work. In October 1993, NDI brought an international delegation of women to Nairobi, Kenya, to support the newly established Education Centre for Women in Democracy. The center had been established a few months earlier to help women increase their role in Kenyan politics. In the four-day conference, international delegates from Germany, Uganda, Ireland, Namibia, Botswana, and the United States met with Kenyan women to discuss assisting female candidates, conducting campaigns, organizing, and educating voters. That NDI received funding for the Nairobi program was a tribute to Amy's "commitment and energy," according to Lionel Johnson. The Institute's support of the Education Centre for Women in Democracy became "one of NDI's more successful programs." Johnson maintains that the issues Amy worked on, such as democracy in Africa, women's rights, and women's participation in politics, are still important to NDI today.

By late summer 1992, Amy brought her work at NDI to a close. Despite the challenges she had faced, she derived a real satisfaction from having worked there. She was proud of the Institute's role in promoting democracy in Africa. She believed that a new era of freedom was dawning on the continent after years of one-party states. "African people from grassroots societies to heads of governments are beginning to recognize democracy as the key to achieving political tolerance, social justice, and economic growth," she wrote just before she left. Although she recognized that democracy on the continent had been assisted by the collapse of communism in Eastern Europe, the end of the Cold War, and the encouragement of donor countries, she believed that Africans themselves deserved much of the credit. "The most significant changes have come from the persistence and resilience of African citizens who are demanding popular participation and accountable government," she wrote. Amy correctly predicted that Africa's path to democracy would not be easy, especially in countries emerging from civil wars. In an essay published in the July 1992 issue of the newsletter *Liberal Times*, she wrote,

> On a continent where population rates spiral out of control and civil conflict is more common than good government, liberal democracy is not just an option. Africans across the continent insist that democracy is necessary to ensure that the growing needs of their societies are met. Africa, and the world, cannot afford another Somalia, where war, famine and political anarchy have claimed millions of lives. Instead, we must strive to achieve more Benins, Botswanas, Namibias and Senegals—democratic societies where Africans are beginning to live up to their continent's vast human potential.

After saying goodbye to her roommate Margaret, Amy left Washington in September 1992 and headed back to southern California to spend time with her family and prepare for her Fulbright trip to South Africa. While on the west coast, she visited Scott in Oregon and friends in the San Francisco Bay area, including her former advisor at Stanford, Kennell Jackson. She told Jackson about her adventures in Africa over the past few years. "She regaled me with all these stories of people and their interests, of a beer she had with this person, of a tea at another African's home, of a woman leader I had to pay attention to in the future in Zimbabwe." She also showed him some of the dance moves she had learned in Africa.

Three years after having graduated from Stanford, some of her college friends were starting families, but Amy was still paving the way for her career. She sensed that adventures still lay ahead of her. "She was so driven and really moving toward some amazing things," Margaret remembered. During the last two years, she had converted her previous academic experience into professional, hands-on work, shuttling back and forth to Africa, helping run workshops and conferences, observing conditions, meeting African leaders and activists, and developing ideas and initiatives of her own. Amy had not only observed prodemocracy movements in Africa, she had actively assisted them. Her next stop was South Africa, home to the continent's most highly anticipated transition of all.

3

Into South Africa

BY THE late twentieth century, South Africa was among the world's most racially divided societies. Its population is not just black and white, but every shade in between, a mixture of different ethnicities, races, languages, and traditions. In the early 1990s, the African majority—commonly referred to as "black South Africans"—constituted about 76 percent of the population, while the white minority, descendants of European settlers, who speak primarily Afrikaans (a derivative of Dutch) or English, numbered about 13 percent. The remaining 11 percent included South Africa's mixed-race population, traditionally known as "Coloureds," and a smaller number of Indians, many of whose ancestors came to South Africa as indentured laborers in the nineteenth century.

Observers frequently note that South Africa encompasses elements of both the developed and the developing world, the North and the South, the rich and the poor. White South Africans have historically enjoyed one of the highest living standards in the world. Many lived in spacious homes in leafy neighborhoods, employed gardeners and domestic workers, had access to excellent schools and services, and enjoyed a wide array of recreational and entertainment opportunities. Black South Africans usually lived in overcrowded, poorly serviced townships or in barren, unproductive rural reserves known as "homelands." Neither domain had adequate schools, healthcare facilities, services, or recreational areas. The contradiction of apartheid was that despite its being a policy to keep the races apart, the economy continually drew them together. Blacks often worked in white neighborhoods as groundskeepers or maids, or commuted to "white" areas to work in mines or factories, and so were constantly reminded of whites' privileges and comfortable lifestyles. But few whites ever entered black townships or rural "homelands," so they rarely saw how the majority of their black fellow citizens lived.

The origins of South Africa's racial conflict stretch back hundreds of years, much like that of the United States. Both societies experienced European colonial conquest, slavery, miscegenation, and racial segregation, both formal and informal. The black freedom struggles in both countries shared key ideas and approaches, and black South Africans often drew inspiration from black American leaders and the American civil rights movement. In his trip to South Africa in 1966, Robert F. Kennedy acknowledged the two countries' striking historical similarities. As he told an audience at the University of Cape Town on June 6, 1966,

> I come here because of my deep interest and affection for a land settled by the Dutch in the mid-seventeenth century, then taken over by the British, and at last independent; a land in which the native inhabitants were at first subdued, but relations with whom remain a problem to this day; a land which defined itself on a hostile frontier; and land which has tamed rich natural resources through the energetic application of modern technology; a land which once imported slaves, and now must struggle to wipe out the last traces of that former bondage.
>
> I refer, of course, to the United States of America.

But the two countries' differences were equally striking. In the United States, whites were an overwhelming majority of the population, whereas white South Africans were a small minority. The cultural divide separating black and white South Africans was considerably larger than that between white and black Americans. The two countries' legal systems were vastly different as well. In the United States, the Constitution and the Bill of Rights suggested that all of its citizens had equal rights, and although this principle was not always observed, victims of discrimination could eventually seek legal recourse through the nation's courts. South Africa had no such constitution proclaiming equal citizenship for all. A sign once carried at a political demonstration in the United States said it best: "Negroes in American fight for their rights, Negroes in South Africa have no rights."

Although slavery, European colonial rule, and racial segregation had existed in other parts of the world, the history of South Africa and other racially divided societies began to diverge after the Second World War. The United States slowly began dismantling legalized racial segregation, and European colonial rulers gradually began transferring power to Asians and Africans. But in South Africa, white rule became harsher. In 1948, the Afrikaner National Party came to power promising to implement apartheid ("apartness"), an all-encompassing system of legalized racial discrimination, so as to advance and defend white South Africa. By playing on fears of *"swart gevaar"* (black peril), the National Party would remain in power for the next 46 years. During that time, its policy of apartheid would become the most notorious system of racial segregation in the modern world.

Not surprisingly, South African politics became increasingly confrontational after 1948. Soon after the National Party's accession to power, the leading vehicle of black politics, the African National Congress (ANC), was revitalized by a new generation of younger members, including Nelson Mandela and Walter Sisulu. They were determined to transform the ANC into a more radical, militant, mass-based movement. But the incident that led to the white regime's first major crisis was precipitated not by the ANC but by a breakaway group of hardline African nationalists, who called themselves the Pan Africanist Congress (PAC). On March 21, 1960, they urged their followers to protest against the law that required Africans to carry a pass book entitling them to reside and work in the "white" cities. At a protest in Sharpeville, a black township south of Johannesburg, police fired into an unarmed crowd, killing 69 and wounding more than 100. The massacre made headlines all over the world and led to unprecedented international condemnation of apartheid. Just days after the tragedy, the government banned the ANC and the PAC. Now forced to operate in secret, the ANC established an armed wing known as Umkhonto we Sizwe (Spear of the Nation) and launched a sabotage campaign. Mandela, then a young lawyer and a leader of Umkhonto, was arrested in 1962 after 18 months of clandestine activity. He and other key leaders of the sabotage campaign were sentenced to life in prison two years later. After the PAC was banned, some of its sympathizers in the western Cape established Poqo (Africans alone), a resistance movement that promoted violence against white South Africans. Poqo killed a handful of whites and African chiefs before it was crushed by the government's security forces in 1963. Both the ANC and the PAC would be virtually wiped out internally, creating a significant void in black protest politics.

In the 1960s, opposition to apartheid arose from a new quarter—black South African students. Drawing inspiration partly from the Black Power movement in the United States, the black medical student Steve Biko and his peers developed a potent new political ideology stressing the need for black pride and self-reliance. Proponents of this ideology, which became known as Black Consciousness, believed that black South Africans could liberate themselves politically only once they shed their inferiority complex and distanced themselves from white liberals, whose commitment to genuine racial equality they questioned. The Black

Consciousness Movement greatly reenergized black protest. A bold new generation of activists stepped forward, eager to challenge the perceived timidity of the older generation and confront "the system" as never before. Their ideas soon spread to black high schools, where they had explosive results.

The most serious student uprising took place in Soweto, the huge black township south of Johannesburg. Sparking the protest was a new government edict requiring black high schools to conduct some classes in Afrikaans, which many students viewed as "the language of the oppressor." Students boycotted classes by the thousands, expressing their anger not just at the new language policy, but at their inferior education and apartheid in general. On June 16, 1976, police opened fire on a mass march in Soweto, killing young student demonstrators and sparking a wave of unrest that would spread throughout the country. When protests finally subsided six months later, almost 600 people had been killed, the majority of whom were black South African students. In the aftermath of the crisis, many student activists fled South Africa to join the ANC in exile in Tanzania and elsewhere. Black South African youth would play a key role in resisting apartheid from then onward. The government's brutal response to the Soweto protests, plus the murder of Steve Biko in police custody a year later, sparked international outrage, and sustained efforts to isolate South Africa began to gain momentum.

In response to rising internal and international pressure, the white minority government began a pattern of reform and repression that would last more than a decade. But as the unrest sparked by Soweto turned into endemic civil strife and instability, the movement of popular resistance spread faster than the government could crush it. The upsurge in unrest led to a massive security crackdown. President P. W. Botha declared a partial state of emergency in 1985 and extended it to the whole country the next year. By the late 1980s, South Africa was under siege. The government was still in control, but it faced a grim future of economic decline, international isolation, and fierce internal resistance. Seemingly crushed in one area of the country, unrest would break out in another. In the words of the American journalist Steven Mufson, the white minority government faced a "half-extinguished fire." Neither side could defeat the other.

Ever since the mid-1980s, groups of South Africans had begun exploring ways of resolving the country's crisis diplomatically. Between 1985 and 1989, delegations of prominent white businessmen, Afrikaner intellectuals, and students met with ANC representatives in exile. Although the South African government publicly condemned these meetings, its own officials began meeting secretly with ANC exiles in Europe and with Nelson Mandela, who had initiated a dialogue with the government from prison. Eventually several factors combined to break South

Africa's stalemate. The end of the Cold War eased the government's longstanding fears of a communist takeover. F. W. de Klerk succeeded the ailing and intransigent P. W. Botha in late 1989 and proved ready to take risks and change direction. Mandela's rare combination of grace and gravitas convinced the government that its most famous political prisoner was not bent on revenge. Internal opposition could not be fully contained, and international pressure was seriously damaging the South African economy.

In early 1990, De Klerk announced that he was ready to end apartheid and build a new South Africa through negotiations. He lifted the bans on the ANC and the PAC, repealed apartheid laws, and released Mandela, catching even his own closest colleagues by surprise. The country's political landscape had changed in an instant. Just months after the fall of the Berlin Wall in Germany, apartheid seemed to be crumbling in South Africa, and Mandela strode free after spending more than 27 years in prison.

Mutual suspicions on both sides were not easily dissipated. Decades of antagonism had built up, not just between the government and the ANC, but among rival liberation movements, political organizations, and homeland leaders. Initially there was little consensus on the way forward. Negotiating teams disagreed on the formula for writing a new constitution, the structure of a new government, and future economic policy. Complicating matters further, black and white extremists frequently boycotted the negotiations and even tried to sabotage the negotiation process itself. Tragically, violence intensified during the transition period. Random attacks on black commuters and township residents claimed dozens, then hundreds, of lives. Fighting broke out between the ANC and Inkatha, a Zulu organization led by Mangosuthu Buthelezi, the chief minister of the KwaZulu homeland. The government and the ANC blamed each other for the violence and often seemed more like bitter enemies than negotiating partners. After almost two years of violence and sporadic peace talks, most of South Africa's major political parties converged at the Convention for a Democratic South Africa (CODESA) in December 1991. But problems persisted. At CODESA II in May 1992, delegates became deadlocked over how decisions would be made in a proposed constituent assembly. When no agreement could be reached, CODESA permanently collapsed.

Violence and instability worsened in 1992. On June 17, 1992, 39 people were killed in Boipatong, a black township south of Johannesburg, during a nighttime attack. The ANC charged that much of the country's violence was being orchestrated by a government-backed "third force" to weaken the ANC and derail the transition to majority rule. After the killings in Boipatong, the ANC pulled out of negotiations. More violence was yet to come. On September 7, 1992, between 70,000 and 80,000 ANC supporters marched in Bisho, the capital of the Ciskei homeland, hoping to spark a popular revolt against the homeland government. During the march, troops loyal to Ciskei's leader opened fire, killing 28 of the marchers and wounding 200 more. Relations between the South African government and the ANC seemed headed toward a new low. But then both sides drew back from the edge of the abyss and, three weeks later, signed a Record of Understanding recommitting themselves to talks, though formal negotiations would not resume for another six months. In the meantime, white-minority rule continued.

HAVING traveled to South Africa several times between 1989 and 1992, Amy was well aware of the country's uncertain prospects. "Although there are no guarantees that South Africa will successfully complete its transition to a multi-party democracy based on individual rights and majority rule," she had written in her Fulbright proposal, "it is currently moving in this direction." Amy was entering an unstable, volatile atmosphere. Expectation was in the air, but negotiations had yet not resumed and violence was worsening. Democracy still seemed a long way off. Although many black South Africans were dying, whites were still largely shielded from the violence. They were not being targeted—at least not yet.

As Amy prepared to leave the United States, Linda and Peter Biehl worried about their daughter's safety, "but we would never have tried to stop her from going to South Africa," Linda said later. "Peter and I raised our children to be independent, free-thinking, and strong. This was Amy's chosen path, and we supported it." Amy left for South Africa from Los Angeles International Airport on October 14, 1992. Linda dropped her off at the airport. As they hugged each other and said goodbye, Amy said, "Don't cry, Mom," never suspecting that she would not see her mother or any of her family again. After traveling via London and Johannesburg, she eventually landed in Cape Town on October 17.

To the first-time visitor, Cape Town can seem like a different country from the rest of South Africa. Its stunning location on the tip of Africa, unique flowers and plants, Mediterranean climate, and colonial architecture are not all that set it apart. Its ethnic mixture is also unique. Whereas black South Africans are the majority in the rest of the country, in Cape Town people of mixed race predominate, giving the area a distinct historical, cultural, and linguistic flavor. If South Africa has sometimes been referred to as a beautiful, cruel land, Cape Town is even more so. With its rare combination of the mountains and the sea, it is breathtakingly beautiful, but this lovely city was also the setting for extraordinarily harsh government policies that caused years of suffering and tragedy.

One of Cape Town's central tragedies during the apartheid era was that the majority of its people—its mixed-race inhabitants—were turned into outcasts in their own city. Before 1948, Cape Town was "one of the least segregated cities in sub-Saharan Africa," according to the geographer John Western. But during the apartheid era, white government officials remade the city, with dire consequences for Cape Town's Coloured population. In an effort to make the most centrally located areas of Cape Town all white, the government forcibly moved mixed-race citizens from neighborhoods where their families had lived for generations and dumped them on the Cape Flats, a vast, sandy plain far to the southeast of the city center.

Conditions facing black South Africans in Cape Town were even worse. The government declared the city a "Coloured labor preference area" during apartheid, and so relatively few Africans were given official permission to live and work there. Those who tried to find work in Cape Town without official government permission were denied government housing and often survived by building tin shacks wherever they could, without water, electricity, and city services. Crossroads became the most infamous of the black squatter camps in Cape Town. Its residents lived under constant threat of eviction and often narrowly escaped as their shacks were demolished by government bulldozers. Cape Town's complexion became more African beginning in the 1980s. By then, government policies limiting the black influx into the city had been abolished—first, the labor policy favoring Coloureds (1984) and then, the pass laws (1986). With such controls lifted, the city's African population rose dramatically, more than tripling between 1982 and 1992. Xhosa-speaking families from the Transkei, Ciskei, and the Eastern Cape flowed in daily in search of a better life, but the urban influx into Cape Town far outpaced the number of available jobs and homes. Unable to find formal housing, the new African residents built a vast sea of shanties on the sand dunes southeast of Cape Town. The area's growing African population was most apparent in Khayelitsha ("Our new home"), which became Cape Town's largest black settlement. Nonexistent in 1980, Khayelitsha had approximately half a million inhabitants by the mid-1990s.

The gap between the haves and the have-nots in Cape Town is arguably the starkest in the country. The contrast between lush suburbs like Constantia and Bishopscourt and the sprawling shanties of Khayelitsha defies description. The scenic beach enclave of Camps Bay seems a world away from the townships of the barren Cape Flats. The situation parallels the contrast between the wealthy seaside community of La Jolla, California, and densely populated Tijuana, Mexico, except that, instead of being separated by an international border approximately 26 miles (42 kilometers) away, no such barrier divides Cape Town's rich and poor. The manicured gardens in central Cape Town are less than 6 miles (9 kilometers) from the Cape Flats.

Amy had been to Cape Town before and was well acquainted with conditions in South Africa. In fact, because of her academic work and experience with NDI, she was probably much more knowledgeable about South African history and society than many other foreigners living in the country. She wasn't the only American in South Africa at the time. Several thousand Americans lived and worked there for extended periods, just as they had for decades. After 1990, more arrived as apartheid crumbled. Some worked for businesses or NGOs, others were students, teachers, researchers, missionaries, humanitarian workers, or journalists. South Africa was still a major international news story, especially after the release of Mandela and the country's uncertain path to freedom. Many white visitors stayed within the boundaries of white South Africa, not venturing far from the places where local whites lived, worked, and played, but Amy consciously shunned such confinements. She was "determined not to live within a white prison," recalled Larry Diamond, one of her mentors from Stanford. She wanted to understand the area's majority mixed-race and black population and to live and socialize with them.

Amy rented a room from Melanie Jacobs, a mixed-race woman who lived in Mowbray, a neighborhood about three and a half miles (six kilometers) from downtown Cape Town. Melanie lived with her 13-year-old daughter, Solange, and worked for Randi Erentzen at the Centre for Development Studies at the University of the Western Cape (UWC). Erentzen had met Amy when she worked for NDI, and it was his idea that she live with Melanie. At first Melanie was decidedly unenthusiastic. She had also been asked to share her office with Amy, and the prospect of living and working with a stranger was unsettling, especially when the stranger was a white American. Like many black South Africans, Melanie regarded whites cautiously and believed that Americans tended to be loud and overbearing. She first said no, but then changed her mind as a favor to her boss. At first, the two "agreed to keep out of each other's way," but they soon warmed to each other. Melanie hadn't had an easy life. Twenty-nine when Amy moved in, she was 15 when she had given birth to Solange and had raised her daughter as a single parent. Her place in Mowbray was an apartment she rented above a small grocery store on Main Road. She charged Amy the equivalent of about $100 per month in rent, which Amy recognized as being quite a bargain.

Mowbray was an old, somewhat bohemian neighborhood near the University of Cape Town and Groote Schuur Hospital, where Dr. Christiaan Barnard had conducted the world's first human heart transplant 25 years earlier. In the early twentieth century, Mowbray had been home to a sizeable community of middle-class Coloureds, but it was declared a whites-only suburb during the height of apartheid. Its mixed-race inhabitants were forced out beginning in 1966, just as the more famous mixed-race community of District Six in central Cape Town was being evicted. By the early 1990s, some Coloureds had trickled back to Mowbray. The Group Areas Act hadn't been strictly enforced everywhere for years, and it was repealed in 1991, a year before Amy arrived. Mowbray was in a good location, relatively near the city center, shops, the railway line, and major motorways.

It wasn't near UWC, however, where Amy would be working. The campus was located in Bellville, a town about 9 miles (15 kilometers) east of Mowbray. Because public transportation between Mowbray and Bellville was limited, Amy decided to get a car within days of her arrival in Cape Town. She bought a used Mazda, intentionally getting a "crappy car" so she wouldn't stand out. Sometimes Amy would forget to drive on the left, Melanie remembered, narrowly missing other cars. On the rear bumper was a sticker that read "Our Land Needs Peace."

Amy's next order of business was getting established on campus. The University of the Western Cape was a product of apartheid but over the years had developed a strong antiapartheid character. Founded in 1960 as an institution of higher learning for Coloureds when the government was creating separate universities for racial and linguistic groups, it eventually became a highly politicized "university of the left." By the time Amy arrived, it was home to many ANC supporters among both students and faculty. A leaflet from the Centre for Development Studies described UWC as "absolutely committed to the post-apartheid ideal in its teaching, research and service activities." Almost all of its students were mixed-race or black.

Contrary to later news reports, Amy wasn't an "exchange student" in South Africa and wasn't enrolled in a degree program. As a Fulbright scholar, she was a research fellow affiliated to UWC's Community Law Centre, where she worked under the supervision of Brigitte Mabandla and Dullah Omar. Also contrary to later news reports, Amy wasn't in South Africa to conduct voter education but to study the role of women in South Africa's transition. Omar, the director of the Community Law Centre, was a member of the ANC's National Executive Committee. He had spent much of his career as a human rights lawyer and had represented Nelson Mandela when he was imprisoned on Robben Island. As a leading member of the United Democratic Front in the 1980s, Omar had been targeted by a secret government hit squad—the notorious Civil Cooperation Bureau—which twice tried to assassinate him. It nearly succeeded when its agents replaced his heart medication with poison. One of the ANC's most prominent leaders by 1992, he would work closely with Amy during the next 10 months. Another of Amy's close contacts at the university was Randi Erentzen at the Centre for Development Studies, which coordinated research on South Africa's future policy options. Erentzen had recommended Amy for the Fulbright, arranged her accommodation, and introduced her to his colleagues. Later he admitted that he was not generally fond of Americans, but Amy broke down his stereotypes.

Several of Amy's colleagues at UWC were destined to become even more important once apartheid finally ended. In 1994, Mandela appointed Omar to become minister of justice in South Africa's first democratic government. Mabandla became deputy minister of arts, culture, science, and technology and eventually minister of justice herself. Bulelani Ngcuka, deputy director of the Community Law Centre during Amy's tenure there, became head of the National Prosecuting Authority under Mandela's successor, Thabo Mbeki. UWC was clearly a training ground for some of South Africa's future leaders. It was a workshop where ideas about the new constitution were researched, proposed, and debated. By being there, Amy could witness, analyze, and even contribute to the constitutional process all at once.

Mabandla was Amy's most important colleague at UWC early on. The two had first met in Namibia in 1991, and it was Mabandla who had initially encouraged Amy to come to UWC. Mabandla had long been on the frontlines of the struggle for democracy and women's rights in South Africa. Born in 1948, she became active in the South African student movement as the Black Consciousness Movement spread in the late 1960s. She was expelled from the University of the North in 1971 because of her political activism, detained for five months, and then banned in 1974–75. Once her banning order expired, she went into exile and became active in the ANC, earning a law degree from the University of Zambia in 1979. While in exile, she represented the ANC at United Nations forums and joined the ANC's legal and constitutional affairs department. When she returned from exile in 1990, she had been a member of the ANC's constitutional committee for two years and was appointed coordinator of the Gender Research Project at UWC's Community Law Centre. She was one of the ANC's legal advisors at CODESA and had become a leading figure in South Africa's Women's National Coalition. She was impressed with Amy's command of human rights issues and found the young American well organized and hardworking. Besides sharing a good personal chemistry, the two were committed to ensuring that women's rights were part of the political settlement in South Africa. They would work closely together in the months ahead.

Amy decided to study three aspects of women's roles: women's participation in the negotiation process, the efforts to enshrine women's rights in the constitutional proposals, and women's activism at the grassroots. She worked in a systematic way from the outset and made a list of things to do that could occupy a team of researchers for years. Amy's research agenda was too broad and inchoate at first, but she had always set ambitious goals for herself. She was eager to assist Omar, Mabandla, and Ngcuka as they drafted policies for a postapartheid South Africa. She and Mabandla began working on several articles on women in South Africa for which Amy did a significant amount of research and writing. Brigitte "seems to have a lot for me to do," Amy wrote shortly after arriving at the university.

Within a week of her arrival in Cape Town, Amy began attending a wide array of women's meetings and conferences. She developed a modus operandi at these events that she would stick with for the next 10 months: she would take notes on the proceedings, type up reports, and then distribute them to the meeting sponsors and the Community Law Centre, thus building up a resource base for the center's Gender Research Project and the women's organizations themselves. On October 23, 1992, she attended a seminar at UWC titled "Exploding Myths about Gender, Race and Class Development." The men at the seminar expressed support for cultural traditions that preserved their dominant status in South Africa, Amy reported, while the women argued that some traditions needed to be changed. The men supported race-based affirmative action but not gender-based affirmative action. Clearly South African women had a long way to travel on the road to equality. Amy also began meeting women in other organizations, including the ANC Women's League and the Women's National Coalition.

As eager as she was to meet academics and leaders of women's organizations, Amy was particularly interested in making contact with ordinary black women at the grassroots. This was easier said than done. Although black women in the townships realized that they had some white support, they didn't necessarily trust whites, given the legacy of apartheid. But women began inviting Amy to attend their meetings in townships and assented when Amy asked if she could take minutes. She would find a place in the back to set up her laptop and would quietly type notes as the meetings proceeded, trying to be as unobtrusive as possible. She wanted to stay in the background, observing and listening, rather than being the vocal American out front. Although she believed passionately in the women's efforts to achieve equality, she didn't believe it was her role to impose solutions. She was also careful how she dressed. Abandoning the more stylish clothing she wore in Washington, D.C., she often came to meetings in South Africa in jeans so that people would be comfortable with her, although she couldn't resist wearing her cowboy boots occasionally. She also stopped wearing makeup.

Part of establishing a rapport with black women was speaking their language. At some of the early meetings she attended, the women spoke a combination of English and Xhosa and likely helped Amy translate when necessary. She began studying Xhosa shortly after her arrival in Cape Town. Her UWC classmates remember how much she enjoyed learning the language and how uninhibited she was about practicing conversation, even though she found the pronunciation difficult at times. In her postcards to Scott, she would often write a few sentences in Xhosa and then print the English translation in tiny letters below. She clearly viewed learning an African language as a great adventure.

Amy's efforts seemed to pay off. She soon built a sizeable network of contacts in the women's movement, first in Cape Town and then beyond. One of Amy's early contacts was Sandra Liebenberg, an active member of the National Association of Democratic Lawyers. Sandra briefed her on the legal status of women in South Africa and the efforts to address women's issues in the legal profession. Another contact was Hloni Maboe, a staff member at the Institute of Child Guidance at UWC. She told Amy about the formation of a women's support group on campus to address sexual harassment and rape and invited Amy to attend meetings of the Western Cape branch of the Women's National Coalition. Around the same time, Amy introduced her to someone at the local ANC Women's League office and learned about the league's plans to mobilize women for the upcoming elections.

Both her research and her living situation began to work out even better than she had hoped. At first her housemate Melanie had been worried that Amy might be "the proverbial pushy American," but, ironically, Amy seemed reserved and even "boring" at first. The pair quickly warmed to each other, especially after they began going to bars and clubs together. In a postcard written just days after her arrival, Amy described her housemates as "very cool" and their house "very funky." The easy familiarity went both ways. Eventually Melanie came to regard Amy as a combination friend, sister, and even coparent for her daughter.

Not everything was perfect. Melanie's mother had committed suicide years earlier, and Melanie sometimes had dramatic mood swings. Linda Biehl later learned that Melanie was bipolar and sometimes took medication to ease her symptoms. Melanie also smoked, which couldn't have been pleasant to someone as health-conscious as Amy. Of course, Amy had her quirks as well. "She wouldn't clean up," Melanie later told a British journalist. "She didn't know how to. She couldn't cook, apart from Mexican food. She'd stay in the bath forever and there'd be no hot water left." Sometimes Amy would intervene during Melanie and Solange's "catfights," although she soon realized that the two loved each other very much. The Jacobses had "very little money," Amy observed, "but they both have very expensive taste!" Amy would sometimes help Melanie pay her bills and would buy her dinner when she was broke.

Amy was the partner Melanie needed and the second parent Solange needed, Linda Biehl came to believe. Melanie and Amy indeed began to share the responsibility of parenting Solange. Solange attended high school at Zonnebloem College in the old District Six, and Amy would often accompany her mother to school meetings and programs. Melanie and Amy took Solange on her first trip to a nightclub as well, and Amy would sometimes pick Solange up from parties. The three began to joke that Amy was becoming Solange's "dad." When the trio went out to eat and the waiter arrived, Amy would sometimes even ask, "And so what will our daughter have?"

"Amy quickly became part of our lives," Solange recalled. "She became my father." The two would leave each other notes occasionally, testifying to their close relationship. In one, Solange thanked Amy for money; in another, Amy reminded Solange to get food for herself. Amy's habit of giving money to Solange did not always please Melanie, who sometimes confronted Amy about it. "She didn't have much, but she did have pride," Solange remembered. "My Mom didn't want Amy to pay me." Solange trusted Amy and talked with her about her skin, clothes, and school issues. In fact, Solange confided in Amy so much that Melanie sometimes got angry. As Melanie later admitted, "I remember snapping at her [Solange] that I am her mother, and that report cards should be seen by me first. Of course we all laughed at my petty jealousy later." Amy and Melanie had a lot of fun together. They hosted parties at their apartment in Mowbray and went out dancing on Thursday nights, often staying out until well past midnight. They frequently went to clubs without a male escort. Men sometimes made advances toward Amy, but, according to Melanie, she "just told them that she had a great big boyfriend back in the States and he wouldn't like it." Even if they didn't return home until 4 a.m., Amy would be up by 7:30 a.m. typing her research papers. Her friends from Stanford and Washington would not have been surprised.

Because interracial friendships were still the exception rather than the rule in South Africa, Amy and Melanie would often be regarded as curiosities when they were out in public together. But instead of taking offense, the two reveled in the attention. "We went into a shop," Melanie recalled later. "I said, 'My sister will have a medium and I will have a large.' And people looked at us and stared." Amy found living with Melanie and Solange to be liberating. "I'm so glad not to be living with white people," she wrote a friend. "It really changes one's experience. For instance, I can move around better with my black and 'coloured' friends—so I go to black and coloured clubs, visit people in black and coloured areas, etc. and I'm accepted because I'm with them. When I go to white people places, I'm appalled! Melanie and I are always getting strange looks from people no matter where we go because nobody can believe we hang out together. We even dance together and stuff."

Amy found plenty of opportunities to enjoy herself in Cape Town. Within a month of her arrival, she began taking dance classes at the city's Jazzart dance studio so that she could learn the "pantsula," a unique style of South African street dancing. "Quick, athletic, it fit Amy's style completely," one of her classmates commented. "Capped with her effervescent smile, she bounced to its crisp cadences with grace and verve." Amy and her friends began frequenting clubs where the Johannesburg-based band Loading Zone performed. Listening to them perform with a Windhoek Lager in her hand, Amy couldn't have been happier. Often the two were joined on their nights out by Gregory Williams, nicknamed "Bucks," a close friend of Melanie's and an architect in the city.

As much as Amy enjoyed frequenting Cape Town's night spots, she loved the peninsula's natural beauty and felt exhilarated being there. She liked going to Cape Town's beaches, especially Camps Bay on the Atlantic side. She also ran regularly to stay in shape and find an outlet for her competitive spirit. In November 1992, she finished 111th out of 873 women in a race sponsored by the retailer Truworths and ran a women's 10-kilometer race in early December. The night before that race, she and some friends had listened to their favorite band, Loading Zone, and didn't arrive home until 3 a.m. Amy had befriended the band's drummer, Paco from Mozambique, and the two had begun running on the beach together. "You should see the looks we get from whites," Amy wrote to her friend Miruni. "Apartheid is not dead!"

As full as Amy's life was in Cape Town, she made sure that she kept in touch with family and friends back home. She regularly wrote her friends by hand, and because email had not yet fully taken over, some of her letters and postcards were saved. She often sent her friends postcards at the same time, writing in small, cursive letters that curled around the cards to fill up every millimeter of space. Amy didn't tend to write her family in California, but she would call home on most Sunday afternoons (morning in California), filling her parents in on all she was seeing and doing. Several of Amy's friends worried about her safety and warned her to be careful. On October 20, 1992, shortly after Amy arrived in Cape Town, one of her friends wrote, "Take care of yourself, as you know it's a very shaky situation there—lots of people get caught under it." Another friend, writing six weeks later, mentioned the State Department's travel advisory for South Africa and its warnings about violence against whites in the Cape. How and if Amy responded to the concerns of her friends remains a mystery.

What is clear is that Amy refused to be constrained by the racial boundaries that limited the lives of most whites in South Africa. She wanted to transcend the country's racial barriers, which was not easy in such a segregated society. The American author William Finnegan called such attempts "crossing the line," the title of his account of teaching in a Coloured school in Cape Town in 1980. Amy "wouldn't accept that as a white woman she couldn't have African friends," her Stanford friend Michael McFaul observed. She began offering to take students home to Gugulethu, a poverty-stricken black township between Bellville and Mowbray. She attended political gatherings of the ANC and even went to some political funerals. One friend remembered that even the vagrants in Mowbray knew Amy because she sometimes gave them money. While reaching out or "crossing the line" in these ways, Amy didn't usually sense hostility from blacks. In fact, she once told a friend that racial tension in Cape Town seemed milder than in the United States.

The many photographs Amy took show that she didn't stay in safe white suburbs—or at UWC for that matter. She traveled extensively and spent as much time as she could with blacks, Indians, Coloureds, youth, and women. She frequently joined predominantly black crowds, whether at schools, parks, performances, or gatherings. Both political and social events attracted her attention. She attended many rallies, marches, and demonstrations in South Africa. One photo she took in late 1992 shows a black marcher in a crowd wearing a "Boipatong" T-shirt, in honor of the victims of the massacre earlier that year. She photographed mixed-race demonstrators carrying the banner "Hands off our teachers." Another photo shows South African police cordoning off a street where blacks and Coloureds were marching. She never reported feeling threatened at any of these events. Many photos show Amy at social occasions, drinking and dancing with men and women of all races. Those who posed for Amy invariably had warm expressions. She often trained her lens on black children and youth and produced some striking images. In one, a small black child of one or one and a half is shown with Amy's white arm reaching out to hold the child's hand. Another photo shows Amy with Melanie, probably at home in Mowbray, beneath a poster showing black and white faces, with the caption "Human rights for all."

In a society where the relationship between white and black women was usually that of "maids" and "madams" (employers), Amy befriended many black

South African women, both at the university and through the women's organizations she became involved in. As several of Amy's closest friends observed, she began to forget she was white. Brigitte Mabandla described Amy as "one of those people you forget is white." They both transcended the typical stereotypes whites had about blacks and blacks had about whites. In a country still divided by race, not only did Amy forget she was white, but so did many of her South African friends.

Amy made a particularly strong impression on Maletsatsi Maceba, a first-year law student at UWC. The two met shortly after Amy arrived at UWC and became better acquainted through their involvement in women's organizations. In a country where history, geography, and politics conspired against interracial friendships, the two young women quickly bonded, and Amy became Maletsatsi's first white friend. Maletsatsi had not had an easy life. She grew up in the Eastern Cape and moved to Cape Town with her mother and siblings when she was about 11. Because no formal housing was available when they arrived, they settled in Crossroads, a vast squatter camp of metal shacks on the Cape Flats. The family had barely enough to live on. Maletsatsi's father died when she and her siblings were in primary school, and her mother supported the family by working as a domestic servant in a white suburb. Maletsatsi didn't graduate from high school until she was 25. Her education was delayed not only by her late start, but also by school boycotts and stints of work to help support the family. When Amy met her, she lived in New Crossroads; much of old Crossroads had been destroyed during police-supported vigilante violence in 1986. Maletsatsi had an on-campus job to help pay her way through law school, and she was an active member of the ANC Women's League

When Amy discovered that she and Maletsatsi were interested in attending many of the same meetings, she offered to give Maletsatsi rides. As they went back and forth between UWC, meeting venues, and black townships, the two talked about politics, the women's movement, and each other's future plans. Instead of keeping them apart, their two very different backgrounds seemed to draw them together. Amy believed Maletsatsi had a bright future and wanted to do what she could to boost her friend's prospects. Amy spent time at Maletsatsi's home in New Crossroads and encouraged her to get even more involved in women's organizations. She introduced her to other women activists and two white women in parliament, Sheila Camerer and Dene Smuts. Although Amy usually tried to keep a low profile at the meetings she attended, she did speak out during one meeting of the Women's National Coalition. When white women there were nominating only other white women to a steering committee, Amy's natural outspokenness got the better of her. She nominated Maletsatsi to the steering committee, and her friend was duly appointed.

Like Melanie's daughter, Solange, Maletsatsi admired and trusted Amy. "She related to me as if there were no differences," she remembered. Amy was not just a student, working on her own project, she said, but a person who went into the community to help improve women's lives. Maletsatsi also noted that Amy didn't want just to associate with famous people, but to work with everyday people, and, by doing so, she gained a true picture of conditions at the grassroots. She particularly admired how Amy would go into the black townships alone. Few white South Africans ever ventured into black townships, except policemen; it was virtually unheard of for lone white women to do so. Amy's forays into black townships enabled her to know more about conditions there than most white South Africans. And unlike many whites, Amy was learning to speak Xhosa. She would frequently implore Maletsatsi to "teach me one word in Xhosa today."

Amy's ability to make friends across the color line enabled her to become more deeply involved in women's organizations. One day she would attend a meeting of women lawyers seeking to draft a "women's charter"; the next she would attend the launch of a new branch of the ANC Women's League. She became particularly involved in the Women's National Coalition. Established in April 1992, the coalition was designed to bring women together across racial and party lines so they could draft a charter of women's rights and ensure that South Africa's new constitution would guarantee equality for women. Amy joined discussions about how women's rights could be protected and participated in two key conferences during her first few months in South Africa that focused her thinking and paved the way for much of her future research.

The first was a workshop on a women's charter sponsored by the Western Cape branch of the Women's National Coalition. Held in the mostly mixed-race suburb of Athlone in late November 1992, the conference was designed to produce a document outlining women's demands. Local women of all races came to discuss the barriers they faced in South African society and how these barriers could be addressed. Amy attended along with Maletsatsi, Sandra Liebenberg, and 23 other women who represented organizations as diverse as Call of Islam, the ruling National Party, the ANC Women's League, the Institute for a Democratic Alternative for South Africa (IDASA), and a women's group from the University of Cape Town. Amy took notes and photos and decided to write two reports: a formal one "for the record" and a shorter "popular" report with photos, hoping that the latter would encourage participating women to stay involved. By attending such meetings, taking notes, and writing and distributing reports, she was doing more than just giving the participants a tangible record of their proceedings, important though that was. She was also spreading an awareness of women's issues and concerns to a broader audience, particularly to men like Dullah Omar on the ANC's constitutional committee.

The campaign for a women's charter would gain momentum and have real historical significance. As the political scientist Hannah Britton has observed, "The WNC's [Women's National Coalition] Women's Charter ensured that women's interests would be recognized in the constitution. South Africa's constitution has one of the broadest and most inclusive antidiscrimination clauses in the world. Its equality clause establishes that neither the state nor a person may 'unfairly discriminate directly or indirectly against anyone on one or more grounds, including race, gender, sex, pregnancy, marital status, ethnic or social origin, colour, sexual orientation, age, disability, religion, conscience, belief, culture, language and birth.'" After generations of legalized discrimination, South Africa would eventually ban discrimination in all its forms.

Amy recognized that she was participating in a historic transition that might ban discrimination on the basis of both race and gender. After the workshop on the women's charter, she made plans to attend a workshop in Durban on "Empowering Women in a Democratic Government." At the December 1992 conference, 80 South African women met to discuss ways of ensuring that women played a role in the future government. They talked about the possible establishment of a "women's ministry" to address their concerns and listened to international delegates discuss the role of women in their respective governments. The delegates represented an even wider array of perspectives than had those at the workshop in Athlone two weeks earlier. Besides the Women's National Coalition, IDASA, the National Party, and the ANC Women's League, women attended from the Pan Africanist Congress, the Democratic Party, the Inkatha Freedom Party, the Azanian People's Organization, and the South African Communist Party. Among those attending were Frene Ginwala and Nkosazana Zuma, two of the most influential women in the ANC (and thus South Africa). Ginwala would become Speaker of the National Assembly after the 1994 election and Zuma minister of health and then foreign affairs. Amy introduced herself to many of the women whom Mabandla had encouraged her to meet and found the meeting extremely useful. "I did my best to keep a low profile and I took lots of notes," she wrote Omar, "which is the reason my report is not finished yet—too many notes!"

Before taking a break for Christmas and New Year—summer holidays in the southern hemisphere—Amy began making plans for her future, both in South Africa and back in the United States. She developed proposals for several research projects, which she gave to Omar and Mabandla for comment. She termed her most important prospective topic as "Towards a Women's Package—An Examination of Options for South African Women." Motivated in part by the conference in Durban she had just attended, Amy wanted to analyze structures that other governments had used to address women's issues, particularly those in Canada, Brazil, and a yet-to-be-determined African country. As she was plotting her research strategy for the New Year, she was also applying to graduate schools so that she could enter a doctoral program in political science once she returned to the United States in the fall of 1993. Setting her sights high as usual, she applied to Harvard, Yale, Princeton, and the University of California, Berkeley, intending to study southern Africa, international and comparative politics, and women in democratic transitions in Africa.

After only two months in South Africa, Amy had established herself as a serious researcher at UWC, made substantive connections with a wide variety of women's organizations, and earned the respect of leading academics and women's activists. She had developed a huge range of contacts across the political spectrum in an environment with a fair amount of anti-American stereotypes. Part of her success was due to the persona she had consciously adopted. As outspoken as she was back home, in South Africa she didn't want to be perceived as being the dominant white person or the overbearing American. Mabandla and Omar found her useful to have on their staff because she was efficient and hardworking and wasn't seeking the spotlight. Even Kader Asmal, a professor of human rights at UWC who didn't know Amy as well as Mabandla and Omar, noticed that Amy was developing unusually good relationships with her South African colleagues. He remembered Amy as being outgoing but humble. Even granting the fact that most future descriptions of Amy would be eulogistic in tone, the respect she earned was undeniable. Far from being "the ugly American," she was eager to learn from South Africans and wasn't foisting herself or imposing her values on South Africa. That, plus her "spirit, warmth, and commitment," won her many friends.

Before year's end, Amy's boyfriend came to visit. Scott was now in law school at Willamette University in Oregon, and he flew to Cape Town to spend the holidays with Amy. When he arrived at the airport, it was 95 degrees Fahrenheit (35 degrees Celsius). On his first day in Cape Town, he and Amy had beers with Randi Erentzen, Dullah Omar, and Albie Sachs, a top ANC legal scholar who had barely survived an assassination attempt four years earlier. Secret agents of the South African government had rigged his car with a bomb when he was in exile in Mozambique. Although he survived the blast, the bomb tore off one of his arms and blinded him in one eye. As the group talked, the famed jazz pianist Abdullah

Ibrahim performed; Allan Boesak even stopped by to chat. Scott could hardly believe he was in such august company. He marveled at Amy's ability to connect with leading people inside the struggle, but, knowing Amy as well as he did, he wasn't surprised. Nor was he surprised when, during his visit, opposition leader Aleke Banda telephoned Amy from hiding in Malawi. Banda was hoping someone from NDI could advise his movement as Malawi's upcoming referendum on multiparty democracy approached, and Amy promised to contact her former colleagues at NDI on his behalf. But Amy happily put her work aside to show Scott the city she loved. They toured the Cape Peninsula, drove to Cape Point, went hiking on Table Mountain, attended musical performances, and spent time in at least one black township where Amy had friends.

Just after the New Year, Amy and Scott took a trip along the Indian Ocean coast to the Transkei. The drive, known as the "Garden Route," is one of the most scenic in South Africa. It skirts beautiful beaches, dramatic mountains, rocky coves, and magnificent, sparkling lagoons. They left Cape Town on January 2 and headed east toward the Transkei's "Wild Coast." Scott remembered that as soon as they entered the Transkei, the telephone poles and the power lines disappeared, a sure sign of the underdevelopment plaguing South Africa's homelands. They would barrel down the deserted highways and then suddenly "300 cattle would be in the road." The Transkei had a distinctly different feel to it from South Africa proper, and Amy and Scott welcomed the chance to "get in the middle of nowhere." Once they stopped at a resort at Mbotyi, just inland from the Transkei coast, beyond Port St. John's. When they saw a group of young African children playing in a lagoon, Amy went right up to them, spoke to them in Xhosa, and proceeded to give them swimming lessons. Much as Amy delighted in speaking in Xhosa, the kids spoke to her in English.

During their time on the road, Amy and Scott saw another South Africa, a quieter, rural side. They also saw the "white" parts of each town they passed and then the ubiquitous black townships that adjoined them, which Amy called "a real political education." Of course, Amy's "real political education" had only just begun.

4

Year of the Great Storm

AS 1993 dawned, South Africa's future was uncertain. Three years had passed since F. W. de Klerk unbanned liberation organizations and freed Nelson Mandela, yet the white minority government was still in control. Formal negotiations were on hold and no date had been set for democratic elections. But a potential breakthrough came from an unlikely source. In late 1992, the leading white communist in the ANC, Joe Slovo, developed the idea of a "sunset clause" to push negotiations forward. Under this plan, after elections, the majority party would share power with minority parties in a government of national unity, and white civil servants would be guaranteed job security. Discussion of these issues and others at a series of private meetings in December 1992 and January 1993 brought the ANC and the governing National Party closer together.

Formal negotiations resumed in early March when 26 parties attended a planning conference for the Multiparty Negotiating Forum. These were the first formal negotiations since the breakdown of CODESA II in June 1992, and they attracted more participants, including the Conservative Party and the PAC. The stage was set for further negotiations at the World Trade Centre in Kempton Park, near Johannesburg's international airport.

In the months ahead, South Africa's transition to democracy became more turbulent than ever, as black and white extremists on the left and right tried to sabotage negotiations. They nearly succeeded. The year 1993 would be the most violent year of the transition—3,706 people would lose their lives in political violence. Black attacks on whites increased, some of which were perpetrated by the

PAC or its affiliates. But despite some well-publicized incidents involving whites, most victims of South Africa's political violence were black. Some black victims were killed by government security forces or by operatives of a covert "third force" directed by elements in South African intelligence. Others were killed in clashes between the ANC and Inkatha. There were also a disturbing number of racially motivated attacks against blacks perpetrated by white civilians. In January 1993, members of the Wit Wolwe ("White Wolves") announced that their organization regarded "every black man as an enemy" and that it would begin to attack "soft targets" among the black population unless the government took action against the military wings of the ANC and PAC. The violence was so serious in 1993 that most newspapers referred only to black body counts, not individuals.

Although the ANC and Inkatha were the two largest black South African political parties in the early 1990s, the PAC began to make headlines more than ever before. The PAC had been established in 1959, when a group of activists critical of the ANC launched an organization based on "Africanism," a militant form of African nationalism. Led by Robert Sobukwe, the PAC opposed the ANC's partnerships with non-Africans and believed that Africans should lead the liberation struggle in South Africa. It opposed the Freedom Charter, the landmark document endorsed by the Congress Alliance stating that South Africa belonged to all who lived there, black and white. Under the slogan "Africa for the Africans," the PAC demanded that South Africa's land be returned to the African majority. It believed that the country's future should be defined by Africans, not by a coalition of different racial groups. Although its leaders sometimes denied it, antiwhite feeling in the PAC was noticeably stronger than in the ANC.

Partly in an effort to outmaneuver the ANC, the PAC had organized the large anti–pass demonstration at Sharpeville in 1960. After the tragic loss of life there, the government declared a state of emergency and banned both the PAC and the ANC. Leaders of both organizations were jailed, driven underground, or forced into exile. During the next several decades, the PAC would be overshadowed by the ANC, both in South Africa and internationally. It became known more for infighting than fighting apartheid, and its bitter rivalry with the ANC continued.

When sustained protest in South Africa reemerged in 1984, the PAC's presence in the country was negligible (unlike the ANC's, which had the high-profile UDF as its unofficial internal wing in South Africa). But after the PAC was unbanned in 1990, its profile in South Africa rose considerably, out of proportion to its actual numerical strength. Many of its members initially opposed negotiations with the government and favored intensifying the armed struggle. These militants regarded the government as illegitimate and insisted that it surrender power immediately. But others in the PAC favored participating in negotiations. Divisions between PAC leaders and the organization's more militant armed and student wings would continue to fester as the transition unfolded.

As South Africa's transition dragged on, youths loyal to the PAC became frustrated by their continued powerlessness and the slow pace of negotiations. They remained loyal to the organization, but they sometimes acted independently, without instructions or approval from the PAC itself. The PAC withdrew from formal negotiations in late 1991, just before CODESA, whose format it rejected. When the ANC remained committed to CODESA, the PAC accused it of selling out. Impatient with the slow pace of change, PAC hardliners seemed more interested in toppling the South African government than in the negotiation process. The PAC's armed wing, the Azanian People's Liberation Army (APLA), launched a series of attacks targeting white civilians. In late November 1992, its operatives attacked whites at a party at the King William's Town golf club, killing four. Days later APLA bombed a restaurant in Queenstown, killing one and injuring seven. Before these attacks, South Africa's rising political violence had hardly touched whites at all.

APLA declared 1993 the "Year of the Great Storm." Despite ongoing negotiations in the country, it planned to intensify the armed struggle. APLA spent much of 1993 operating underground, stockpiling weapons, planning attacks, looking for safe havens, and dodging the police, not always successfully. Although most black South Africans supported the ANC's strategy of negotiations and not the PAC's armed struggle, the PAC was popular in some areas, particularly in the Transkei and Cape Town's black townships. In February 1993, the PAC president Clarence Makwetu said, "The PAC would fight to the bitter end as long as there were vestiges of imperialism and colonialism. It would fight for self-determination and not settle for crumbs from the master's table." That month, representatives of the government and the PAC met in Botswana to discuss the suspension of the PAC's armed struggle, but the PAC refused to lay down its arms, even though it joined the Multiparty Negotiating Forum at the World Trade Centre in March and engaged in negotiations. Tension between the government and the PAC rose in the months ahead.

In late March 1993, the *Weekly Mail* newspaper reported a growing divide between the PAC leadership and members of the PAC's student wing, the Pan Africanist Students Organization (PASO). Disillusioned with the leadership's talks with the government, students were inspired by APLA's attacks against whites and were sometimes training to undertake such attacks themselves. These young activists believed they were in a war to overthrow the apartheid state. The *Weekly Mail* identified an ominous new trend: "spontaneous attacks by youth and student groupings which have access to arms and are disillusioned by the negotiations, escalating violence in the townships and the continued education crisis."

The PAC's militancy was best captured by its slogan "one settler, one bullet," which activists began to chant more frequently at PAC rallies. Not all of the organization's leaders favored the slogan. In March 1990, the returned PAC exile Barney Desai said, "I wish also to caution my brothers and sisters that the slogan of 'one settler, one bullet' is inconsistent with our stated aims. No mature liberation movement has ever had as its stated policy an intention to drive the white people into the sea." But the slogan continued to be popular in the organization, especially among young PAC supporters in the black townships. The rising anger among black youth in general was undeniable. In March 1993, students from the ANC-aligned Congress of South African Students (COSAS), PASO, and the Azanian Students' Movement chanted "one settler, one bullet" at a demonstration in central Johannesburg. That month, the senior ANC leader Chris Hani criticized the PAC for its "one settler, one bullet" slogan and for continuing the armed struggle, prompting a defiant response from the PAC secretary of political affairs. Despite Hani's rebuke, the slogan would continue to be a potent rallying cry in the months ahead.

AMY was clearly concerned about the upsurge in violence in South Africa. She read about it, talked about it with friends and colleagues, and thought about it. As Amy pondered the issues she wanted to write about during the rest of her Fulbright period, she considered doing a study of South Africa's violence. "[It's] clear that South Africa is caught in a spiral of violence," she wrote in notes to herself. Although she remarked that political violence received the most attention, violence was "particularly brutal and damaging to women." Apartheid lay behind much of the violence, because it broke up families and eroded men's sense of self-worth. For the problem to be eradicated, "drastic measures" would be required, such as "emphasizing women's human rights in the constitution and favoring women in legal reform; education and counseling; and monitoring the issue."

As Amy resumed her work after her holiday with Scott, she was brimming with ambitious ideas and plans. She saw 1993 as a key year for women's efforts to gain equality because negotiations for a new government would lead to democratic elections and a new constitution. Women had demonstrated their determination to achieve equality and participate in negotiations, the election, and a new government, but they were divided by race, class, religion, and custom, which challenged their efforts. Amy planned to analyze women's contributions to the transition process and evaluate the strengths and weaknesses of their efforts. She wanted to be both comprehensive—by examining women's organizations across the social and political spectrum—and impartial. She wanted to reach people all over the country, of all races and languages, in urban and rural areas, at both the leadership level and the grassroots. As part of her research, she would also "observe and play a supporting role" in the Women's National Coalition and work with groups of progressive lawyers. Amy's research framework was incredibly broad and could have taken a team of researchers years to complete. But that was Amy—she'd always set a high bar for herself, and now was no exception.

One of the people who helped Amy with her research was Rhoda Kadalie, UWC's gender equity coordinator. Amy befriended Rhoda in early 1993, when she attended a workshop on gender that Kadalie led at the orientation for the university's residence assistants. Amy noted that while most students were highly attuned to racism in South Africa and enthusiastically backed the struggle for democracy, they hadn't spent much time thinking about gender discrimination. "Rhoda did an outstanding job of making students think about sexism in the same way they think about racism," she wrote. A Capetonian of mixed race, Rhoda was a feminist and a critic of the liberation movement at the time, although she fully supported the transition to democracy. She recalled that when she tried to befriend Amy early on, Amy was cool toward her, perhaps having been warned by ANC women that she was too critical of the liberation movement. Rhoda speculated that like many international students, Amy might have romanticized the antiapartheid struggle at first. Eventually Amy came to Rhoda's office hoping she would comment on her work. In the months ahead, the two became friends. Rhoda served as a valuable resource for Amy's work, and Amy kept Rhoda informed on a host of issues relating to her research. Like so many other South Africans who got to know Amy well, Rhoda marveled at Amy's seemingly inexhaustible energy:

> In the short space of time that Amy was here, she had more black friends
> than I had. She knew where all the clubs were in the townships. She
> would go and dance and party with her friends. She loved the beach; she
> ran marathons; she played hard but worked equally hard. She was the
> model student, researching, following all the leads, taking advice, writing
> essays, volunteering to organize and help with conferences, writing up
> notes of conferences, and generally monitoring the debates at CODESA
> and the negotiations between the political parties prior to 1994.

The more Amy delved into her research, the more conscious she became of the challenges facing her as an outsider. An important discussion she had with

Brigitte Mabandla in late January crystallized the issue. Mabandla was pleased with Amy's work but warned her not to get too involved in the women's groups she was studying. Her work had to be viewed as impartial to be respected. Mabandla also warned Amy that "the same people who will often encourage my involvement in various projects can also turn around and criticize me for being an American doing South African work. I have taken Brigitte's advice to heart." Her self-consciousness as an American scholar-activist became stronger than before. In a fax to a colleague in early February, Amy mentioned that because of her "sensitivity to being an American doing this type of research," she would wait until her paper drafts were approved by Dullah Omar before distributing them more widely. Amy sensed that Mabandla and Omar—her two supervisors—seemed to have different ideas about her objectivity. "Brigitte thinks it is extremely important that I be viewed as impartial, while you are of the opinion that trying to portray myself as impartial would be false," Amy wrote in a memo to Omar. "I do think it is important that my research methodology be impartial and sound. When I am interviewing people—particularly outside of the liberation movement—I don't want them to perceive that I have chosen sides." Although her view was closer to Mabandla's, she promised to consult with Omar frequently to ensure that he was comfortable with her activities. As he said later, "She thought as an American, she didn't want to interfere. She always felt South Africans must decide for themselves."

Ever since she worked for NDI, Amy had been very conscious of the negative impressions of Americans abroad—that they sometimes came into other countries and dictated solutions, often knowing very little about conditions on the ground. Amy wanted to avoid this and support her South African colleagues from behind the scenes, not in front. Balancing the roles of participant and observer could be difficult. She strongly supported the struggles for liberation and women's rights but believed that South Africans should take the lead, even when she sometimes wanted African women to be more proactive. She knew that South Africans sometimes resented foreigners who gave them unsolicited advice on how they should conduct their struggle. Amy's friend Stephen Stedman said, "She understood that solutions to South Africa's problems would ultimately come from South Africans, not foreign visitors with instant expertise about the country and its conflicts." To complicate matters, Amy had to be conscious of her status as both an American and a white woman. She wanted to avoid the white paternalism that too often surfaced in multiracial settings. "She seemed to believe that when black and white women were together in the same organizations, the white women tended to dominate," Kennell Jackson recalled. The problem came later when some South African women urged Amy to be more active than she wanted to be.

Amy attended meetings of different organizations almost daily, sometimes more than one a day, both at UWC and off campus. Her list of contacts among women's organizations was extensive, but she wasn't just meeting women's activists. She attended conferences and workshops featuring prominent speakers such as Cyril Ramaphosa, Neville Alexander, George Bizos, and Alex Boraine. She continued to attend meetings of the Western Cape Women's Coalition and the gender desk of the National Association of Democratic Lawyers. Meetings did not have to be tedious, however. After Amy attended a workshop on racism and sexism in the student residences at UWC in January 1993, the students invited her to be a judge for their talent show. She agreed and went to the party afterward. "When the music started, everyone got up to dance, and all of a sudden, all eyes were focused on me, the only *white girl* in a room full of 200 people. 'Can she dance?' they were thinking to themselves. Well, I started groovin', and all of a sudden, *everyone* was groovin'! I had passed the test!"

Amy was also making headway with her major research projects. By January she had completed a draft of her comparative study of structures for women in decision making and began revising it for publication after receiving comments from Mabandla, Kadalie, Erentzen, and Sachs. She also began work on what she called her "Fulbright paper," which focused on women's role in the transition and prospects for women's rights afterwards. As busy as Amy was, she also found time to continue her advocacy for Malawi's prodemocracy movement.

Suddenly a wonderful thing happened: Amy got the chance to meet her long-time hero Nelson Mandela. She described the February 1993 encounter to Kennell Jackson at Stanford. "By the way, I met Nelson Mandela the other day. My boss at the Community Law Centre, Dullah Omar, introduced me to him, knowing that it would make my day! I spoke to him in Xhosa and then we talked, in English, about Bill Clinton and the saxophone. We agreed that he should learn some Mbaqanga—township music!" Amy was obviously thrilled to meet her idol.

As Amy met with individuals and groups, she sought to bring people from different backgrounds together. Around the same time she met Mandela, she attended a luncheon organized by the US Information Service (USIS) in Cape Town and met Sheila Camerer (National Party) and Dene Smuts (Democratic Party)—two female members of Parliament—and Mamphela Ramphele, a prominent physician, academic, and one of the cofounders of the Black Consciousness Movement. Although Amy appreciated the work of the USIS, she worried that it was not "meeting enough of the 'right women' to network with" when important American speakers came to Cape Town. She encouraged it to support education and leadership training for black South African women and brought along her

South African friends to USIS events. In March she organized a meeting between female law students from UWC and their counterparts at the predominantly white University of Cape Town. About a week later she showed two visiting American women around Cape Town's black townships with two members of the Langa branch of the ANC Women's League. Amy also reportedly organized at least one meeting between the Women's League and a group of white women lawyers. In these initiatives and others, she hoped to build bridges between black and white women in a society still thoroughly segregated by race. Women on both sides of the color line appreciated her efforts and told her so.

Several of Amy's friends and colleagues noticed how integrated Amy had become into the liberation movement despite her nationality. She saw an excellent opportunity to harness her energy on the movement's behalf when the white minority government released its Bill of Rights in early February 1993. On the day the bill was made public, Omar asked Amy to analyze its provisions for women in two hours, because he was going to debate a government representative on the radio that very evening. In a letter to a friend, Amy called the bill "completely bogus," but she was pleased that Omar had asked for her analysis. That was a sure sign that he trusted her judgment and analytical skills. The debate between Omar and Camerer was broadcast on Radio Metro on February 4, 1993. The next day, Amy wrote an urgent memo to Omar, congratulating him on his performance. She also drafted a lengthy response that she offered to submit in his name as an op-ed piece for a newspaper. "I know that this type of thing must be consulted fully within the ANC, so I just offer it as an idea. But I know that you are busy and that timing is important if you are to respond quickly."

Her response, just over two typed pages, was bold and well written, though not strident. She compared the government's proposals for women unfavorably with those in the ANC's proposed bill of rights. She criticized the government for trying to dictate women's rights without consulting women themselves, who needed to be part of the debate on how their rights should be protected. Consultation and consensus building were essential. She also criticized the National Party for putting a small section on women's rights toward the end of its charter. In her view, women's rights needed to be integrated into a bill of rights, not "ghettoized" in its own section. She agreed with the government's statement that religious values needed to be respected but insisted that women's rights shouldn't be compromised, even if they clashed with religious values. "The right to free practice of religion and custom must be strongly supported, but a future Bill of Rights should ensure that religious and cultural rights are protected in a manner that does not interfere with the attainment of full equality for women in law and practice," she wrote. Finally, she insisted that the rights of black women couldn't be fully protected until they had the right to vote, for which they were still waiting. In her memo to Omar, Amy said that she would understand if he didn't think publishing her response was appropriate, in which case she would incorporate it into her own research. "I hope you don't think I'm being too aggressive," she wrote. She wanted to contribute, if possible, but behind the scenes and anonymously.

Her research on the government's proposals for women continued in the weeks ahead. In late February, Amy gave Omar a 23-page briefing comparing the ANC's draft bill of rights and charter for social justice with the government's proposals on a charter of fundamental rights. Then in early March she traveled to Pretoria to attend a conference titled "Women and a Charter of Fundamental Rights" sponsored by the Ministry of Justice. The conference gave Amy the chance to learn firsthand about the government's draft legislation on women's equality. She must have rolled her eyes during Minister of Justice Kobie Coetsee's opening address. "Minister Coetsee began by joking that if the conference was successful, he would have to declare the male population of South Africa an 'endangered species,'" she wrote. Despite believing that the government's draft legislation was "merely an electioneering exercise," Amy found her trip to Pretoria worthwhile because she learned more about the government's perspective on women. She wrote a 16-page report of the conference, which she submitted to the Community Law Centre at UWC upon her return to Cape Town.

As she traveled back and forth between the different worlds of black and white women in Cape Town, Amy often reflected on the enormous gulf in culture and experience that divided them. Sometime during March or April 1993, as she contemplated South Africa's future from Melanie's apartment in Mowbray, with its view of Devil's Peak and Table Mountain, Amy wrote a poem she called "Mowbray Morning":

> I wake to the sights and sounds of a Mowbray morning
> Cars and trucks rush by below my 2nd story student's flat
> Dark shadows of workers rush by to boldly face another day
> The wind whistles as it glides down the shadow of Table Mountain
> The ageless mountain sees all
>
> The wind from the mountain whispers a story of two women
> The first has scrambled out of a crowded taxi and waits for a bus
> Thinking of her children's future and inspiring hope, she faces the day
> She boards the bus to take her around the impenetrable mountain

Where another woman awakes to the soft rhythm of the sea
   and the smell of clean salty air
   thinking of her children's future with fear and gnawing guilt

The ageless mountain whispers this story of two different women
   two different worlds
An uncertain future
Only the mountain knows

I listen to the tale of the wind
   the messenger of the mountain
For some hint of what the future holds
   for these two women of different worlds
   but the wind and the mountain grow silent
It is not for me to know

As Amy pondered South Africa's future, she pondered her own. She decided to apply for a Jacob Javits Fellowship from the US Department of Education to help pay for graduate school, which she hoped to begin in the fall. She wanted to continue her study of women in democratic transitions by comparing women's efforts in South Africa, Namibia, and Zambia. "Upon the completion of a PhD, I hope to teach and write in political science and Africa area studies," she wrote on the Javits application. "As a woman in this field, I feel a special responsibility to encourage young women—both American and African—to pursue careers in political science and to write and teach about the experiences of women in Africa." Then bad news arrived. Amy received rejection letters from all of the graduate schools she had applied to—Harvard, Yale, Princeton, and Berkeley. She was devastated. A journalist who later interviewed Melanie and Solange reported that Amy was "hurt and incredulous" and "wept for several hours."

Amy wasn't about to slow down, but she didn't let her heavy workload stop her from enjoying herself. In addition to her South African friends, Amy had begun socializing with a handful of Americans who arrived in Cape Town in early 1993. Steve Stedman, whom Amy had befriended at Stanford, was a political science professor at the School of Advanced International Studies at Johns Hopkins. He and his wife Corinne arrived in South Africa in early January 1993 so that Steve could begin his work as a Fulbright scholar at UWC's Centre for Southern African Studies. To the Stedmans, Amy was fun, not a stuffy intellectual. She had energy, "chutzpah," a great sense of humor, and frailties just like everyone else. Anna

Wang, another American in Cape Town, had first met Amy at NDI in Washington, D.C., in June 1992. She got to know Amy better beginning in February 1993, when NDI sent her to Cape Town to work on voter education projects. Anna would join Amy and others on Friday and Saturday nights to hear music and dance. "All of the boys were in love with Amy," Anna remembered. "She was vivacious and pretty, from California. She had a very infectious laugh. She was self-confident and really smart. But she was also down to earth."

Throughout her 10 months in South Africa, Amy called her parents back home on Sunday mornings (California time). "She would talk for 20 minutes nonstop," Peter later told a reporter. "She was excited with everything. It gave me so much satisfaction just listening to her. I felt really proud of her these mornings. She was so alive, so into it." Amy told her parents about the amazing people she was meeting, from Mandela to members of parliament to unknown but hardworking women at the grassroots. In one phone call home, Amy half-jokingly told her Republican father, "You know, Dad, some of my best friends are communists."

Then the sudden death of a communist threatened South Africa's entire transition. Chris Hani, one of black South Africa's most revered leaders, was shot and killed outside his home in suburban Boksburg on April 10, 1993. Fifty years old at the time of his death, he was murdered by a Polish immigrant with ties to white extremists. The gunman was arrested shortly after the murder, thanks to Hani's Afrikaner neighbor, who glimpsed the license plate of the fleeing car and reported the number to the police. It was as if an earthquake had struck South Africa. An opinion poll in November 1992 indicated that Hani was the second-most-popular leader in the country after Nelson Mandela. He was general secretary of the South African Communist Party, a leading member of the ANC's national executive committee, and formerly head of Umkhonto we Sizwe. He was hugely popular among black South African youth, who regarded him as a courageous fighter for justice. In the words of one South African journalist, Hani stood up for the "poor, oppressed, and dispossessed." Amy's friend Steve Stedman called Hani "a crucial link between the leadership of the ANC and its most marginalized constituencies—youth and Umkhonto we Sizwe cadres." Although he had a reputation for being militant, he had supported the negotiation process and called for the PAC's military wing, APLA, to lay down its arms. His loss threatened to tear South Africa apart—and perhaps even spark a civil war.

Sensing the gravity of the crisis—and his own limitations—South African president F. W. de Klerk asked Mandela to appear on national television and appeal for calm. Mandela did so the very night of Hani's death. "A white man, full of prejudice and hate, came to our country and committed a deed so foul that our whole nation now teeters on the brink of disaster," Mandela said. "But a white woman, of Afrikaner origin, risked her life so that we may know, and bring to justice, the assassin." That Mandela, not De Klerk, addressed the country in its moment of crisis showed how the balance of power in South Africa had fundamentally changed.

Many feared that Hani's death would set South Africa on fire. After news spread, thousands marched in central Cape Town to protest the killing. In the looting that followed, people smashed car windows, broke store windows, and set fire to vehicles and garbage cans, filling the air with black smoke. Police fired tear gas and then shot into the crowds, killing at least two and injuring 120 more. Protestors put up burning barricades in Cape Town's black townships. Some crowds chanted, "No more peace, no more peace!" Others shouted, "Where is Hani? Who killed Hani?" A reporter for the *Weekly Mail* called the mood not just angry, but "maniacal." As one demonstrator said, "You can't kill a leader of the people and expect nothing to happen." Clashes between black activists and police broke out elsewhere in the country, claiming at least 68 more lives. In three days of nationwide protests after Hani's death, 90 percent of South Africa's workers went on strike in what was probably the largest stayaway in the country's history. ANC Youth League leader Peter Mokaba appeared at a rally with Winnie Mandela and told the crowd, "Kill the Boer! Kill the farmer! We are tired of endless talking. We have been hit very hard. And we must hit back!"

Amy called home the day of Hani's death. A longtime admirer of his, she was "heartbroken" over the killing and feared a possible antiwhite backlash. She described the disenfranchised youth to her parents in order to help them comprehend the volatility of the situation. Scott soon realized that Amy's concerns were justified. With Hani's absence, the ANC—and other black political organizations—lost some control over the young militants in the townships. Amy was touched when some of her friends from the townships called her to make sure she was all right. But when some family and friends from the United States kept calling her to ask the same thing, she said, "My God, who cares about me?" Peter Biehl had been concerned about Amy's safety in South Africa ever since he first heard about her Fulbright. Linda shared his concerns. "I was very worried about her, but she would say, 'Mom, I'm okay. I'm doing this because I want to do this. You can't live your life in a shell.'" Amy continued venturing into black townships even though the climate was changing. The antiwhite mood in South Africa grew significantly in the aftermath of Hani's death. But those closest to Amy agree that she wasn't naïve or irresponsible or unaware of South Africa's dangers. As Scott later observed, Amy understood the hatred that apartheid created, but not necessarily the chaos that hatred could cause.

In the weeks after Hani's death, the mood in South Africa darkened considerably. Black anger toward whites grew, particularly among black youth. Antiwhite slogans and sentiments became more common at rallies. Whites reacted angrily to the upsurge in racist slogans, but few fully understood the depths of black rage. The Rev. Frank Retief, pastor at St. James Church in the Cape Town suburb of Kenilworth, felt the rising tension. White welfare workers affiliated with his church stopped going into Khayelitsha because of the perceived antiwhite mood there. Just three days before Hani's murder, a young white church volunteer from the United Kingdom was shot in Khayelitsha during a youth soccer match he'd organized. He survived the attack but lost sight in one eye. Hani's assassination days later made even the most experienced white community workers think twice before venturing into South Africa's black townships.

Negotiations between the government and the ANC quickened after Hani's death, sparking ominous reactions from both the left and right. In May 1993, the Fort Hare political scientist Sipho Pityana commented on the growing impatience with the negotiation process. The ANC had abandoned the armed struggle but hadn't achieved enough to satisfy many of its young supporters. "Hani's murder not only angered the black community," Pityana wrote, "it also unleashed the previously dormant frustrations with the negotiation process. . . . The anger of the masses is reaching a bursting point. . . . The voice of reason is increasingly losing ground. The theatre of war is becoming more attractive."

Frustration from the white right was also about to boil over. On June 25, right-wing Afrikaners stormed the World Trade Centre and trashed the facilities to show their disgust with the negotiation process. Many of the rabble-rousers were members of the Afrikaner Resistance Movement (AWB / Afrikaner Weerstandsbeweging) who came dressed in battle fatigues. They were angry at the impending changes to South Africa and blamed De Klerk for selling them out. Despite the disruption, a date was set for South Africa's first democratic election: April 27, 1994. Most of the major parties agreed, with some important exceptions—Inkatha, the Conservative Party, and some homeland leaders. Their representatives walked out of negotiations after the election date was set, but the PAC stayed. Negotiations moved forward when the ANC and the National Party discussed forming a transitional executive council to govern the country until elections. Despite such progress, the fight waged by black and white extremists was far from over.

The PAC seemed intent on escalating the armed struggle. On April 28, APLA attacked a white farm in the northern Transvaal and killed the white landowner's wife. PAC leaders announced that white farmers were legitimate targets because they were allegedly well-armed and often members of "commando units." On

May 1, gunmen attacked the Highgate Hotel in East London, killing five white civilians and injuring several more. Although no APLA members applied for amnesty for the attack, the Truth and Reconciliation Commission later suspected that APLA was involved. At the time, APLA was actively recruiting youths into its ranks. Later in May 1993, South African police arrested more than 70 PAC activists in nationwide raids, including many members of the national executive. Then the government threatened to restrict the PAC's participation in constitutional negotiations. But PAC leaders were defiant. In June, Sabelo Phama, PAC secretary for defense and APLA commander, called for the armed struggle to be intensified. After all, he said, people's lives in South Africa hadn't changed after years of struggle, and the enemy was still in control.

The PAC's militancy needs to be kept in perspective. While the organization was attracting much attention for its highly charged rhetoric, the white right was equally hostile to the negotiation process and was contemplating civil war. Each time negotiations inched forward, extremists from both sides hardened their attitudes. The PAC was becoming more emboldened and planning more attacks against whites, but PAC supporters were still far outnumbered by the ANC, which had suspended its armed struggle in August 1990. The PAC lacked a leader of the stature of Mandela, who was a national icon. But even though the PAC was much smaller than the ANC, radical elements within the organization could still wreak considerable havoc—especially in the Western Cape, where its support base was relatively strong. According to a poll conducted in mid-1993, 10 percent of blacks in South Africa's largest urban areas supported APLA's attacks on white civilians. Forty-five percent completely opposed such attacks, and 40 percent said that while they didn't support the attacks, they understood why they occurred. The highest support for APLA attacks against whites came from young Xhosa-speakers in Cape Town. As it turned out, the poll proved to be chillingly accurate.

Well versed in the politics of the time, Amy was still determined to transcend South Africa's racial boundaries. She had black friends from the university who lived in the townships and continued to offer them rides home when they asked. She probably felt that the anger there wouldn't affect her. Anna Wang felt the same way. She and Amy knew about the unrest but saw themselves as part of the liberation movement. "We were aware of the risks, but I didn't think bad things could happen," Anna said. She noticed that Amy often dropped students off in the black township of Gugulethu. "She has always said that she doesn't mind because she has a car and most people don't." Others close to Amy agreed that she was fully aware of the dangers of traveling in and out of black areas, but that she overcame her fears in order to challenge herself, much as she always had.

Amy faced other challenges by late April 1993. She felt the first pangs of homesickness after about six months of being away. Her car had been hit twice in three days while parked in front of Melanie's apartment, and she was also experiencing some cash flow problems—her Fulbright check was late and NDI hadn't yet sent some money it still owed her. But her positive experiences far outweighed her negative ones. As Amy's younger sister Molly remarked on Amy's birthday on April 26, "Remember, you've done more in your 26 years than most of us will do in a lifetime!" And Amy wasn't done yet. She was pleased when an article she and Rhoda coauthored was published in the *Weekly Mail* on April 30, 1993. In "Women's Voices Will Be Heard at Last," Rhoda and Amy praised the eventual inclusion of women at the World Trade Centre talks and called for women to be included in every phase of the upcoming election process. "Negotiators must remember that women are more than 53 percent of the voting population," they wrote. "A transition process that does not consider their safety, their equality, and their unique experience of racial and gender discrimination will be inherently flawed." Amy was also earning praise from others in the South African women's movement. A May 1993 letter from the gender consultant Gill Noero shows that the posthumous praise Amy received wasn't overblown. After Amy drafted a report for an IDASA conference, Noero wrote, "Well, dear child, you put us all to shame with your extraordinary competence and industry." She thanked Amy for her "ably objective" report and offered to pass it on to members of parliament and legal scholars at the University of the Witwatersrand.

After months of research, writing, and revisions, one of Amy's major papers was ready for publication. Her essay "Structures for Women in Political Decision-Making" was published as a booklet in mid-1993 by the Gender Project at UWC's Community Law Centre. The article was one of the two most substantive articles she wrote during her 10 months as a Fulbright scholar. In it, Amy surveyed the structures different countries had established to ensure women's participation in government. The subject could hardly have been timelier, because South African women were working to gain access to government decision-making structures at that very moment. Amy's essay was thorough and well-documented. It demonstrated her ability to write for an academic audience and provided a good resource for women leaders as they strategized about how to gain access to government positions and influence policy. According to Amy, South African negotiators were moving toward a constitutional commitment to "non-sexism," but problems remained. There were still too few women leaders of political parties and too few women in transitional structures. "The differences among South African women are great," she concluded. "Apartheid has divided women and resulted in the positioning of black women at the lowest level of the socio-economic ladder with the least access to the very decision-making structures designed to improve their status. Nevertheless, South African women have come together in a debate about what types of decision-making structures for women will empower the broadest spectrum of women in their country. This debate must be fostered and facilitated." Amy's article would be a key resource for Brigitte Mabandla, who played an important role in promoting the interests of women during the constitutional negotiations and who would later become a cabinet minister in the new government. She drew on Amy's report in her own article, "Choices for South African Women," which was published in the feminist journal *Agenda* in 1994.

Besides studying how women could be incorporated into governmental structures, Amy became interested in the impact of "customary law" on women. Under "customary law" in South Africa—as it had been interpreted and codified by white authorities—African women were defined as perpetual minors who could neither enter into contracts nor inherit land. This inferior legal status was unacceptable to women's activists of the 1990s, who saw the opportunity for change during negotiations for a new constitution. In early 1993, Amy and Mabandla decided to organize a major conference on the subject. Here Amy took on an active role, planning, mobilizing, and articulating issues on behalf of South African women. She first drafted a proposal and budget for the conference in February and then wrote letters of invitation on Mabandla's behalf in April. Women needed to have a dialogue with traditional leaders on "customary law" "in order to promote the full citizenship and democratic participation of African women in a new dispensation." The conference would mark "the first step of a process by which South African women hope to influence the course of the debate on custom and religion."

The conference, "Custom and Religion in a Non-Racial, Non-Sexist South Africa," was held at UWC from May 14 to 16, 1993. The event brought together women from South Africa and abroad not only to exchange ideas on "customary law," but to develop strategies for how women could actually influence the negotiation process. At the end, women representing the National Association of Democratic Lawyers drafted a resolution to be presented to negotiators. It affirmed that the constitution for a postapartheid South Africa must guarantee women's right to equality in both the public and private spheres, and that no group of women should have fewer rights than another. South Africa's future constitution eventually reflected those very principles, but twenty years later, the country's legislators and activists would still be debating different versions of "customary law."

Once the conference adjourned, Amy worked to make its proceedings more widely known. She and Mabandla coauthored an article titled "'God-Given'

Oppression Upheld by Tradition," which was published in IDASA's journal *Democracy in Action* in July 1993. In it, they noted that although some conservative and traditional leaders sought to preserve those aspects of "customary law" that gave men power over women, "more progressive traditional leaders believe that tradition must be brought in line with the democratic principles of a bill of rights." Women's rights to own land, to have reproductive choices, to receive support if a husband remarried, and to have access to health and educational services needed to be protected in the future, even in areas governed by traditional leaders. When the conference papers were published by the Community Law Centre in 1994, the booklet was dedicated to Amy and included her executive summary. Her summary was also published in the journal *Women against Fundamentalism* that year.

Just a week after the custom and religion conference, Amy was scheduled to attend an ANC Women's League conference in Stutterheim in the Eastern Cape. But her usual enthusiasm was flagging. "I'm supposed to go to an ANC Women's League conference this weekend and they are paying my way," she wrote Scott. "But I'm no longer sure I want to go! Can you believe *I* am saying this about the Women's League? I think I am sick of conferences." The conference turned out to be worthwhile. It aimed to help the Women's League strategize about constitutional negotiations and eventual elections in South Africa. Members of the organization discussed their struggle to be included in the World Trade Centre negotiations and interacted with international women who spoke about democratic transitions in their countries. Women's League president Gertrude Shope gave the opening address and vice president Albertina Sisulu closed the conference. Both women posed for a photo with Amy, who was designated the official "rapporteur" (reporter) for the conference and who prepared a summary of the proceedings. In taking such detailed notes and compiling conference reports, Amy was not only assisting the sponsors of the events she attended but also documenting women's efforts to influence South Africa's transition to democracy. At one point she took time off from her note taking to write a letter to Scott. She wrote that although she sometimes wished Mabandla was more organized, her strengths were on full display at the conference. "She is in her element here and she is able to relate to women's league people in their own languages about very complicated issues. But she also continues to challenge the old ma's—the older generation of ANC women—who do not have the modern constitutional ideas that she has . . . Viva, malibongwe igama lam akhosikazi! [Viva, praise to the women!]"

Amid her papers and conferences, Amy undertook one of the greatest physical challenges of her life—the Comrades Marathon. The race, first held in 1921, was legendary for its arduousness. Its route spans 54 miles (89.9 kilometers) from Pieter-maritzburg to Durban and tests the endurance of even accomplished marathoners. Those who manage to finish sometimes collapse at the end. Amy was determined to take up the challenge. She wanted to reach and then transcend her "pain bar-rier," just as she had during swimming practice at school years earlier. Even though she was in excellent shape and had run standard marathons before, she had never entered a race of this magnitude. "I hope I don't die!" she joked in a letter to Scott. The Comrades Marathon of May 31, 1993, began at Pietermaritzburg city hall and ended at Kingsmead Stadium in Durban. Amy finished in 10 hours and 25 minutes, at 4:28 p.m., 32 minutes before the race officially ended. A photograph taken as she crossed the finish line shows her exhausted but elated. Marathon organizers and signatories of South Africa's National Peace Accord had agreed to call the race "the 1993 Comrades Marathon for Peace." Officials gave runners peace badges and cer-tificates to sign, affirming their support of peace and freedom in South Africa. The statement that Amy signed after finishing the race read, in part, "I pledge myself with integrity of purpose to make this land a prosperous one where we can all live, work and play together in peace and harmony." Empty words to some, perhaps, but to Amy the pledge undoubtedly had real meaning.

She barely had time to catch her breath before being absorbed in another commitment—the WNC's Shopping Centre Campaign. Although Amy usually tried to avoid assuming leadership roles in South African women's organizations, she did play a key role in this effort. Ever since she had arrived in Cape Town in late 1992, she had been attending meetings of the Western Cape branch of the WNC. In early 1993, the group began planning a shopping center–based campaign to educate women about their rights. The campaign would solicit women's views and raise their awareness of women's rights. It was part of an effort to collect women's ideas for a Women's Charter, which the WNC was drafting for submis-sion to constitutional negotiators. Amy was one of the main organizers for the Shopping Centre Campaign. On June 12, 1993, 15 women—likely including Amy—launched the WNC's Shopping Centre Campaign at Town Centre in Mitchell's Plain, a traditionally mixed-race community on the Cape Flats. Volunteers set up a booth at the shopping center and distributed pamphlets on violence against women, women's legal rights, the WNC, and the campaign itself. They asked women their thoughts about a wide range of gender issues, including the division of household responsibilities, abortion, and women in government. In two and a half hours, 163 women were interviewed.

The Shopping Centre Campaign was not the only example of Amy moving from observer to participant in South African political activism. She was also moved to publicly defend the *Cape Times*'s controversial black columnist Sandile Dikeni. Dikeni, a year older than Amy, grew up under apartheid in Victoria West in the Cape province. Generally pro-ANC, Dikeni often wrote very bitterly about South Africa's apartheid past. He had a good reason for doing so—his father had been harassed and tortured by the South African police. Dikeni was not afraid to ruffle the feathers of white liberals, and his column elicited many angry responses from white readers. When the *Cape Times* published a letter from one such reader, T. B. Griffin, on June 21, 1993, accusing Dikeni of stirring up bitterness and antiwhite sentiments in his columns, Amy felt compelled to respond. That day she wrote a letter to the editor of the *Cape Times* titled "In Defence of Dikeni" and asked that that her full name and address not be printed:

> As a white follower of Sandile Dikeni's weekly article, "Township Life," I was disgusted by the ill-informed attack against Dikeni by TB Griffin on 21 June.
>
> Griffin accuses Dikeni of "bitterness and implied retribution." If he or she would read more carefully and more frequently, he [sic] would see that nothing is farther from the truth. Dikeni is honest about the anger blacks feel, and if TB Griffin had visited Khayelitsha or Guguletu lately, he or she would see that Dikeni's anger is much softer than that of the average township dweller.
>
> Dikeni uses humor and sarcasm to help expose whites to township life, and perhaps also to warn them that there is a great distance between what is going on in Griffin's so-called "amiable negotiations" and in the everyday lives of township dwellers. Perhaps if white South Africans had not been sheltered from black opinion by press censorship, this opinion would not come as such a shock.
>
> Dikeni's is often a message about anger, but it is also a message of reconciliation. Racism in South Africa has been a painful experience for blacks and whites, and reconciliation may be equally painful. However, the most important vehicle toward reconciliation is open and honest dialogue. The anger that Dikeni expresses, as well as the pain that Griffin feels, will be part of this process.
>
> The Mayibuye Centre at UWC has published a book of Dikeni's poetry. I might not advise Griffin to read this book, as much of the poetry is filled with the anger of a young man who was detained and abused by "white" perpetrators of apartheid. However, I would point to the end of

a particular poem "Victoria West," where Dikeni writes, " . . . They told their story to the children, they taught their vows to the children that: we shall never do to them what they did to us."

This, TB Griffin, is a far cry from "kill the boer"!

A.B.

Mowbray

For some reason, Amy's letter was never published. But it illustrates how attuned Amy was to the frustration felt by black South Africans after years of discrimination and poverty. She understood the roots of black anger but saw signs of hope as well.

Around the same time she wrote her letter to the *Cape Times*, Amy finished a major paper titled "Dislodging the Boulder: South African Women and the Democratic Transition." The paper was a culmination of Amy's eight months of Fulbright research. Amy's self-confidence had been bruised by her graduate school rejections, but it received a boost when Steve Stedman offered to include Amy's essay in the book he was editing, *South Africa: The Political Economy of Transformation.* The book would be published in 1994. The title of Amy's essay, "Dislodging the Boulder," came from the song 20,000 women sang during a protest against the pass laws in Pretoria in 1956. Angered that the government planned to extend the pass laws to women, they marched on the offices of the white prime minister at the time, J. G. Strijdom, singing, "You have struck the women. You have dislodged a boulder. You will be crushed." Thirty-seven years later in 1993, women marched on the World Trade Centre in Kempton Park to demand that they be included in the negotiation process. "As in 1956," Amy observed, "the message was clear—the boulder had been dislodged. After decades of resisting apartheid, women would not be excluded from negotiations for a democratic government."

Her article, written for an academic audience, drew on her interviews, the conferences she had attended, and the documents she had gathered from women's organizations. First, she profiled South African women, noting their legal and economic inequality and the domestic and political violence that they faced. Then she provided an overview of women's political activity between 1990 and 1993, some of which she had witnessed firsthand. She discussed the establishment of the WNC, women's struggles to be included in negotiations, and their efforts to influence the transition. In discussing the many obstacles to women's participation in the transition, Amy noted, "The security situation and prevailing atmosphere of violence are likely to remain threatening to the participation of large numbers of women in the process." She also showed that she could be critical of the ANC. Noting that males dominated political organizations and processes on all sides of the spectrum in South Africa, she wrote, "Although the ANC has made significant progress in developing policy proposals designed to ensure women's equality, the organization has a long way to go before the policies will be practiced by the majority of its members." South African politics were still dominated by men in black, white, and multiracial settings. As Amy saw it, the impediments to women's progress were the lack of adequate access to decision-making structures, the persistence of patriarchy, and divisions among women. The need for a coordinated national effort among women was more important than ever.

By mid-1993, the balancing act that Amy was performing as a scholar-activist had grown more difficult. On the one hand, as a white American academic, she wanted to avoid playing a leading role in the movements she studied. But on the other, she wasn't content merely to observe and report; she wanted to help the causes she so passionately believed in. Her assertive, activist side took over on several occasions. She felt she was part of the struggle, part of the ANC. Being so heavily engaged in the movement brought both risks and rewards. Amy was greatly admired by the UWC units she was involved in. But despite her offers to help, she was once accused of being a rich white American. This hurt her deeply, because she thought her race and nationality no longer mattered. Rhoda Kadalie remembered it this way: "As a white middle class American woman, Amy had to navigate her stay very carefully through the murky waters of racial and gender politics, anti-Americanism within the movement, class differences, [and] the turbulent policies of the early '90s. . . . She felt hurt when she was told by comrades, 'You Americans want to take over' when she just honestly offered her services to help with conferences or seminars. By then she thought she was a comrade and that her origins were no longer an issue."

But Amy's work was also exacting a toll on her. Her father, for one, saw the signs of stress. "In the last few phone calls I had from her, she was very aware of being used for different people's agendas," he reported. "She was tired, she was really exhausted. The whole time she was there she was trying to be the appropriate person for everyone. These women were devouring Amy." She admitted as much in her final Fulbright report:

> I would caution ambitious student researchers that politics in South Africa are very sensitive—particularly when it comes to foreigners—especially Americans. One must approach people carefully and be prepared to do

a lot of listening and very little speaking. Much of my research involved observing meetings and one must be careful not to become *too* active. The same people who want your assistance will turn around and criticize you for being an outsider. I think I struck an appropriate balance, but it was not easy.

Amy clearly needed a break from South Africa's politically charged, pressure-cooker atmosphere. When Rhoda encouraged her to get away for a while and meet her boyfriend somewhere, it sounded like just what she needed. In May she and Scott began planning a trip to Paris together. Realizing that Amy needed a break from South Africa, Peter and Linda donated some of their frequent flyer miles so that Amy could make the trip. In a May 1993 letter to Scott, Amy admitted to feeling somewhat incomplete. "So, while I am having these amazing experiences, I am finding that I am really lonely. This has never really happened to me before so I don't know what to make of it. I have lots of friends and I always have things to do but I feel really empty." Her extended time away had also caused her to reflect on her relationship with Scott: "What I guess I am saying is that I really miss you and I really need you and I am slowly beginning to realize that. Maybe this 'adventure' has been an important milestone for me in terms of accepting a relationship and making the appropriate sacrifices—don't hold me to it, but maybe . . ." She ended by writing that she hoped their trip to Paris would materialize "and that we both don't get even broker!"

Two weeks before she left for Paris, Amy had a visit from one of her friends from Stanford. Becky Slipe had been Amy's roommate during her junior year and flew to Cape Town during the last week in June 1993. She kept a journal that provides a unique window into Amy's world after eight months in South Africa. Becky was initially concerned about traveling there because of the violence she had read about, but her fears subsided somewhat after she arrived. The two had a wonderful time together and were on the go nonstop. Amy took Becky on drives around the Cape Peninsula, from the Atlantic beaches to Cape Point to the black townships. She took her to UWC, the waterfront, nightclubs, restaurants, and a play. Becky met Amy's friends, both American and South African. During her week in Cape Town, Becky got a clear picture of Amy in her element. She was amazed at how involved Amy had become in the country's politics. Her friend was "becoming a fixture in Cape Town" and had "fans" of all races.

Becky was often justifiably concerned about safety in and around Cape Town. She noticed that armed policemen were stationed on overpasses near black townships to prevent people from stoning cars. One night she accompanied Amy and some friends to a nightclub in a black area and admitted to being "terrified." Becky had heard that a young white woman had recently been stabbed at a similar establishment. When Becky shared her misgivings with Amy and her friends, the group decided the club was too crowded and moved on to another nightclub. Amy drove into townships and mixed-race neighborhoods several times during the week, taking people home, visiting friends, and showing Becky around. Becky felt nervous during those drives and saddened by the extreme poverty. As they drove through the townships, Amy gave Becky a kind of crash course on the history of apartheid. She told her about the housing policies that had relocated blacks and mixed-race citizens far from the city center, thus forcing them to pay more for transport, although they were the least able to afford it. The townships were overcrowded, lacked basic services, and were home to structures that looked like they could blow away in a strong wind. When it was time for Becky's "send off," Amy and Melanie took her to Club Lenin, one of their favorite nightclubs. Becky enjoyed the evening but was unnerved by a sign at the door that read "Check firearms here." Besides noting some of her own fears, Becky's journal also reveals—without saying so explicitly—how Amy had become somewhat desensitized to South Africa's dangers.

Shortly after Becky left, Amy began packing for Paris. She hadn't been out of South Africa since her arrival in October 1992, eight months before. On July 7, 1993, she left Cape Town for London, where she arrived on July 8. A day later she took a Hover Speed cross-channel boat to Paris to join Scott. The two hadn't seen each other in six months and relished their reunion. During the next week, they saw the sights of Paris together—they went to museums, strolled along the river Seine, and enjoyed the French food and wine. In the photos from the trip, she and Scott seem to glow with contentment. Then it was time for them to part once again. Amy left for London on July 19 and boarded a flight to southern Africa later that day. Her work was not yet finished.

1　The Biehls in Tucson, c. 1972. *Left to right:* Linda, Kim (top), Amy, Peter, and Molly. (Biehl family)

2　The Biehl children in Tucson in 1977. *Left to right:* Molly, Kim, Zach, and Amy. (Biehl family)

3   Amy's 1988–89 Stanford swimming and diving photo. (Stanford athletics)

4   Scott Meinert and Amy at Stanford graduation, June 1989. (Biehl family)

5   With women in Soweto, South Africa, 1989. (Biehl family)

6   In Namibia with NDI colleague Sean Carroll, 1991. (Biehl family)

7   With Namibian president Sam Nujoma, 1991. (Biehl family)

8   On an NDI trip to Guyana, 1991. (Biehl family)

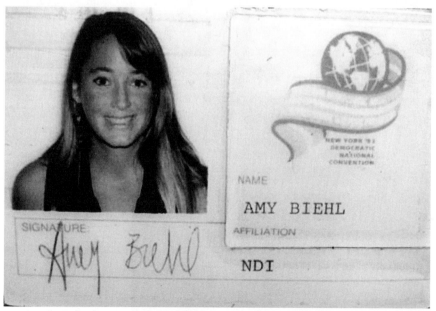

9   Amy's ID for the 1992 Democratic National Convention in New York. (Biehl family)

10 (*above*) The Biehls just before Amy began her Fulbright trip to South Africa, 1992. *Left to right:* Kim, Amy, Peter, and Linda. (Biehl family)

11 (*left*) Amy with Melanie Jacobs, her South African housemate, c. 1992–93. (Biehl family)

12 (*above*) With Maletsatsi
Maceba, c. 1992–93.
(Biehl family)

13 (*right*) Running the
Peninsula Marathon in
1993. (Biehl family)

PENINSULA 1993

14   With Greg Williams (a.k.a. "Bucks"), c. 1992–93. (Biehl family)

15 (*above*) With Albertina Sisulu (*left*) and Gertrude Shope (*right*) at an ANC Women's League conference in the Eastern Cape, 1993. (Biehl family)

16 (*left*) Amy reaching out to a South African child, c. 1992–93. (Biehl family)

17 With housemates Melanie and Solange, c. 1992–93. (Biehl family)

18　Scott and Amy in Paris, July 1993. (Biehl family)

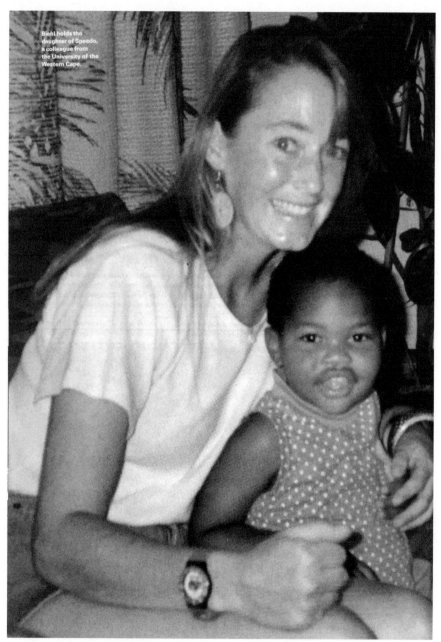

Biehl holds the daughter of Speedo, a colleague from the University of the Western Cape.

19 One of the last photos of Amy. She is with the daughter of her friend Speedo, c. August 1993. (Biehl family)

5

Gugulethu

WHEN AMY returned to Cape Town, Rhoda organized a special luncheon so she and Amy's other female friends at UWC could hear all about her trip. "We prized personal details from her, as only girls can do, about her reunion with her boyfriend!" Rhoda later wrote. Amy's trip to Paris had convinced her that she wanted to plan a future with Scott. But for the time being distance was still a barrier. "A year is a *very* long time in a lot of ways," she wrote Scott upon her return, "but I guess it's short in the big picture. I guess all I really want to say is that I miss you as much now as I did before we got to Paris if not more."

Rhoda noticed that after Amy's rendezvous with Scott in Paris, she began to look forward to going home. In a letter to Scott, Amy sounded glad to be back in South Africa but was also "feeling fine about heading into my last couple of months." She still had several projects to finish up and was receiving recognition for some of her earlier efforts. IDASA had just published one of her articles, and she was being credited for research for an article in *Femina,* a well-known South African women's magazine. "So all in all," she wrote, "things should wind up nicely, full of excitement until the very end!"

But all too often in 1993, political turmoil and violence clouded South Africa's future. On Sunday, July 25, 1993, four days after Amy's return, black gunmen attacked worshippers at St. James Church in Kenilworth, a white suburb of Cape Town. Two operatives from the PAC's armed wing burst into the evening service, sprayed the predominantly white congregation of more than a thousand with machine-gun fire, and threw hand grenades into the pews, killing 11 people and injuring 58 more. This was the single worst attack targeting white South Africans during the entire transition to democracy.

The incident signaled not only that black militants were still on a war foot-ing, but that the PAC was intent on escalating its attacks against white civilians. Immediately afterward, an APLA official said that his organization didn't make a distinction between hard and soft targets in South Africa. He suggested that because most white civilians were armed, they were legitimate targets.

The attack made headlines all over South Africa and shocked people of all races. The killing of innocent worshippers convinced some citizens that the country had sunk to a new low. If a sanctuary could be attacked so brutally, was nothing off limits? Afterward, President F. W. de Klerk visited St. James Church to show his sympathy. The archbishop of Canterbury and the pope sent messages of condolence to the congregation; Archbishop Desmond Tutu came to pray with senior minister Frank Retief. Kenilworth was only about three and a half miles (six kilometers) from Mowbray, the neighborhood where Amy lived with Melanie and Solange. Although concerned by the upsurge in violence, Amy had seen signs of danger ever since Chris Hani's death in April and saw no reason to panic. She wrote Scott, "Did you hear about the church bombing? Well that is right up the main road! Whew, I'm glad Becky is gone—she would have freaked!" When Amy spoke to her mother Linda on the phone after the attack, she asked, "Aren't you glad I don't go to church?"

The church attack was covered widely on SABC-TV and in the white-owned media. But blacks continued to be victimized by political violence considerably more often than whites. Black attacks against white civilians were still comparatively rare, and when they did occur, such attacks received a disproportionate amount of publicity. This kind of imbalanced reporting was all too familiar to Amy. As her friend and colleague Steve Stedman later observed, "Amy was appalled at the dis-tinct reactions of the media to violence in South Africa. 'White deaths,' she said, 'involve individuals with families, friends, and most importantly, names. Black deaths involve numbers.' She once told my wife that if anything ever happened to her in South Africa, she hoped that she would be just another nameless victim."

In the last stage of her stay, Amy continued to reflect on ways women expe-rienced discrimination in South Africa. It was often more than just a matter of gender but also involved race, class, and culture. She pondered how South Africa could build a culture that respected the rights of all people. In order to further develop her ideas, she attended programs and lectures on creating democracy and advancing women's rights. On August 2, she was present at a seminar on civil society in an emerging democracy sponsored by IDASA, the US Information

Service, and the American Centre in Cape Town. The keynote speaker was Larry Diamond, an Africa specialist and senior fellow at the Hoover Institution, whom Amy had known as an undergraduate at Stanford. Besides talking at length with Diamond, Amy heard the views of a host of prominent South African academics, journalists, and political commentators, including IDASA head Alex Boraine, former *Cape Times* editor Tony Heard, Stellenbosch professor Sampie Terreblanche, and University of Cape Town academics Neville Alexander, Barney Pityana, André du Toit, and Cheryl Hendricks. At about the same time, the August 1993 issue of *Femina* hit the stands, in which Amy was credited for some of the research for Marianne Thamm's article "Storming the House." The article discussed how women's rights could best be guaranteed in South Africa's future democracy—through a bill of rights and a set of structures that actively promoted gender equality. The piece helped bring Amy's views to a wider audience than had her more academic papers. "There is still a lot of work to be done but we can't wait for men to take up our cause," the article concluded. "The time is right for women all over the country to start voicing our needs and concerns, and ensure that we are not left behind when our first democratic government takes office."

There was still more that Amy wanted to do, but her time was coming to an end. Amy seemed to be in overdrive during her last month in South Africa; her schedule was as frenetic as ever. And in the middle of winding up, she had to make plans for the future. Amy had originally planned to stay in South Africa until the end of September. She still wanted to pursue a PhD in political science and teach and conduct research in African studies and women in politics. She was also interested in working on international human rights issues and political development. But because she hadn't been admitted to the graduate schools she'd applied to the previous fall, her short-term future was still uncertain. She applied for admission into a course on gender at the University of Greenwich in London and was accepted at the end of July. Then in early August, Amy was awarded a Javits Fellowship, a US Department of Education grant worth $9,000 a year for four years of doctoral study in the United States. The fellowship director gave Amy a week to find an American PhD program that would admit her, because she'd have to begin using the fellowship during the coming 1993–94 academic year.

Amy was in the odd position of having a lucrative fellowship, but no university. She wrote friends that she'd be coming home sooner than expected— provided she could find a graduate school that would admit her in time. The scramble for a university began. Amy compiled a list of graduate programs in political science that interested her and soon focused her efforts on UCLA, close to her parents in southern California and home to a long-standing African studies program, and Rutgers University in New Jersey, which had been recommended to her by several women in Cape Town. Having just interacted with Larry Diamond in Cape Town, Amy faxed him "an urgent plea for assistance" and asked if he would help her contact the right people at UCLA and Rutgers. He agreed, as did Stedman, who was finishing his last month as a Fulbright professor at UWC. Rutgers called in mid-August to offer Amy admission into its PhD program, which was scheduled to start on September 1. The university gave her a week to respond. But she still hadn't even received an application form from UCLA and was worried that she wouldn't have enough time to apply. After several days of pondering her options, Amy decided Rutgers would work and accepted the offer of admission. The vice-chairman of graduate studies in Rutgers's political science department later wrote that it was unprecedented for the university to admit someone into its doctoral program "at such a late date," but it made an exception in Amy's case because the faculty was so eager to work with her. In order to visit her family in California and then begin classes at Rutgers, Amy would have to leave South Africa by late August, a month earlier than she had initially planned. She was in for a hectic last few weeks.

Suddenly it was time for Amy to take stock of her 10 months in South Africa and submit her final Fulbright report. Like other Fulbright recipients nearing the end of their grant periods, she was asked to reflect on the results of her project and her adjustment to her host country. "The contacts, materials, and information I gained have far exceeded my expectations," Amy wrote. "I am overcome with a sense that I must continue this research as the negotiations continue and the transition process gets underway." Amy believed that although women had made some gains during her stay, they still had a long way to go. They had secured a place in the negotiations, but it was unclear how they would be represented in future government structures. Amy's comments on her adjustment to a new culture showed how immersed she had become in South African society. She had learned how to speak elementary Xhosa and some Zulu, become familiar with Cape slang, taken eight months of street dancing, attended plays, concerts, and community meetings, and befriended people of differing backgrounds. It was not an exaggeration. She ended her report this way:

> While South Africa, because of the fact that racial divisions have evoked a great deal of mistrust, can be a difficult place at times, the benefits of such a unique experience are well worth the difficulties!
>
> Academically, I have grown a great deal here. I have received lots of encouragement from South Africans and others to pursue a Ph.D.

I have gained so much information that I must now give it a theoretical framework. I hope to write more articles and books on South Africa, on women in democratic transitions and about ethnicity and gender. Too often academics and particularly political scientists lump women together as a homogenous "group" whose lack of participation has become an interesting phenomenon. However, women are affected by the same ethnic divisions, class divisions, etc. as men, in addition to their particular situation as women. These are the areas I would like to focus on.

AS Amy was finishing her work in Cape Town, racial tension was rising in South Africa. The results of an opinion poll released in mid-July reflected the growing racial divide. The number of black South Africans who believed that race relations were deteriorating had risen from 15 percent in May 1992 to 49 percent a year later. The number of whites who agreed had increased from 18 percent to 48 percent. The percentage of those characterizing race relations as good had dropped by more than half. It was not hard to understand why. Nineteen ninety-three was the most violent year of the transition to democracy in South Africa, and more people died in political violence in July (547) and August (451) than in any other period that year. The violence was so serious that in early August 1993 Archbishop Tutu called for international peacekeepers to restore order in the country.

The roots of the violence were not just political, but socioeconomic. South Africa had one of the most unequal societies in the world. Between 5 and 8 percent of the population—almost all whites—owned 88 percent of the goods and property, and over half of black families lived below the poverty line. Black citizens also lacked adequate housing, electricity, running water, health services, and schools. These inequalities had fueled black frustration for years. The drawn-out negotiations, political violence, and continued poverty brought black anger to a boiling point, especially among the younger generation.

Black South African youth had long been on the front lines of the country's political struggles. High school students in Soweto had risen up in 1976 to challenge apartheid education, sparking the most widespread unrest in South Africa since apartheid began in 1948. Black townships became battlegrounds again in 1984 when the government sent in troops to crush protests, many of which were led by young activists known as "comrades." During each wave of protests, youths risked their lives in the struggle against apartheid. They developed a hatred for "the system" and were ready to sacrifice in order to liberate the country:

they were no longer prepared to accept the third-class citizenship that had been imposed on their parents' generation. Leaving their classrooms behind and taking to the streets, thousands of students nationwide had rallied around the slogan "liberation now, education later" for almost two decades. The combination of police repression, disrupted schooling, and poor job prospects turned them into what many commentators called "a lost generation."

Youth activism had continued into the 1990s. After having their hopes raised by the unbanning of antiapartheid organizations and the release of Mandela, militant youths had become exasperated after more than three years of negotiations. Little seemed to have changed in the townships—poverty, joblessness, and poor education were still the order of the day. After the murder of Chris Hani, anger among black youth rose dramatically, and antiwhite slogans such as "one settler, one bullet" became more popular.

These attitudes were especially common in the PAC's youth wing, PASO. Many PAC youths believed that the liberation movements were selling out by negotiating with the white government and allegedly agreeing to share power. In PASO's view, the oppressed shouldn't compromise with their oppressors: they should destroy them. Given the fiery rhetoric of some hardline PAC leaders in 1993, it's no wonder that PAC youth could be whipped into a frenzy at rallies. The PAC enjoyed far less support than the ANC nationally, but the PAC had a strong support base among young people in Cape Town's black townships. The Western Cape was probably the PAC's strongest region. The organization's leaders there opposed PAC participation in the scheduled April 1994 elections, as did PASO. PASO had a branch at UWC and enjoyed a particularly strong following in the Gugulethu township.

Gugulethu ("Our pride") was established in the 1950s, when apartheid officials intensified their efforts to segregate the city. Like its older neighbor, Nyanga, Gugulethu was on the Cape Flats, away from the city center, with few facilities and services. Not only did the new residents of the township face higher transportation costs, but they could not own their houses. Instead, they had to pay rent to the white government. Most of Gugulethu's earliest dwellings were single-sex hostels built to house migrant workers who were only allowed in Cape Town for fixed periods. Migrants were also prohibited from bringing their families with them. Eventually employers sought a more stable workforce, and so the government built small family housing units. Built in a standardized, stark design, the typical home had four rooms—a lounge, two bedrooms, and a small kitchen. Toilets were usually placed in an outhouse in back. The government insisted on providing only the lowest standard of accommodation for black residents. Instead of using regular street names, authorities used the letters "NY"—short for "Native Yard"—and a series of numbers to designate different roads. Officially, the township was named "Our pride" in Xhosa, but, as former resident Sindiwe Magona noted, some blacks jokingly called it "Gugulabo" ("Their pride"), because only the authorities could have been proud of a place like that.

Political unrest and violence erupted in Gugulethu in the mid-1970s as the Soweto unrest spread to other cities in the country. During the next decade, a culture of protest and defiance took root. In the 1980s, youths were exposed to violence more than ever before, whether as protestors, detainees, or innocent bystanders. Violence and repression dehumanized many young people who faced it on a regular basis. Some of those young people turned to crime. According to Mamphela Ramphele, Gugulethu had the highest per capita murder rate in the world in the 1980s. The combination of political violence and criminal violence made it a very dangerous place. Some criminals participated in political protests, and some political activists committed crimes, blurring the distinction between crime and politics. The overlap between "comrades" (political activists) and "tsotsis" (thugs) yielded a uniquely South African term—"comtsotsis," of which Gugulethu had more than its fair share. Children there grew up seeing corpses, violence, police hostility, and gang activity. Ramphele and her young sons left Gugulethu in mid-1986 "when the violent repression of the local population by the security forces took on the proportions of open warfare. This included the burning of shacks in squatter areas in a vain attempt by police to flush out political activists." For many of its residents, living in Gugulethu in the 1980s was like being in a war zone.

Gugulethu had a notorious reputation among white residents of Cape Town, who regarded it as a dangerous place to be avoided at all costs. Most whites had never ventured into Gugulethu or any other black township. Under apartheid, whites were generally not allowed into black townships unless they had a permit. As a sign outside Gugulethu once read: "Warning. Proclaimed Non-European Township. Unauthorised persons are forbidden to leave this road, or to stop in this area."

On March 3, 1986, one of the most tragic incidents in Gugulethu's history took place. At 7:30 that morning, South African police shot and killed seven black youths at the corner of NY111 and NY1, claiming afterward that they had come under attack and returned fire in self-defense. The state-run South African Broadcasting Company reported that "seven terrorists died in Cape Town" when police foiled ANC plans to ambush a patrol. Several of the youths' parents only found out that their sons had been killed when they saw it on television that night. A videotape made by police at the scene showed the dead youths with weapons on or near their bodies. They were mostly in their early twenties and had all died of multiple gunshot wounds. Devastated and in shock, the parents of the dead youths believed that police planted the weapons on their sons, but they could do little about it but grieve.

At an inquest later that year, the court held that no one could be held responsible for the youths' deaths because they were killed in a legitimate police operation. White officials at another inquest in 1989 reached similar findings, and no one was held criminally responsible. Thanks to a high-level police cover-up, the truth about the incident would remain hidden for a decade.

South Africa's Truth and Reconciliation Commission launched an investigation in 1996. At the commission's hearings that year, police involved in the incident revealed that the youths hadn't been involved in a terrorist attack when they were killed. Instead, they were the victims of an elaborate, secret police operation designed to eliminate young activists in the townships. The operation in Gugulethu was authorized by Eugene de Kock, the notorious commander of a security police death squad, and was conducted by a joint force of more than 25 black and white policemen. In early 1986, three black policemen posing as Umkhonto we Sizwe operatives from exile were sent into the township to infiltrate a group of politicized youths, train them, and then lure them into a trap. After two months of preparations, an undercover black policeman drove the youths straight into a police ambush. All seven were killed at close range and had multiple bullet wounds. The deaths and the resulting cover-up further embittered a community already suffering from years of poverty, discrimination, and police repression.

Despite seismic shifts in South Africa's political landscape beginning in 1990, conditions in Gugulethu remained bleak. Cape Town's African population had risen from 200,000 in 1982 to more than 900,000 in 1992. A government official speculated that Cape Town was one of the fastest-growing cities in Africa at the time. This unprecedented rate of population growth compounded the problems already faced by many black residents of the area—namely, overcrowding, unemployment, poverty, and crime.

Mamphela Ramphele conducted a major study of young people in the township of New Crossroads near Gugulethu between 1991 and 1993. Youths here faced many of the same conditions as did their peers in Gugulethu, particularly regarding their schooling. Years of school boycotts had severely disrupted students' educations and showed no signs of abating. During school boycotts in the early 1990s, students in the area often congregated in large groups on township streets and sometimes stoned police vehicles. Tension between parents and children and between teachers and students was growing. As Ramphele observed, adults in the townships had lost control over their children. Because of teachers' strikes, school boycotts, and having to repeat grades, students were often 20 or older before they finished high school, if they finished at all. Ramphele painted a portrait of a whole generation of township youth growing up resentful over poverty, discrimination, overcrowding, poor schools, limited opportunities, and the inability of their elders to change the situation. Because black parents were away working long hours to make ends meet, they often left their children without adequate material and emotional support—and without adequate supervision. Thanks to the legacy of apartheid, townships were plagued with dysfunctional families, schools, and neighborhoods.

Much the same could be said about Gugulethu. By 1993, the township's population was just over 100,000. The shacks, stagnant pools of water, muddy streets, and sand that had characterized the area since its founding were still there, only in greater quantities. Gugulethu is within sight of Table Mountain and Devil's Peak, but it was a world away from the tree-lined white suburbs closer to Cape Town. By the early 1990s, anger and resentment was spreading among politicized youths in Gugulethu. Hostility toward whites was palpable. Youths began stoning cars from overpasses on the main highway between the airport and the city center. Many students had engaged in running battles with the police for years and had become fearless. They were eager to confront authority, whether white or black, real or symbolic. Sometimes innocent whites found themselves targets of the growing black rage. In June 1993, a white woman from the United Kingdom was assaulted in Gugulethu while driving through the township with her black South African husband. Judith and Siya Twani had just visited some friends in the area. As they were preparing to leave Gugulethu, the two encountered a group of students who were apparently returning home from school. When the youths spotted Judith in the car, some of them began chanting "Burn, settler, burn." Then a student approached the car and punched Judith in the face. When Siya stopped the car to tell the youths that Judith was his wife, one of them said, "We'll burn you too." Deeply shaken, the couple drove away. "I was shocked and angry," Siya later told a journalist. "But I have a deep compassion for those kids who abused my wife. I was there myself 14 or 15 years ago. I was a very bitter young man and I hated whites from the depths of my heart." The anger the couple faced reflected the darkening mood in Cape Town's black townships in mid-1993.

Mzikhona "Easy" Nofemela had spent all his life in Gugulethu. Born in the township on June 6, 1971, Easy grew up in difficult circumstances. His father worked as a gardener and at the discount department store OK Bazaars, and his mother worked variously at a clothing factory and as a domestic worker. They struggled to provide for Easy, his brothers and sisters, and his cousins, who shared the same small house. The children sometimes fought over bread and had to compete for attention and love. More often than not, Easy recalls, tear gas was his "daily breakfast, lunch, and supper." At times sad, at times angry, Easy was one of South Africa's countless "children of apartheid."

He came of age in the 1980s during a period of increasing political activity. As nationwide protests against apartheid escalated from 1984 onward, Easy witnessed shacks burning, police shootings, and protestors throwing stones and burning tires. As young teenagers, Easy and his friends sometimes threw stones at police vans and followed older activists who were singing freedom songs. Easy's father and uncle supported the PAC, and so Easy began reading the banned political literature they showed him. He also learned about the ANC and the Azanian People's Organization (AZAPO) when he was in the equivalent of seventh grade. When he went to his first PAC rally at about the same time, his morale lifted and he felt free. "Something was inspiring me inside," he recalled. The Gugulethu Seven were killed in Easy's neighborhood, and he remembers seeing police prepare for the ambush on his very street. When he and his friends attended the young men's funeral days later, he became determined to join the freedom struggle. "I wanted to serve, suffer, and sacrifice for this country," he said.

Easy enrolled at Mvuzemvuze High School in Khayelitsha in the mid-1980s, and there his commitment to the PAC deepened. When Easy began attending secret PAC meetings in the townships, he noticed how people's spirits soared. "I thought this was where I belong," he remembered. He took an oath of allegiance and loyalty to the organization and began attending PAC rallies and workshops. He embraced the PAC's central tenet wholeheartedly—that South Africa's land belonged to the African majority. On the street where he lived in Gugulethu, all the boys were PAC members. They would have meetings, talk politics, and invite PAC activists to workshops. Politics permeated life in the late 1980s. Easy and his friends would even talk about national liberation strategies after soccer matches. If they saw a police van on their street, they would throw stones at it. More and more, the streets of South Africa's major black townships resembled those of Gaza and the West Bank, where Palestinian youths were launching the first intifada around the same time.

Eventually Easy's political involvement supplanted his studies. He became a member of the Azanian National Youth Unity, a community organization affiliated to the PAC. When he was 16 or 17, he began leading marches and running workshops at school in an effort to recruit other students into the liberation movement. He did all he could to spread the word about Africanism, the PAC's ideology. During his canvassing sessions, he would tell his fellow students that South Africa was their country and that they needed to take it back from the white enemy, who raped their women and stole their land. Easy remembers one particular student debate he participated in. During the debate, Easy asked, "How do you fight apartheid? By sharing toilets? No, you must attack the people who support apartheid." That is why he supported the "one settler, one bullet" slogan. "If you're attacked by a person holding a sjambok [whip], you don't fight the sjambok, you fight the person," he told the cheering crowd.

Education was indeed taking a backseat to liberation in those days. School boycotts constantly punctuated the academic year, and when students were in school, classes were sometimes disrupted by young political activists. Easy and his peers left their fears behind as they took to the streets and protested white minority rule. Once when Easy was at a Gugulethu shop, a riot erupted outside and police hit him with a sjambok as they were chasing and whipping people. For Easy, revenge was the best answer. He and his friends made slingshots and fired iron marbles at police in armored vehicles. There was a competition to see who could hit policemen in the eye. Politics engulfed Easy as the years progressed. His uncle was arrested; he saw people getting shot in front of him and police whipping people as they ran away. Such violence only increased Easy's anger and determination to fight.

The events of early 1990—the unbanning of liberation movements, the release of leaders, the return of exiles—raised people's expectations about apartheid's impending demise. Easy was part of the huge crowd that waited for hours to hear Nelson Mandela's first public speech after his 27 years in prison. Listening to the great man speak from a balcony at Cape Town's City Hall, Easy remembers Mandela saying that he had fought against black domination. Easy and his friends were puzzled, because they viewed white, not black, domination as the enemy. As Mandela and the ANC engaged in talks with F. W. de Klerk's government, Easy and his comrades became disenchanted. They believed that because South Africa "was taken by the barrel of a gun, so it must be returned by the barrel of a gun." Easy remained committed to the PAC's armed struggle. He helped PASO recruit students in the Western Cape, an effort that would gain momentum in the years ahead despite PASO's rivalry with COSAS, the ANC's student organization. Once school was dismissed in the afternoon, Easy and his peers would burn government vehicles and look for whites to attack. Their slogan was "maximum damage to the enemy, minimum damage to Africans." Easy believed that Africans needed to fight for their country, just like the nineteenth-century African heroes Shaka and Dingane had done. When soldiers from APLA (the PAC's armed wing) began entering South Africa, Easy and his friends wanted to support them. Despite having received some training from APLA, he hadn't become a formal member. He also evaded the police dragnet when the government cracked down on APLA in mid-1993. In fact, before August 1993, Easy had never been arrested. His bitterness toward the white government was as strong as ever because it had ruined the lives of so many black South Africans. When unrest broke out, police seemed to attack everyone just because of the color of their skin, whether they were involved in protests or not. That is why Easy justified attacking whites, even if they weren't directly involved in enforcing apartheid. "How do we stop the violence?" he asked at the time. "By talking? No, we hit back. It's self-defense."

Easy's friend Ntobeko Peni agreed. The two lived within a block of each other on the same Gugulethu street, NY111, and had grown up together. They played in the same soccer club, went to movies and political rallies together, and became highly motivated PASO activists during the dying days of white rule. Ntobeko was born on September 28, 1973, and grew up with his paternal grandparents. He started school at the age of seven. Under apartheid, black families had to pay for their children's education. "Our parents earned peanuts, but pupils had to pay for school," Ntobeko said. He soon realized that the policy was deliberately designed to keep blacks from getting an adequate education.

Violence and insecurity confronted all children growing up in Gugulethu, Ntobeko included. Even as young as eight years old, he saw people being kicked and shot by police. His first school was situated near the township's police station, and he regularly witnessed police firing tear gas and assaulting people. Confrontations between residents and police became more common after 1984, and Ntobeko inevitably became more politically aware. When the Gugulethu Seven incident occurred in 1986, he was on his way to school and joined other students to see what had happened. As he got older, he began reading PAC documents that his father's friends possessed and became attracted to the organization's militant position. "The PAC called a spade a spade and said that the land belonged to Africans," Ntobeko recalled. Because the land was taken by force, it had to be returned by force.

Like so many other black youths, Ntobeko's political engagement deepened in high school. He enrolled at Langa High School in 1990 and joined his friends at the city hall when Mandela gave his first speech as a free man. Even though Ntobeko and his peers were aligned with the PAC, they still cheered Mandela's release. But they eventually viewed the ANC as selling out when it began talking with the white government. The PAC's view, which Ntobeko shared, was that "the oppressed can't negotiate with their oppressors"—they must defeat them.

In 1991, Ntobeko was elected as a national member of the PAC and worked with organizers and secretaries. Like his friend Easy, he didn't formally join APLA, but he did receive some training from the organization. Throughout 1992 and 1993 Ntobeko joined fellow students in protests against continued white minority rule. Their motive was to make South Africa ungovernable. "There was no reason to negotiate [for] what rightfully belonged to us," Ntobeko believed. He was arrested several times for his political activity in 1992–93 but was never formally charged. His education was severely disrupted by protests and boycotts, and sometimes classes would be suspended for two months at a time. With his mind focused squarely on politics, Ntobeko failed the equivalent of 8th grade but had progressed to 10th grade by age 19 in 1993. His formal schooling would go no further.

By mid-1993, rage among militant black students in Cape Town was stronger than ever. Slogans such as "one settler, one bullet" and "kill the Boer, kill the farmer" were clear evidence of "the hate that hate produced," a phrase originally used to characterize the black nationalist movement in the United States decades earlier. As the novelist Sindiwe Magona described it, the poisonous mood permeating Cape Town's black townships was "an outcome of 300 years of racial hate. Black South Africans had been so oppressed that they had begun to hate whites. These children didn't originate slogans. They answered what was in the air. History had molded South Africans."

Nancy Scheper-Hughes, a Berkeley anthropologist who arrived in Cape Town for a year of fieldwork in mid-1993, sensed hostility almost immediately. While walking down the street in Mowbray one day, she smiled at a young black student who then whispered "Die, settler!" in her ear as she passed by. Signs of the growing antiwhite sentiment were multiplying. In mid-August 1993, approximately 500 PASO supporters marched on Caledon Square police station in central Cape Town to demand the release of three PAC leaders being held in connection with the attack on St. James Church. During the march, PASO youths hit a white American tourist in the face and stole his glasses. "This is ridiculous," the visitor told a reporter after the incident. "I support their cause." Other youths threw a brick at a mixed-race photographer who collapsed after he was hit. One of the youths then shouted, "One settler down!" Upon leaving the police station, others attacked and robbed two white women. Striking out against anyone who resembled a "settler" was becoming the order of the day.

An expatriate South African writing in the *Times* of London captured the prevailing mood in a column later that month. "The Cape squatter camps and townships are home to the most alienated, angry and bitter section of South Africa's entire black population," wrote R. W. Johnson. "The ordinary Cape Town resident knows only that the road to the airport, flanked by vast squatter settlements on either side, is chronically unsafe. The stoning and shooting at 'white' cars by squatter residents has become so commonplace that soldiers with automatic weapons and armoured vehicles are stationed every few hundred yards along the road and on all the bridges over it."

Soon black students were out on the streets in greater numbers. On Monday, August 16, 1993, black teachers from the South African Democratic Teachers' Union (SADTU) launched a nationwide strike for higher pay. Seventy-five thousand black teachers participated, affecting approximately two million students whose schooling had already been severely disrupted by boycotts and unrest. Schools in Cape Town's black townships felt the effects immediately, including those in Gugulethu. Events took a dangerous turn as the strike entered its second week. Students in Cape Town relaunched a violent protest campaign they called "Operation Barcelona," named after the Olympic host city (1992) and its flaming torch. The operation had originally been held in April 1993 to protest government-imposed exam fees on black students, which the authorities were then forced to abolish. Having won their battle against exam fees, students were ready to go on the offensive once again. They resumed Operation Barcelona in order to show support for the teachers' strike and again prepared to destroy government and commercial vehicles that entered the townships. With the relaunch, an already highly charged situation escalated considerably. On August 23, youths attacked and burned at least eight vehicles in Gugulethu, Khayelitsha, and Nyanga. Youths also attacked a furniture delivery truck and a van delivering books to Gugulethu. "We can turn the whole thing upside down," one of the students told a journalist.

Whites could be targeted in the townships even if they weren't connected with the government or business. On the Monday that Operation Barcelona was relaunched, a white healthcare worker from the South African Christian Leadership Association was attacked in Khayelitsha. The vehicle that Fiona Loubser, 27, was driving was clearly marked with her organization's name, but that didn't matter this time. As she drove through the vast township, a group of youths stoned her van, forced her out, set fire to her vehicle, and assaulted her. She was pulled to safety by some local women and taken to a hospital, where she was treated for serious head injuries. White skin had clearly become a red flag in Cape Town's black townships, regardless of what kind of vehicle was being driven.

As the teachers' strike and Operation Barcelona continued, the perception spread that townships were becoming "no-go areas" for whites. A group of visitors from the Iona community in Scotland were scheduled to visit Gugulethu in mid-August but decided not to because of the escalating attacks. Amid the rising violence of August 1993, how aware was Amy of the dangers? Did she ever consider that she might be at risk? Ever since she'd arrived in South Africa the previous October, she had systematically followed the news. Amy undoubtedly knew about the teachers' strike because 4,000 of the striking teachers held a rally at UWC on the first day of the walkout. And because she passed black townships on her drive from Mowbray to Bellville each day, she would have known about the occasional stonings of vehicles and seen police patrolling the overpasses. Amy expressed concerns about the township violence to Melanie, but she "refused to stop driving her black friends home after work." At one point Rhoda told Amy that she wouldn't go into the townships as frequently as Amy did, "but she'd dismiss me as a nagging old woman."

Perhaps Amy didn't keep up with the news as carefully as she usually did during her last few weeks in Cape Town. Because she was leaving a month sooner than she'd originally planned, she had a great deal to do to prepare for her departure and very little time in which to do it. Her habit of reading the newspapers and collecting articles may have been a casualty of her frenetic schedule during her last few weeks. Alternatively, she might have kept up with the news but become somewhat desensitized to the reports of violence after a while. Perhaps she thought that she could still slip in and out of the townships without incident, just as she had so many times in the past. Her friends insist that she was very aware of the risks in South Africa but probably thought that the youths' anger wouldn't affect her. "She was intellectually aware of the risks and dangers, but I don't think she incorporated it into her behavior," Larry Diamond said. "Like many young people, she had a sense of wonder, discovery, a sense of invulnerability that 'I'm going to be okay.' When people are young, their calculation of risk isn't governed enough by experience and the weighing of realities." Like many of her friends, including Melanie and Rhoda, Amy "forgot she was white." "It's an enormous tribute to Amy that she forgot she was white," Diamond said. "There were risks as well forgetting you were white. It could produce moments when you weren't sufficiently mindful of anger against whites." Amy's friend Anna Wang agreed. She and Amy went into the townships frequently and were aware of the violence but didn't think bad things could happen to them personally. They were young, idealistic, politically informed and well connected. "We knew there were risks, but we saw ourselves as part of the movements," Anna recalled. She could identify Amy's mindset because she shared it:

> [Amy] may not have been completely fearless, but she was an unqualified idealist. She believed in people, she believed she was a sister among the Africans. Who would harm their sister? I had that naiveté as well. When you are in a foreign community that you so much want to embrace, you

can only assume that the other(s) also want to receive you. Because you trust, you also presume that it will be returned. You see violence, you read about cruelty, you experience pain, but rarely do you think you can be the victim. When people expound on the security situation in South Africa, you dispel the panic. You say, there are parts of Washington, D.C., that are more dangerous than the heart of a black township. I believed, as Amy did, in all of my declarations. Coupled with that self-confidence, we felt untouchable.

Amy planned to leave Cape Town on Friday, August 27. She would arrive in southern California the next day, spend the weekend at her parents' house in Newport Beach, and then head to New Jersey the following Monday to prepare for graduate school at Rutgers. She was eager to be reunited with her family, whom she hadn't seen in 10 months. Because she was leaving sooner than she'd initially intended, she had to scramble to get ready. She had to pick up her plane ticket, wrap up her work at UWC, pack her belongings, send her books and notes to Rutgers, and say goodbye to her many South African and American friends in Cape Town.

Saying goodbye to her friends in Cape Town was bittersweet. As excited as she was to begin the next chapter of her life, she felt deeply connected to South Africa on many levels. She had become part of the women's movement, the prodemocracy movement, UWC, the Cape Town jazz scene, and a long-distance runners' club, and she had a South African family to boot—Melanie and Solange. Sunday the 22nd was Melanie's birthday, and that evening she and Amy hosted a combined birthday and farewell party. Many of Amy's South African friends attended, including Dullah Omar, who held Amy's hand during some of the festivities. After the party, Amy and several others went to a nightclub and danced together until dawn. "She was particularly alive that night," Anna Wang remembered, "dazzling all of the Africans with her blonde hair and African movements."

Amy's last three days were a whirlwind of activity. The Community Law Centre at UWC threw a farewell party for her on Monday. To Rhoda, Amy seemed radiant but had a touch of melancholy because she was preparing to leave South Africa. Amy's colleagues at UWC were not the only ones sorry to see her go. Just days before her scheduled departure, Amy received a letter from a member of the Women's National Coalition in Cape Town thanking her for all of her efforts on the organization's behalf during the past year. "Your advice and common sense helped us over the 'teething problems' with this new organization," the correspondent wrote. "I hope that all your efforts will be richly rewarded!" But as she was preparing to leave South Africa, Amy had a premonition that she shared with

Rhoda and a few other close friends in Cape Town. She felt lucky that nothing bad had happened to her during her long stay in the country. Rhoda later told a reporter, "She said to me repeatedly, 'My stay here was too good to be true. I'm convinced something's going to happen.' We were walking across campus and she had this absolute premonition." Her parents heard about it as well. "Whether that was a premonition or fear, I don't know. I'm not sure it necessarily indicates that. But she did tell several people that she was surprised to be coming out of this unscathed," Peter said.

Wednesday, August 25, was going to be another busy day. Amy was getting so many calls from friends wanting to say goodbye that she unplugged the phone in her room so she could finish packing. But she did have time to help with a student election at UWC that day. She then said goodbye to Randi Erentzen and Omar, both of whom were sorry to see her go. "She said she would come back," Omar recalled, "but only to a free South Africa." That afternoon Amy spoke to Greg Williams on the telephone so they could make some plans for her last two days in Cape Town. Along with Melanie and Solange, he had spent the most time with Amy and had become a close friend.

Amy and Rhoda spoke at length over the telephone that Wednesday. Amy sounded both homesick and nostalgic about South Africa. As she told Rhoda, "I find it so difficult to leave this place. I've got South Africa in my heart." She said again how surprised she was that nothing bad had happened to her after 10 months in South Africa. "Now that she was about to go back she had a feeling something was going to happen," Rhoda remembered. Before they hung up, Rhoda told Amy that she'd heard reports about unrest in the townships and that a white health worker had been attacked. She asked Amy to promise her that she wouldn't go into the townships before she left. Amy promised. After all, she was too busy packing up her things to make extra trips at this point. Rhoda had originally planned on going into the townships herself that day to show some Swedish visitors around, but they decided to go to the botanical gardens at Kirstenbosch instead. Rhoda wasn't the only one to warn Amy away from the townships that week. Scott told her not to take anybody home the day before she was due to leave because he'd heard that "the vitriol had picked up."

Then Evaron Orange asked Amy if she could give him a ride home to Athlone, a mostly "Coloured" neighborhood on the way to Mowbray. Evaron, a mixed-race 19-year-old, worked for the Rapping for Democracy project, a voter education program based at the Centre for Development Studies. He was a cousin of Melanie's and had met Amy shortly after she'd arrived in Cape Town in October 1992. He didn't know Amy all that well, but he had attended one of Amy's farewell parties. He'd just finished a performance on Wednesday afternoon when his ride left without him. But Amy was happy to help out.

That day Amy's friend Maletsatsi and another female UWC student, Sindiswa Bevu, 26, had also been trying to find a ride home without success. They both lived in New Crossroads, a black township near Nyanga. In the late afternoon, after Evaron approached Amy, they too asked if Amy could give them a lift. That morning had been quiet in the townships, Maletsatsi later recalled, and so it did not seem risky. Amy hesitated. She often gave people rides home to the townships, but she was behind schedule now and had to get home. But Maletsatsi was a good friend whom she had helped so many times in the past 10 months. Sensing Amy's hesitation about the ride, Maletsatsi asked if she could just drop them off on the main road in Gugulethu, where they would find another ride to New Crossroads and thus help Amy save time. Amy agreed; after all, Gugulethu wasn't very far out of her way.

Amy thus broke her promise to Rhoda. She did so, Rhoda speculated, because she was "generous to a fault." She didn't know when to say no, whether it was helping Melanie financially, doing work for people at UWC or in the liberation movement, or giving friends rides home. She also didn't fully consider the risks that day. Her mindset resembled that of Todd Shields, an American journalist stationed in Somalia in the early 1990s. As Keith Richburg chronicles in his book *Out of America,* Somalia had become one of Africa's most volatile regions as followers of different warlords battled for supremacy, mercilessly shelling each other on the streets of Mogadishu. Shields recalled intervening in an argument between two armed Somali gunmen and then questioning the wisdom of his actions. As Richburg put it, "He knew he had been there so long it was all starting to seem normal and not so dangerous—which is precisely when foreigners let down their guard and are most at risk." Amy let down her guard in precisely the same way. She had been in South Africa for 10 months and gone into the townships so often without incident that it all seemed normal to her, despite her awareness of the potential dangers.

Amy left UWC at about 4:30 p.m. to drop off Maletsatsi and Sindiswa in Gugulethu and then Evaron in Athlone before heading to Mowbray. As she was leaving the university with her three passengers, her friend Marva told her to drive safely. "Yes, I'll drive safely," Amy replied. "I don't want to die on South African roads."

Meanwhile, Operation Barcelona was in its third day. Supporters of COSAS and PASO were not just attacking government, commercial, and service vehicles that entered the townships, but they were seeking to make the townships "ungovernable." Support for the campaign seemed to be growing. On the afternoon of the 25th, a branch of PASO was launched at Langa High School in Cape Town's oldest black township. Several hundred students from different black schools in Cape Town attended, including friends Ntobeko and Easy from Gugulethu. Ntobeko, then 19, was elected chairperson of the new branch. Students cheered as two speakers stepped to the podium: Simpiwe Mfengu, regional secretary of PASO, and Wanda Mathebula, regional chairperson. Their words electrified the crowd. The battle to win back the land was not just APLA's, they said, but the duty of all of the assembled students. APLA had dubbed 1993 the Year of the Great Storm, and PASO needed to do all it could to make the country ungovernable. That meant not just supporting the current teachers' strike but destroying the current education system. It meant taking violence to white communities, churches, and restaurants. It meant destroying government property and vehicles driven by whites. The white government was the enemy, and therefore white people were the enemy. "One settler, one bullet!" the speakers shouted. "One settler, one bullet!" the crowd chanted in response. "Maximum damage to the enemy, minimum damage to Africans!" As they chanted slogans and sang freedom songs, the crowd's emotions built to a fever pitch. This was no ordinary political meeting but a highly charged launch of PASO, one of the most militant youth organizations in South Africa. Urged to regard whites as enemies, students were fighting a war for freedom. The future was theirs; they just had to seize it.

Ntobeko's election as PASO chairman at his school made him especially eager to assist APLA. He and Easy had been receiving training from APLA operatives in Gugulethu. Easy, 22, was not just a PASO member at the time but a PASO organizer at his school in Khayelitsha, which had been renamed Joe Slovo High School after the legendary white communist leader. Ntobeko and Easy regarded themselves as young warriors ready for battle. So did Mongezi Manqina and Vusumzi Ntamo, two other students in the crowd who didn't know Ntobeko or Easy. Mongezi, 21, was in the equivalent of eighth grade at Gugulethu Comprehensive High School. He lived with his mother in a tiny concrete blockhouse about a block and a half from a Caltex service station in Gugulethu. Vice-chairman of the PASO branch at his school, Mongezi hoped to become an APLA soldier one day. His friend Vusumzi, celebrating his 22nd birthday on August 25, 1993, was equally committed. Vusumzi lived in Langa and had only attended school up to sixth grade. He wasn't a formal member of PASO, but he attended PASO meetings because some of his friends did so. Inspired as they were with the fiery words at the PASO launch, all four young men—along with scores of others in the crowd—were ready to head into the streets for battle.

It wasn't just the PASO launch that motivated the youths that Wednesday afternoon. A few days earlier, another black student had been shot by police during an outdoor political rally. "In the week that this thing happened, a student died at Nyanga Junction," Mongezi said later. "His name was Shaubry. Before my eyes, he was shot by a Boer [white policeman] while we were singing freedom songs. I felt terrible because he died in my arms." As if they weren't angry enough, the death of Shaubry gave his comrades additional motivation to seek revenge against whites.

The students left Langa High School highly charged and ready to hunt vehicles to attack. Students divided into groups and headed to Gugulethu, Khayelitsha, and other locations in Langa, where they would find targets and meet later. They would attack at least a dozen vehicles that day. Ntobeko, Easy, Mongezi, and Vusumzi were part of a group of approximately 200 students that walked to Bonteheuwel train station looking for vehicles to attack. As they surged forward, the students sang, toyi-toyied, and chanted "one settler, one bullet!" They spotted a furniture truck at the intersection of Washington Street and Vanguard Drive and threw stones at it. Then they told the African driver to get out, and when he did so, they set the truck on fire. Suddenly police arrived and the crowd found a new target. As they stoned the police van, white policemen inside opened fire, as did some whites from unmarked vehicles. "What happened with the police is that they shot at us," Easy remembered. "Some of the white people who were passing by also helped the police. That made us to be very emotional, that each and every white person we met we will try and do something to that person." As if the earlier political rally hadn't inspired them enough, the students' running battle with police escalated matters considerably. Enraged, the students' desire to fight and attack whites intensified.

After the skirmishes on Vanguard Drive, the students split up. Mongezi, Vusumzi, and 50 to 60 others headed to Langa station and boarded a train bound for Gugulethu. Ntobeko and Easy's group of approximately 80 to 90 students boarded a train at Bonteheuwel station and got off two stops later at Heideveld station in Gugulethu. Both groups had now arrived in Gugulethu, adrenalin pumping after their clash with police, determined to find new targets.

At about the same time—roughly 4:30 p.m.—Amy and her friends left UWC in her rickety beige Mazda 323. Years old and well worn, it wasn't a flashy or expensive car that would normally attract attention in a black township. The sticker "Our Land Needs Peace" was still on the rear bumper. Evaron sat in the front seat next to Amy, while Maletsatsi and Sindiswa got in back, Sindiswa directly behind Amy on the right-hand side. The mood was bright, the conversation light-hearted.

Amy was excited at the prospect of seeing her parents and her boyfriend soon, but she was sad to leave South Africa because she'd made so many friends there. Ten minutes or so later, Amy drove onto NY1 in Gugulethu heading south. NY1 was one of the main roads in the township, and because it was late afternoon, it was busy with traffic and pedestrians returning home from work. It was an open, public thoroughfare with long rows of connected houses on the right and a Caltex service station ahead on the left.

Students from the PASO launch had arrived in Gugulethu minutes earlier. Between 50 and 100 of them headed toward NY1, toyi-toyiing, chanting, and singing political songs as they went. Mongezi and Vusumzi were part of the procession; Easy and Ntobeko hitched a ride on a pickup truck. The youths headed toward the corner of NY1 and NY132 near the Caltex service station, where they spotted a large truck. At about the same time, Amy's car approached and pulled up right behind it. Fresh from their skirmish with police, the students were ready to launch another attack. At first they didn't see Amy's car, but the truck was target enough. They launched a barrage of stones at the truck from the right side of the road opposite the Caltex station. Vusumzi joined in the attack while his friend Mongezi stood nearby talking to a girl; Easy and Ntobeko would arrive moments later.

Suddenly someone in the crowd saw Amy's car and shouted, "Here comes a settler!" pointing at Amy. None of the youths had ever seen Amy before, but they aimed their stones at her. One of the first rocks crashed through the driver's side and hit Amy in the head. Then bricks and stones came flying from all directions, shattering the windows. The "stones" were not mere pebbles, but large chunks of concrete that lay strewn around the township. Amy was particularly vulnerable because the driver's side was on the right, facing the bulk of the crowd. As rocks crashed into the car, Evaron began to pray, and then shouted to Amy, "Drive! Drive!" But she couldn't. The truck in front blocked her car, traffic was coming from the opposite direction, and she was reeling from a rock that had struck her right eyebrow. Evaron then put Amy's head on his lap to protect her from more stones while Maletsatsi and Sindiswa crouched in the back to protect their own heads. One stone hit Evaron in the arm. As the crowd approached the car chanting "One settler, one bullet," someone reached in and snatched Amy's watch from her wrist. Evaron turned to someone in the crowd and asked what he should do. He was told to get out of the car and that the youths were interested not in him but "the settler."

All four got out of the vehicle. Maletsatsi and Sindiswa pleaded with the students to leave Amy alone. She was not a settler, they shouted, but an American and a comrade who supported the ANC. She was a UWC student who was working with them. Some of the youths listened, but others said that the woman deserved to die "because she is a settler." Motioning toward Amy, a bystander told Evaron, "You must go, go rescue her," but he sensed that would be suicidal. Someone in the crowd tried to grab Maletsatsi's bag from her arm, but she resisted. Then several males ran toward them with knives. Someone tried to stab Evaron, but he managed to avoid the blow; Sindiswa was stabbed on the hand; and Maletsatsi suffered two fractured ribs. The three of them ran to the Caltex station for help as the crowd converged on Amy.

Many subsequent articles, particularly those in American newspapers, reported that Amy was "dragged from her car" during the attack. But eyewitness accounts suggest otherwise. Dazed and bleeding, Amy stumbled from the car on her own accord as about a dozen youths rushed forward. She was holding the side of her face where she'd been hit and ran toward the houses opposite the Caltex station shouting for help. As the youths pursued her, she grabbed the arm of a bystander, Pamela, and said, "Please help me." Pamela tried to shield her from the crowd but was soon overpowered and shoved aside. Amy then ran across the road toward the Caltex station. In normal circumstances, Amy might have been able to outrun her attackers. But she was suffering from a serious head injury, was being pelted with stones, and was wearing the high-heeled boots she'd bought in Paris a month earlier. As she was being chased on the grass near the service station, Mongezi tripped her and she fell. She was trapped between a white pole fence and a metal Caltex sign.

Between seven and twelve youths wearing PAC T-shirts then swarmed over Amy, including Easy, Ntobeko, Mongezi, Vusumzi, and, according to one eyewitness, at least one female. They kicked Amy, smashed rocks against her head and body, and stabbed at her with knives. Amy sat up and tried to ward off the blows with her arms, but she eventually collapsed amid the furious assault. Mongezi got a knife from someone in the crowd, moved toward Amy, and stabbed her in the chest. Another PASO youth tried to stop the attack but was told, "How can you stop us? She is a settler and she deserves to die." Individually the youths might not have attacked Amy that afternoon, but together they were a gang out to cause mayhem and attack anything white. Together, they fed each other's fury. As a South African–based reporter for the New York Times later wrote, when "impromptu mob justice" takes hold, "an apprehended suspect becomes the sacrificial culprit for a thousand grievances." Amy's only crime that day was that she was white. Many of those who witnessed the attack on their way home from work were horrified and in tears afterward.

But the youths were not yet finished. Sometime during or immediately after the attack on Amy, some in the crowd set their sights on Amy's abandoned car. They stole the backpacks still inside, turned the car on its side, and then asked for matches so they could set it on fire. By then, someone had called the Gugulethu police station to report the attack. The station was only a few blocks away—no more than 400 or 500 meters—and a yellow police van quickly screeched onto the scene, scattering the crowd. Covered in blood, Amy somehow managed to stand up, step over the low fence, and stagger toward her friends at the Caltex station. She reached Evaron and then collapsed. She groaned but could not speak. Evaron, Maletsatsi, and Sindiswa helped her into the police van. As they sped toward the police station, Constable Leon Rhodes radioed for an ambulance. Amy was struggling to breathe, but her eyes were wide open.

Once at the station, Amy was laid down outside and surrounded by her three friends. Constable Rhodes washed blood off Amy's face and put gauze on her forehead. Neither he nor her friends knew the seriousness of her injuries at that point. As they waited for the ambulance to arrive amid the encroaching darkness, Evaron thought about putting her back in the police van and taking her to a hospital himself despite having been taught not to move an injured person.

But even a hospital wouldn't have been able to help. Amy had been stabbed through the heart and had sustained a fractured skull. Accounts differ as to how long it took the ambulance to arrive: possibly 10 minutes, possibly 20 or even 30. Amy was covered in a blanket when ambulance driver Victor West pulled up. He examined her and found no vital signs. He placed a sheet over Amy's head and told the onlookers that their friend was dead.

6

"Comrades Come in All Colors"

NEWS OF Amy's death spread quickly. Randi Erentzen came to the Gugulethu police station immediately and was soon joined by township residents with whom he'd worked in the past. "They were distraught, they were angry," he recalled. Then ANC leaders from the Western Cape arrived, including Dullah Omar, Ebrahim Rasool, and Allan Boesak. In the darkness, a photographer from the *Cape Times* focused his lens on Boesak and several other men as they stood next to Amy's body, which was covered by a white sheet. The shutter clicked as Boesak said a prayer over Amy's body. At around the same time, someone telephoned Rhoda at home to tell her what had happened. Rhoda then tried to contact Melanie, but Solange was home alone and picked up the phone. Later, Melanie telephoned her daughter and said she was going to identify Amy's body. "The world came crashing down," Solange remembered. "The press came swarming in. . . . I felt like I was in a daze." That evening Erentzen called Pat Keefer, who was in Johannesburg on an NDI mission. Keefer then telephoned the US embassy in Pretoria, the consulate in Cape Town, and NDI in the United States, asking that someone inform the Biehl family about Amy's death before they heard about it on the news.

Molly, 23, was the first in the family to get the news. She was working at the Watergate building in Washington, D.C., when someone from the State Department called to tell her that something bad had happened in South Africa. It was about Amy. "Is she dead?" Molly asked. "Yes, she's dead," the person answered. Molly then telephoned her father Peter in Oregon and her sister Kim in California.

Peter, vice president of marketing for Agripac, an Oregon-based packaging company, was in a meeting in Salem when his secretary told him he had a phone call about a family emergency. He listened to what Molly told him in a state of disbelief. On the flight back to California, he decided to write Amy a letter. "It was the only way I could communicate with her at that point," he said to reporters later. He told her how proud he was of how she had lived her life and that the family would try to honor her "with some sort of action." Kim, 27, was at work at Neiman Marcus in Newport Beach when Molly called to tell her that Amy was dead. "I think I fell to the floor," Kim recalled. Her coworkers comforted her and urged her to call her mother. Linda and her son Zach, 16, had spent the afternoon at South Coast Plaza, a massive Orange County shopping complex, to get Zach some things for the start of the new school year. Their mood, like the day, was bright. Looking forward to their reunion with Amy over the weekend, they lowered the top of Linda's white Mustang convertible and drove to nearby Costa Mesa in the warm August sunshine. When Linda and Zach returned home, the phone rang. "Mom, are you sitting down?" Kim asked. "Amy's dead." When she heard her mother scream, Kim rushed home to be at her family's side. Scott Meinert had been in law school classes all day at Willamette University in Oregon. By the time he returned to his apartment, Peter had left four messages for him. Scott called back and Peter told him the news. "He told me she'd hung in there for a little while, but one lucky blow had got her. I don't remember much after that for ten hours." When Peter arrived home in Newport Beach a few hours later, reporters had already started to surround the Biehls' house, but Peter avoided the media crush by sneaking in through a back fence. That night, US ambassador to South Africa Princeton Lyman telephoned the Biehls to explain what had happened to Amy and to express his condolences. "I hope she did some good," Linda told him, still in shock. "She so loved the people there."

The shock the Biehls felt over Amy's death was compounded by the way in which she died. But neither Peter nor Linda blamed anyone for the tragedy. Ironically, Linda had worried more about Amy in Washington, D.C., than she had when Amy was in South Africa. As she thought of the youths who killed her daughter, she said to herself, "Lord, forgive them, for they know not what they do." She was devastated, but not angry. "The low point was looking at the faces of my children afterward," Linda said. "We hadn't seen Amy for so long and that was hard." Linda was particularly concerned about Molly, who became bedridden shortly after she arrived from Washington. Scott came down from Oregon but lay immobilized on the family's couch much of the time. Linda felt "hollow and empty—a very physical feeling." Though not physically ill, Zach was not as stoical as his parents seemed to be. "From day one my parents weren't angry," he recalled years later. "I would've killed the guys [who murdered Amy]." As the family reflected on their ordeal, Peter read aloud the letter he wrote to Amy as a sort of tribute. Although the family did not yet know the extent of Amy's involvement in South Africa's liberation movement, they began talking about how to carry on her legacy. But in the fog of shock and grief that first day and night, they were not sure how they would do so.

Almost immediately, letters and faxes started to come in from all over the world expressing sympathy to the Biehls and praising Amy's work. Among those sending their condolences were President Bill Clinton, Nelson Mandela, and Coretta Scott King. Ms. King, who was in Washington for the 30th anniversary of her husband's "I Have a Dream" speech, wrote, "I am deeply and personally saddened to learn of your daughter Amy's death. Your loss is shared by all people of conscience in South Africa, at the King Center, and around the world—people, who, like Amy, have devoted their lives to the quest for worldwide freedom, peace and justice." NDI's team in South Africa faxed the Biehls a letter signed by Mandela, hailing her work on behalf of South African women and her contributions to the country's future democracy. Amy's friends in South Africa sent the Biehls countless letters of condolence, many of which were deeply moving. They praised Amy for her kindness, warmth, and spirit and opened the Biehls' eyes to the work Amy was doing in South Africa. Even people who hadn't known Amy reached out to express their sympathy. The messages of condolence were not only numerous—flooding in by the hundreds—but were often substantive as well. Most had a common theme: that Amy had touched people in South Africa in extraordinary ways, and that despite being a white outsider, she had become part of the struggle, "a sister and a comrade."

The day after Amy died, three black South African students from the University of California–Irvine came to the Biehls' house and asked if they could mourn with the family. Once the Biehls invited them inside, the students sat vigil with the family, grieving with them calmly and quietly. Prominent ANC member Jeff Radebe was in Los Angeles at the time, and he too came over to the Biehls' house to express his solidarity. The visits by these South Africans so soon after Amy's death made the Biehls realize that Amy was part of a broader movement, which helped ease the family's sorrow. The many calls and faxes from South Africans were comforting as well. "We sensed that Amy was a part of history, something big," Linda said. "We were moved by this."

The day of August 26, 1993, was a complete blur. Besides grieving with their South African visitors, the Biehls received phone calls from the State Department, the White House, Commerce Secretary Ron Brown, the *Today Show,* CNN, and reporters from all over the world. News crews had begun camping out in front of the house and inundating the family with interview requests. In the days ahead, representatives of all the major television networks asked to accompany the Biehls if they decided to visit South Africa to retrace their daughter's footsteps; producers and screenwriters offered to dramatize Amy's story; and publishers proposed doing books on Amy. It was truly a media feeding frenzy. "We were so surrounded and inundated by the press that it was three weeks before I really got out of my house, except for a couple of trips to the store," Linda said. In their many interviews, the Biehls were careful not to say anything that might exacerbate South Africa's racial and political divisions in the wake of Amy's death. After all, they reasoned, Amy had worked to bridge those divisions. Their magnanimity astonished many reporters. Not only did Peter and Linda avoid sounding bitter, but they refused to criticize the people who killed their daughter. No one in the family publicly condemned Amy's killers in the weeks and months ahead. Amy wouldn't have wanted that, they said, nor would she have been comfortable with all of the publicity her death was generating. But Linda and Peter were determined to tell Amy's story. "We made the decision that we want her work and her anti-violence beliefs to be heard," Linda told a local reporter. "We're doing this out of love and respect for her."

The Biehls began a pattern whereby they would refuse to condemn Amy's killers or demand vengeance; instead, they used Amy's death to call for reconciliation in South Africa and an end to violence. "[Amy] was a very humanitarian person," Linda told reporters. "And she would not want anyone, I'm sure, condemned for this act." She was asked to describe Amy's work in South Africa and comment on her daughter's murder. "She wanted to give herself to the African people," Linda said. "She wanted to do whatever she could to help them. I was very worried about her, but she would say, 'Mom, I'm OK. I'm doing this because I want to do this. You can't live your life in a shell.'" Once Linda and Peter began to view the media as a means to get Amy's message out, they quickly became comfortable with the multitude of reporters and cameramen congregating on their front lawn waiting to interview them. Linda told South Africa's *Star* newspaper that she was proud of her daughter. She told another journalist that

> I don't have any anger, we're just sick her life is over. She was contributing so much. She wanted to be there. She felt it was a mission she needed to do. She loved all your people. My reactions are what my daughter's would have been. I am totally supportive of what Amy's goals and values were.

She was a great believer in democracy, that's why she was there. She hated the violence. She wanted to be friends with all your people and I believe she was. I want to keep that memory of my daughter and want to do something to continue her tradition. I just haven't decided what.

Peter and Linda appeared on the *Today Show* on NBC the day after Amy died, at 4:10 a.m. Pacific Time. As Katie Couric looked on from the New York studio, the couple took their places in a makeshift studio at Newport Harbor High School across from their house. Linda blinked somewhat nervously and held a tissue in her hand, but Peter looked as if he had been on television all his life. Linda began the segment by reading a statement that she and Peter had prepared:

As parents who have lost a daughter of great personal worth and value, we have been comforted by an incredible outpouring of support and appreciation for Amy, and what she was. And we think she was a force for good in South Africa and the world. Calls and faxes have poured in continuously from many corners of the world expressing love and respect for Amy. Expressions of caring from the people of South Africa have been particularly moving. And as her very close friend Scott said, "Amy made more than friends, she made believers."

Thanks to the *Today Show,* Amy's story was now being watched by millions of people throughout the United States and beyond. And the media attention showed no signs of slowing down. Jim Maceda reported on the Biehls on NBC *Nightly News* that same evening; CBS *Evening News* featured a story on Amy that night as well. The Biehls were repeatedly asked if they were angry and if they were going to go to South Africa. "We're at peace with Amy, we're at peace with ourselves, we're at peace with the people she was working with and trying to help," Peter told CBS. As for whether they would visit South Africa, the Biehls told reporters that they intended to, but they had not yet determined when. Before planning such a trip, they wanted to continue to publicize the issues Amy cared about—democracy, nonviolence, and women's rights in South Africa—and plan her memorial service.

The fact that Amy was the first American killed in South Africa's racial violence, and that she was killed in a racially motivated attack by the very black South Africans she felt she was there to help, was bound to make headlines, but the extent of the coverage was truly extraordinary. In the United States, Amy's murder seemed destined to become the biggest news story from South Africa since Mandela's release from prison three and a half years earlier. It brought renewed attention to South Africa's racial divisions at a time when many Americans were concerned about race relations in their own country, particularly in the aftermath of the 1991 beating of black motorist Rodney King and the violent Los Angeles riots the following year. Reports of Amy's death featured prominently in scores of American newspapers, including the *New York Times,* the *Washington Post,* the *Christian Science Monitor,* the *Los Angeles Times,* and many other local and regional newspapers across the nation. Often on the front page, the stories discussed Amy's commitment to racial justice in South Africa, the many black friends she had made, and the irony that she was killed because she was white. *Time, Newsweek,* and *People* published in-depth magazine articles. On television and radio, NBC *Nightly News,* ABC *World News,* CBS *Evening News,* CNN, the *MacNeil-Lehrer NewsHour,* local television stations in California, and National Public Radio (NPR) provided coverage.

It wasn't just the American press that took a special interest in the story. The British wire service Reuters provided in-depth reporting, as did the *Times* of London, the *Independent,* the *Daily Telegraph,* the *Daily Mirror,* the *Daily Mail,* and the *Guardian.* Journalists sensed that Amy's murder was a profound symbol of the damage that apartheid had wrought, damage that was possibly irreparable. In his article "The Tragedy of Amy," published in the *Times* on August 29, 1993, correspondent Richard Ellis opened with Amy's physical description: "She was the epitome of the all-American young woman, a bright, blue-eyed blonde in a baseball cap whose energy seemed as limitless as her devotion to help build a new South Africa." That she so imbibed the culture and spirit of black South Africa was also an important part of the story. Ellis continued: "In between researching her university thesis on women's rights, Amy Biehl ran marathons, learned township dances, studied Xhosa, preached peace and developed voter education programmes. Black friends dubbed her an honorary African." He then suggested that Amy's naïveté was fatal: "Her crime was to forget, or never to learn, the first rule of survival in a South Africa that stands on the brink of a race war: that the colour of a person's skin is reason enough for murder. It was a mistake that cost Biehl her life."

In South Africa, Amy's death gripped the nation and set off a media frenzy. Her murder was covered on SABC television on the night she was killed; the next day, SABC radio and television reported that her death was "condemned across the political spectrum." The story made the front pages of the country's major newspapers. The sensational headlines were impossible to ignore: "Murdered Girl Had Packed for Home" (*Cape Times*); "Amy's Agony . . . Chased by Youths Then Mercilessly Hacked to Death" (*Argus*); "Gentle Amy Loved by All" (*Weekend*

Argus). Many of the white-owned papers had multiple stories featuring color photos of Amy, interviews with her friends and parents, and detailed profiles of her life in the United States and her work in South Africa. Most accounts focused on the racial nature of the attack and reported that the youths who killed Amy regarded her as a "settler." Once again, the tragic ironies of the attack—that Amy was killed by the very people she was trying to help as she was giving black friends a ride home, two days before she herself was to return home—took center stage.

Like her family in the United States, Amy's friends in South Africa were shocked by her death. Dullah Omar was horrified at the loss of his young American colleague and lamented the senselessness of her death. On the evening of her murder, Omar told reporters that Amy had been "absolutely dedicated to the cause of the oppressed" and that her murder "tarnished" the struggle for freedom in South Africa. That night, in a letter to Peter and Linda, he paid tribute to Amy's work on behalf of women's rights. "Your beloved Amy became one of us in her spirited commitment to justice and reconciliation in South Africa," he wrote. Amy's housemates Melanie and Solange were distraught after Amy's murder. They had become Amy's second family during the past ten months. That Amy had been killed by black South African youths, whose cause she so passionately advocated, was unthinkable. But, as Melanie told reporters, Amy would have been the first to explain why the youths lashed out. "She would have said they learned to hate by looking around at how white people hated them and how white people treated them. And it is a matter of many, many years of hate just boiling up. . . . I'm crying for this country. We're in such trouble. We need a few million more Amys," she said. Brigitte Mabandla had been instrumental in encouraging Amy's work in South Africa and was deeply traumatized by Amy's loss. "She was truly part of us, you know, and she didn't deserve to die," Mabandla told an ABC news team months later. "The worst thing, she didn't deserve to die like she did. . . . There were many people like myself who felt guilty. Guilty being black."

The grief spread like a growing wave of sadness and loss. Although UWC law professor Kader Asmal hadn't known Amy as well as the others, his remarks summed up the shock and grief that descended on the university in the immediate aftermath of Amy's death. "She was one of the liveliest, most intelligent and most committed young people I knew. She had this life-enhancing and lovely presence," he said. "She was in and out of the townships and was received well always. She was so gentle and so genuinely concerned with the emancipation and freedom of black South Africans. She had become . . . part of the struggle."

UWC held a memorial service for Amy on August 26, 1993. At least 1,000 mourners crowded into the university's main hall to pay tribute to someone whom they viewed as a fallen soldier in the struggle for freedom. Those attending included Amy's friends and colleagues, university students and officials, and representatives of the ANC, the Women's National Coalition, and the Black Sash. Organizers of the memorial service wanted to use Amy's death to rally South Africans around the values they believed Amy embodied—namely, justice, peace, and equality. After mourners sang the moving antiapartheid hymn "Senzenina" (What Have We Done?), speaker after speaker lamented the circumstances of Amy's death and praised her for making such a valuable contribution to the university and the country. Before the service ended, someone read a message from the Biehl family, cementing the university's admiration not only for Amy, but for her parents and siblings. It read, "We want to thank all of you who have been so much a part of Amy's recent and amazing life for gathering in her honor to remember her. It helps us to know that you are with Amy and us at this moment. Amy cared so much for you and was completely committed to your incredible potential. She was with you because it was what she wanted to be doing, what she believed was important to do. We are incredibly proud of Amy, we love her deeply and we pray for you and your future."

After the service, members of the ANC Women's League asked for volunteers to march with them to the spot in Gugulethu where Amy was killed. They invited white and mixed-race women to join them, so they could demonstrate that all people should be welcome in the township and that no one should be excluded from the area because of their race. With the press not far behind, about 300 people headed to Gugulethu to retrace Amy's last steps along NY1. Although most of the marchers were black or mixed-race, a handful of whites joined the procession. As they walked along NY1, the crowd sang freedom songs and carried signs and banners. A black marcher in front held a sign that read "Forward to democracy." Other signs read "Comrades come in all colours"; "Amy fought for women's rights"; and "Stop the senseless violence." Although the march proceeded through Gugulethu without incident, more than one participant sensed hostility from some of the young black men watching from the sidelines. As the marchers approached the Caltex station where the attack took place, they could see the bloodstained fence where Amy was killed. Bricks and stones still lay scattered on the grass nearby. As they approached the service station, many marchers placed wreaths or flowers next to the fence, some moved to tears as they did so. Mourners sang the liberation anthem "Nkosi Sikelel' iAfrika" and prayed while members of the press photographed the scene. Albie Sachs, a high-profile constitutional law expert, had known Amy well and spoke to the gathering. "When we were abroad fighting for freedom in this country, we got support from millions and millions of people in the northern continents," he said. "Amy was one of them. Her blood joins the blood of so many thousands who died for the spirit of freedom." Later that day, rain washed the blood from the white fence where the crowd had gathered.

AMY'S death rocked South Africa's political landscape. The ANC, to which Amy had the closest ties, reacted first. ANC Western Cape leaders Allan Boesak and Tony Yengeni called a press conference hours after Amy's murder. "We are deeply concerned and shocked, disgusted by the senseless killing of Amy Biehl," Yengeni said. "Those who are calling for violence in Cape Town must take responsibility for creating an atmosphere in which such terrible and shocking incidents take place." Boesak, who had met Amy, told reporters, "This incident can only be described as racism in its crudest form and the ANC is deeply shocked and angered that such acts should take place at a time when all should be united in their efforts to achieve peace and racial tolerance in our country." Both he and Yengeni blamed the PAC's student wing for the killing. They noted that the youths who attacked Amy had worn PASO T-shirts, shouted PASO slogans, and called Amy "a settler." "We regard the killing of Amy . . . as a declaration of war against the ANC," Yengeni said. Appalled by the attack on their young white colleague and sensing an opportunity to weaken the rival PAC, the ANC clearly hoped to seize the moral high ground in the aftermath of the tragedy.

The situation was more complicated than it seemed. It was the ANC's student wing, COSAS, which had relaunched Operation Barcelona, the violent campaign of stonings and property destruction in Cape Town's black townships. The chaos and violence resulting from the campaign led directly to Amy's death, although it had been students from PASO, not COSAS, who attacked her. ANC leaders in the Western Cape had endorsed the Operation when it began on August 23, 1993. This put the ANC in an awkward position. In a statement released the day after Amy's death, the Western Cape ANC called on both COSAS and PASO to explain their actions in the townships. Western Cape ANC officials said that although they understood the education crisis (which led to Operation Barcelona), they could not accept the role of student organizations in creating an atmosphere of violence in the townships. Tony Yengeni conceded that Operation Barcelona should be condemned if it had led to the death of Amy Biehl.

The ANC's high-profile reaction to Amy's death can be viewed in several ways. Certainly, many ANC leaders and members had genuine remorse because Amy had worked closely with the organization from her base at UWC. Her racially motivated murder contradicted the ANC's long-held policy of nonracialism. ANC officials could also have been worried that Amy's murder might set off a backlash among whites that would slow down the transition to democracy. Getting "out in front" of the story and condemning the act would reassure jittery whites that such an attack completely violated ANC policy. Some speculated that the ANC sought to use Amy's death chiefly to mobilize against the PAC, which was relatively strong in the Western Cape. If the ANC could be seen as taking the moral high ground in the aftermath of the killing, it might increase its chances of attracting support among mixed-raced voters, who formed the majority population in the region and tended to view the ANC with considerable skepticism.

The PAC quickly denied responsibility for the attack. Bathembu Lugulwana, the PAC's secretary in the Western Cape, said his organization was shocked by Amy's death. He insisted that the PAC was not involved and pledged that it would do everything it could to find out who was responsible. PAC officials also sent an official letter to US ambassador Lyman expressing regret for Amy's death and asking that he convey the organization's condolences to the Biehl family.

Not only was the PAC on the defensive, but some of its members resented what they perceived as the undue publicity surrounding the young American's death. "How many blacks have been killed since 1976? Why were we so upset about the death of one white person?" Mgwebi Mtuze, a PAC supporter in the early 1990s, recalled thinking. He remembered one fellow PAC activist saying, "Amy Biehl's death leaves me cold," echoing Justice Minister Jimmy Kruger's dismissive remark about the death of Black Consciousness leader Steve Biko in 1977. An article in the *Times* of London suggested that such sentiments were shared by some PAC leaders, although they were not always voiced publicly.

In the period after Amy's death, the long-standing tension between the ANC and the PAC escalated. The day after Boesak and Yengeni's press conference, the PAC held a press conference of its own in Cape Town. PAC officials said that contrary to ANC allegations, their organization did not attack individual whites, but the system of white domination. "They [the ANC] must not use Amy Biehl's death as a political ballgame to win votes," declared Western Cape regional secretary Lugulwana. Facing such damaging charges from its rival, the PAC attempted to blame the ANC for Amy's death, "claiming it was the product of township anger over a national teachers' strike, to which the PAC [was] opposed." The back-and-forth accusations triggered a wider debate over the ANC's recent actions. On the positive side, the influential *Star* newspaper ran an editorial praising the ANC for pledging to find Amy's killers. But a black reader of the *Weekly Mail & Guardian* criticized the ANC for allegedly pandering to white fears and neglecting "its core constituency—blacks." He accused the organization of expending more energy trying to track down the St. James and Amy Biehl perpetrators than bringing to justice those who had killed blacks. Others charged the ANC with hypocrisy for tolerating violence and racist slogans in the past. A lead editorial in the *Natal Mercury* criticized the ANC for allegedly feigning outrage over the murder of Amy Biehl, who worked with their organization, while it continued to use the slogan "kill the farmer, kill the Boer" at its rallies. Residents of Cape Town called their morning newspaper to make similar points. Sensing an opportunity, another of the ANC's chief rivals—the Inkatha Freedom Party—joined the chorus of disapproval. Its spokesman said it was "curious" that the ANC was blaming the PAC for Biehl's death, when its own slogans had done the most to create antiwhite hostility. With South Africa's first democratic elections scheduled for early 1994, the ANC was clearly not the only political party trying to seize the moral high ground in the wake of Amy's death.

In the early morning hours of August 26, Easy Nofemela and Mongezi Manqina were arrested in connection with Amy's death. Some residents of Gugulethu had broken with tradition and tipped off the police to help them locate the perpetrators. Township dwellers rarely went to the police to turn each other in for political murders, but that they did so in this case showed how much some Gugulethu residents disapproved of the attack. PAC spokesmen eventually admitted that the youths who killed Amy were members of PASO, but they insisted that the PAC did not condone the murder. On August 30, Nofemela and Manqina appeared at a preliminary hearing at the magistrate's court in Mitchell's Plain. As they left the court hearing, Easy raised his fist and led a crowd of about 50 young supporters in the chant "One settler, one bullet." The defiant, antiwhite mood was stronger than ever.

The controversy over Amy's death revealed significant tensions within the PAC, both generational and ideological. The gap between the senior leadership and the youth after the murder showed that the elders had lost some control over their juniors. They disagreed about key issues, including negotiations, violence, and racial slogans. While senior leaders of the PAC denied that their organization was targeting white civilians, antiwhite sentiment persisted among militants. The day after the attack on Amy, PASO Western Cape chairman Tsietsi Telite struck a defiant tone. "We are not surprised at what happened yesterday," he said. "Looking at the situation on the ground, the youths and the students are so angry and frustrated that when they see anyone identified with the dispossessing classes, anything can happen—and could happen again." In fact, the PAC's position on the targeting of white civilians was ambiguous. The issue provoked more than a generational divide, because the PAC's armed wing, APLA, had been stepping up attacks against whites since November 1992. PAC leaders publicly distanced themselves from violent acts against white civilians, while its armed wing continued to plan and conduct such attacks. As the *Weekly Mail & Guardian* pointed out, the PAC often had a double agenda. It used antiwhite attacks to generate support among township militants but then publicly distanced itself from them.

The controversies swirling around the ANC and the PAC threatened to put both organizations on the defensive. Of the two, the PAC was hurt the most. Its reputation for extremism was heightened, whereas the voice of moderates and those favoring negotiations was strengthened. The South African press harshly criticized the PAC in the days after Amy's death. The *Star's* lead editorial on August 27, 1993, titled "A Horrible Catalyst," read in part as follows:

> If it is true that Amy Biehl's murderers shouted "you deserve to die because you are a settler," then no PAC official can possibly still pretend that the "one settler, one bullet" slogan is not an incitement to racial violence. The PAC's leadership should instead hang their heads in shame at having failed to condemn the deadly chant when it first made its appearance . . . Amy Biehl's death is made especially horrific by the crude racism which apparently inspired it . . . and by the fact that she was a guest in our country; a guest who, moreover, was deeply concerned about the future of the underprivileged.

These criticisms and others took a significant toll on the PAC. Polls before Amy's death suggested that less than 5 percent of black South Africans supported the PAC; it would win only 1.2 percent of the vote in South Africa's April 1994 elections. Leading PAC member Patricia de Lille later conceded that her organization's reputation had suffered as a result of Amy Biehl's murder.

The ANC Women's League took Amy's death particularly hard. Its leaders lamented not only the loss of a colleague, but that women were increasingly being drawn into the country's political violence. Albertina Sisulu wrote to the Biehls on behalf of the league, telling the family that Amy was greatly respected for her commitment to women's and children's issues in South Africa. "We deplore and are deeply grieved by her brutal and senseless murder," she wrote. The Biehls had lost a daughter and a sister, while the ANC Women's League had lost "a comrade in the struggle for democracy." The Centre for Adult and Continuing Education at UWC also rallied to defend women's rights in the wake of Amy's death. It condemned her "senseless killing" and noted that she had worked "tirelessly" to promote women's causes. Their statement continued: "The killing of

Amy in daylight in a Cape Town township is a horrifying and graphic example of how women's ability to move around the townships and suburbs of South Africa is being continually curtailed through the threat of physical violence. Women are unable to go out freely at night because of the continued threat of physical violence. Now their mobility is threatened in the day time as well, whether they are traveling on foot, in taxis, in buses or private vehicles." As these statements suggest, Amy's death brought South Africa's gender divisions into sharper relief, not just its political ones.

Amy's killing was condemned all across the racial and political spectrum. Diverse groups that had never agreed on anything agreed that the murder brought South Africa to a new low. Even the radical Azanian People's Organization (AZAPO), a product of the Black Consciousness Movement, felt compelled to speak out. "If it should transpire that the perpetrators of such bestiality are associated with any black organization, the organization must publicly distance itself from them," said AZAPO publicity secretary Gomolemo Mokae. The killing of people because of their race or political beliefs was barbaric and did not advance the liberation struggle. AZAPO's publicity secretary in the Western Cape, Jimmy Yekiso, was slightly more equivocal. His organization would always deplore senseless killings, he said, but blacks still saw whites as part of their oppression. The National Association of Democratic Lawyers (NADEL) released a statement that echoed wider sentiments. Besides deploring Amy's "senseless and brutal killing," it noted how her death highlighted "the deepening crisis of violence and racial polarization in our society."

Compared with the outrage and grief being expressed in the rest of the country, the South African government's response seemed unusually muted. President F. W. de Klerk was on a week-long Latin American tour between August 22 and 29. The only official reaction to Amy's murder by the South African government seems to have come from a Law and Order Ministry spokesman, who said that the incident proved how racist slogans could lead to politically motivated killings. The day after he returned from his South American trip, President De Klerk called for a special cabinet meeting to discuss "the constitutional crisis and the escalating violence," but he did not comment publicly on Amy's death, either immediately after the meeting or later on. Although the Biehl family never heard from De Klerk after Amy's death, South African diplomats based in the United States did reach out. Officials from the Los Angeles consulate wrote messages of sympathy and sent Linda a massive protea, South Africa's official flower. South Africa's ambassador to the United States, Harry Schwarz, expressed his condolences in a brief telegram to Peter and Linda the day after Amy was killed. "It is particularly tragic that this should have happened to a young person who was seeking to help others in my country," he wrote.

The widespread condemnation of Amy's killing had an immediate impact on South Africa's political environment. ANC officials in the Western Cape urged students to stop their violent protest campaigns. Under pressure from their elders, COSAS called off Operation Barcelona on August 26, 1993. The next day, a regional organizer for COSAS acknowledged that the killing of Amy Biehl had contributed to the decision. Then the South African Democratic Teachers' Union (SADTU) ended its two-week-long strike, though SADTU officials rejected accusations that the strike was somehow linked to Amy Biehl's death. But by ending its protest, the union was tacitly admitting that its walkout had contributed to the recent unrest in Cape Town's black townships. Seeking to stanch the damage to its own reputation, PASO agreed that teachers and students in the Western Cape should return to school. Two major protest campaigns were thus ended within days of each other, helping to stop the chaos in the townships that had brought racial tension to a boiling point. In the words of the *Sunday Times*, South Africa's most widely circulated newspaper, "The shocking death of 26-year-old Amy appears to have touched a nerve within Cape Town's violence-plagued black areas and has led to political organizations reassessing their role in the violence." Had they done enough to stem violence and promote a positive vision for the future? Were their actions hastening or delaying the transition to democracy?

AMY Biehl's death triggered an unprecedented wave of soul-searching among South Africans of all races. They began to reflect more deeply on the violence that was claiming so many lives and threatening to derail the transition to democracy. It was as if by losing Amy, South Africans felt they were losing their dream of a harmonious society in which citizens of all races could live together in peace. They feared losing the cherished idea—among the majority, at least—that South Africa belonged to all of its citizens, black and white. Only Chris Hani's death four months earlier had provoked such an outpouring of collective anxiety. Voices rose up from all over the country, from private citizens to political, religious, academic, media, and human rights organizations, expressing outrage and shame over Amy's death. South Africans collectively asked, "What kind of society have we become? What happened to our ideals? Is there any hope for our country?"

Many South Africans feared that the racially motivated killing of "an unselfish and idealistic young woman" from overseas boded ill for their country's future. It convinced some that South Africa's violence was bringing the country closer to an all-out race war. In a letter of condolence to the Biehl family, a resident of Hout Bay in Cape Town noted how "[Amy's] death has touched us all deeply. It has awakened feelings of anger and profound frustration amongst those of us who seek a new order in South Africa. A peaceful order. Amy's death reminds us all of how horribly far we have still to travel and the cost that remains to be paid." In the minds of many South Africans, Amy's death sparked fears of worsening racial violence and a derailed transition to democracy.

There was a growing fear that black anger had escalated beyond the point of no return. Even some black activists who opposed the violence worried that black anger was reaching a boiling point—not just because of the delay of democracy, but also because of the still glaring socioeconomic inequality. These concerns bespoke the wider tragedy that was engulfing South Africa, reminiscent of that dramatized in Alan Paton's literary classic *Cry, the Beloved Country*. In that novel, Msimangu, an African priest based in Johannesburg, said, "I have one great fear in my heart, that one day when they [whites] turn to loving they will find we are turned to hating." This was a real fear among many white South Africans and some older Africans, during both the apartheid era and the transition to democracy. The fear was magnified by Amy's death. The anguish surrounding Amy's murder was particularly intense because apartheid was being dismantled, and real democracy seemed to be around the corner. Perhaps South Africa's racial animosities were indelible, despite the miracle of Mandela's release and the encouragement of the wider world.

South Africans of all colors felt increased apprehension toward young people who were perpetrating violence. At Amy's memorial service at UWC, Rhoda Kadalie described her friend's killers as "young monsters" created by apartheid. "Now they are afoot in the land and no one can stop them. They are eating us and eating each other," she said. Anthropologist Nancy Scheper-Hughes, who attended the memorial service, found that Kadalie's fears were widely shared. "South African political leaders of all stripes began to worry that township youth were totally out of control."

Amy's death sparked a period not only of intense soul-searching among South Africans, but of widespread gloom. Just as their country was trying to overcome centuries of institutionalized racism, racial differences and hostilities were growing. One American reporter believed that Amy's death raised doubts about South Africa's ability to hold its first democratic elections in April 1994. Karin Chubb, a prominent member of the Black Sash in Cape Town who had met Amy, felt the despair spreading over the country. Amy's death came at a fragile time, when violence was multiplying. After Amy was killed by the very people she'd come to help, Chubb recalled, many South Africans began to lose hope in the country's future. It wasn't just whites who despaired of the country's future. On August 26, the All Structures Forum, which represented student organizations at UWC, hailed Amy's work in preparing the country for its first democratic elections and her work on behalf of South African women. The recent township violence that claimed Amy indicated that "the fabric of our society is disintegrating with greater rapidity than at any point in our history."

Even though South Africans of all races began to worry more about their country's future after Amy's death, white anxieties were most acute. Her death occurred during a time of transition not just for the country, but for white South Africans in particular, many of whom generally favored reform but hadn't yet reconciled themselves to black majority rule. Amy's death came after a series of highly publicized attacks against whites, the St. James attack being the most notorious. White fears and anxiety—about their future under black rule, about crime and potential revenge—were rising. It took the death of a single white person—a young white American woman—to bring home their vulnerability in the face of change. In particular, whites feared that the anger among black youth was becoming irrational and uncontrollable. Keith Richburg, one of the *Washington Post*'s Africa correspondents, noticed such fears when he traveled in South Africa after Amy's death. "Amy Biehl's death doesn't fall into the category of random criminal violence," he wrote. Instead, he noted, "She was killed specifically because she was white. And maybe that's why her death, more than the other daily incidents of crime and mayhem, terrified white South Africa even more. A black mob had set upon a white exchange student—an American no less—and killed her because she was in the wrong place at the wrong time, an incident that reached to the dreaded core of white terror—the fear of black retribution for decades of oppression, and whites being randomly targeted because of their color."

Amy's death reinforced antiblack stereotypes among some white South Africans, particularly those on the right. An editorial published in *Die Burger* on August 27 was among those that blamed Amy's death on the atavistic violence among black people. In condemning the murder, the paper's editors used phrases such as "blind racial hatred," "unbridled bloodlust," and "frustrated and irresolute mob." Such language concerned black journalists elsewhere, who worried that Biehl's killing would confirm racial stereotypes—that blacks were irrational, inherently violent, and bent on revenge. Many observers knew that the anger of Amy's killers was not representative of most black South Africans, but, in the words of a British journalist, "among conservative elements of South Africa's 14 percent white population, [Biehl's] murder will once more raise the spectre of a race war." His reporting was startlingly accurate, at least as far as white extremists were concerned. "We've warned in the past that in the end it all comes down to the color of your skin," Koos van Rensburg, spokesman for the Afrikaner People's Front, said days later. "Nobody is going to ask you if you support the ANC or the PAC or the AWB [Afrikaner Resistance Movement]—it's the fact that you have the wrong skin color that counts." An American journalist heard one Afrikaner use Amy's murder to justify long-held stereotypes. "They [blacks] are like that," he said. "They go into a frenzy, in a mob." The simmering sense of horror over what befell Amy revealed an undeniable irony. Some of the people most upset about Amy's death—conservative white South Africans—were least supportive of her work in South Africa.

The country's white liberals were dismayed as well, but for different reasons. Amy's murder, although an aberration, triggered fears among white liberals that their own security was endangered and that their good intentions would no longer matter. Such sentiments were particularly evident in Cape Town. Like most white South Africans, whites in Cape Town had been shielded from black anger for decades, when political violence claimed only black victims. Many white Capetonians were proud not only of the physical beauty of their city, but of their liberal tradition. They had consistently voted for opposition parties that questioned apartheid and falsely believed that racial harmony predominated in the Western Cape, because they saw themselves as more humane and enlightened than the Afrikaner Nationalist government. But as *Chicago Tribune* correspondent Liz Sly observed, the St. James and Amy Biehl killings shocked Cape Town's whites and shattered their illusions. "The attacks exposed decades of pent-up resentment of which whites were only dimly aware but blacks always knew was there," she wrote. Cape Town mayor-elect Clive Keegan, long active in liberal causes, captured the mood well days after Amy's death. "Cape Town has lost its innocence," he said. "This is the last place where we expected such things to happen. We have a tradition of liberal political and multicultural tolerance that was for years the envy of South Africa."

Another attack two days after Amy's murder compounded white fears. On August 27, 1993, two APLA operatives fired on a luxury bus carrying mostly white passengers as it traveled near Beaufort West, a small town approximately 265 miles (426 kilometers) northeast of Cape Town. Eight passengers were wounded in the attack, bringing antiwhite violence to South Africa's front pages once again. After three highly publicized attacks on whites in the space of a month—on St. James Church, Amy Biehl, and now the luxury bus—South African officials became increasingly concerned about the future of tourism and academic exchanges.

Amy's death probably also helped accelerate white emigration. The number of whites leaving South Africa increased noticeably after she was killed. In 1993, about 8,100 South Africans emigrated (the majority of whom were white), an increase of 88 percent from 1992. It was the highest emigration figure since 1987. If emigration rates were a barometer of white insecurities, then those insecurities rose dramatically between early 1993 and early 1994. During the first five months of 1994, South Africa experienced a net loss of 2,857 people. Antiwhite violence during the second half of 1993 had clearly taken a psychological toll. Gail and Anthony Mosse, two young Americans who had graduated with Amy's class at Stanford in 1989, visited New Zealand in late 1993 and met a South African couple who had just immigrated there with their two teenage sons. They told the Mosses that Amy's death had been "one of the catalysts prompting them to leave the random and increasing violence." In 1992, 382 South Africans immigrated to New Zealand; in 1993, 2,800 did so.

Black South Africans also reacted strongly to Amy's death, but in different ways. Many regretted having lost a comrade in the struggle for democracy and felt anger and shame that Amy had been murdered in their name. Jonathan Jansen, then a professor of education at the University of Durban-Westville, had been in a class with Amy at Stanford in 1987 but had not known her personally. His first reaction upon hearing of Amy's death was, "Oh my God! Don't the students know she's one of us?" He felt terrible, because "white Americans like Amy were in solidarity with us. We're losing a valuable ally." Freeman Bukashe, a black South African who lived near Soweto, was also angered by what happened in Gugulethu. He wrote this in a letter published in the *Star*: "I am sure every sane and decent South African, notwithstanding his or her political inclinations, was appalled and disgusted at the brutal murder of Amy Biehl. The sadists who perpetrated this ghastly crime regard themselves as champions of freedom. If their struggle entails the slaughter of the very people who strive for democracy and freedom, God help us all. Ironically, the name Gugulethu when translated means 'our pride.' After this incident, who can be proud of such a place?"

Some prominent black South African journalists feared that "unfortunate racial stereotypes" would be reinforced in the wake of Amy's death. Editors of the *Sowetan*, for example, worried that certain groups would use the incident to "confirm their worst racist prejudices"—that blacks were inherently irrational, vengeful, and violent. But other black citizens were more apathetic. When Neliswa Solatshu of Cape Town first heard about Amy's death, it hardly registered. After all, she recalled, "How many blacks have been killed?" She did not initially know that her cousin was involved in the attack. "But even if he was, I would still feel the same. She's a white woman. What the hell must I care about her?" As her response suggests, some black South Africans were so embittered by years of oppression and so numbed to the violence that they were unmoved by yet another death. They might not have cheered when Amy was killed, but they did not grieve.

Reactions in Gugulethu varied according to age, political affiliation, and other factors. Some young militants were unrepentant. Themba Mbane, a young supporter of PASO, told an American reporter that anger and a desire for revenge characterized the mindset of many people in the area. Historically, blacks had had particularly difficult experiences in Cape Town. As a result, there was a deep reservoir of bitterness and rage in Cape Town's black townships. In an interview with a South African journalist days after Amy's death, another PASO member admitted that he still hated "white oppressors." "If I have to kill white people, I'll do it," he said. "I'm not sorry about Biehl's death."

Many Gugulethu residents, however, disapproved of the murder. The community's willingness to help police identify the assailants was an early sign of scorn for PASO's attack. Local reporting at the time indicated that most township residents supported nonracialism and believed that whites should be able to come into their areas unharmed. They did not want whites to view townships as "no-go" areas, particularly because whites helped staff health clinics. Many were shocked by Amy's death and resolved that such attacks should never happen again. Nomzame Sodladla, 34, told a reporter, "People are very angry, they are ashamed that it happened in our township. . . . I didn't even think things like this could happen. This can really haunt me for the rest of my life." Sodladla had brought white friends to Gugulethu before to show them around and had helped organize a fashion show in the township, which whites attended. She feared that she'd never again feel comfortable asking white friends to visit her in Gugulethu, which hurt, because she wanted to bring the races closer together.

Gugulethu residents held no less than three memorial services for Amy in the week following her death. On August 26, township women organized an interdenominational service for peace at Ndaliso Memorial Baptist Church, which lay only about 100 meters from where Amy was killed. Several of those present had either seen Amy in the township before or recalled how Amy always greeted people on the street. Organizers asked for those who knew Amy to come forward. Among those who did was Hilda Ndude, a leading member of the ANC Women's League in the Western Cape. She had first met Amy in May and described the day she died as the saddest of her life. "Some whites are standing with us," Ndude told those assembled. "They are not foreigners. Let us correct slogans, they are misleading." Another woman led a prayer: "O Lord, we call upon you to bring down a flag of peace. Our children are dying, including the white one killed last night. We pray for an end to the violence, whether white or black. Enter and restore love in the hearts of blacks and whites, our children and their teachers who are now roaming the streets. Make us one." Following the service, a group of women walked through the rain toward the fence where Amy was struck down, singing as they went. The leader of the service, Ms. N. C. Mquqo, said a short prayer there; then 40 of the mourners traveled to the US consulate in central Cape Town to express their condolences.

Members of St. Gabriel's Catholic Church in Gugulethu planned a memorial service of their own. Led by Basil van Rensburg, a white priest and longtime opponent of apartheid, the church placed an ad in the *Weekend Argus* inviting other whites to come to Gugulethu and join residents in a service celebrating Amy's life. On Sunday, August 29, 1993, between 700 and 1,000 people crowded into St. Gabriel's, including a handful of whites and more than a few reporters. Cape Town journalist Anthony Heard reckoned that the congregation was about twice the size it usually was on a Sunday morning. After a large color photograph of Amy was placed in front of the altar, six girls performed a dance in her honor; other members of the congregation read poems and messages to Amy's parents thanking them for their daughter, moving some of the black mourners to tears. "She showed her courage when she came to Gugulethu knowing that she could be risking her life," one young woman said. "She believed in us and never thought of us as being black but as human beings just like her." Three days later, Gugulethu hosted yet another church service in Amy's honor, this one attended predominantly by schoolchildren.

SOUTH Africans did more than just express grief over Amy's death; many became more determined to work for positive change. In the wake of the tragedy, South Africans engaged in a national dialogue and collectively concluded, *We're risking throwing away the progress we've made after years of effort and struggle, risking the democracy that is so close, because of exploding violence and racial hatred. We must step back from the precipice, recommit ourselves to nonviolence and nonracialism, and actively curb racist hate speech before our dream of democracy is destroyed. Let us use the tragedy of Amy's death to make South Africa better.*

Hopes rose that Amy's death would be a catalyst for peace and reconciliation. Some of the country's most prominent newspapers took the lead in promoting this message. The *Star* used Amy's death to suggest that despite its noble sentiments, South Africa's Peace Accord was being flouted by political leaders. It called for the National Peace Secretariat to be given more power before the death toll mounted further; then Amy's death could at least be a catalyst "for stopping the horror." A *Cape Times* editorial urged that more effective action be taken against those who promoted racial hatred. The Black Sash released a statement saying that Amy's death must lead to an urgent commitment to peace. The coordinator of a civic association in Durban wrote Melanie to express its condemnation of Amy's killing. The letter shows that progressive organizations not only wanted to express their repugnance toward Amy's death but also sought to use the tragedy as a springboard for something positive—an intensified march to democracy. In a letter published in the *UWC Women's Bulletin,* Amanda Botha, a member of the Women's Coalition in the Western Cape, was determined to honor Amy's memory by urging that peace efforts be intensified. "May Amy's death inspire us to work together as never before to overcome all gulfs and may we work until reconciliation, reconstruction, and freedom has been achieved," Botha wrote. Observers noticed that South Africans of all races were coming together to reject racial hatred and violence. Perhaps Sindiwe Magona said it best. Acclaimed for her novels and autobiographical writings, Magona was working for the United Nations in New York at the time of Amy's death and had lived in the Gugulethu neighborhood where Amy was killed. She believed that Amy's death was "an indictment on all of us for having allowed race hate to get to the level it did. We must all work for reconciliation." Many other South Africans felt the same way.

Calls for an end to violence intensified in the days after Amy's murder. Archbishop Tutu urged black political leaders to acknowledge wrongdoing in their own organizations, so that those working for a just and peaceful South Africa could retain the moral high ground. All over the country, South Africans expressed dismay over their country's escalating violence. As one American journalist put it, Amy's death became synonymous with "no more bloodshed." The many memorial services, marches to Amy's death site, and the end to Operation Barcelona were local manifestations of a wider movement for peace that was gaining momentum throughout the country.

South Africans also began to condemn racist slogans more vigorously than ever before. Here the white-owned press took the lead. In an editorial on August 27, 1993, the *Cape Times* wrote that racist sloganeering had created the environment that led to Amy's death. It called for both the ANC and the PAC to curb such slogans, which had allegedly been used to drum up support among youth ahead of the country's first democratic elections. The *Argus* saw welcome signs of a backlash against racial hate speech. "It would be a fitting tribute to Amy Biehl if her death were to mark the dawn of a new effort by all political groups to put an end to hateful language, and to recognize that strategies which capitalize on anger and political passions increasingly threaten the national reconciliation which so many purport to support," the paper wrote. Other print media expressed similar sentiments in the week after Amy was killed. Whether they were liberal, conservative, or somewhere in between, South Africa's white-owned newspapers were united in their condemnation of racist slogans in the wake of Amy's death.

Important sections of the black South African community also called for an end to racial hate speech. Archbishop Tutu scolded political leaders who should have realized how dangerous "blood curdling" slogans could be in South Africa's volatile atmosphere. Prominent leaders of the ANC also condemned racist slogans, despite the fact that some of its own people had used such slogans in the past. In a speech in Stellenbosch the day after Amy's murder, Tokyo Sexwale said that ANC Youth League leader Peter Mokaba's slogan "Kill the farmer, kill the Boer" was inconsistent with ANC policy and pledged to stop such slogans from being used. Even ANC firebrand Harry Gwala, not known for being conciliatory, publicly criticized racial hate speech in the days following Amy's death. That he joined the growing campaign against hate speech showed how truly powerful it had become.

As the backlash against racist slogans gained momentum, South Africans strongly reaffirmed the principle of nonracialism. Despite the occasional utterances of its Youth League leader, nonracialism lay at the core of the ANC's identity, and it vigorously defended the principle in the wake of Amy's death. In his speech in Stellenbosch, Tokyo Sexwale said that the struggle for democracy could not be allowed to degenerate into the killing of whites. Since its founding, the ANC had conducted a nonracial struggle, he said, and if attacking whites became part of the struggle, the ANC's foundation would be destroyed. Guy Berger, editor of the prodemocracy newspaper *South*, agreed. In the columns of his newspaper, he urged South Africans to stand firmly behind nonracialism in the aftermath of Amy's death. "We know that South Africa needs political justice as a precondition for peace in this country. Nonracialism is just as fundamental. We must use September Peace Month [*sic*] to make South Africa a no-go area for violent racists across the racial spectrum."

The greatest living symbol of nonracialism in South Africa was of course Nelson Mandela. Despite opposing white-minority rule with every fiber of his being for virtually all of his adult life, he had worked side by side with whites in the struggle for freedom and believed that South Africa belonged to all its people, black and white. All should recognize each other's humanity regardless of skin color. No race was the enemy of another. But he was keenly aware of white fears as the country's democratic elections grew closer. In a speech to a crowd of 30,000 in Khayelitsha on September 12, 1993, Mandela said that while the problems of blacks would be a top priority under an ANC government, whites were important to South Africa's future as well, because they had critical skills that the country needed. He called whites "our brothers and our sisters." Then he moved on to Amy Biehl, whom he called "a wonderful student, cruelly murdered." "It is not military action to kill innocent civilians," he told the overwhelmingly black crowd. A day later, Mandela spoke to a mostly white audience in Cape Town and tried to reassure them. "This is not the time for panic," he said. "This is not the time to think of emigration to Australia." At a time of escalating white fears in the weeks after Amy's death, Mandela felt it essential to address such fears head on. He had done so before and would do so again.

The strengthening consensus around nonracialism was undeniable, and it had been triggered largely by Amy's death. Observers began to sense that amid the tragedy of her death, South Africa had a chance to steer away from racial hatred and violence and to redeem itself. An American academic based at Stellenbosch recognized the shift in a letter to the Biehls five days after Amy was killed. As blacks and whites expressed their horror over "this inexcusable atrocity," he wrote, "your loss seems likely to contribute to bringing people to their senses and moderating the practice of politics in South Africa." He hoped that the Biehls could take comfort in the fact that while Amy's contribution to the world in her life was extraordinary, so was her contribution in death. One mother of another Stanford undergraduate who had spent time in South Africa hoped that Amy's death would "bring a new understanding to the meaning of 'umlungu [white person].'" That turned out to be the case. Amy's death reminded black South Africans of the humanity, commitment, and comradeship of some whites, thus moderating antiwhite feeling and strengthening the concept of nonracialism.

South Africans didn't just talk about the need for peace and nonracialism, they took concrete steps to promote them. On August 30, 1993, ANC Western Cape chairman Allan Boesak organized a meeting in Gugulethu to discuss ways of ending violence and invited representatives of all groups and communities to attend. Those who did so included members of the ANC, COSAS, the South African Civic Association, the National Peace Campaign, Gugulethu residents, and a number of whites—though not the PAC. Those present decided to hold a procession in Gugulethu on the following Sunday morning, and they especially hoped that mixed-race, Indian, and white citizens would participate. Peace committee official

Zilila Dubasi encouraged "our comrades from outside the township to join us in demonstrating nonracialism and to undermine the notion of no-go areas."

Alarmed at the rising political violence during July and August 1993, officials from South Africa's National Peace Campaign decided to launch what they called "Operation Peace Campaign" in September. Amy's death, while not being the only precipitating factor, was very much in the minds of organizers in the Western Cape. They and other South Africans were worried that the country's violence was spinning out of control and, if not stopped, could escalate into a racial civil war. Operation Peace Campaign was scheduled to begin with a "Peace Day," during which traffic in South Africa would come to a standstill at noon so that the country could engage in a moment of silence for peace. The Western Cape Peace Committee planned a busy month of follow-up activities.

Peace Day was observed on September 2, 1993. In an editorial titled simply "Peace!" the *Cape Times* wrote that the violent incidents of 1993, including the Hani assassination, St. James church attack, and Amy Biehl murder, had finally "drawn the people of the Cape closer together in a new determination to advance the cause of reconciliation. The way in which the people of Gugulethu, shamed by the murder of Miss Biehl, have flocked to churches in the township to mourn her death, has made a deep impression at home and in the United States." The editors urged people in the Cape to renew their commitment to peace and justice from that day forward. After the paper hit newsstands, mayor-elect Clive Keegan presided over a service at St. Mary's Catholic Cathedral in Cape Town to mark the first day of the peace campaign. Some residents of the city wore blue or white ribbons to show their support for the campaign. At noon, church bells rang and balloons were released, and some motorists, pedestrians, and workers stopped to observe a moment of silence.

Millions of other South Africans observed the country's national day of peace in some way. "All over South Africa, millions of office workers, shoppers, and motorists linked hands and meditated for a minute," one eyewitness reported. Even in violence-ridden townships like Katlehong in the Transvaal, people linked arms. There was a noticeable easing of tension around South Africa that day, and the number of violent incidents dropped dramatically. Both F. W. de Klerk and Nelson Mandela talked about the need for peace as well, with Mandela criticizing those who were engaging in "senseless violence to prevent the advent of democracy." The only groups that held out were PASO and the right-wing Conservative Party, both of which "openly derided" the occasion. After Peace Day, stickers reading "I am dedicated to peace—are you?" were printed and sold on the streets of South Africa. Organizers believed their campaign was off to an excellent start.

As part of the peace campaign, a peace march was held in Gugulethu on Saturday, September 4, 1993. Kader Asmal and other ANC officials in the Western Cape planned the march to "assert the fundamental principle of nonracialism and isolate those who do not support this value." Approximately 200 people, including a handful of whites, marched through Gugulethu in the rain, singing freedom songs and waving peace flags. When the crowd arrived at the fence where Amy was killed, Allan Boesak said a prayer: "We must reaffirm our commitment to peace, the liberation of all of our people and nonracialism." After marchers planted a peace flag at Amy's death site, they continued toward New Crossroads and Nyanga, attracting the curiosity—and in some cases the participation—of township residents as they went.

In the months ahead, South Africa's violence did not end completely, but it did begin to decline. Political deaths peaked in July and August 1993, the most violent year of the transition to democracy. Thereafter the fatalities began to decline until flaring up briefly just before the April 1994 elections. Clearly the National Peace Campaign in September had some positive effects. Perhaps South Africa was turning the corner on its recent violence as ordinary citizens became fed up and actively assisted the peace process.

AMID all of the public statements and events commemorating Amy, hundreds of South Africans who had no connection to her contacted the Biehls to express their support. Their letters displayed the humanity of ordinary South Africans, their gratitude for Amy's life and work, and the fact that her killers represented an aberration, a fringe group. The majority of the correspondents were white South Africans. Amy's death had touched them as no other political death had in ten years of mounting unrest. But black South Africans also wrote, expressing solidarity with the Biehls and showing that a reservoir of goodwill still existed toward whites who declared common cause with the oppressed and actively worked for democracy. Amy had become a hero in many people's minds and a symbol of democracy. In the aftermath of Amy's death, it was as if much of Cape Town had adopted her.

Many South Africans wrote not only to express their condolences but to express admiration for the way the Biehls were handling their grief. They admired the way Peter and Linda refused to condemn South Africa and instead affirmed the need for peace and democracy in the wake of their daughter's death. A black high-school student attending a predominantly white school wrote to the Biehls from his township in the Eastern Cape to express his sympathy. He praised the Biehls for the "meaningful, forgiving and deep-rooted Christian way" they had reacted to news of their daughter's death. The student wished he had known Amy, because he shared her sentiments, and if it were not for financial difficulties, he would have attended Amy's funeral service. The hundreds of moving letters like this showed not only that large numbers of South Africans were deeply disturbed by Amy's death, but that they found a larger meaning in the tragedy—namely, that the violence had to stop before it destroyed South Africa. The Biehls drew enormous strength and comfort from the letters, which inspired them to publicize Amy's ideas and learn more about South Africa themselves.

Just weeks after her death, Amy had become a phenomenon in South Africa, memorialized in church services, marches, editorials, speeches, letters, and even poetry and art. In South Africa in particular, the national conversation about Amy was just beginning. The shock waves had also reached the United States.

7

The Amy Phenomenon

AMY'S DEATH struck a nerve not just in South Africa, but in the United States. Americans had their own history of racial struggles and a longstanding interest in South Africa. Now, one of their own had become a victim of the very racial divisions she sought to heal. Americans were drawn to the story of this gifted young American woman who died so tragically trying to promote racial justice in a land long defined by apartheid. While the American press had provided detailed coverage of South Africa's difficult transition to democracy ever since Mandela's release in 1990, Amy's death brought renewed attention to that country's persistent racial divisions and turmoil. It awakened Americans to the randomness and senselessness of South Africa's political violence in a way that the more common killings of black people had not. In the words of one journalist, Amy's death "brought home to many Americans, for perhaps the first time, the ferocity of the battle being waged among South African blacks."

Because news of Amy's murder was covered so extensively in the media, Americans couldn't ignore the story. People from all over the country reacted strongly to the news, both those who knew her and those who did not. Black Americans and white Americans expressed their thoughts in newspaper columns, letters to the editor, and in hundreds of cards, messages, and letters they sent directly to the Biehl family. The diversity of those who commented touched the Biehls deeply and gave them a renewed appreciation of Amy's life and work. Some of the country's most prominent citizens reached out to the Biehls. Besides President Clinton and Coretta Scott King, other high-profile citizens sent the family messages, including Vice-President Al Gore, Secretary of State Warren Christopher, Secretary of Education Richard Riley, and former Vice-President Walter Mondale. Former Assistant Secretary of State for African Affairs Chester Crocker, the subject of Amy's senior thesis, hoped that Amy's loss would spread awareness of her ideals and contribution. "No one I know personifies better than your daughter Amy the hopes and ideals we Americans have had for South Africa, and no one has paid a higher price for them," he wrote Peter and Linda.

Naturally, those with more personal connections to Amy and the Biehls reached out in large numbers—friends from Tucson and Santa Fe, coworkers at Agripac and Neiman Marcus, and those Amy knew in high school, college, and Washington. Her peers from Stanford were particularly hard hit by Amy's loss. Amy had mailed her American friends postcards in mid-August, and most of them arrived a few days after she died. Becky Slipe, one of Amy's roommates at Stanford, talked about her week visiting Amy in Cape Town. Like a growing number of others, she found Amy an inspiration, because she combined compassion for her South African friends, a conviction that things must change, and effective, "on the ground" work. In her letter to the Biehls, the mother of Amy's freshman-year roommate paraphrased Edward Kennedy's famous eulogy for his brother Robert: "How sad that one who saw injustice and tried to right it—who saw suffering and tried to ease it—should be cut down by the very ones she was trying to help. . . . Millions of people the world over have been saddened by Amy's death."

Amy's mentors and professors also mourned the death of one of their most promising and memorable students. Kennell Jackson was heartbroken over her loss and appalled at the way she died. "I was so crushed when I read that morning that she had been killed," he confided to a friend months later. "I was doubly crushed when I read later about the viciousness of the mob and of its racism. It hurt me so that she, a young idealistic white person, was struck down for all the world to see in this manner. Honestly, it made me worry that people might conclude that Africans are racist and brutal." Larry Diamond, another Stanford scholar who had just seen Amy in Cape Town in August, felt a mixture of "shock, horror, outrage, and sadness" at Amy's death. He admired Amy's determination not to "live in a white prison" but to reach out to blacks in order to understand their struggles. Perhaps the most meaningful letter the Biehls received from Stanford came from David Abernethy, the political science professor whose course on southern Africa sparked Amy's interest in the region. "As you reflect with justifiable pride on Amy's many accomplishments in South Africa," he wrote, "I hope you will also consider a more intangible but nonetheless significant accomplishment back at her alma mater. She helped her teachers fulfill their calling."

Amy's colleagues at NDI were appalled by her death. For Lionel Johnson, Amy's loss was "a very personal blow." He had worked with her closely at NDI and had traveled with her in Africa. He felt some sense of responsibility for her being in South Africa, because he was among those who nominated her for the Fulbright award. Johnson kept thinking how admirable his young colleague's motives had been, going to South Africa to support democracy. Brian Attwood, the head of the US Agency for International Development and president of NDI when Amy was a staff member, also reached out to the Biehls. Echoing and perhaps reinforcing Peter and Linda's sentiments, Attwood hoped that "in [Amy's] death, her life's work and her beliefs will gain more attention. She would want her example to be used in the battle against racism, violence and non-democratic behavior."

Some Americans who expressed their sympathy to the Biehls had lived in South Africa and felt that apartheid's poisonous legacy was ultimately responsible for Amy's death. Many South Africans living in the United States wrote supportive letters to the Biehls and offered their thoughts on the violence that claimed Amy and so many others. Black South Africans in the United States who wrote the Biehls revered Amy for her ideals, efforts, and ultimate sacrifice. Like their compatriots back home, they embraced Amy as part of the struggle for democracy. As painful as Amy's loss was, such communications meant a great deal to the Biehls and boosted their spirits immeasurably.

Some of the most heartfelt letters came from African Americans, many of whom admired Amy's efforts to promote democracy and racial equality. Like many South Africans, they too were moved by her sacrifice. African Americans saw in Amy—and by extension the Biehls—white Americans who reached out to blacks, which was encouraging at a time of racial polarization in the United States, as evidenced by the recent police beating of black motorist Rodney King. Their cards and messages came in from all over the country. An African American man from Harlem wrote one of the most moving letters:

> As a black man from Harlem in NY I was shocked and deeply saddened when I heard what had happened to your lovely young daughter.
>
> Although American blacks & Africans are very different, I want to apologize to you on behalf of the entire world's black community for taking your daughter's life.
>
> Unfortunately she joins a long list of people who have died due to racial hatred including Martin Luther King Jr., Medgar Evers, Steve Biko.
>
> Your attitude concerning your daughter & South Africans is unbelievable! If all people, both black & white, were like you, the world would be a beautiful place to live, for all people.

I'm still crying over your daughter & wish I could bring her back. The
only positive is that her place is secure in history as a person who cared
about people & who rose above the stupidity of racial politics and racism.
The black community is forever in your debt. You (the Biehl family) are
great Americans.

I love you all.

So many letters came pouring in that it is impossible to quote from them
all. Among others who wrote the Biehls were parents who had lost children suddenly; those with children who had traveled in the developing world; and those
whose children had worked in or died in Africa. Strangers with no connection to
the Biehls kept reaching out, so mesmerized were they by the media reports that
continued for days after Amy's death. Many of the cards and letters from around
the United States were simply addressed to "The Biehl family, Newport Beach,
CA." Americans' admiration of Amy seemed to grow by the day. In editorials,
letters to the editor, columns, public pronouncements, and personal letters to the
family, Amy was being mythologized as a beacon of freedom, democracy, and
racial equality. Many Americans began to view her as a martyr, as someone who
had died for democratic ideals and deserved to be honored. Numerous observers,
from academics to journalists, from politicians to private citizens, proclaimed that
her example should inspire other Americans to continue her work to make a better world. Although Amy had always said she wanted to be merely a statistic if
South Africa's violence ever claimed her, she became a symbol of human rights
and the highest American ideals. She underwent a transformation from person to
victim to news story to icon in a matter of days.

The press did its part to memorialize Amy as a beacon of democracy. A
headline in the *San Francisco Chronicle* was typical: "Slain Student Remembered for
Idealism: A Champion of Democratic Rights, She 'Wanted to Make the World a
Better Place.'" Editorials all over the United States praised Amy for having "made
a difference"—for doing something positive with her life when she could have
basked in privilege. These headlines and editorials deeply resonated with many
Americans, who were moved to commemorate Amy in their own ways. In eulo-
gizing Amy, large numbers of Americans were collectively expressing solidarity
with her values. In so doing, they sometimes made Amy larger in death than she
was in life, as important as her contributions undoubtedly were.

Many Americans began to compare Amy to famous heroes of the past, especially those of the civil rights and antiapartheid struggles. In her letter to the
Biehls, Coretta Scott King wrote about commemorating her husband's 1963 "I

Have a Dream" speech while simultaneously remembering "Amy's valiant effort and supreme contribution." Her private comment to the Biehls foreshadowed how Amy would become another symbol of the worldwide struggle for racial justice. In another letter to the Biehls, a Stanford professor of engineering who had grown up in South Africa hailed Amy as "a heroic and altruistic volunteer, working to promote free elections in that tortured country." He hoped that the efforts underway in South Africa would lead to free elections, based in part on "the ultimate sacrifices made by dedicated young idealists like Chris Hani and Amy Biehl who have given their lives in support of . . . peaceful change." As proud as Amy was of her work in South Africa, being compared to her hero Chris Hani would certainly have embarrassed her. But that such comparisons were being made showed that in death, she had become an icon of freedom and equality in the minds of many Americans.

Stanford professor David Abernethy's belief that Amy had the potential to inspire others turned out to be true. She inspired more than just her professors, but also many young Americans who wanted to promote democracy and human rights in the wider world. Many young women in particular wrote to the Biehls saying how much they admired Amy, identified with her, and were inspired by her. They wanted to know how they could continue Amy's work on behalf of racial and gender equality. The president and chairman of the National Endowment for Democracy recognized Amy's potential to inspire others in a letter they wrote to the Biehls a week after Amy died. The two first compared Amy to earlier civil rights workers: "Your daughter represented the best of her generation and the hope for the country's future. She was a scholar and an idealist, a person who believed that being an American entails a responsibility to work for all. She is a direct descendant of the civil rights workers of an earlier era who marched for racial justice and registered voters, often at the cost of their own lives. They were driven by a vision of freedom and democracy that is the heart and soul of our nation." Judging from the number of young people who wrote the Biehls, the inspirational power of Amy's story was very real.

Numerous Americans believed that in order for Amy's death to mean something, South Africa's democracy needed to become a reality. Journalists and private citizens alike felt that the struggle in South Africa should be carried on in Amy's memory. In a letter to the *New York Times*, Christine Keener from Cambridge, Massachusetts, urged people not to give up on South Africa after Amy's death. Instead, they should redouble their efforts to promote democracy there. "I don't think that Amy Biehl would want us to despair or give up the struggle for equality and democracy in South Africa," she wrote. Instead of succumbing to despair, "we have to remember Amy Biehl's courage, compassion and desire to fight injustice." American support for South Africa's transition to democracy clearly grew in the wake of Amy's death.

Amy was becoming the lens through which many Americans viewed South Africa on the eve of the elections, at least for those who hadn't read about, studied, or traveled to South Africa before. Amy's death also led some Americans to reexamine their own country's difficult racial past and present. The many letters, columns, and editorials on her death illuminated not only American thinking on South Africa and the legacy of apartheid but also the fraught state of race relations in the United States in the early 1990s. Between 1991 and 1992, the Los Angeles police beating of African American motorist Rodney King was shown countless times on American television, sparking renewed debates about racism and police brutality all over the country. In April 1992, a predominantly white jury in Simi Valley, California, acquitted four police officers in King's beating. The worst race riots in the United States in a generation exploded almost immediately, causing the deaths of more than 50 people in the Los Angeles area and almost $1 billion in property damage. During the unrest, several black men in South Central Los Angeles brutally beat white truck driver Reginald Denny, who almost died in the racially motivated assault. The beating was filmed by a helicopter news crew and broadcast repeatedly on television, just as the King beating had been. These incidents, unfolding within about 50 miles of the Biehls' affluent suburb in Orange County, reignited racial tensions in the United States that had been smoldering since the 1960s.

Some observers drew parallels between the assaults on Amy and Reginald Denny—and the legacy of racial injustice in the United States and South Africa that led to the attacks. Richard Hamer drew such parallels in a perceptive letter to the *Los Angeles Times* the week after Amy was killed. He worried that Amy's murder might cause undue resentment in the United States, that people would condemn the act of violence without understanding the root causes. He noted that Amy put herself in harm's way because she wanted to make a difference in the world. "This pretty girl was killed by apartheid and not a mob," he wrote. "Hate and anger fueled by oppression and discrimination took her life, just as the beating of Reginald Denny was caused by bigotry in this country. It is easy to see the symptoms in acts of violence and ignore the causes." Hamer believed that the historical exclusion of blacks caused resentment in South Africa, just as joblessness among black Americans caused resentment. Before people condemned the mob for Amy's death, he reasoned, they needed to consider the underlying causes of the tragedy. "A group of people is just a crowd until angered by injustice," he concluded.

Some believed that Amy's death should be a catalyst for the United States to improve its own society. Robert Wozniak, who had met Amy in Washington in 1990, hoped that Americans would draw lessons from Amy's death. In a letter to the Minneapolis *Star Tribune,* Wozniak wrote, "All Americans must begin to hold themselves more accountable for our current social conditions. If we fail to do so, we face the unfortunate prospect of more Rodney Kings, Reginald Dennys, Malice Greens, and Jerry Haafs. In South Africa, Amy Biehl paid the price for hatred created by years of racist oppression. Let us hope that we can all learn a valuable lesson from this tragedy. I am sure that is what she would want."

American Christians sometimes reacted to Amy's death in an entirely different way—by infusing her story with religious meaning. Some who wrote the Biehls saw Amy as a martyr and quoted scripture in an effort to comfort the family. Besides writing directly to the Biehls, many Christians chose to honor Amy by donating to religious orders in her name. Naturally the donations sprang from people's admiration of Amy, but oftentimes donors were also motivated by the forgiving spirit Amy's parents displayed when discussing their daughter's death with the media. American Christians found equally powerful meanings in Amy's death and her parents' response, whose magnanimity seemed to be a shining example of Christian forgiveness.

Praise for the Biehls' magnanimity and understanding was not just based on religious sentiments. People all over the United States, Christians and non-Christians, were moved by the Biehls' response to Amy's death. Peter and Linda did not condemn their daughter's killers or South Africa, but talked instead about Amy's ideals, her love of South Africa, and how impressed they were with the South Africans she knew. Initially, some of Amy's close friends from Stanford, NDI, and her Fulbright year had more anger than the Biehls, but their bitterness melted in the wake of the Biehls' magnanimity. A colleague of Amy's at NDI, who worked with her on a voter education program in South Africa in 1991, was one such friend. In a letter to the Biehls a week after Amy's death, she wrote, "Your encouraging words have inspired me to look past the pain and see the positive of her work and what she accomplished." The Biehls were comforted by many such letters of support, and by the conviction that they were reacting in a way Amy would want. Their empathy and sincerity quickly became part of the story; eventually the Biehls would become *the* story.

Not everyone had kind words for the Biehls. A San Francisco resident wrote to express sympathy to the family but scolded Peter and Linda for allowing their daughter to go to South Africa in the first place. "A USA citizen has no business making bigger trouble in South Africa than they already have." Letters expressing such sentiments were relatively rare, but in an era when many Americans were concerned with rising crime, some observers were indeed worried that the extensive coverage of Amy's death was diverting attention from pressing issues closer to home. The Biehls also received some hate mail. These letters were generally from white racists who called Amy a "n——r lover" and said that she got what she deserved for trying to help blacks. The Biehls read even these letters before throwing them away.

While overtly hateful reactions were uncommon, there was discomfort with Amy's story in some circles. Some Americans worried that the intensive media coverage led to a distorted portrayal of black South Africans as perpetrators rather than victims. They criticized the imbalanced media coverage that tended to downplay or ignore black victims of South Africa's violence. Others feared, with some justification, that antiblack stereotypes would spread. A columnist for the *San Jose Mercury News* overheard two women talking about Amy over lunch at the Stanford Shopping Center a few days after she was killed. As they discussed the fact that she was killed by the very black people she wanted to help, one said, "You see? You can't help these people." Still others feared that coverage of Amy's death was diverting attention from crime in the United States, as did the San Francisco resident who wrote to the Biehls. In a letter to the *San Jose Mercury News,* one reader criticized the paper for reporting that in two more days, Amy would have been "safe at home." Given the high rate of crime in the United States, as evidenced by the frequency of murder and sexual assault, such wording seemed inappropriate to the reader.

The massive media coverage surrounding Amy's death clearly made Americans more cautious about traveling in South Africa. Of the estimated 10,000 Americans living in South Africa, few ordinarily ventured into the black townships apart from journalists and humanitarian workers. Bill Keller, then the *New York Times* correspondent in South Africa, noted that some of these Americans began to have second thoughts about returning to the townships in the wake of Amy's murder. Even before the incident, the State Department had issued a travel advisory warning American citizens about the dangers in parts of South Africa. Two weeks after Amy's murder, American consular officials in Johannesburg recommended that the State Department strengthen its travel advisory and warn Americans of the recent volatility of some of South Africa's black townships. State Department officials also warned other Fulbright recipients in South Africa of dangerous conditions in the country after the tragedy. Stanford's exchange program with the University of the Western Cape continued, although the committee administering the program began warning students of the potential dangers in South Africa.

A representative of the Harvard-based organization Worldteach-Score said his program had stopped sending volunteers into black townships ever since Chris Hani's death; Amy's death threatened the program's viability even more seriously.

American businesses were also cautious about investing in South Africa. Some commentators publicly speculated that Amy's murder might deter much-needed foreign investment in the country. Business people interviewed for a story published in the *Orange County Register* in September 1993 reflected some hesitation about expanding their operations in South Africa because of the crime and political violence. South Africa hosted a "Made in USA Expo" that month and invited representatives of approximately 200 American companies to sample the business climate in the country. Six exhibitors dropped out after Amy's murder, but her death was not the only reason US businesses were hesitant to invest in South Africa. There were many other incidents of violence plaguing the country, plus uncertainty over the ANC's commitment to free markets and private property. Some potential investors were waiting to see how South Africa's transition to democracy turned out. Many companies were still hesitant about reengaging in South Africa in September 1993, and while Amy's death wasn't the only deterrent, it certainly added to the anxiety.

AMY'S story had become a phenomenon—a media sensation that captured the public's imagination in South Africa, the United States, and elsewhere. One American working in South Africa said that the press coverage was unlike anything he had seen in 25 years of working overseas. The story spread all over the world and came to symbolize the tragedy that seemed to be engulfing South Africa. Escalating racial hatred threatened to derail the country's long-awaited transition to democracy and send the country into a downward spiral of worsening violence. South Africa's racial tension had become so intense that it claimed the life of a young, idealistic outsider who had worked tirelessly for racial justice. The tragedy sparked a national dialogue among both South Africans and Americans about their countries' racial past, present, and future. But the disproportionate attention bestowed on Amy troubled some observers who wondered why it took the death of one white woman to awaken people to the dangers of racism, when the deaths of black victims failed to elicit similar outrage.

As press attention mounted, Amy was turned into a human rights icon and an object of veneration. But the widespread admiration for Amy in the media risked obscuring the real person behind the myth. So did the comparisons with Martin Luther King Jr. and Steve Biko, which would have surely embarrassed Amy. While the Biehls wanted to publicize Amy's values, Linda knew Amy would have been uncomfortable being portrayed as a martyr. Some of Amy's colleagues at Stanford and NDI agreed. While admiring Amy's contributions, they knew that thousands of others had worked equally as hard at promoting democratic change in South Africa and the wider world. Amy became a symbol of democracy because of her murder, and in death she became larger than life.

The imbalance of media coverage was undeniable. The South African and American media covered Amy's life and death in unprecedented detail, but initially revealed only the names of the black suspects arrested for the murder. Newspapers provided almost no background on the suspects and frequently misidentified them, misspelled their names, and misstated their ages. In 1993, the most violent year of South Africa's transition, most victims of the country's political violence were black, but these victims usually died anonymously. Amy's death, by contrast, was covered on the front pages and in lengthy stories, columns, and editorials for weeks, in both South Africa and the United States. Although large numbers of South Africans were deeply moved by Amy's death and admired her, others were troubled that it took the death of a single white person to draw attention to the violence in South Africa's townships. Anna Wang came face to face with such frustration several months later. In April 1994, she walked into a women's bathroom in Johannesburg and found graffiti on a wall that read, "A hundred blacks die every day and no one cares. One f——ing white girl dies and the world goes nuts."

As unique as Amy's story was, what befell her wasn't completely unprecedented. A few other whites dedicated to the well-being of black people had been killed during political unrest before, although such incidents were highly unusual. One such incident occurred in a black township near East London in November 1952. On edge because of the recent Defiance Campaign, police baton-charged a black political gathering in Duncan Village and then opened fire, killing at least seven people in the township before the day ended. A white medical nun, Sister Mary Aidan Quinlan, had run a health clinic in Duncan Village for several years and was popular with local residents. Unaware of the residents' bloody confrontation with police earlier in the day, she drove into the township just as an angry, antiwhite political demonstration erupted. The crowd threw stones at Quinlan's car and then stoned and stabbed her to death, ignoring an African man who tried to stop the attack. Fifteen African youths were eventually charged with Quinlan's murder, five of whom were ultimately convicted.

In 1976, history repeated itself to some extent. During the first day of the Soweto uprising on June 16, a white sociologist was attacked and beaten to death by a group of black youths near his office in the township. Dr. Melville Edelstein worked at a Soweto youth center and set up workshops for disabled township residents, but he found himself at the wrong place at the wrong time. He was killed after black students had been shot by police and their enraged comrades vowed to continue the battle. "People stoned anything that symbolized the state or white power," one student leader recalled decades later. Edelstein was killed in the driveway of the West Rand Administration Board's office, the white authority that governed Soweto.

The publicity surrounding Amy's death far surpassed that of Quinlan and Edelstein. The tragic ironies of her death were even more jarring: she was a young, idealistic visitor killed by the very people she had come to help, two days before her return home, while doing a favor for her black friends. Her death came just as South Africa was making the transition from apartheid to democracy, when many South Africans believed they were on the verge of transcending the racial divisions of the past. That Amy was the first American to be killed in South Africa's racial violence gave the story added currency. But the outpouring of grief and publicity didn't just occur because Amy was a young white American killed by those she was there to help. It also pierced the public's consciousness because of her substantive and sustained contributions on behalf of women's rights and the democratic movement. Amy had become unusually integrated into the liberation movement, which was quite uncommon for a young white foreigner. Her death resonated so widely because of the quality and quantity of her connections in South Africa, which encompassed the ANC, universities, women's organizations, and her many social networks. Her friends and colleagues from these constituencies had been touched by her life and gave interviews, spoke at memorials, and participated in marches, dramatizing the importance of her story and her values. Amy had made a lasting impression on many people. Her sincerity, energy, and involvement had touched South Africans of all races, and her uniqueness and vitality deeply impressed her wide circle of contacts. Amy's impact had been not merely political but personal as well.

There was another factor to the "Amy phenomenon"—her physical attractiveness. Countless articles referred to Amy as blonde and blue-eyed, the very picture of a youthful all-American girl. South African and American newspapers published numerous photos of Amy, including those from her years as a diver at Stanford. In an interview with John Carlin of the *Independent,* Kader Asmal described Amy as "a very attractive blond." Many people who sent their condolences to the Biehls commented on how beautiful Amy was. An official from the Investor Responsibility Research Center had met Amy in Washington, D.C., and "was struck by Amy's intelligence, self-assurance and quiet commitment to fostering democracy in southern Africa." "On top of that, she had the glowing, healthy looks that I think of as quintessentially Californian," she told the Biehls. Such sentiments were common among friends and strangers alike. Some of Amy's friends speculated that Amy's physical attractiveness helped propel media interest. They were right.

The massive publicity surrounding Amy wasn't just driven by the ironic and tragic circumstances of her death, or by her youth, idealism, beauty, and substantive contributions. It was also driven by her parents' embrace of the media. Peter and Linda were eager to talk about Amy and her values, and as they did so, they displayed a lack of bitterness that attracted considerable attention. Their magnanimous attitude elicited strong emotions, widespread admiration, occasional puzzlement—and additional press coverage. Well after Amy's death, her story took on a life of its own.

BACK in South Africa, Amy's cremation was one of the ongoing events that kept her story in the news. Melanie had organized the details in consultation with the Biehls. On August 30, between 20 and 35 of Amy's colleagues from UWC attended a service in her honor at the Maitland Crematorium in Cape Town. In his remarks at the service, Dullah Omar said that the morality of the liberation movement must always be superior to that of "our oppressors" and the movement must not tolerate racism but embrace everyone. Bulelani Ngcuka was ashamed that Amy became a victim of the community she served. "It's painful to say, I'm sorry," he told the gathering. "I'm part of the community with whom Amy worked and for whom she gave her life in the end. She did not die by the deeds of the enemies, but by our own hands."

Some of Amy's belongings had already been packed and shipped to the United States by Anna Wang; Melanie and Solange gathered her remaining possessions and her ashes to take with them to the Biehl family. When the two arrived in Los Angeles on September 1, they were escorted off their plane to avoid the press. American Airlines invited them to their lounge at the airport, where they could meet the Biehls without the intrusion of the media. Peter and Linda were the first to embrace the two South Africans who had become their daughter's second family. Kim, Molly, Zach, and Scott were also there to welcome them. Solange remembered feeling a mixture of sadness, guilt, and anger, because young South Africans like her had killed Amy, who had been a big part of her life and an inspiration. "I was probably angrier than the Biehls," she added. After having their own spirits buoyed by the outpouring of support they received, the Biehls now consoled Melanie and Solange.

Amy's memorial service in Newport Beach was scheduled for Friday, September 3. In the days leading up to the service, the Biehls hardly left their house. They received a constant stream of visits from Amy's friends, relatives, colleagues, and mentors. The Biehls showed Amy's friends all of the letters they'd received about Amy, and they marveled at how people from all over the world had reached out to the family. Scott was still in a state of shock and was unsure how he would go on with the rest of his life. As he told *People* magazine, "I've had my life taken away from me—everything is gone now." But as devastated as he was at Amy's death, he didn't want to be consumed by anger. "If they can make you hate, then they win," he said.

Between 600 and 700 people crowded into St. Andrew's Presbyterian Church in Newport Beach on the afternoon of September third. In addition to family and friends from Stanford and NDI, a number of South Africans attended, including the chairman of the ANC's California chapter. Newspaper reporters and an ABC camera crew took their places as well. The pain of Amy's loss was overwhelming for those who had gathered in her honor. But as emotional and somber as the service was, there were both tears and laughter. Peter and Linda did not speak at the service, but other family members did, each in their unique way. Both Kim and Molly gave emotional tributes. "Amy was my little sister, and a world changer," Kim said. "Singing, swimming, dancing and drinking, graduating, moving, learning, leaving, changing lives, changing the world. Amy, I'm so impressed." Molly called Amy her friend and her hero. "What words could I say to my sister—who never let me get in a word edgewise? So it won't be with words, but with action. I will dance as I never danced and sing as I never before sang. And now I have your spirit in me, Amy, I won't let you down." Sixteen-year-old Zach got up to speak, wearing an armband in ANC colors given to him by the black South Africans at the service. With a calm and steady voice, he compared his sister to the flag bearers in the Civil War, who were strong, brave, and determined. "Unfortunately, our flag bearer has fallen," he told the gathering before him. "It is up to each and every one of us to pick up the flag and march on. It is our responsibility to make sure that Amy's dreams become reality. And when that beautiful day comes, we'll raise the flag of a changed country."

The most gut-wrenching tribute came from Scott. At times struggling to speak, he began, "I was going to ask Amy to marry me today. I don't regret not having asked her before. The time was never right before. In the last letter that she wrote to me, she told me [*pause*] . . . 'One year isn't so long in the big picture.' How could we have known? How could I have known?" He talked about how captivated he had been by Amy's eyes, her competitive spirit, her ability to make friends—"like other people make mistakes"—and her love for South Africa. She had the heart of a warrior, and her determination shone in everything she did, from her role on the Stanford diving team to her efforts to promote democracy in South Africa.

As the mourners filed outside into the warm California afternoon, American and South African reporters were waiting outside, eager to get some reactions for their stories. Peter answered a few questions as well. "We are so proud of our daughter," he said after the service. "She has set examples for all of us. We want her work to continue." After reporters scribbled their final notes, they filed stories on the memorial service that were widely published in the American and South African press. Some of the service was even broadcast on CNN-International, where friends of the Biehls saw it in Germany. As the service in Newport Beach proceeded, congregants at the First Presbyterian Church in Santa Fe held a simultaneous memorial, organized by friends of Amy and the Biehl family. The Biehls, who had attended the church during their years in New Mexico in the early 1980s, sent a message that was read out at the Santa Fe service. It said simply, "Let us rejoice in friendship and in the gift of a unique and special life, which stood for good."

After the memorial service in Newport Beach, the Biehls wanted to lighten the atmosphere after a week of grieving and took Melanie and Solange to Disneyland. Meanwhile, as publicity about Amy continued to spread, more letters to the family poured in. The flow of correspondence would continue for months after Amy's death. As before, reactions to Amy's death emanated from even the most remote parts of South Africa. A black resident of the small town of Nqanduli in the Transkei was moved to write the Biehls, even though he didn't know them or their daughter. "Each time I read from the newspapers about the death of your loving daughter Amy something seems to say—write to her parents. So, I do so now," he wrote. "I sympathize very deeply with you upon what befell you. Take it that God wants her in His Kingdom. She is one of the chosen, were it not so, she would still be with us. Wipe away those tears. All from your dear friend from now on." Ilze Olckers, director of the Women's Desk at Lawyers for Human Rights, wrote the Biehls on September 3, 1993, and captured the importance Amy's story had assumed in South Africa:

> Maybe it's because I knew and worked with her, maybe it's because I'm based here in Cape Town with links to Gugulethu, maybe it's just because we so desperately need a unifying force in this country, but I do think that it's not melodramatic or overstating the case to say that it has been one of

the most meaningful and potent political deaths in our country's history.
It has jolted the whole country like an electric shock to the collective psyche
and whilst the youth in the township is [sic] still threatening people's lives,
a new consciousness has sprung up whereby other township residents
actively protect and support [those] who venture in.

As this and other letters demonstrated, Amy had become part of a national conversation in South Africa.

American tributes to Amy continued to flow in as well. But along with the
tributes and public recognition of Amy, her family and friends continued to receive occasional hate mail. Amy may have become a human rights icon in the
eyes of many Americans and South Africans, but, to a lesser extent, she was also
becoming a lightning rod of criticism from the white right. Some conservative
newspaper columnists used Amy's death to criticize American liberalism. Such
criticisms, sometimes worded quite harshly, provoked heated debate and angry
responses from those who knew Amy. Often the critics had been longstanding
opponents of the ANC. They suggested that Amy was naïve and misguided for
having aligned herself with the organization and, by implication, for ever having
trusted blacks in the antiapartheid movement at all. They reserved some of their
harshest criticisms for her American professors for allegedly having nurtured a
false idealism in their dead student. Although such right-wing backlashes toward
Amy and those close to her were relatively rare, such sentiments would persist in
the years to come, countering the image of Amy as an unvarnished hero.

Two days after Amy's murder, R. W. Johnson obliquely criticized the young
American in his opinion piece in the *Times* of London. He suggested that Amy
was a stereotypically well-meaning American who had stumbled into South Africa
thinking that its problems were no different from those faced by the American
civil rights struggle. "Virtually without exception such Americans embrace the
African National Congress as the 'good guys,' often without understanding the
dense South African political context with its nuances and shades of grey," he
wrote. "Any denizen of Cape Town, black or white, would have told Miss Biehl,
26, she was taking her life in her hands by driving at dusk into a Cape township
or squatter camp; the fact that she supported the ANC would cut no ice. The civil
rights struggle was not like this." A white South African expatriate, R. W. Johnson
would have been considered a liberal in his home country, but he viewed the ANC
with considerable skepticism.

Simon Barber criticized Amy and her American professors in his syndicated
column, which appeared in several leading South African newspapers. Adopting

an anti-American, antileft bias, Barber took direct aim at Kennell Jackson and Larry Diamond, two of Amy's mentors. In his column published on August 31, 1993, he quoted Jackson and Diamond as saying that if Amy's attackers had paused to talk to her, they would have spared her life. Barber viewed such statements as evidence of American naïveté. "Both epitaphs betray the kind of attitude that gets nice Americans into trouble in nasty places," he wrote. "So trusting are they in their own goodness that they cannot understand why anyone would want to harm them." He went on to mock Amy and her professors for having such faith in their ability to promote democracy overseas. "Into this maelstrom stumbles Amy Biehl, convinced by her upbringing and professors that the world, however full of oppression and other beastliness, is at root a rational place and that all that is required to tame the beasts of its unrulier elements is a good, strong dose of democracy, which she, burning with love and justice, is determined to help deliver."

Diamond wasted little time in drafting a response. His letter was published in the *Cape Times* on September 12, 1993. "It is pathetic that Simon Barber must trample the memory of Amy Biehl to find another vehicle to vent his bitterness over the state of South Africa and the world," he wrote. Amy was not a naïve do-gooder, Diamond insisted, but a thoughtful researcher doing substantive work who "was determined to bridge racial divides rather than be confined by them." Furthermore, she was very aware of South Africa's violence and its underlying causes. She knew the risks in the country, but it was her misfortune to encounter a mob while driving friends home. In Diamond's view, Amy deserved admiration, not contempt. He accused Barber of being detached from the real issues facing South Africa.

The debate over Amy was just getting started. American Samuel Francis, a syndicated columnist for the conservative *Washington Times,* launched an even harsher critique of Amy and her supporters. Francis was well known for his right-wing views, and he used Amy's death as an excuse to launch an extraordinarily bitter, demagogic rant against American liberalism. His column, titled "The Tiger and the Murdered Lady," was published on September 3, 1993, the day of Amy's memorial service in Newport Beach. Amy's supporters in Washington were furious. Stephen Stedman, based at the Johns Hopkins School for Advanced International Studies, called Francis's column a "vile missive of hate" and accused him of using Amy's death "to further his own twisted political agenda." Stedman's letter was published in the *Washington Times* on September 14, 1993. He lambasted Francis for misrepresenting both Amy and South Africa. Far from being a "bubblehead," Amy was the "single most impressive candidate for doctoral study" that Stedman had ever encountered. She wasn't undertaking "experiments in do-good talk" but believed South Africa's problems would be solved by South Africans. She disdained Americans who came to South Africa briefly, advocated radical solutions, and then moved on. Furthermore, she sought to "ignore the de facto apartheid that still exists in South Africa and . . . connect to the majority of the country's people." Interacting and communicating with black South Africans wasn't naïve. Stedman accused Francis of suggesting that apartheid restrained racial hatreds and that blacks sought an all-out race war. On the contrary, Stedman argued, blacks in Gugulethu helped identify some of Amy's assailants. Polls suggested that "no more than 10 percent of blacks in South Africa support racial violence, a truly astonishing figure given the history of white subjugation of blacks." Stedman wrote that Francis's "diatribe amounts to blaming the victim." Furthermore, Francis's assertion that those who reach out across the color line were instigating a race war was "a mirror image of the racial hate-mongers of the left." In the end, asked Stedman, who was more simpleminded, Amy Biehl or Samuel Francis?

Two more of Amy's admirers rushed to her defense: Joseph Duffey, director of the US Information Agency, and Karen Clark, a senior program officer at NDI, who both wrote in response to Francis in the *Washington Times*. Soon the debate petered out for the time being. But such heated exchanges showed how some observers were using Amy's fate to debate wider issues, such as prospects for democracy in South Africa and America's role in a post–Cold War world. At its most vitriolic, the debate wasn't really a discussion about Amy but a series of angry diatribes against American liberalism.

Amid all the press coverage of Amy, the Biehls began making plans to travel to South Africa. They had been deeply moved by the many messages of support from Amy's friends and colleagues and wanted to see the land and people that Amy loved so much. Other families might have wanted to wash their hands of a country in which their daughter and sister had met such a brutal death, but not the Biehls. They hoped that in making such a trip, they could find ways of connecting to Amy's legacy and perhaps even contribute to it. The mayor of Cape Town, Clive Keegan, helped make the visit possible. Angered that the young American visitor was killed in his city, he wanted Cape Town to do something to show that it abhorred the murder. He contacted South African Airways and the Cape Sun Hotel to see if they would donate tickets and provide accommodation for the family. When both organizations agreed, Keegan informed the Biehls, who accepted his invitation to visit. "I invited the family of Amy Biehl to visit Cape Town so that the citizens of the Mother City could express to that family our love and affection, and to recommit ourselves to a peaceful future for all our people," he told a rally in Cape Town on September 13. Apart from humanitarian motivations, Keegan was undoubtedly mindful of the blow to Cape Town's international reputation after the murder. He wanted to repair the city's image and make sure that investment and tourism did not suffer long-lasting damage. As for the Biehls, they believed that because so many South Africans had paid tribute to Amy, they should embrace the opportunity to visit. It would be a way to strengthen the connection between the United States and South Africa and to ensure that Amy's legacy was positive and ongoing. "The people that she touched have touched us," Linda told a reporter. "How can you ignore that?"

By mid-September, members of the family had gone back to work and Zach returned to school, but handling the many issues related to Amy still seemed like a full-time job. Amy's computer arrived from Cape Town by air cargo, as did her files and belongings. Letters, faxes, and phone calls continued nonstop; reporters still besieged the family with interview requests; and the South African itinerary needed to be finalized. The family hoped that their upcoming trip would help them "deal with our many emotions." During an interview with *People* magazine shortly before the trip, Linda said, "We are confident that Amy's work will not die. We are going to see that it doesn't."

There was still one more memorial service scheduled before the Biehls' departure—at Stanford, where Amy's interest in Africa had blossomed. Approximately 300 people attended the service at the university's ornate Memorial Church on October 7, 1993. Kennell Jackson and Katie Bolich had organized the service with the help of the International Relations program. Peter, Linda, Kim, Zach, Scott, and cousin Karra Shewalter came to represent the family. For those who had been touched by the story for the past six weeks—including this author—the service was deeply moving. In his tribute, Steve Stedman talked about how Amy chose not to withdraw from the world and live comfortably but to face problems head on and try to find solutions, despite the risks. "Amy was not fearless, but she was brave," he told those assembled. "Bravery is acting in the face of fear and overcoming fear, and Amy was the bravest person I've ever known." With remarkable poise and composure, Amy's father Peter walked up to the front to speak. "How did a person so small accomplish these things?" he asked. "It leaves hope for all of us."

The Biehls left for South Africa the next day.

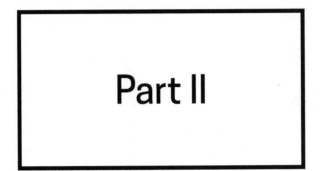

Part II

8

"Welcome to the Struggle, Family"

THE BIEHLS had never been to South Africa before. They knew the country only from a book or two they had read, some school reports, sporadic news coverage, and, of course, conversations and letters from Amy. They learned more from the flood of condolences after she died. Now they were preparing to go to the country that had claimed Amy, the country that so captured her imagination and changed the family forever.

Even before they had begun formally planning their trip to South Africa, the Biehls had been besieged by media outlets—print, radio, and television—that were competing to tell Amy's story and publicize the family's reaction. Amid all of the requests, one stood out to the Biehls—that from ABC News producer Lisa Soloway. Soloway hoped to tell Amy's story in a one-hour, prime-time documentary, which would be designed to educate the American public about both Amy's work and the larger struggle for democracy in South Africa. Soloway proposed that Amy's story be interwoven with that of an unknown black South African, so that the program could capture the struggles of ordinary people, whose stories usually went untold. Given Amy's concern about nameless black victims of apartheid, such an approach appealed to the Biehls. "Perhaps you might consider this program a 'tribute' to Amy's life and the thousands of South Africans who have dedicated their lives fighting for what they believed," Soloway wrote Peter and Linda. With these factors in mind, the Biehls agreed to cooperate with Soloway and allow an ABC News crew to travel with them to South Africa and film their visit. They also authorized a reporter from the

Orange County Register, Kim Christensen, to accompany them and document their trip by filing daily news stories.

By mid-September 1993, the Biehls were ready to make their plans public. All of the Biehls had spoken to the press and would appear in public events commemorating Amy, but Peter became the family's unofficial spokesman. In a handwritten letter faxed to the University of the Western Cape, he thanked Amy's friends for their moving letters of support and revealed the family's plans to visit South Africa so they could meet the people who had befriended and worked with Amy. He also affirmed the family's interest in assisting South Africa's transition to democracy. "It is fair to say that Amy's friends and colleagues are now ours," he wrote, "and we are proud to have this opportunity to come to know and to appreciate you more fully and to work, to the best of our abilities, in the democratic transition struggle with which you and Amy are so deeply involved."

While the Biehls looked forward to meeting Amy's friends and learning about the work she did in South Africa, they were worried that their visit might be used for political purposes. Peter expressed his concerns in a letter to the US consul general in Cape Town, David Halsted, in the weeks before their departure for South Africa. The family had decided to visit South Africa to thank Amy's friends, "to participate in a few low-profile events in Amy's honor," and to focus American attention on women's rights and the transition to democracy in South Africa. "We have no interest in 'symbolic' visits to Amy's death site or in other such potentially inflammatory appearances," Peter wrote. He hoped Halsted could advise the family about how "to avoid the pitfalls of perceived political sponsorship or other potential self-serving manipulations of our visit." The last thing the family wanted was for their trip to become "a political three-ring circus." Molly expressed similar concerns. She thought the family should voice support for democracy in South Africa but not align itself with any particular group or party. In voicing these concerns, Peter and Molly echoed a dilemma that Amy herself faced—how to support the transition for democracy in South Africa without being identified solely with one political party. Consul General Halsted sympathized with the Biehls' dilemma but believed that it might be difficult to prevent the family's visit from being politicized, given the highly charged environment at UWC and in Cape Town in general. One thing was certain, according to Halsted—the family's visit would generate intense media coverage.

Dullah Omar was particularly interested in coordinating the Biehls' visit. He wrote the Biehls with a flurry of ideas for their itinerary, including a tribute at UWC, a service at a Gugulethu church, and a visit to the site where Amy died. Although the Biehls had serious reservations about the proposed visit to Amy's death site, they welcomed his offer to help. They wanted UWC to coordinate their trip because of Amy's close association with that institution. Linda believed that the services and tributes in South Africa would be very meaningful—even necessary—for the family to heal. "We are trying to maintain some order and dignity throughout this chaos," she wrote Omar.

The Biehls didn't need to be reminded about South Africa's continued volatility. In fact, Peter feared for the family's safety during their upcoming trip. When Molly began to enquire about the family's security arrangements, a contact at NDI in Washington recommended that some form of American security be used. The contact advised against using security from the ANC and, in particular, from the South African Police, who were "resented by black South Africans." As it turned out, officials from the US State Department escorted the family during their stay in South Africa, although the ANC also provided an armed guard on at least one occasion.

All five of the Biehls made the trip—Peter (50), Linda (50), Kim (27), Molly (23), and Zach (16), a junior in high school. Amy's fiancé-to-be, Scott (28), joined the family on the marathon 27-hour voyage to South Africa. All six wanted to make a connection with the land and people Amy had come to embrace. En route to South Africa, Peter told a journalist that he didn't need to make the trip on a personal level, because it would probably just upset him. But he felt that South Africans needed the opportunity to express their sorrow to the family directly, to ease the burden of guilt so many felt. In order to cope with her grief, Linda had tried to stay focused on Amy's life, not the circumstances surrounding her death. She hoped the trip would help her understand South Africa better. "Amy is no longer just our child," she told Kim Christensen of the *Orange County Register*. "She's a child of a world and a culture we don't even know. I just want to go and meet these people and open up a dialogue. From a symbolic point of view, I hope we can be a bridge between the two cultures, just as Amy was."

The Biehls arrived in Cape Town on Saturday, October 9, 1993—spring in the southern hemisphere. The press coverage began as they descended the steps of their jumbo jet on that rainy night. At the airport to greet them were Cape Town mayor Clive Keegan, US ambassador Princeton Lyman, and Amy's housemate Melanie Jacobs. Once everyone was in the terminal, the visitors and their welcoming committee held a press conference. In his statement to the assembled reporters, Peter said that his family bore South Africa no ill will. "We are here in peace to reach out to you as you have reached out to us. We are looking forward in these few days to becoming one with you—and again with Amy." He spoke of Amy's unbreakable bond with South Africa, a bond that the entire Biehl family now shared. "Amy loved the people of South Africa and was a believer in your prospects as a nation," he said. "We have nothing but love and respect for you and prayers for your peaceful future."

If anything, racial tensions had been escalating, not diminishing, as the Biehls arrived in Cape Town. The night before the Biehls arrived, a young white American woman was stabbed by two black youths in the old District Six, a neighborhood near central Cape Town from which residents had been forcibly removed in the 1960s. The victim, a graduate student from Brown University, was seriously injured in the attempted robbery but survived. Another violent incident the day before the Biehls arrived made even more headlines. On Friday, October 8, the South African Defence Force (SADF) killed five black youths during a raid in the Transkei, increasing political tension in an already volatile environment. The government insisted that those killed were either members of APLA, the PAC's military wing, or collaborators with the organization. Family members of the victims said they were innocent children. United Nations observers in South Africa at the time condemned the raid.

Looking out of his hotel room window on Sunday morning, Zach saw Lion's Head on his left and Robben Island in the distance straight ahead. "It's hard to imagine a place so beautiful is also in such a horrifying state," he wrote in his journal. The first item on the family's itinerary that morning was a service at St. Gabriel's Catholic Church in Gugulethu. Some 700 township residents and guests packed the church to welcome the Biehls and to pay tribute to Amy, whose large color photo was prominently displayed up front. During the service, conducted in both English and Xhosa, some young black children sat with the Biehls, much to Peter and Linda's delight. They watched and listened as a choir sang in both languages, accompanied by congregants playing marimbas. Father Basil van Rensburg told those present, "Since the struggle began in our country, 16,000 people have given their lives. Amy was 16,001." Peter then spoke on behalf of the family and was followed by Dullah Omar. With the Biehls standing up front at the altar, Omar talked about the antiapartheid struggle and said that, although he abhorred Amy's death, the recent killing of five black students in the Transkei was "a hundred times worse. That was a cold-blooded killing." As much as the Biehls were grateful for Omar's mentorship of Amy, they were uncomfortable with the way in which he used Amy's death to make a political point. Still, they remained intent on listening to what he and other South Africans had to say.

As people filed out of the church, many members of the congregation offered their personal condolences to the Biehls. "I tell them we were broken-hearted about what happened to their daughter," one black parishioner said. "We cried tears about it, but now we are better." Peter and Linda felt uplifted by the service and kept telling reporters how embarrassed Amy would be by all the attention her death received. Both insisted that they felt no anger toward South Africa and hoped the family's presence would help South Africa heal and move forward toward democracy. "Our coming here was to say we have no anger or remorse with respect to Cape Town or South Africa," Peter told a South African reporter. "Our daughter was doing exactly what she wanted to do. We came, also, to bring attention to the fact that elections are very important—and that there are two million people still unregistered to vote. We thought that by coming here it would keep attention focused on the process." The Biehls' magnanimity, evident from the outset, was becoming a story in itself.

Now came the part of the visit the Biehls dreaded. The family had not wanted to go to the Caltex station where Amy was killed, but they discovered that Omar had put it on the family's agenda for the day. They had no personal interest in visiting the death site, saturated as it was with painful associations, nor did they want to be prevailed upon to make a symbolic visit for the benefit of a political party or the press. When Peter voiced his reservations, Omar insisted, so the family reluctantly complied. But Peter in particular was unhappy that a political agenda took precedence over the family's wishes on this occasion.

The scene near the Caltex station was crowded with onlookers, the press, and ANC officials as the Biehls arrived. Melanie Jacobs was there to support the family, as were Ambassador Lyman and his wife Helen. After the Biehls got out of the van and looked around, their unease grew until they felt suffocated by sadness and grief. They were also appalled by how open the site was and that Amy could have died in such a public place without anybody helping her. As township dwellers stared and camera crews and reporters swarmed around them, the Biehls' discomfort intensified. An onlooker gave Linda some flowers, which she took to the white fence where Amy was killed. "Rest in peace, Amy," she said, her voice quivering with emotion. Then she and Peter embraced. Each member of the family took turns placing flowers at the fence, some fighting back tears. For his part, Scott hadn't wanted to visit the site and hated being forced to do so. He stood well away from the fence at first, but then approached it after all of the others. Overwhelmed by emotion, he collapsed to his knees and placed some flowers next to the fence before leaning forward and burying his head in his hands. Photographers scurried toward him to capture the moment on film. Afterward, he and the Biehls were quiet as they traveled back to the city center, emotionally drained and numb from the experience.

The Biehls' visit to the Caltex station—as well as their entire trip—was widely covered by the South African media, keeping Amy in the headlines more than six weeks after she had been killed. The day after the Biehls placed flowers at Amy's death site in Gugulethu, the *Cape Times* published a front-page photo of Scott kneeling at the fence where she was stabbed and included an accompanying story on page two. The news coverage tended to be sympathetic, portraying the Biehls as magnanimous Americans who wanted to honor their lost loved one by learning more about South Africa and encouraging the country's transition to democracy. In a prominent editorial titled "Atoning for Amy," the *Cape Times* hoped that the Biehls' visit would contribute to healing and reconciliation in South Africa. The paper echoed Peter's recognition that for South Africa to progress toward a brighter future, its citizens needed to get involved in the democratic process and confront the country's problems to a greater extent than ever before. That, the editors wrote, would be the ideal tribute to Amy Biehl.

On Monday the 11th, the Biehls were scheduled to visit a park in Wynberg where some of her South African friends had planted a yellowwood tree in her honor, but the family canceled it. They wanted a break from the emotional events of Sunday, so Melanie Jacobs took them on a four-hour sightseeing tour around the Cape Peninsula while Peter stayed behind and worked at the hotel. The beauty of the Cape Peninsula took their breath away. As the day drew to a close, the sadness and pain the Biehls felt the day before had eased considerably.

The next item on the Biehls' agenda was attending a ceremony in their honor at the University of the Western Cape. On Tuesday, October 12, hundreds of black and mixed-race students packed into a lecture hall early in anticipation of the family's arrival. As they waited, they swayed, clapped, and sang jubilant freedom songs, and when the Biehls entered the auditorium, the crowd gave them a standing ovation. The family came up to the front, deeply moved by the outpouring of support. Each of the Biehls was introduced to additional rounds of applause and cheers. As Zach later recalled, the family wasn't prepared for the extent of the response—they hadn't yet grasped the depth of Amy's impact. Alongside the Biehls stood Maletsatsi Maceba, Evaron Orange, and Sindiswa Bevu, the three South Africans who were in the car when Amy was attacked. UWC rector Jakes Gerwel, Professor Kader Asmal, and Rev. Allan Boesak joined the family up front.

"UWC still hurts after the loss of a person dedicated to peace and democracy in South Africa," Gerwel told the crowd. He hoped that Amy's family would find solace by learning about the valuable work she did in the country. Some UWC students read poems in Amy's honor. The most stirring words came from Boesak, still chairperson of the ANC in the Western Cape. "What you see here today is an outreach to tell you that when Amy came to South Africa and committed herself to the struggle of which we are a part, she became part of our family," he told the

Biehls. "Today you are here and we are telling you that you are part of this family. Welcome to the struggle, family." He then told the crowd, "Take a message to Amy as you pray and tell her we shall have our freedom."

Speaking for the family, Peter told the audience that his daughter had been in good company in South Africa. "Amy was no more and no less than one of you," he said. "We love you. We pray for you and wish you only your full potential that you're entitled to as intelligent and wonderful people." Once again, Peter managed to say just the right thing, in just the right tone, with a sincerity and eloquence that listeners found irresistible. Just as UWC had bonded with Amy, they were now bonding with her family. Scott also inspired the listeners, telling them that the young people of South Africa could "really shape [the country] into something marvelous. And there are people in America who really care about the situation in South Africa and we would help in any way we can." At the end of the ceremony, the crowd sang "Nkosi Sikelel' iAfrika," the anthem of the liberation movement. As the family left the hall, they were surrounded by well-wishers who wanted to shake their hand, hug them, and offer words of encouragement. Although the crowd was overwhelmingly supportive, there was at least one dissonant voice. As the family was leaving, a man yelled "One settler, one bullet!" but other students told him to be quiet. Zach kept his cool. "I was not going to let one man affect my opinion toward such amazing and beautiful people," he told a reporter afterward.

Molly later admitted to being somewhat uncomfortable during the event. "All these [singers and poets] who were so intense about their feelings toward my sister. I thought, 'How can they feel so intensely about my sister?' She's my sister and I hated to share her with so many people. As much as she was a warrior and a soldier and all that, she was just my sister, and my dancing partner, and my pal," she said. Scott found the ceremony at UWC even more difficult. At one point, he left his seat by the family as students read poems dedicated to Amy. Molly's and Scott's reactions foreshadowed a developing problem: the more Amy was memorialized, the more she became mythologized, thus obscuring the real person behind the myth.

Scrambling for more footage, the ABC news crew asked to film Kim, Molly, and Zach walking through a squatter camp later that afternoon. For about an hour, the Biehl siblings were filmed walking through the KTC squatter camp in the bright sunshine, mostly interacting with children from a day-care center. All three were shocked by the extent of the poverty they encountered, particularly the small tin shacks and latrines that dotted the sandy landscape. Despite the bleak setting, the residents gave the Biehls a warm welcome. Zach later wrote about being followed by children as he walked through the settlement. Two young, preschool-age boys latched onto him and held his hand, letting go only when he carried them. "I felt terrible as we jumped in our cars and left," he wrote in his journal afterward. "These people can't leave. I gave one boy my hat and he smiled so warmly." The poverty of KTC was further magnified once the Biehl siblings returned to the Cape Sun, the family's luxury hotel in central Cape Town. Staying at such a sumptuous property amid such widespread deprivation troubled all of them. "It's just ironic that we're here, staying at the Cape Sun Hotel and being treated like royalty," Molly told a reporter. "It bothers me a great deal. The whole time you just think, 'What would Amy be doing? What would she be thinking about this whole thing?' I just hope it would not upset her." But the visit to the squatter camp had a long-term value. Although it was a staged photo op, it gave the Biehls a greater appreciation of the poverty and deprivation facing blacks in Cape Town. Linda realized that if nothing was done to help those young children in the townships and squatter camps, they could grow up to be angry and bitter, just like the people who had killed Amy.

Public reaction to Amy's death continued, largely generated by press coverage of the Biehls' visit. Varying reactions to the family reflected continued divisions in the country at large. A number of South Africans wrote moving letters to the family to express their condolences and profound regret at the Biehls' loss. But evidence of youth bitterness still surfaced, even after the peace movement had been reenergized in the weeks immediately following Amy's death. Some militants in PASO were still unrepentant about what happened to Amy. During the Biehls' visit, the organization's leaders vowed to win freedom by continuing the armed struggle. PASO president Tsietsi Telite spoke at a rally in Khayelitsha on October 13 in honor of the Transkei youths killed by the SADF. In front of an estimated 800 PASO members, Telite urged the PAC to "stop appearing on television to answer for the things our organization is doing." Amid loud cheers, he continued, "The whole world was crying recently when one American was killed in Gugulethu, but there is a deafening silence now because those killed by the Boers are African people. The PAC leadership will never again go in front of the press to account for things we are doing to the enemy in the townships. The situation among the students is that the enemy should be wiped away from the face of the earth." After the rally, youths stoned several cars in Khayelitsha.

On their last full day in Cape Town, the Biehls met with staffers at the US Information Service office in the city. Their meeting coincided with the announcement that the 1993 Nobel Peace Prize would be awarded to Nelson Mandela and F. W. de Klerk. Asked by the press for comment, the Biehls praised the choice and said that the award would draw attention to the problems of South Africa, which were so important to the family. Later that day, the Biehls opened a conference on juvenile justice dedicated to Amy's memory and to all victims of violence across South Africa, sponsored by UWC's Community Law Centre. More and more, the Biehls began to ponder how they could work on behalf of South Africa's children to honor Amy's memory in tangible ways.

The Biehls left Cape Town on Saturday, October 16, to see more of South Africa. Their next destination was Pietermaritzburg, the capital of KwaZulu-Natal, where they were invited to attend the opening of a new community center and preschool named after Amy in the Happy Valley township. As the Biehls drove into the township, hundreds of children waving peace flags lined the streets to welcome them. The township's leaders said they were naming the new facility after Amy "to express our solidarity with the causes she stood for: non-racialism, non-sexism, and democracy." At the dedication ceremony, Peter told the audience, "You do Amy a great honor by dedicating this marvelous facility to her memory. Nothing could have meant more to Amy, to us, or to her memory. . . . We are committed here forever and want to do what we can for South Africa." Residents at the event greeted the Biehls warmly and the Biehls reciprocated; a large photo of Molly kissing a young black child from the township appeared in the *Sunday Star* and the *Citizen* newspaper the next day.

After their brief stay in Pietermaritzburg, the Biehls headed to Johannesburg for the final leg of their South African trip. On Sunday, October 17, they first visited Katlehong, a black township southeast of Johannesburg that had been racked by violence during the transition to democracy in the early 1990s. The Biehls were there "to show their solidarity with other families who [had] lost parents or children" in the country's political violence. Producers from ABC arranged for the family to meet Tokyo Sexwale, a high-ranking ANC leader, while they were in the township. Popular and charismatic, Sexwale had been among the first to condemn Amy's murder and reaffirm the need for nonracialism in the days after her death. He introduced the Biehls to Katlehong residents and told the family, "You're part of the ANC now. You've given everything to us."

Heading east, the Biehls then went to see the family of Chris Hani, the popular ANC leader whose assassination by white extremists earlier that year had threatened to derail the transition to democracy. Hani had been one of Amy's heroes. The Biehls traveled to Boksburg's Dawn Park neighborhood to meet with Hani's widow Limpho and 14-year-old daughter Kwezi. With cameras rolling, the Biehls and the Hanis greeted each other and talked about the loss of their loved ones. They agreed on the need to transcend their grief and stress racial healing instead. Despite the pain of her loss, Hani's widow told the Biehls that she had not become embittered, because bitterness would only delay the democracy for which her husband and her fellow South Africans had fought. Her words meant a great deal to the Biehls, because as Molly put it, "they've experienced the violence." As young Kwezi reflected on the loss of her father, Linda offered words of comfort, noting how Amy had felt such sadness that day that she called home. Despite the fact that the families' encounter was filmed by a camera crew, their bond seemed genuine. They had both lost loved ones in racially motivated attacks that year and drew strength from each other's commitment to a democratic South Africa. As the families' meeting drew to a close, Linda embraced Limpho, a powerful image of racial healing and solidarity that was captured in both American and South African newspapers the next day. Peter thought that the meeting between his wife and Limpho Hani was the most important part of the trip for Linda. As Linda said afterward, "It's just like meeting someone I've always known." Her meeting with Mrs. Hani had given her "a lot of inner peace," as had the entire trip. Encounters with black South Africans like the Hanis brought home to Linda—and all of the Biehls—just how many South Africans had lost family members during the struggle against apartheid. The Biehls' loss, linked to many others, now seemed all too common.

The Biehls left South Africa that evening and headed back to the United States. They had found their trip highly worthwhile. In Peter's view, one of the goals of the trip had been to help South Africans heal, and in that respect he believed it had succeeded. Linda was overwhelmed that her daughter had affected so many people and that those people wanted to celebrate Amy's life. For much of the trip, she was "in awe" of her daughter. She derived satisfaction from learning how Amy had contributed to positive change in South Africa. She also enjoyed the personal encounters with South Africans, although the country's continued violence troubled her. The trip left a deep impression on Kim, Molly, and Zach. They felt a bond with the many people who had been close to Amy, and they hoped that the publicity surrounding the family's trip would raise South Africa's profile in the United States and make Americans more aware of the challenges the country faced.

The pain of Amy's death still overwhelmed Scott, and the trip only made it worse. It was an ordeal that constantly reminded him of his loss, which was still fresh after six weeks. When asked by a reporter to share his impressions of the trip, Scott confessed, "I have pretty much hated every minute of it." He had grown tired of all the media attention and the public memorials to Amy, which he found very impersonal. He had agreed to go on the trip to support the Biehl family but had wanted to leave almost immediately after they arrived. Recalling the trip years later, Scott confirmed these feelings. "Everybody was celebrating her in a way I felt disconnected to," he said. At one point he became so frustrated that he told Peter that "I had to get on a plane" and leave the country. "The Biehls were getting energized by it all, but I felt angry."

Praise awaited the Biehls back home. In an editorial timed to coincide with the family's trip, the *Los Angeles Times* described Amy and the Biehls as representing the best American values. The paper's editors praised the Biehls for not focusing on Amy's death, but for promoting her cause—a brighter future for South Africans of all races. The editorial closed by saying that South Africa's future "depends mightily on the efforts of those like the Biehls. Their contribution is made without guns or angry words, but it is powerful. It lies in the American notion that a better day for all is indeed possible."

The Biehls were thinking carefully about their future involvement with South Africa. Peter knew that his family was interested in supporting scholarship funds in Amy's name, but he also believed that they wanted to return to a normal routine. "I don't think we are going to go around and build shrines to Amy Biehl," he told Kim Christensen of the *Orange County Register*. "We will get along with our lives. But she will always be with us." But at the event in Pietermaritzburg, he had hinted at the family's ongoing commitment to South Africa. As a result of their trip, the Biehls developed strong bonds with South Africa and became determined to work on behalf of the country in honor of Amy. Exactly how they would do so was not yet clear.

The Biehls were not just pondering their own future, but the future of Amy's killers. At the time of their visit to South Africa, seven people had been arrested in connection with Amy's murder. Although Amy's absence left a permanent void in his family, Peter sounded philosophical. "I have never felt any anger about this," Peter told a reporter. "I just feel very sad for those people. Those who killed Amy will carry that image with them for as long as they live." During his remarks at the juvenile justice conference in Cape Town, Peter had said that those accused in his daughter's death should have educational opportunities rather than face imprisonment. Scott Meinert expressed similar sentiments. He believed that the killers should not be given the death penalty, which neither he nor Amy favored, but an education. "They killed Amy, the single most important thing in my life, and I am very angry for that," he said. But as angry as he was, he believed that apartheid was ultimately responsible for Amy's death, because that racist policy caused the youths to lash out. "I'm infuriated and will always probably be until it [apartheid] is completely stamped out." It was now time for the accused to have their day in court.

9

Time of Trials

THE TRIALS of Amy's killers provided another sustained wave of publicity that kept the Biehls' name in the headlines, both in South Africa and the United States. The first trial—in which several suspects faced charges—was shrouded in controversy and uncertainty. Few knew whom to believe or what the outcome would be. In the eyes of one perceptive journalist, the central questions of the trial revolved around oppression and accountability. To what extent was oppression a valid excuse for those who killed Amy Biehl? To what extent was oppression an excuse for all crimes under apartheid? There would be no easy answers.

The seven initial suspects in the murder ranged in age from 15 to 22: Mankenke Lungilisa, Mongezi Manqina, Mzukisi Mxoli, Mlungisi Ngxaza, Mzikhona "Easy" Nofemela, Thembisile Nojozi, and Vusumzi Ntamo. Most had been identified through tip-offs to police after Amy's death and were arrested within days of the murder. Usually those accused of crimes, even murder, could be released on bail, but authorities invoked a special law for unrest-related offenses to keep the young men in jail, with the exception of the 15-year-old. He was released into the custody of his family while awaiting trial. A pretrial incident foreshadowed the bumpy road ahead. On Monday, September 13, 1993, Manqina and Nofemela appeared at the magistrate's court in Mitchell's Plain for an initial hearing. At their court appearance, approximately 30 supporters of the two young men demonstrated outside the court building after they were denied permission to attend the hearing. Angered by the white authorities in charge, they chanted "Settler, settler, war, war, one SAP [South African Policeman], one bullet!" and "We want war!"

as reporters captured the raucous scene. The supporters of the defendants would continue to make their presence known in the months to come.

The trial was held at the Cape Provincial Division of the Supreme Court in central Cape Town. The indictment charged the seven young men with being part of a group of approximately 40 people who stoned Biehl's car, assaulted her three passengers, killed Amy, and stole a wristwatch, a camera, and a backpack. At a hearing in early October 1993, approximately 50 protestors entered the court building and shouted "Every settler deserves a bullet!" and "Kill a cop a day!" Later they danced in the street chanting "War! War! War!" The crowd's actions indicated just how much the trial would reflect South Africa's political and racial divisions in the dying days of apartheid. The judge was an English-speaking white South African, the prosecutors were Afrikaners, and the defense lawyers were black South Africans. According to one report, Judge Gerald Friedman was "the Cape's most senior jurist." South Africa's legal system did not include jury trials, and so the fate of the defendants was in Friedman's hands. Nollie Niehaus, deputy attorney general for the Cape, would lead the prosecution with the assistance of Leon Nortier. They faced a steep challenge from the start—their evidence was confined to confessions and witness testimony. Inexplicably, police investigators had not gathered any physical evidence from the crime scene: no clothing, finger-prints, weapons, or other proof. Despite the dearth of evidence, the prosecutors decided to seek the death penalty.

Recruiting defense lawyers proved difficult. Because of the intense stigma at-tached to the crime, the state couldn't find a lawyer from Cape Town willing to defend the young men. The Defence Aid Fund for Southern Africa traditionally paid for defense teams in political trials, but it refused to do so in the Biehl case because, in its words, the crime "did nothing to advance the cause of peace and democracy." The PAC then agreed to provide the legal defense. Although the or-ganization had not accepted full responsibility for the crime, youths affiliated with the Pan Africanist Students' Organization had perpetrated the attack. The PAC re-cruited a Durban-based lawyer to defend the suspects. Aptly named, Justice Poswa was an experienced lawyer who had defended black political activists during the height of apartheid. He had represented both PAC and ANC members in political trials and had gained a high profile in the process. By Poswa's own admission, not everyone was happy that he had taken on the Biehl assignment. Archbishop Tutu was particularly troubled. Horrified by Biehl's murder, Tutu wondered how Poswa could defend the indefensible. Poswa's partner in the defense effort was Nona Goso. During the early days of the trial, she described the defendants as follows: "In every sense, they are children . . . in fact, lovely children, like any other. Under normal circumstances, they would have had a wonderful, normal life. But they are children of apartheid. Most come from broken homes and from deprived families where no one is working. Education is out of the question. . . . They have experienced everything, been exposed to everything." In Goso's view, the suspects' environment and the oppression they suffered under apartheid made them do what they did.

The court proceedings were formal and reflective of South Africa's Roman-Dutch legal tradition. Like Friedman, most judges in South Africa were white at the time, delegitimizing the court system in the eyes of many black South Africans. Usually only one judge presided at South African trials, but in cases where the death penalty could be imposed, a panel of "assessors" attended to certify that the proceedings were conducted fairly in their eyes. These jurists were trained lawyers. Two such assessors—one black and one white—were assigned to assist Judge Friedman during the Biehl trial. The pace of court proceedings was slow, because spoken Afrikaans, English, and Xhosa had to be translated. Niehaus spoke in English and Afrikaans, Poswa in English and Xhosa, the police in Afrikaans, while the accused listened in Xhosa.

The planned opening of the trial proved to be a false start. On November 8, 1993, the 15-year-old accused in Biehl's death, Thembisile Nojozi, failed to appear after having been released into the custody of his family. Learning that he had fled to avoid prosecution, officials issued a warrant for his arrest and postponed the opening of the trial for two weeks. It was not a good sign.

When the trial began on November 22, police cordoned off the court building with razor wire in order to discourage potential demonstrators from invading the premises. Just minutes after the trial began, prosecuting attorney Niehaus announced that he was dropping charges against three of the accused because a witness, Charles Benjamin, had suddenly decided not to testify. It was the second major setback for the prosecution in as many weeks. Benjamin, an ANC member, withdrew from the case because he feared for his physical safety. The ANC had apparently urged him to testify, but it hadn't offered to protect him from possible PAC retaliation. Without a well-established witness protection program in South Africa, Benjamin's fears were not unreasonable. The three against whom charges were dropped—Mankenke Lungilisa, Mzukisi Mxoli, and Mlungisi Ngxaza—immediately walked free. A crowd of cheering supporters greeted the young men outside, hoisted them on their shoulders, and sang and danced in triumph. Security personnel stood watch as cameras recorded the crowd chanting "One settler, one bullet!" and "Every settler deserves a bullet!" The young demonstrators, many of whom were under 18 and wearing their school uniforms, clearly enjoyed the press attention and the festive atmosphere. Their impromptu street demonstration showed that in round one at least, they had triumphed over the system. Like the trial as a whole, their jubilant celebration made news in South Africa and around the world.

A woman from Soweto, 900 miles away, was so troubled by the conduct of the young people outside the court that she wrote to the *Argus*, one of Cape Town's leading newspapers: "Never have I wept more for our beloved country than when I saw on TV how our children rejoiced when the three accused in the Biehl case were released. May I ask, where were the parents of those children? Have we reprimanded our children for their atrocious behavior? Do we realize that we will one day reap the whirlwind of this kind of behavior? Women of South Africa, let us unite to bring this country to its senses." Not only was the trial being watched carefully beyond Cape Town, but the generational divide in black South African politics was as strong as ever. South Africans of all races would become increasingly troubled by the youths' conduct during the trial. And although few people could have predicted it at the time, a trial that was initially expected to last six weeks would drag on for the next 11 months.

Despite the fact that many people had witnessed the attack in Gugulethu, Niehaus was having trouble lining up witnesses. People feared for their own safety and that of their families if they testified. On November 26, the trial adjourned early because, according to the prosecution, another witness had been intimidated and refused to testify. Niehaus requested more time to try to persuade the potential witness to come forward. As Niehaus and others knew, there were historical reasons why witnesses hesitated to testify. During the apartheid era—which had not fully ended—township residents who assisted police by identifying activists were known as *"impimpi"* (informers) and often faced harsh retaliation from young township militants. Being labeled an informer could be deadly. "Anyone who talks to the police is seen as a collaborator," said David Welsh, a University of Cape Town political scientist. Suspected collaborators had often been attacked and even killed by members of their community during the antiapartheid struggles of the past decade.

Even before Niehaus requested more time to locate witnesses, another issue arose that delayed the trial. Defense lawyer Poswa argued that one of the assessors, Renata Williams, could not be regarded as impartial because of her membership in the ANC. After Poswa voiced his concerns, Ms. Williams requested that she be recused from the case. Judge Friedman believed that her impartiality was beyond question, but he granted her request nevertheless and appointed a replacement. The defense team's strategy of questioning the inner workings of the legal process would continue in the days ahead.

The three young men in court still facing charges—Manqina (21), Nofemela (22), and Ntamo (22)—pleaded not guilty to murder, public violence, and robbery. All three were members of PASO, a group that advocated attacks on whites and opposed the negotiated political settlement. As each morning's proceedings began, the three would greet their supporters in the gallery by grinning and saluting. Manqina reportedly smirked during the early days of the trial and "occasionally sucked his thumb," according to one observer. Ntamo often fell asleep, prompting Nofemela to nudge him and wake him up.

One of the first to testify was police constable Leon Rhodes. He was the driver of the first police vehicle on the scene and drove Amy and her friends to the Gugulethu police station. He said it took an ambulance 30 minutes to arrive, too late to help Amy. A forensic pathologist later made it clear that even had an ambulance arrived sooner, it would have been too late, given the seriousness of Amy's injuries. Amy's three passengers also testified during the first week of the trial. Evaron Orange described the moments when the car was stoned and when he and his fellow passengers attempted to flee, but he couldn't identify the specific individuals who attacked Amy. Sindiswa Bevu, who had sat behind Amy, gave a fuller account. She and Maletsatsi Maceba had tried to persuade the crowd that Amy wasn't a settler but an American and a comrade. Sindiswa identified Nofemela as having participated in the attack on Amy. After she left the witness stand, a supporter of the accused threatened her outside, saying she would "end up the same as Amy." Sindiswa returned to complete her testimony the next day, telling Judge Friedman that "I feel intimidated but I will carry on." When she said that she was no longer sure if Nofemela was involved in the attack, "the crowd in the public gallery began to hiss until the judge said he would clear the court" if such behavior continued. Upon leaving the court after her second day of testimony, she told a journalist, "We were shocked by what happened in court, because we thought all people would condemn this inhuman act. . . . They killed Amy because she was white. That's why it is high time political organizations must educate people. They judge an enemy only by the color of the skin. . . . But I think this is also an excuse—they were just thugs."

Maletsatsi also testified, despite the potential risks. "I'm not testifying because they [the accused] are PAC, but because what happened is morally unacceptable," she told a reporter. "I would have testified even if it was ANC people who did it." In excruciating detail, she described how Amy was covered in blood and groaned after the attack, but couldn't speak. As she described how Amy moaned, laughter erupted in the public gallery. Young supporters of the accused chuckled and even cheered. "Judge Friedman, revolted by their outburst, cleared the courtroom," an observer wrote.

The laughter in the gallery was widely publicized, often with emotionally laden language. "Jeers at Amy Agony," screamed one local headline the next day. A story in the *Times* of London read, "The clerk to the court, a woman, sobbed quietly as Maceba spoke. Biehl's friends, black and white, held their heads in their hands. But the public gallery, packed with supporters of the three youths accused of Biehl's murder, erupted with glee. Depravity had penetrated the court." The young people in the gallery didn't just laugh at awkward moments; when Judge Friedman would enter the court, the youthful PAC supporters refused to stand (as was customary), showing their scorn for the white man's court, which they deemed illegitimate. Before and after daily proceedings, some of the youths would harass white visitors, chant, toyi-toyi, and make shooting motions at the courthouse. Some in the gallery even shouted "Kill the settler!" at white spectators.

Defense lawyer Goso disapproved of such behavior but said that the township youth had become so desensitized to violence that human life had lost its meaning for many of them. According to a PAC official, shouting antiwhite slogans inside and outside the court was the youths' way of supporting the struggle and showing solidarity with the victims of the system. The youths saw the accused as victims, much like themselves. "Most [of the black youths attending the trial] are here to support their peers being prosecuted for their race and politics, by an unjust system that ignores the oppressing circumstances of their lives," one journalist observed.

White South Africans weren't the only ones troubled by the lack of decorum at the trial. Some leaders in the ANC and the PAC wondered whether youths had become so alienated that they would be difficult to control. "Were these young militants children at all, they worried, or were they 'monsters' beyond repair?" wrote Nancy Scheper-Hughes, who observed parts of the trial while conducting anthropological fieldwork. Worried that the youths' conduct was damaging the reputation of his organization, the PAC's regional secretary in the Cape decided to attend the trial on November 29, 1993. Bathembu Lugulwana hoped his presence would restrain the unruly PASO members in the gallery who had been disrupting the trial.

The rebellious conduct at the trial was directly linked to the situation in Cape Town's black townships, where antiwhite sentiment still festered in some circles. In late 1993, *New York Times* correspondent Bill Keller noted that antiwhite rage lingered among militant black youths in Gugulethu, more than three months after the attack on Amy Biehl. He found that PASO youths were unrepentant about Biehl's murder and didn't believe a white court had a right to judge those accused of her death. The youths whom Keller interviewed were so embittered by their lack of prospects that they viewed all whites with hostility.

Distinguishing between oppressive and nonoppressive whites was a distinction they didn't have the luxury to draw. They viewed whites as the cause of their suffering, standing in the way of their advancement, occupying their land. At one point Keller spoke with Easy Nofemela's father, whom he described as deferential to whites, unlike the younger generation in the township. "Our parents, they are cowards for the Boer," Easy's girlfriend told Keller. "The youth are not scared, and they have the power."

Meanwhile, in court, Judge Friedman was determined to restore decorum. Annoyed that some youths in the gallery had been violating court etiquette, he threatened to clear the court if they refused to rise when the court assembled each day. When proceedings began on November 30, 1993, the youths rose when Friedman entered the courtroom. But outside the court, young supporters of the accused kept up their demonstrations, toyi-toyiing and chanting slogans. Some had been denied entry into the court by security personnel. In order to curb protests and demonstrations, police began allowing people into the gallery only if they were over 18. They also put up a barbed wire barricade in front of the court entrance, which kept demonstrators at a distance. As members of the Internal Stability Unit patrolled outside, police began searching those who entered the courtroom.

Thousands of miles away in Newport Beach, the Biehls were growing concerned about the trial's troubled start. They were understandably upset when they heard that people in the gallery had laughed when Amy's last moments were described. But they refused to succumb to anger, at least in public. Neither were they surprised when they learned that witnesses had refused to testify. "I understand it," Linda said. "I think we could perceive that fear is just under the surface of everything over there. I would have been shocked if this had not happened." Linda told reporters that rather than focusing on the trial, the family preferred to ponder what they could do to help South Africa's multiracial society develop. But the trial would claim much of their attention nevertheless, partly because the press was constantly asking them to comment.

The Biehls were particularly concerned about the safety of Maletsatsi and Sindiswa. Both young women had been threatened after testifying at the trial. Peter wondered whether arrangements could be made to spirit the two out of South Africa to ensure their safety. He expressed his concerns to the US Consulate in Cape Town, to Dullah Omar, and to the American ambassador in South Africa, Princeton Lyman. State Department officials worked with the University of the Western Cape to provide Maletsatsi with safe housing and transportation until well after the trial ended and probably did the same for Sindiswa, although her arrangements were not documented.

Suddenly, on November 29, 1993, the focus of the trial shifted. Defense attorney Poswa claimed that the statements his clients gave to police after their arrest were invalid because the police had allegedly assaulted them and forced them to confess. In his statement, Manqina had admitted to being in the area when Amy was killed but denied participating in the attack. Nofemela had admitted throwing stones at Amy's car but not attacking her. Most damaging of all was Ntamo's statement, in which he admitted throwing bricks at Amy and seeing Manqina stabbing her. According to Ntamo, Manqina later boasted that "he was proud to have killed a white woman." Before Judge Friedman could determine the guilt or innocence of the accused, he needed to determine whether their statements were admissible or whether the "police had used force to extract confessions." So began what Friedman called a "trial within the trial," an ordeal that would last nine months.

Casting doubt on police methods was a shrewd move by Poswa. The policeman who obtained Manqina's statement was being investigated at the time for assaulting a suspect in the St. James Church attack. The officer denied the allegations of assault, both in the St. James and the Biehl cases. Not surprisingly, all of the policemen who testified denied assaulting any of the accused. They also denied that the suspects were harassed or intimidated while giving their statements. But Poswa's claim that the police forced the confessions wasn't far-fetched. Police assaults were all too common during the apartheid era, when they had free rein with detainees, battering, torturing, and forcing "confessions" from prisoners at will. The defense team's wider strategy was clear. They sought to cast doubt on a judicial system in which forced confessions and police mistreatment had been commonplace under apartheid. In this way, they would draw attention away from the alleged actions of the accused and instead shift focus to the police. If the police were on trial, that could create reasonable doubt in the mind of the judge as to whether the suspects' rights had been violated and whether their statements were thus tarnished. In short, Poswa planned to use apartheid as his clients' defense—that they were victims of oppression, not criminals. The implications of the "trial within the trial" were clear. Without any physical evidence, the case depended on the confessions, and if those started to melt away, the whole trial would collapse.

As Judge Friedman began to weigh evidence of police misconduct, the atmosphere in the court calmed down—for the time being. By the middle of December 1993, the pro-PAC demonstrators were gone and the three accused were back in court, while their mothers and a few family members sat in the gallery. The trial adjourned just before Christmas and was scheduled to resume in late January 1994.

To many observers, the trial seemed to be on shaky ground. Some of Amy's friends and colleagues, who initially thought the government had a strong case, were stunned that the trial seemed to be unraveling "because of shoddy police work and crude intimidation of witnesses." Omar was worried that after the police obtained confessions, they didn't pursue other evidence. Those more sympathetic to the three defendants were also troubled by the trial, but for different reasons. "It's a horrible incident, and it was such a tragedy, because she was an American who had come to South Africa to help the people," Manqina's brother Gary told a reporter. "But if she had been black and poor and from some other country, would the world have ever heard about it?" Amy, no doubt, would have agreed.

As the problems in the trial mounted, some observers began to seriously question South Africa's legal system—and the rule of law in a democratic South Africa. With witnesses refusing to testify, audience members laughing at testimony of death and suffering, and demonstrators chanting racist slogans, what might the future hold? "Symptoms of a growing contempt for law and order have become alarming," wrote the *Argus*. "Defendants fail to appear in court, or abscond while on bail. Witnesses are intimidated—most recently, and disturbingly, in the Amy Biehl murder trial. Political demonstrations are challenging and disruptive." The trial had clearly unnerved a segment of South Africa's white population in particular. Some viewed it as a bad omen for South Africa's future under majority rule. Would the justice system be flouted? Would human rights be respected? Would the rule of law survive? Would racial strife abate? The Biehl trial set off a new round of preelection jitters, just as her murder had done.

Linda and Molly decided to attend part of the trial when it resumed early in 1994. The family wanted to go beyond patchy press reports and occasional telephone calls and observe the court's proceedings themselves. Given reports about demonstrations and intimidation of witnesses, they wanted to learn how the trial was being conducted. "I also thought that some respect and dignity needed to be added to the trial," Linda said. "We are real people, not just some abstractions from California 10,000 miles away. There was a real human life that was taken, a very lively human life." When the Biehls informed Ambassador Lyman about their plans, he responded cautiously. He worried that Linda's presence might rekindle the noisy demonstrations that had occurred during the early days of the trial. But he also understood why she wanted to attend and promised to assist her if she did so.

As Linda and Molly began planning their trip to South Africa, the kind of anti-white violence that had claimed Amy struck again. This time it was premeditated. On December 31, 1993, five black gunmen affiliated with the PAC attacked the

Heidelberg Tavern in Observatory, a pub popular with students at the predominantly white University of Cape Town. The gunmen fired into the crowd of New Year's Eve revelers, killing four patrons and wounding five others. It was another of APLA's racially motivated attacks that had begun earlier in the year. As British journalist Alec Russell reported, "The latest massacre seems to confirm growing suspicions that in the Cape there is a group of black fanatics dedicated to terrorizing local whites." Antiwhite extremists were still a minority, but they could cause considerable disruption and anxiety, despite their relatively small numbers.

On January 16, 1994, the PAC announced that it was suspending its armed struggle. The organization's leaders undoubtedly realized that their affiliate's high-profile attacks against white civilians—launched the previous year under the banner "Year of the Great Storm"—were hurting its image among South Africa's population. Whether the announcement would curb the behavior of militants in the organization was unclear at that point, but it signaled a major shift and indicated the PAC's desire to compete in elections rather than wage war. PAC regional secretary Lugulwana noted that the PAC was also trying to phase out the "one settler, one bullet" slogan and to convince black youths that whites weren't the enemy, just white domination. He had the three defendants in the Biehl trial in mind when he said so. "We have failed in our political education and these boys are an albatross around our necks," he admitted.

Linda and Molly arrived in South Africa in late January 1994. They both hoped their second visit to the country would be low key and less publicized than the first. They stayed with the family of Paul Welsh, a Methodist minister in Rosebank. They went to Amy's favorite beach and restaurants and didn't schedule any high-profile events. "We've seen things the first day here we never even saw the last time we were here," Linda told a reporter. "Amy really loved it here and last night I stood on the beach and understood why. It's really schizophrenic, it's so beautiful." There were security precautions to attend to, however. At the request of US consular officials, the South African government provided two bodyguards for the visiting Americans. In addition to their security detail, Linda sensed that she and her daughter were being followed by officials from the State Department or the CIA.

Shortly after their arrival in Cape Town, Linda and Molly met with Nollie Niehaus, the lead prosecutor. He told them that two additional witnesses had been found, aged 11 and 14, but, fearing retribution, their parents refused to let them testify. He admitted that without any material evidence and other eyewitness accounts, his case depended on the three defendants' confessions, whose admissibility was now being questioned. Sindiswa and Maletsatsi had identified two of the accused, but only as robbers. "I'm sure hundreds of people saw what happened and I have no case," Niehaus said later. "It happens all the time." Linda and Molly realized that a conviction was far from certain.

The Biehls were in for some other surprises when the trial resumed on January 31, 1994. The three defendants stared at Linda and Molly as they entered the courtroom, where they sat just in front of the prisoners' dock. Manqina looked right at Molly and grinned, unnerving her. "Was he smiling at me or was he laughing at me?" she asked a reporter afterward. Molly bore a striking resemblance to Amy. "I feel sorry for them. I hope that by looking at me somehow they could realize that they've stopped a life, killed a very good person," she said. As Molly and Linda left the court building the first day, a young black man shouted "settler, settler" when he saw them, but the large crowds that had been so boisterous before the holidays had not yet reappeared. Molly had expected Amy to be the focus of the trial. Instead, she and her mother were subjected to a trial of technicalities that seemed far removed from Amy's life and work. Amy's name was hardly mentioned in the court sessions they attended. Instead, the proceedings focused on whether the police had pressured or assaulted the defendants and whether their confessions were admissible as evidence. As for the defendants, Linda said, "We really know very little about them and I don't want to know. I was interested on the second day that they didn't look at us. They were told not to." At first, Linda felt neither compassion nor hatred for the accused. But she could not suppress her curiosity for very long. "I know that not long ago they were shiny-eyed children," she said, "and I wonder what happened to make them what they are today." Although she wanted justice to prevail and sensed that the defendants were guilty, she had no thoughts of anger or retribution. Asked later what she would say if she could send one message to the suspects, Linda replied, "Hey, guys, she was there for you. You made a big mistake."

Soon word spread among the defendants' supporters that the Biehls were attending the trial. On Tuesday, February 1, about 20 young demonstrators returned to the courthouse steps and shouted "One settler, one bullet!" and "Kill the Americans!" as Linda and Molly tried to leave the premises. As the pair threaded their way through the hectoring gauntlet of protestors, their two white bodyguards trailed behind them. The harassment continued throughout the week and the number of demonstrators grew to 40 or 50. As Molly and her mother walked in and out of the court building, the youths jeered, pretended to fire machine guns at them, and even mimed slitting Molly's throat. Linda and Molly remained composed during the daily taunting. "I am quite entitled to attend the trial and they won't keep me away," Linda told a reporter from the *Cape Times*. "I can't be hurt more than I already am." Court officials offered to let Linda and Molly use a rear door, but the pair said no. "We are not going to give in to them," Molly said. She later admitted that before the harassment, she hadn't known what it felt like to be hated solely because of race. Linda speculated that the young people were playing to the cameras. "There was a five-year-old with them—how could they possibly know what they were doing? If their presence was organized by a political group, all they got out of it was adverse publicity," she said later. Having had many positive interactions with black South Africans, both Linda and Molly knew that the behavior of the youths was atypical in its vehement antiwhiteness. Linda still felt no anger. "Anger and bitterness weren't what Amy was about. It would diminish us, and her memory."

Before Linda and Molly left South Africa, a high-level PAC leader reached out to them and expressed regret for the conduct of the youths outside the court. Ahmed Gora Ebrahim, the organization's secretary for foreign affairs, wrote Linda and acknowledged that the trial had been "an ordeal" for the family. He condemned the "unbecoming behavior" shown toward them during the trial and said that his organization would take action against those involved if they were affiliated with the PAC. He hoped that the Biehls would "emerge from this trying ordeal with courage and faith." Although just short of a formal apology—neither the word "sorry" nor "apologize" was used—the letter was sincere. After receiving Ebrahim's letter, whose sentiments she welcomed, Linda gave the PAC a book dedicated to Amy's memory, titled *Uneven Paths: Advancing Democracy in Southern Africa*. Linda's inscription read, "Mr. Ebrahim and the PAC, we are hopeful for a peaceful transition in South Africa."

When they weren't at the trial, Linda and Molly seized the opportunity to meet black South African leaders. At a dinner hosted by Ambassador Lyman, Linda sat next to ANC elder statesman Govan Mbeki, whom she found charismatic and relaxed. The two talked about music and the antiapartheid struggle, a long-standing interest of Amy's. Linda and Molly met Nelson Mandela on February 2. Mandela was visiting Paarl, near Cape Town, to light a "flame of freedom and reconciliation" outside Victor Verster prison, where he had been housed during his last year of confinement. Inching forward amid a crush of Mandela supporters with Allan Boesak at their side, Linda and Molly greeted the leader. Mandela hugged Molly and kissed her on both cheeks. When she introduced Mandela to her mother, he became somber and told Linda, "We were really devastated by that tragedy." "Well, [Amy] loved you, she loved your country," Linda replied. As they posed for a photograph, Mandela's solemn expression gave way to a broad smile, matching Linda's and Molly's. Their delight in meeting Amy's hero was obvious. Mandela had wanted to convey his sympathies to the Biehls and said afterward, "The death of Amy Biehl gave us a pain which is beyond words." A South African journalist, Sahm Venter, had helped set up the encounter, and she took Linda and Molly to meet Desmond Tutu the next day at his official residence, Bishopscourt, in suburban Cape Town. Tutu would become a great source of support for the family in the years ahead.

After Linda and Molly departed South Africa in mid-February, the atmosphere surrounding the trial calmed down. Police removed the barbed wire from outside the court and the number of youths attending the trial dropped, although some school-aged supporters of the defendants continued to gather on the court steps each afternoon. The "trial within the trial" continued. Poswa highlighted allegations of police brutality to suggest that his clients' self-incriminating statements were forced out of them. But he still felt it would be difficult to get an acquittal. "Because the ANC and Nelson Mandela are behind the state 100 percent and want a conviction, my job is that much tougher," he said. At one point, a policeman testified that Nofemela had been examined "at the time of his confession to check for evidence of police assault." The examiner allegedly found no recent injuries but did find nine scars on his body, including those inflicted by knives, a brick, and a machete—testimony to how dangerous it was for black males to come of age in townships like Gugulethu.

Amy Biehl would have celebrated her 27th birthday on April 26, 1994, the day before South Africa's first democratic election. Millions of South Africans voted for the first time in their lives, sometimes waiting hours in endless lines that snaked across fields and stretched around city blocks. The sense of joy and relief was palpable as South Africa's democratic dawn finally arrived. As her sister Kim noted, Amy would have been elated that Mandela was elected as South Africa's first black president. "She would have been ecstatic, but she would have been ready to work, too, for the future," Kim said. The ANC swept into power with approximately 63 percent of the vote. The incumbent National Party received just over 20 percent, while the Inkatha Freedom Party came in third with 10.5 percent. Only 1.2 percent of voters had cast their ballots for the PAC, which finished in sixth place. In an interview after the election, a PAC official discussed his party's dismal showing. He admitted that the PAC had been associated with Amy Biehl's murder in the eyes of the public, which "tainted it with racism," even though he denied that the PAC or any of its affiliates were responsible. As it turned out, the PAC would find it difficult to recover from its 1994 election debacle.

Mandela's inauguration on May 10, 1994, signaled that apartheid had finally ended, along with more than three centuries of white minority rule. South Africa had truly become "another country." Ambassador Lyman believed that South Africa's election had gone better than expected and that the country was turning the corner on its turbulent history. "Many persons worked and sacrificed for this achievement," he wrote Linda. "Amy was one of those, and I am sure that she would have glorified in this outcome."

Meanwhile, the Biehl trial inched forward against the backdrop of a free South Africa. An order prohibiting bail for the defendants expired, and the three defendants were released on bail on May 23, 1994. The prosecution was required by law to set bail at an amount that the defendants could afford, and so bail was set at R250, the equivalent of $70 each. As the three young men were released from police custody, they were cheered by supporters outside the court, some of whom reportedly taunted whites who were watching.

The court was in recess from late May until mid-August. In June, Thembisile Nojozi, the youngest of the accused who had been released to his family and fled, was rearrested. Now 16, he was ordered to remain in custody until the trial resumed. Although pleased that another suspect was in custody, the Biehls were still concerned about the direction of the trial—and its length. "If they would have gotten more physical evidence from the start, perhaps there would have been a conviction already," Linda said, unable to hide her frustration. Ambassador Lyman warned the family that the trial's outcome was uncertain. Not only was the investigation poorly handled by police, but the statements from the defendants might not be accepted, weakening the case considerably. He also told the family that amnesty legislation was being prepared that might pave the way for the defendants' eventual release. The prosecution wondered "whether to proceed with a weak case and risk acquittal, or let the amnesty application take its course," because "an amnesty decree would at least constitute a kind of admission of guilt." In order to receive amnesty, applicants would have to disclose their crimes. In Lyman's view, the prosecutors might drop the case if the judge rejected the defendants' confessions. This was hardly reassuring.

Nine months into the case, the Biehls still felt they needed to know more about the trial. Linda decided to return to South Africa, this time traveling with eldest daughter Kim. The pair arrived in mid-August and immediately sensed the new mood in the country. When the case began, South Africa was in turmoil, with racial tensions flaring before democratic elections were held. By August 1994, the turmoil had dissipated as the Mandela-led government was stressing racial reconciliation. Linda and Kim attended the first day of the trial's resumption on August 15, 1994, at which defense lawyer Poswa argued that the defendants' statements to police should be ruled inadmissible because they were allegedly assaulted and coerced by police. No sooner had the trial resumed than Judge Friedman ordered yet another recess so he could have more time to determine whether the statements were admissible. Linda and Kim had a busy week despite the trial's unexpected postponement. Foremost on Linda's agenda was discussing the possibility of amnesty with Dullah Omar, now the new minister of justice in Mandela's government. "I just want to remind him that Amy was still an important person to us and there should be some accountability in some way for the loss of her life," she told a reporter. "We're understanding, but we're not forgetting. There's a balance there." Linda was troubled by the prospect that the defendants might receive amnesty for Amy's murder. During Linda and Kim's meeting with Omar, he briefed them on the status of the trial and on the amnesty legislation he was drafting. The Biehls attended Mandela's 100-day state of the nation address two days later, given against the backdrop of reduced violence and growing optimism, particularly among black South Africans. The new government's honeymoon was still going strong. Before they left South Africa, Linda and Kim attended a service at St. Gabriel's Catholic Church in Gugulethu to mark the first anniversary of Amy's death. They headed back to the United States the same day.

On August 31, 1994, Judge Friedman ruled that the statements made by Nofemela and Ntamo were admissible, but not Manqina's. He believed that undue pressure might have been imposed on Manqina, whereas similar claims regarding Nofemela and Ntamo were weak and unpersuasive. The decision gave new life to the prosecution. "At least now, I think there will be some accountability," Linda told journalists, clearly relieved by the decision. "I'd like to see this resolved. I wish that these guys could be remorseful."

Another breakthrough in the case was announced by prosecutors days later. The police had located four additional witnesses to the attack, three of whom agreed to testify if they could do so privately, "in camera." Judge Friedman agreed to let the three witnesses—all women—testify behind closed doors to preserve their anonymity. Identified only as Miss A, Miss B, and Miss C, the women described the attack on Amy in detail, Miss A weeping as she did so. Their testimony directly implicated Manqina, Nofemela, and Ntamo in Amy's murder. Bolstered by the new testimony, the state rested its case on September 27, 1994. The only defendant to testify in his own defense was Manqina, who denied any involvement in the attack.

Both the prosecution and the defense gave their closing arguments on October 12, 1994. Only a few people were in the gallery to hear them. Niehaus said that, based on the evidence, all three defendants should be convicted of murdering Amy. Poswa maintained that his clients should be acquitted because the testimony against them was "inconsistent," "improbable," and even dishonest. Judge Fried-man wanted 12 days to arrive at his verdict.

Friedman ended up writing a 120-page judgment that highlighted both his meticulousness and his fair-mindedness. He was determined to consider all sides fully and render a just decision. He took two days to read his judgment in court. On the second, October 25, 1994, he found all three defendants guilty of murder. "The state has proved beyond a reasonable doubt that each had the direct inten-tion of killing Miss Biehl and that each took part in the attack," he told the packed courtroom. The three accused sat expressionless as the verdict was announced.

The Biehls learned of the verdict at 3:40 a.m. California time. "It's closure on the one hand and on the other hand it's just the beginning," Peter told jour-nalists. "We feel a great deal of sympathy for the families of the accused—now convicted." Although Linda admitted that she would've been "crushed" if the three suspects had been acquitted, she felt Amy's spirit guiding her as she reacted to the news. "I wouldn't like to think it's just a verdict for Amy, but for all the others who've lost their lives working toward democracy [in South Africa]," she said. "This group of people that did this to Amy, this group was not the soul of South Africa." Although relieved by the verdict, both Peter and Linda repeatedly expressed sympathy for the young men's families. "From our viewpoint, we can understand what they've been going through," Peter said. "Every parent wants more for their children. They certainly didn't want something like this, any more than we wanted what happened. This whole thing has been a catastrophe on all sides."

Associated Press journalist Sahm Venter spoke to one of the young men's parents shortly after the verdict. Evelyn Manqina was Mongezi's mother and said that her son was raised by a grandmother because she, his mother, was jailed for shoplifting several times. Now she feared that local youths angry at Amy's death might attack her house because her son was found guilty of Amy's murder. That wasn't her only concern. "I am very worried about Amy Biehl's mother and family because they lost their child," she told Venter. "I am sorry about what my child did to her child." Linda's response was published in AP dispatches all over the United States. "I certainly appreciate her beautiful thoughts, and that is very important for bridging gaps," she said. "It is not just our tragedy. Amy of all people did un-derstand the conditions that [black] children grew up under."

The trial was not quite over—Judge Friedman had yet to announce the sen-tence. When Niehaus called for the death penalty at a hearing on October 25, the defendants' supporters in the gallery "erupted in loud gasps and angry whispers." But Niehaus was undaunted. "This was a racist killing," he told the court. "[Amy

Biehl] was killed because she was white and regarded as a settler." The young men had perpetrated the brutal murder after having been told that Amy was a comrade. Even though he called for the death penalty, Niehaus expected the three to be sent to prison, given the moratorium on the death penalty in South Africa and the ANC government's opposition to it. Defense lawyer Poswa argued for a lighter sentence, saying his three clients had been "swept up" by the "emotional fervor" of the antiapartheid struggle. "The court needs to look at the youth of the accused, their economic backgrounds and the social conditions they come from," he told Judge Friedman. In Poswa's view, the adult leaders of the political organizations shared much of the blame, because they popularized the racist slogans that the youths took literally.

The Biehls hoped that the sentence would be "as rehabilitative as possible." Although the family rejected the death penalty, neither did they support amnesty for the young men at this point. "There has to be accountability. I think there has to be some sentence here that is harsh enough that people feel you can't just get away with it," Linda said. She hoped the sentence would "turn these people around and make them better citizens."

On October 26, 1994, Judge Friedman sentenced Manqina, Nofemela, and Ntamo to 18 years in prison. Upon pronouncing the sentence, Friedman said the murder "was cold-blooded and brutal and carried out by a mob on a defenseless 26-year-old girl who was already seriously injured." He described Amy as "a young girl with her whole life ahead of her. She was an American and an active supporter of the cause of the disadvantaged." He said that the attack was purely racially motivated and that "racially motivated crimes can never be tolerated." He acknowledged, however, that the murder was not premeditated. In mitigation, he noted that the crime was committed during a period of political unrest and that the young men "had been caught up in the spiral of violence." He added that it was possible that the young men could be reformed. After the sentencing, about two dozen youths ran onto the streets near the courthouse chanting "One settler, one bullet!" Some supporters and family members ran after the police truck as it took the three young men to prison.

The Biehls received the news by telephone that morning; faxed messages of support started coming in shortly thereafter. Both Peter and Linda expressed support for the sentence. "Any sentence cannot bring Amy back," Peter said. "If they survive the 18-year term, they'll be 40 or so when they get out. I hope they make more productive use of their lives." Linda was relieved that the trial had finally ended and glad the death sentence hadn't been imposed. "I just don't think more death on top of death would be right in this case," she said. Ntamo's mother

Nomhle expressed sympathy for Peter and Linda after her son was sentenced. "[Their daughter's] gone and they won't see her anymore," she told a reporter. "Our sons are coming back."

Both Americans and South Africans had followed the trial closely and were eager to make their voices heard afterward. Americans, especially Californians, wrote Judge Friedman after the trial, complaining that he should have sentenced the killers to death. But he also received letters from those saying that the 18-year term he imposed was too harsh. The sentence—and the Biehls' reaction to it—had made national news in the United States, including coverage in the *New York Times*. The Biehls' magnanimous reaction to the verdict and to the families of the young men elicited admiration from around the country. Prominent American newspapers such as the *Los Angeles Times* held the Biehls up as role models for other Americans in an age of harsher sentencing for criminals.

Shortly after the sentencing, Manqina, Nofemela, and Ntamo told their lawyer that they wanted to appeal their conviction. When Judge Friedman turned down their appeal application, Poswa announced that he would seek to get the young men pardoned under the provisions of the country's pending amnesty legislation. At the time, there was a bill before parliament paving the way for the Truth and Reconciliation Commission, which would be established a year later. If perpetrators of human rights violations under apartheid could demonstrate that their crime was politically motivated, fully disclose their actions, and admit guilt, they would qualify for amnesty. The amnesty process would usher in an unprecedented period of angst, anger, controversy, and healing when it finally began in 1996. For the time being, however, the process was just in the planning stages.

But at least one of those convicted in Amy's death didn't want to wait. Two weeks after the trial ended, Nofemela and at least seven other PAC prisoners launched a hunger strike, demanding that they be classified as political prisoners and granted amnesty. They ended their hunger strike after a week, but the prospect of amnesty still concerned the Biehls. Mark Hill, the US vice-consul in Cape Town, told them that amnesty was unlikely because Judge Friedman had described the crime as being "racially motivated," not "political." Linda agreed. "I do not think they should be granted amnesty," she told one reporter. "When I saw the three accused, I saw the one particularly that thrust the knife up to the hilt in Amy's heart, and he had no remorse. He looked at us with pride. 'I did this.' It was not a political crime. They didn't know Amy as a politician. They didn't even know who she was. In Amy's case it was just, 'Hey, let's get her; she's white.'" Peter agreed with her.

In an interview years later, Judge Friedman said that Amy's murder did have a political motive, because the young men had just returned from a political rally and were highly charged. The fact that the crime was at least partly motivated by politics was a mitigating factor in his sentencing. Had there been no political motive, Friedman said, the death sentence would have been "competent." At the trial, however, Friedman had stressed the racial/racist nature of the crime. His understandable ambiguity about the racial versus political nature of the crime would reflect similar ambiguity at the amnesty hearings a few years later—and the deeply divided opinions of South Africans about the nature of the crime and of amnesty itself. But in 1994 the question of amnesty would have to wait.

There was still some unfinished business in the Amy Biehl case. Charges against the youngest accused, Thembisile Nojozi, were quietly dropped in early 1995, but police arrested an additional suspect—21-year-old Ntobeko Peni. He had originally been taken into custody in October 1993 but was released after witnesses failed to recognize him in a police lineup. He was rearrested in January 1995 and charged with murder, to which he pleaded not guilty. His hearing, which began in April 1995, had none of the intimidation and histrionics of the first trial, much to the Biehls' relief. It also proceeded much more quickly. On the basis of evidence from the first trial and the private testimony of some of the women who had spoken earlier, Judge Braam Lategan found Peni guilty of murder on June 6, 1995, and imposed the same sentence that Judge Friedman had—18 years of imprisonment. Coincidentally, on the same day that Peni was sentenced, South Africa's newly created Constitutional Court abolished the death penalty.

Peter and Linda returned to South Africa shortly after Peni's trial ended. They met with Nollie Niehaus, who told them that no further arrests were likely, even though more than eight people were probably involved. The case was being closed, and the Biehls were satisfied that justice had been done. As they struggled through the trials, they remembered how Amy had educated them about South Africa's "lost generation." She had told them that the country's black youth "were victims of the system of apartheid, that all they were doing was returning the same treatment they were given," Peter recalled. The Biehls were grateful to those eyewitnesses who testified at the trials and glad that some of the family had attended part of the trial. After the first trial, Linda talked about the family's plans to remain engaged with South Africa. Peter agreed. Reflecting on the guilty verdicts, he said, "It has been a tragedy on all sides, and at the same time we feel that as a family we're just beginning to recommit ourselves to what Amy was starting." The Biehls had developed an unbreakable connection with South Africa, just as Amy had, and that connection would grow in the years ahead.

20 Marchers in Gugulethu honoring Amy the day after her death, August 26, 1993.
    (© Louise Gubb)

21 Women at Amy's death site in Gugulethu, August 26, 1993. (Obed Zilwa/*Argus*/
    Independent Media)

22 (*above*) Memorial service for Amy at St. Gabriel's Church in Gugulethu, August 29, 1993. (Benny Gool/*Cape Times*/Independent Media)

23 (*left*) Dullah Omar (*left*) and Melanie Jacobs at Amy's cremation ceremony, August 30, 1993. (Biehl family)

24 Linda, Kim, Molly, and Melanie (*left to right*) at a church service in Gugulethu, October 10, 1993. (Biehl family)

25 Maletsatsi Maceba (*left*) and Sindiswa Bevu (*right*) at a ceremony welcoming the Biehl family, University of the Western Cape, October 12, 1993. (Biehl family)

26   Kim, Molly, and Zach with children in KTC, a settlement near Cape Town,
      October 1993. (Biehl family)

27   Linda embracing Limpho Hani, the widow of Chris Hani, in Dawn Park,
      October 17, 1993. (David Brauchli / AP)

28　The Biehls with President Clinton in the White House, November 23, 1993. *Left to right:* Peter, Linda, Bill Clinton, Kim, and Molly. (Biehl family)

29   Molly and Linda in Cape Town for the trial, February 1994. (Biehl family)

30   Linda and Molly meeting Nelson Mandela in Paarl, February 2, 1994. (Biehl family)

31 Linda meeting Archbishop Desmond Tutu at his residence in Bishopscourt, February 1994. (Biehl family)

32 Linda with Evelyn Manqina, mother of one of the men convicted in Amy's murder, June 28, 1997. (Sasa Kralj / AP)

33 Linda and Peter embracing Mongezi Manqina's cousin and mother in
Gugulethu, June 28, 1997. (Sasa Kralj)

34 The four young men applying for amnesty for Amy's murder at the Truth and
Reconciliation Commission hearing, July 8, 1993. *Left to right:* Ntobeko Peni, Easy
Nofemela, Vusumzi Ntamo, and Mongezi Manqina. (Mike Hutchings)

35 (*above*) Linda and Peter at the Truth and Reconciliation Commission hearing in Cape Town, July 8, 1997. (Reuters)

36 (*left*) Appearing before the media after the TRC hearing, July 9, 1997. (Reuters)

REMEMBERING AMY

In South Africa, Linda and Peter Biehl uphold a daughter's legacy of hope

▲ "They extend their warmth and love to us," says Linda Biehl (with husband Peter, outside Cape Town) of South African children.

37 Greeting township residents near Cape Town in 1997, shortly before the official launch of the Amy Biehl Foundation Trust. (© Louise Gubb)

38 Easy Nofemela (*left*) and Ntobeko Peni (*right*) on the evening of their release from prison, July 28, 1998. (Reuters)

10

Laying a New Foundation

AS THE two trials unfolded, the Biehls began to support an increasing number of humanitarian projects in South Africa. In fact, within hours of Amy's death, the family had agreed that they needed to do something to honor her memory. Their resolve to contribute to South Africa's new democracy would ultimately result in the formation of the Amy Biehl Foundation. Although they didn't fully realize it at the outset, they were embarking on a journey that would bind them to South Africa and transform their lives. "We didn't set out to do it, but it just evolved," Linda said of the foundation. "There was no intention at the beginning."

Ever since news broke of Amy's death, people from all over the world had written letters to the Biehls, sending money or asking for information on a fund or organization to which they could donate in Amy's name. Peter and Linda put the money in a checking account as they pondered what to do with the donations. They had been astounded by the amount of attention Amy's death had received and that her life had touched so many people. They wanted to parlay all of the attention into something positive for South Africa, to carry on Amy's work in some way, and to do something she would be proud of. Their initial plan was to support two memorial funds that had been created to honor Amy and carry on her work. One, established by NDI in early September 1993, supported projects on democratization and "the political empowerment of women in Africa." After consulting with the Biehls, Stanford set up its own Amy Biehl Fund around the same time. It assisted Stanford students wishing to work on humanitarian projects in South Africa and enabled UWC students to attend Stanford. Thanks to a steady stream of contributions, Stanford created an endowed fund that allowed the program to continue well into the 21st century. The Biehls supported the funds at NDI and Stanford and encouraged prospective donors to do so as well.

Other institutions established scholarships in Amy's memory in cooperation with the Biehls. Two funds originated in New Mexico, where the family had lived when Amy was in high school. One of them was begun by members of Amy's 1985 graduating class at Santa Fe High School who raised funds for an Amy Biehl Memorial Scholarship, which would be based at Santa Fe Community College. A second New Mexico–inspired initiative to honor Amy's memory was conceived in the fall of 1993. An official with New Mexico Advocates for Children and Families had been inspired by Amy's work and wanted to keep her spirit alive so that other young people would work for a better world. The organization created the Amy Biehl Youth Spirit Award to recognize young people who best embodied Amy's ideals of human rights and community service. The $1,000 award, first presented at an event in Albuquerque in November 1994, singled out outstanding New Mexicans and generated considerable publicity in the state in the years to come. Other scholarships honoring Amy were established elsewhere. In 1994, the US Information Agency awarded an "Amy Biehl Fulbright" to a South African student headed to Stanford for graduate studies in political science. A few years later, two Fulbright scholarships would be awarded in Amy's honor—one for a South African student to study in the United States and another for an American to study in South Africa.

As these scholarships were getting started, Amy and her family gained public recognition in other forums across the United States. In November 1993, NDI dedicated its eighth annual Democracy Dinner to Amy's memory. Peter, Linda, and Kim flew into Washington, D.C., to attend the dinner with Molly, who was working at NDI at the time. Commerce Secretary Ron Brown fondly remembered Amy, who had written some briefing papers for him while she was at NDI. When he heard that the Biehls were in Washington, he arranged for the family to be invited to a White House ceremony at which President Clinton would partially revoke sanctions against South Africa. As the Biehls were boarding their plane to head back to California on November 23, 1993, the president summoned them to the White House. President Clinton was preparing to sign the South African Democratic Transition Support Act of 1993, which would lift some of the sanctions that Congress had imposed after the passage of the Comprehensive Anti-Apartheid Act in 1986. As the Biehls were ushered into the Roosevelt Room for the signing ceremony, they were joined not only by Secretary Brown but by a host of high-level administration officials and members of the House and Senate.

President Clinton thanked the guests for coming and for contributing to the end of apartheid, "the realization of a great dream." He said that the ceremony was designed to salute the efforts of those who had "join[ed] with South Africa's oppressed majority to hasten apartheid's demise . . . But I want to especially recognize the presence here of the family of Amy Biehl, who herself did so much to further that cause," he said. Before the family left the White House, Assistant Secretary of State for African Affairs George Moose told Linda, "Your daughter is part of South African history now."

The Biehls' decision to establish a foundation in Amy's name came gradually. After their initial trip to South Africa in October 1993, the family thought they would "go on with [their] lives," but their newly formed bonds with South Africans made them want to stay involved with the country. During their first Christmas without Amy, the Biehls and Scott Meinert discussed how they could perpetuate Amy's legacy. "We all formed the foundation in our living room," Molly later recalled. They agreed that starting a foundation in Amy's name would be a way of keeping her spirit alive. Perhaps they could establish an organization that would work on behalf of South African women, particularly in Cape Town, to reflect Amy's work and interests. Knowing that Amy wouldn't have wanted the attention, Linda and Peter initially hesitated to name the foundation after Amy, but in the end it seemed like the appropriate thing to do. In the weeks after Amy died, the Biehls had received her laptop computer and her other belongings from South Africa. They pored over her notes, journals, correspondence, and papers in order to more fully understand her work and goals. With this understanding, they would steer the foundation toward things that had been important to Amy, such as human rights, women's rights, and education. Linda quit her job at Neiman Marcus by the end of 1993 so that she could work full-time on projects related to Amy. "Parents die in peace," she told a journalist. "But when you lose a child, you need to keep procreating." By expanding their connections to South Africa, the Biehls would find a way to work through their grief. After a lawyer friend helped them file the necessary paperwork, the Amy Biehl Foundation was officially created in February 1994, when it was granted tax-exempt status as a California charitable corporation.

The Biehls' knowledge of local conditions in South Africa increased when Linda and Molly traveled to Cape Town during the early phases of the first trial in late January 1994. Despite the periodic heckling outside the court, the two generally received a warm reception from South Africans, and that redoubled Linda's initial desire to contribute to the country in ways that would have pleased Amy. Not only had she and various members of her family met Dullah Omar,

Ambassador Princeton Lyman, Tokyo Sexwale, Limpho Hani, Nelson Mandela, and Desmond Tutu, but they had been introduced to lesser-known individuals from townships, schools, universities, and NGOs. These contacts would help the fledging foundation identify needs and prospective partners for future projects. Linda explained her mindset in early February 1994 shortly after arriving in Cape Town: "When someone dies very young like Amy, there's a need to feel that they haven't died in vain, that there is a legacy. You kind of want to pick up the torch. If you don't do it, you sink. Amy was here working for hope and justice, so let's all work for hope and justice. Maybe I'm taking my own journey too, in a way." She hoped that improving conditions in South Africa's black townships would help prevent the rise of another lost generation—"another angry mob needing to kill just because of the color of skin." Bolstered by the strength of her family and the support of Mandela, Tutu, and Amy's friends and colleagues in Cape Town, Linda's experiences told her that there was indeed hope for South Africa. "If we pray, hope, invest, and contribute in some small way, maybe we can save lives, stop the bloody violence, and dry the tears of injustice," she later wrote.

Linda's magnanimity toward the country in which her daughter was killed manifested itself in deeds, not just words. Three months before South Africa's April 1994 elections, the PAC decided to suspend its armed struggle and contest the vote. PAC officials then asked NDI for logistical support. Of course, it had been young people affiliated with the PAC's youth wing who had killed Amy. Before responding to the PAC's request, NDI representatives contacted the Biehls to gauge their reaction. "I said, yes, give it to them," Linda recalled. "This is what Amy wanted, for everyone to join the democratic process." The NDI governing board ultimately decided that the PAC would be eligible for assistance, as would other parties that "ascribed to a democratic ethos" and refrained from violence.

The Biehls' generosity of spirit received widespread media coverage in the months after Amy died, and this coverage generated considerable support for their newly formed foundation. The family became as much a part of the story as Amy had. A prime-time television program in April 1994 did much to raise awareness about the Biehls. After Amy died, all of the major American networks had vied to tell Amy's story, and the Biehls ultimately chose ABC. The family asked network representatives not to focus solely on Amy, but to tell South Africa's story, so people could understand the context behind the country's violence. Claudia Pryor, an African American producer with ABC News, agreed to produce the program. When a network executive initially asked her to do a documentary on Amy Biehl, she had hesitated: "While her murder was horrific, I objected to doing a story immortalizing Amy when neither my show nor any network newsmagazine had bothered to notice the thousands of black people who had been killed in South Africa's struggle against apartheid. After hearing my objection, the executive firmly stated that the documentary should include a 'parallel character'—a black South African whose story would unfold along with Amy's. That sold me."

Produced for ABC's *Turning Point* series and titled "Inside the Struggle: The Amy Biehl Story," the hour-long program was broadcast on the evening of April 20, 1994, a week before South Africa's first democratic election. It was one of the few substantive programs on South Africa to be broadcast by the major American networks in the 1990s. The production team put together an engrossing, well-researched documentary that packed an emotional punch. It interwove Amy's story with footage of the Biehls' October 1993 trip to South Africa and showed their visit to the site where Amy was killed, their reception at UWC, and their emotional meeting with Chris Hani's widow and daughter. Alongside Amy's story, the program also told that of Maria Kutuane, a South African domestic worker, to give American viewers insight into the lives of South Africa's black majority. Maria's life of discrimination, poverty, and menial labor had all but crushed her spirit, and after her husband was killed by a white man after a petty dispute, she found it difficult to envision a better future. By watching the program, viewers learned not just about one American's life and death, but about the legacy of apartheid in South Africa. It showed that Amy was one of many who lost their lives in the struggle for democracy in South Africa.

"Inside the Struggle" injected new life into Amy's story and bolstered the newly created Amy Biehl Foundation at just the right time. Letters flooded into the Biehls' home from people wanting to help the foundation. A college student from North Carolina wrote to say that he admired Amy for her commitment to South Africa and considered her a hero on par with Biko and Mandela. A resident of Tuba City, Arizona, also admired Amy's efforts to make a better world and drew a parallel between the treatment of black South Africans and native Americans. Students at a Catholic girls' high school in St. Louis saw the program and wrote about how Amy inspired them to work on behalf of others. Their teacher sent their responses to the Biehls and wrote, "My students and I have a new hero. Her name is Amy Biehl." In one hour, the program did more to raise Amy's profile—and, by extension, the Biehls'—than the reams of newspaper and magazine articles that had been published up to that point. As the ABC reporter Don Kladstrup observed, "Viewers who couldn't have cared less about South Africa called or wrote to say what an eye-opener it was and how much they learned." Many of Kladstrup's peers were equally enthusiastic. At a ceremony at Columbia

University in January 1995, ABC received the Alfred I. DuPont "Gold Baton" award for distinguished television journalism. Among the programs receiving special commendation was "The Amy Biehl Story."

The Amy Biehl Foundation was publicly launched at a benefit concert in Washington, D.C., a week after ABC's program aired. Molly organized the event to coincide with South Africa's historic election. It was held at the Kilimanjaro Club, among Amy's favorites when she lived in the city. Although the concert would be dedicated to Amy's memory, it also honored the thousands who had died in political violence in South Africa since the transition to democracy began in February 1990. Although invited, President Clinton was unable to attend, but he sent a message expressing admiration for all Amy had done to promote the cause of democracy and women's rights in South Africa. "As you celebrate the election in South Africa to the incomparable music of Hugh Masekela," Clinton wrote, "please know that I am there with you in spirit and in harmony." On the evening of April 28, 1994, South African jazz musician Hugh Masekela and his band performed before approximately a thousand people who had gathered to celebrate the birth of a new foundation and a new country. The concert raised more than $40,000, a portion of which came from large organizations that Molly contacted, such as Goldman Sachs and the World Bank. The Biehls shared some of the proceeds from the concert with the Free South Africa Fund. According to the official invitation, the funds going to the Amy Biehl Foundation would support "training and education programs aimed at strengthening the political voice of all South African women."

The evening had been a great success, and it added to the upbeat mood generated by the recent wave of positive publicity. With national exposure, an expanding number of enthusiastic supporters, and a sense of useful work ahead, the future looked bright. Although the challenges ahead hadn't fully manifested themselves, the Biehls were personally and professionally ready to undertake the task.

With momentum from television coverage and the benefit concert, the Biehls set about building the foundation—appointing board members, scheduling meetings, discussing goals, and drafting bylaws. Joining Peter, Linda, Kim, and Molly on the original board of directors were Kennell Jackson, Scott Meinert, who had begun to practice law in Fresno, California, Carole Sams Hoemeke, one of Amy's close friends from Stanford who had experience with nonprofit organizations, and Stephen Stedman, Amy's fellow Fulbright scholar at the University of the Western Cape and an associate professor of political science at Johns Hopkins. In August 1994, the foundation's board of directors held its first meeting in Newport Beach, on the first anniversary of Amy's death. The board agreed that the foundation would focus on southern Africa and on the needs of women in particular. It would raise money and offer grants to individuals and organizations to promote human rights, women's rights, and children's rights.

Peter's business background proved essential as the foundation took its first steps. As he noted on his résumé, "My entire management life has been a progression of broadening experiences—each quite different from the others—which has left me comfortable in a wide range of management functions." With his set of experiences, he was uniquely qualified to help start up the Amy Biehl Foundation. But it was Linda who made many of the early contacts with community-based organizations in South Africa. The transition in Linda's life could hardly have been more dramatic. Whereas before she had spent her days in high-end retail management, she was now coleading a new humanitarian foundation and traveling in and out of South Africa's black townships (with local escorts). Once a relatively apolitical wife and mother, she was becoming an international human rights activist. Helping her bond with this new country was a journalist, Sahm Venter, a white South African reporter for the Associated Press. She had met the Biehls on their first trip to South Africa and they became close. During subsequent trips, Venter provided the family with crucial logistical support as well as facilitating communication between the Biehls and South Africans like Desmond Tutu and Albie Sachs. Without her support in South Africa, launching the foundation's early initiatives there would have been much more difficult.

One early priority for the foundation was assisting Maletsatsi Maceba, Amy's friend and fellow passenger on the day of her death. After Maletsatsi testified in the trial, she received death threats and was forced to leave her home and go into hiding. Despite this, she continued her legal studies at UWC. Amy had recognized Maletsatsi's potential and had gone out of her way to help her. After Amy's death, her friends and family were deeply moved that Maletsatsi risked her own safety to identify Amy's attackers in court. The Biehls and Carole Sams Hoemeke worked together to raise funds for Maletsatsi. After ABC's "Turning Point" program was broadcast, a family in Oregon offered to help pay for Maletsatsi's education. The Palo Alto Rotary Club also stepped forward, awarding Maletsatsi funds to defray her housing and transportation expenses. Thanks to the foundation's efforts, Maletsatsi continued to receive financial assistance for the next several years.

By early 1995, the foundation had raised about $50,000. Many of the donors were "not big money people, but just people who cared," the Biehls observed. They believed that even modest donations could go a long way in South Africa. They didn't want the foundation to become a massive organization divorced from the people, but to remain relatively small and connected to grassroots efforts.

They preferred that approach over working with the South African government or international organizations, at least at first. "You don't have to be a huge foundation to do what we want to do," Peter told the press. Still, in order to remain viable, the foundation constantly needed to find new sources of funding. One creative idea came from Los Angeles–based Global Partners. It had acquired hundreds of surplus ballots from the South African government after the 1994 election and planned to sell them as collectibles. Impressed by the Biehls' humanitarian efforts, the organization's leaders offered to share the profits with the Amy Biehl Foundation. Interested consumers could acquire a historic campaign souvenir and help the foundation at the same time. The Biehls welcomed this creative fundraising idea, which ultimately generated more than $1,000 for the foundation. The Biehls also organized another benefit concert, this one in San Francisco. On April 27, 1995, approximately 500 people gathered at the city's Great American Music Hall to celebrate Amy's birthday and the first anniversary of South Africa's young democracy, enjoying dinner and dancing to the music of several bands. In the six months between March and September 1995, the foundation received almost $30,000 in donations and earned additional revenue from the ballots and T-shirt sales. Despite its growing number of grants and expenses related to concerts, travel, and publicity, the foundation managed to stay comfortably in the black. Peter's business expertise was paying dividends once again.

During its early years, the foundation had another valuable ally—Dullah Omar, Amy's mentor at UWC and now minister of justice in Mandela's government. He strongly supported the Biehls' work and was interested in actively promoting it. "The generosity with which you and the rest of the family have come forward and your compassion shown to the disadvantaged sectors of our society is indeed remarkable, taking into account the circumstances in which Amy met her death," he wrote Peter and Linda. "I hope that we shall be able to display similar compassion and generosity." The Biehls heard from Sahm Venter that Omar might be willing to "facilitate some quiet reconciliation sessions with families of the convicted" and representatives of the PAC. The Biehls would be interested, Peter wrote, as long as the meetings were private. Not only was Omar one of the principal authors of South Africa's new democratic constitution, but he was also a "point man for the Mandela government's mission of reconciliation."

In mid-1995, the Biehls moved to La Quinta, California, after Zach graduated from high school in Newport Beach. La Quinta was a desert town near Palm Springs, much smaller and quieter than bustling Orange County. They would no longer need a large house after Zach left for college, and they wanted a place to start afresh, where they could work on the foundation without distractions

and live "very frugally." Their priorities had shifted from raising a family to focusing on their South African work. Just weeks after they moved to La Quinta
in July 1995, Peter and Linda embarked on what Peter called the couple's first
"exploratory, fact-finding" trip on behalf of the foundation. It was Peter's first trip
to South Africa since the family's visit in October 1993. He and Linda wanted to
learn more about the country's needs and make new contacts with a minimum
of publicity. The problems facing Cape Town's vast population of disadvantaged
people were endless, given the legacies of apartheid—poverty, unemployment,
poor housing and education, inadequate healthcare, and more. The Biehls faced a
dramatic learning curve, because they had had no real knowledge or experiences
in South Africa before Amy's death. But they were determined to learn and to
expand the foundation's work. When looking for projects to support, the Biehls
sought to "identify the need via talking to the community, scope out a program
idea, and wait until the right person emerges." They continued to identify and
support projects like this on an ad hoc basis for the next two years. During their
July trip, the Biehls renewed their support of St. Gabriel's Community Centre in
Gugulethu and provided funding for some new programs, including a youth club
in Khayelitsha, the sprawling, sandy township that was Cape Town's largest.

One community assistance program that particularly intrigued the Biehls
was known as Mosaic. Founded in 1993 by Rolene Miller, a white South African
who had worked for the National Institute for Crime Prevention and Rehabilitation of Offenders (NICRO), Mosaic was a "training, service, and healing center
for women" based in the townships of Cape Town. Miller developed a one-year
program to train black women as community workers, since qualifying as full-
fledged social workers required a university degree, which was beyond the financial reach of most black women. At that point, most social workers were white,
didn't speak African languages, didn't live in the townships, and weren't on call
on weekends or at night, when many township women needed help. The women
selected to participate in Mosaic's training program came from the townships and
would provide health and educational services to women and offer support to
victims of domestic violence. The Biehls met the instructor and the first group of
trainees just before the first training program began, and they were moved by the
women's wisdom and commitment. Convinced that Amy would have embraced
the program, the Biehls awarded $1,600 to support Mosaic's training course. The
foundation continued to raise funds for Mosaic in the years to come, and the
Biehls regarded it as among the foundation's most important undertakings.

In the fall of 1996, Peter and Miller wrote about the partnership between
Mosaic and the Amy Biehl Foundation for *Reflections*, a journal published by the

Department of Social Work at California State University–Long Beach. The journal also published commentaries on the partnership by specialists in the fields of sociology and public health. Some of the scholars voiced pointed criticisms of the project, illustrating the potential minefields that sometimes awaited the Biehls in South Africa, where outsiders, Americans, and whites were not always trusted. Alosi Moloi, a black South African teaching at CSU–Long Beach, was somewhat skeptical of American-based foundations wanting to help black South Africans, arguing that this reflected an outdated, paternalistic model of well-intentioned foreigners coming to the rescue of poor, helpless Africans. Moloi suggested that all too often, white outsiders with little knowledge of South Africa came to help and preferred partnering with white South Africans because they were uncomfortable interacting directly with blacks. Despite these cautionary notes, the author still felt Mosaic was a worthwhile project. Wilma Peebles-Wilkins, an African American academic and dean of the School of Social Work at Boston University, also expressed some discomfort over the partnership between the Biehl Foundation and Mosaic, worrying that it downplayed black South African efforts to help themselves. She objected to Peter's tone in the article, especially when he referred to black "mamas" in townships and "traditions of paternalistic tribalism" that he suggested sometimes condoned the abuse of women. Peebles-Wilkins called Peter's use of such terms "paternalistic and patronizing." While accepting that Mosaic's efforts had potential, she believed that the training of black South African women as fully qualified social workers should be prioritized.

Kenneth Lutterman, a high-level official at the National Institute of Health in Maryland, supported the efforts of the foundation and Mosaic to help victims of domestic abuse but noted that the problem was systemic. Unemployment, poverty, and other legacies of apartheid exacerbated the phenomenon, and until these underlying problems were dealt with, violence would continue to be endemic. In other words, Mosaic was treating the symptoms of the problem—which he believed was necessary—but not the causes. Ruthann Rountree, an African American lecturer in CSU–Long Beach's Department of Sociology, refrained from commenting directly on the foundation and Mosaic. Instead, she cautioned well-meaning outsiders to make sure they learned about past and current efforts within oppressed communities to improve themselves. In other words, outsiders wishing to help shouldn't impose solutions but listen, learn, and support. It was advice that Amy would have given and that Peter and Linda understood. Peter seemed to take the critiques in his stride, realizing that he and Linda had much to learn but rejecting the idea that white involvement in black communities was inherently inappropriate.

Another endeavor that meant a great deal to the Biehls was assisting Solange Jacobs, the young daughter of Amy's South African housemate Melanie. Amy had told her parents about Solange, who she believed had unlimited potential if she could get an American education. Just 13 when Amy was killed, Solange had long dreamed of studying in the United States. With the help of the Biehl Foundation, Solange received a full scholarship to Rolling Hills Preparatory School in San Pedro, California, and later to Stanford University, Amy's alma mater. "I was the first project of the Biehl Foundation," Solange recalled years later. Among all its early activities, the foundation's support of Mosaic and Solange Jacobs made the Biehls the proudest.

Peter and Linda ran the foundation from their home office in La Quinta, with no staff or corporate sponsorship. They returned to South Africa in July 1996, thinking they might be able to proceed unnoticed, but they were widely recognized. Besides maintaining their support for Solange, Maletsatsi, Mosaic, and other projects in Cape Town, they contributed funds to the Los Angeles–based Artists for a New South Africa, which was involved in shipping medical supplies to South Africa. The Biehls paid for their own travel expenses to South Africa but constantly needed to look for new ways to keep the foundation sustainable. Much of the foundation's income came from small donations from family and friends, so the Biehls began to apply for outside grants and partner with other individuals and organizations. But the Biehls did not accept every offer that came their way. In late 1996, an executive with the Nelson Mandela Children's Fund asked for Linda's thoughts on the possibility of a community center in Crossroads (near Cape Town) being named after Amy. "You have much of [President Mandela's] traits of tolerance, forgiveness, [and] understanding in your heart," he wrote, "and it is important to spread such traits right across the globe." The Biehls believed that Amy would support such a community center, but they were careful to limit the number of things named in her honor. Consistent with her beliefs, they always sought to highlight the many others who sacrificed anonymously for South Africa's freedom, even if their deeds hadn't been widely reported at the time. The Biehls wrote that although they wanted to learn more about the proposed community center, "We are quite certain that Amy would not wish to be singled out for recognition in the identity of such a venture, to the exclusion of the many South Africans who struggled and died."

The Biehls did express an interest in making more connections with American educators and students. Their efforts in this regard also originated from media coverage. When ABC's "Turning Point" program on Amy first aired in April 1994, Judy Kendall, a middle school teacher in suburban St. Louis, recorded it, believing that she might use it in her teaching one day. Her daughter Tracy was student-teaching at another middle school in the St. Louis area when she was asked to teach a unit on South Africa. Tracy decided to use the program as a teaching tool in her sixth and seventh grade classes. When she asked for her students' reactions, many wrote movingly about Amy's work on behalf of others and her commitment to democracy and human rights. Tracy and Judy thought the Biehls might want to read the students' comments, so they sent them to Peter and Linda, who were highly appreciative. That began a connection between the Biehls and the Kendalls that would grow in the years ahead. The Kendalls then invited the Biehls to St. Louis to speak about Amy and the foundation at local schools. Learning that the Biehls had been invited to speak at St. Louis University in December 1996, the Kendalls arranged a speaking tour for the Biehls that would take them to six middle and high schools. The Biehls reveled in the student assemblies, at which they showed photos illustrating Amy's life and work, read from her journals, and talked about South Africa's painful past and current challenges. The programs were designed to be more than history lessons, but motivational talks on the role individuals could play in making a better world. "The students were shown that, just as Amy touched thousands of people with her strong belief in democratic values and reconciliation wherever injustices occurred, they can also be a powerful force for positive change," Tracy observed.

In the years ahead, the Biehls would return to St. Louis many times, visiting numerous schools and addressing thousands of students. Their friendship with the Kendalls blossomed in ways neither family would have imagined. After reading Mark Mathabane's best-selling memoir *Kaffir Boy* in 1997, the Kendalls decided to visit South Africa. When they contacted the Biehls for advice, the Biehls invited the family to accompany them on their upcoming trip, which they did that summer. The trip was such a rewarding experience for the Kendalls that they expanded their involvement with South Africa in the years to come, developing teacher training programs for South African schools and conducting workshops for South African teachers. The Kendalls' commitment to these workshops—and to the Amy Biehl Foundation—lasted well into the 21st century and shows no signs of stopping.

A New Jersey school also developed a special connection with the foundation. Like Tracy Kendall, a teacher at Hillsborough Middle School in Dance-Somerville, New Jersey, showed the ABC documentary to his sixth graders in the mid-1990s. Steve Schwartz then asked his class to write the Biehls about how Amy inspired them. "When I watched the movie about Amy I instantly thought, 'Wow! What a strong woman,'" one student wrote. "She did a wonderful thing by risking her life for other people." Another wrote, "It took an enormous amount of courage to go to South Africa at a time of racial strife. . . . Hopefully, many more courageous young people will continue Amy's efforts to try to change racial opinions that have existed for far too many years." Schwartz sent his students' letters to the Biehls, who, to his amazement, replied to all sixty students individually. Then one student suggested that the school hold a dance to raise money for the Amy Biehl Foundation. In May 1996, the Biehls traveled to New Jersey to attend the dance, which raised more than $1,000 for the foundation. Linda told a reporter, "I thought this is really an amazing thing coming from these kids and I think this is what Amy was all about. She loved music and dance, and we didn't get to celebrate her birthday anyway. We thought it might be a great little way to see the kids and get some personal joy for my husband and myself." The students were thrilled that the Biehls actually flew out for the event and enjoyed sampling the South African desserts and music. The next year, sixth graders at the school organized a fundraising dinner for the foundation, contacting local restaurants for food donations and asking the Biehls to speak at a student assembly. The Biehls returned for a second year in a row and then attended the dinner, at which more than $700 was raised for the foundation. These kinds of events, at which the Biehls could speak to students and interact with the public, energized them for months afterward, and they hoped to make such programs a priority for the foundation in the years ahead.

As the Biehls planned to embark on another trip to South Africa in mid-1997, they learned that the four young men convicted of Amy's death would be applying for amnesty from the country's newly established Truth and Reconciliation Commission. After all they had been through during the trials, there was now a real possibility that Amy's killers would be released from prison. Undaunted, Peter and Linda continued preparing for their departure for South Africa, determined not just to expand the Amy Biehl Foundation, but to witness the amnesty hearings—and to participate in them.

11

The Truth and Reconciliation Commission

IN 1995, the South African government passed the Promotion of National Unity and Reconciliation Act, thereby establishing the Truth and Reconciliation Commission (TRC). The commission would invite victims of apartheid-era human rights abuses to testify about their experiences and would offer conditional amnesty to the perpetrators. The basis for the TRC was the belief that South Africans had to forgive each other for past conflicts if the country was to build a better future. Without such forgiveness, racial bitterness would continue—even expand—and threaten the newly democratic nation from the start.

Mandela appointed the famous antiapartheid cleric Desmond Tutu to lead the commission. His cochair was Alex Boraine, formerly an opposition member of parliament and cofounder of the Institute for a Democratic Alternative for South Africa, a progressive think tank. Both Tutu and Boraine believed that South Africa had to come to terms with its troubled past if the fragile new nation was to survive. South Africa's legalized system of racial segregation had been abolished in 1994, but the legacy of apartheid still blighted the country's prospects. Memories of violence and mistreatment still haunted the country.

During the transition to democracy, negotiators had discussed various ways of dealing with South Africa's past. They ruled out Nuremberg-style trials that would have treated former government officials like war criminals. That option would have violated the spirit of compromise that ultimately resulted in the transfer of power. Negotiators also decided against offering former officials a general amnesty. That would have amounted to airbrushing the past and thus ignoring the suffering that apartheid caused. The TRC represented a compromise between a war crimes tribunal and a blanket amnesty. Amnesty would be considered for those who fully confessed to violating human rights. If amnesty was ultimately granted to the applicants, they could not be prosecuted for their past actions. The TRC's central role was, in Tutu's words, "to forgive rather than demand retribution." "Restorative justice" rather than "retributive justice" would be the commission's goal.

The amnesty that the commission offered was conditional. Acts for which amnesty was sought had to have been committed between 1960 and 1994; the acts must have been politically motivated; the applicants must have fully disclosed their actions; and the acts must have been "proportional" to the perpetrators' political objectives. The TRC would not just investigate human rights violations committed by the former white minority government, but by all sides, including the liberation movements, the white right, and others. Tutu and his fellow commissioners hoped that by enabling victims to testify about their suffering under apartheid and enabling perpetrators to confess, South Africans could heal the wounds of the past and forgo the desire for revenge.

The TRC considered only what it termed "gross human rights violations," such as assault, kidnapping, torture, and murder. Investigating all of the human rights violations under apartheid, such as those involving housing, education, employment, and freedom of movement, would have made the commission's work next to impossible. In its three years of major operations from 1996 to 1998, the commission would hear oral testimony from approximately 2,500 victims, consider written testimony from almost 20,000 others, and receive more than 7,000 applications for amnesty. Like Tutu himself, South Africa would become immersed in the "devastating but also exhilarating work" of the commission. But despite Tutu's unparalleled moral authority as its chairman, the commission would be a lightning rod for controversy.

Controversy began even before the TRC held its first public hearings in 1996. Some black South Africans criticized the commission for enabling perpetrators to "walk free." These early critics of the commission believed that it was fatally flawed because it would only investigate past injustices, not hold the guilty parties accountable. On the other hand, some Afrikaners felt that the commission was preparing a "witch hunt" against their people. Many Afrikaners and English-speaking white South Africans harbored serious reservations about the commission. They worried that "reopening" the wounds of the past would hurt the country's chances to unite and move forward. Members of the liberation groups also had qualms about the commission. They argued that they should not be put on the same footing as the apartheid government in the TRC's human rights investigations. Because they were fighting an unjust system, they maintained, any violations they committed in the struggle were secondary to those committed by the apartheid government.

Many of the commission's hearings would be broadcast live on South African radio and television, ensuring that a large audience would tune in to witness the country's unprecedented exercise in truth telling and soul searching. As Tutu told those assembled for the commission's first public hearing in April 1996, "We are charged to unearth the truth about our dark past; to lay the ghosts of the past so that they will not return to haunt us. And that we will thereby contribute to the healing of a traumatized and wounded people—for all of us in South Africa are wounded people—and in this manner to promote national unity and reconciliation."

The Biehls had known about the TRC from the beginning. During the first trial in mid-1994, Ambassador Lyman had told them about the pending amnesty legislation and that the young men charged with Amy's death might ultimately apply for amnesty. Justice Minister Omar had sent them a copy of the relevant legislation. At first, the Biehls were troubled that Amy's killers might eventually receive amnesty. During her August 1994 trip to Cape Town to attend the first trial, Linda planned to express her concern directly to Omar that there should be some accountability for Amy's death. Shortly after the first three accused were sentenced to prison in October 1994, their defense lawyer, Justice Poswa, said that he would seek to get his clients released once the amnesty legislation was finalized. That month, Linda again stressed the need for "accountability." "I think there has to be some sentence here that is harsh enough that people feel you just can't get away with it," she said. Neither she nor Peter thought that the young men should be granted amnesty, because they regarded Amy's death as a racial attack, not a political one. They were also troubled that the young men seemed to have no remorse.

Shortly after the TRC began its work in 1996, leaders of the PAC testified about their role in the struggle against apartheid. They also discussed their role in violence, particularly in 1993, when they had targeted white civilians. PAC leaders were not ready to take responsibility for Amy's death, but they did concede that her murder had been a mistake:

> On the Amy Biehl issue, we wish to state that PASO was not a part of
> APLA. They are a component part of the PAC and not involved in armed
> struggle. This act occurred in the context of a strike for recognition by

[the] South African Democratic Teachers' Union in the Western Cape. To support the strike, "Operation Barcelona" was launched to stop deliveries into the townships. Although the PAC was not involved, PASO acted in solidarity with their teachers and with COSAS. They wrongly targeted and killed Amy Biehl. We expressed our regret and condolences to Amy Biehl's family in a letter to the United States Ambassador. We restate this position yet again through the TRC. But misguided as the deed was, we support the amnesty applications of all those convicted and sentenced for the offence.

Despite the PAC's statement, Linda was confident that the TRC would not grant amnesty to Amy's killers. "We know people on this commission," she told the *Los Angeles Times.* "Amy worked with people on this commission. There was a lot of anger by these people over what happened. Desmond Tutu told me what happened to Amy was an aberration. My feeling is definitely that they will make an appropriate decision." She and Peter still doubted that the perpetrators were politically motivated when they attacked Amy, which was a requirement for am- nesty. "We don't feel it was a political crime," Linda said. "They were roving and they probably would have hit anyone they saw and wanted to get. I don't think politics was a really big part of their lives. I think they were thugs."

Despite their misgivings, the Biehls expected the young men to apply for am- nesty, and so when they received confirmation that the first of their applications had been filed in April 1997, they weren't surprised. At this point their attitude began to shift. As they reflected, they concluded that if they were going to remain consistent with Amy's beliefs, they needed to support the Truth Commission's mission of healing. They decided that they should no longer oppose the amnesty bid, even if they weren't going to endorse it explicitly. Linda and Peter called Arch- bishop Tutu on the day the first amnesty application came through and told him that they wanted to "support the process." They viewed the amnesty hearings as "a South African issue" and that, as Amy's parents, they should attend the hearing and let South Africans determine the outcome. Once the media was informed that Mongezi Manqina would apply for amnesty, reporters immediately contacted the Biehls for their response. "Our feeling is [that] it's their country and their process, and let the case be decided on its merits or the lack of them," Peter said. Linda expressed an interest in meeting the young men's families to see "whether they have any feelings about what the young men did." "We have come to realize that there is no logical sense for bitterness or anger," she said. As always, acting in ways that would honor Amy strengthened the Biehls for what lay ahead.

The amnesty hearing in relation to Amy's killing was originally scheduled for mid-May 1997, but the Biehls requested that it be rescheduled to coincide with their upcoming trip to South Africa in June and July. In his letter to the amnesty committee requesting the postponement, Peter revealed that he and Linda still had mixed feelings about the pending applications. As he wrote to the TRC lawyer Robin Brink, "Amy was completely devoted to a free South Africa. We have committed ourselves and our resources to your rebuilding process. Considering the personal insult represented by this application for amnesty and our public support for the amnesty process itself, we feel we are not being unreasonable in our request for notification of a hearing date." Just days after Peter wrote to Brink, the TRC agreed to move the amnesty hearing to early July. Omar not only urged the Biehls to attend the hearing, but he encouraged them to make a statement that would become part of the historical record. So did Archbishop Tutu. He urged Peter and Linda to "speak from your heart and tell them about Amy." The Biehls embraced the opportunity. "One of the reasons we want to participate in this is to dignify a process that is essential to the new South Africa and which was important to Amy," Peter said.

Some TRC officials told the Biehls that the amnesty bid wasn't likely to succeed because it didn't meet the necessary conditions. For example, the PAC hadn't ordered the young men to kill Amy (or other white people) on the day of the attack, thus casting doubt on their political motivations. Peter agreed, and also doubted whether the attack was "proportional" to the PAC's goals, another requirement for amnesty. "That's going to be a little difficult to prove since this was just the worst and most violent murder," Peter told a journalist. So even though the Biehls decided not to oppose the amnesty bid, they didn't think it would succeed. At a gut level, they were still troubled that Mongezi, the young man who stabbed Amy in the heart, could walk free, especially after expressing no remorse for what he'd done. But honoring Amy dictated their actions. "Amy would have wanted us to move forward," Linda said. Even though Peter could not yet accept that Amy's death was a political act, he understood that "it was a logical consequence of systematic denial. . . . Amy would have said, if she could have, 'I'm sorry you guys did this. I understand where it's coming from. It's the system of apartheid that has driven you to this point.'" He and Linda were concerned that if the young men were granted amnesty and released, they might seek revenge against those who identified them or engage in criminal activity in the townships. Mindful of this possibility, the Biehls thought of starting a rehabilitation program for ex-prisoners, so that such individuals could receive job training and contribute constructively to their communities.

Kim and Molly shared their parents' attitude toward the TRC, although Zach was initially more skeptical. But eventually they all agreed that the family should support the process and not specifically endorse or oppose amnesty, but allow South Africans to decide. They too felt that Amy would have wanted it this way. Scott Meinert took a different approach. While he admired the Biehls' stance and even believed "it was the right thing to do," his personal loss "still hurt me too much to participate." He drafted a statement addressed to the Truth Commission in which he strongly opposed amnesty. He believed that the amnesty bid was misguided because the applicants had brutally murdered a defenseless person who could not conceivably be termed a political target. There was no justification for killing an innocent civilian, he argued, and thus he believed the men should "serve out the remainder of their sentences."

The Biehls arrived in South Africa on June 27, 1997, accompanied by the Kendalls, the educators they had befriended in St. Louis. As the Biehls entered the terminal at Cape Town's airport, a group of women from Mosaic greeted them and sang to welcome them back to South Africa. Despite the long series of flights from California, Peter and Linda always felt energized when they touched down in South Africa. They felt closer to Amy there and connected to the sense of change and possibility in the new democracy. Unlike their past two trips, the Biehls were besieged by the media from the moment they arrived. Wherever they went, they seemed to be trailed by journalists. Although Peter knew that Amy would have been embarrassed by all the attention, he was pleased that a "committed life" was being remembered.

The day after they arrived, the Biehls met Mongezi Manqina's mother in Gugulethu. Earlier, Evelyn Manqina had contacted a journalist and expressed an interest in making a video-recorded statement addressed to the Biehls. In the statement, she tearfully lamented that the Biehls had lost their daughter "for no reason." While she would be surrounded by her family at Christmas, there would be someone missing at the Biehls' household, she said. Hearing Evelyn's emotional message, Linda wanted to give her some support. As they made their way to Gugulethu, trailed by journalists and a camera crew, the Biehls first went to the wrong house. Taking the error in stride, they proceeded next door, knocked, and out came Evelyn. They were not far from the gas station where Amy had been killed. The two mothers embraced as the camera shutters clicked. Linda told Evelyn that she and Peter had been looking forward to the meeting and that they wouldn't oppose her son's amnesty bid. The Biehls hoped he could contribute to his new country. "I looked at her and wondered what her life was like, what she felt about her son and what he'd done," Linda recalled. "I don't feel hatred.

This poor woman has to deal with her son killing Amy Biehl. I gave her a picture of our family." Deeply moved, Evelyn spoke while her niece translated: "It's the beginning of a new life for us, at our home, to be blessed with your presence here. We never knew that you would make peace with our family because we know what [my son] did to your family was very sad. But knowing those things, you've put them behind . . . now what you are encouraging is love and peace and reconciliation."

The meeting between the two families lasted an hour, and by the end the initial awkwardness had dissipated. The meeting was clearly cathartic for both sides. Mongezi's cousins were astounded by the Biehls' kindness and lack of bitterness. "This is what it's all about," Linda told reporters. "This is why Amy was over here, why we keep coming back, because of the heart and soul of the African people. And we just want the races to reconcile, for people . . . on a one-on-one relationship to make differences." Peter felt the same way. "It's liberating to forgive," he said. The Biehls' personal encounter with Evelyn had softened their attitude toward her son and his comrades even before the amnesty hearings began.

The day before the hearings commenced, Peter and Linda accepted an invitation to meet with some senior PAC leaders in Cape Town. Both sides hoped that the meeting would promote reconciliation. PAC secretary general Ngila Muendane attended, as did Johnson Mlambo, who had been commander of the PAC's armed wing when Amy was killed. During the meeting, Muendane and Mlambo told the Biehls that their young supporters had made a mistake and that Amy should not have been killed. They talked about the war the PAC was involved in, which they said was "not of our own choosing." Reaching out to hold the Biehls' hands at one point, the men praised Amy's work among women and young people. Heartened by the PAC's overture, the Biehls thought the PAC's gesture was a good first step. They also hoped that the PAC would admit that their racial sloganeering had deadly consequences. At a press conference the next day, Muendane praised the Biehls for understanding that Amy died in the context of the struggle in South Africa. "We were really humbled by their attitude," he said of the Biehls. "We are proud to have people like this. People who are of good heart, people who have reached out and said, 'Look, we understand how she died,' people without bitterness. I am sure South Africans will learn from the attitude that the Biehl family has taken."

Several high-profile amnesty hearings were scheduled in Cape Town around the same time as the Biehl hearings. One involved former security policeman Jeff Benzien, who tortured political prisoners in the 1980s and was preparing to face some of his victims. Another involved two policemen—one white and one black—who participated in the Gugulethu Seven incident in 1986, during which police lured seven antiapartheid activists into an ambush and killed them in cold blood. Still another involved APLA operatives who claimed responsibility for killing eleven people during the St. James Church attack in July 1993. As the *Cape Times* pointed out, the hearings scheduled for Cape Town would "revive memories of some of the most horrific violations of human rights in this nation's deeply divided past." The ability of the TRC to reveal the truth and promote reconciliation from these cases would be a great test for the commission. That the St. James hearing was scheduled immediately after the Biehl hearing magnified the publicity, as both incidents had shocked South Africa because of their brutality and because white civilians had been targeted. What made the Biehl hearing especially unique was that the victim and her family were outsiders, not South Africans. Domestic and international media swarmed into Cape Town to cover the hearing on Amy's death. "Like the killing itself," one journalist wrote, "this amnesty hearing has attracted national attention as a symbol of the vexing problem of reconciliation."

The Biehl hearing began on July 8, 1997, at the TRC's offices on Adderley Street in central Cape Town. The four young men applying for amnesty—Mongezi Manqina (24), Easy Nofemela (26), Vusumzi Ntamo (25), and Ntobeko Peni (23)—were brought from prison to testify. Paul Haupt served as the TRC's liaison with the Biehls, picking them up from their hotel, escorting them to the hearings, and generally walking them through the process. Privy to their emotions, Haupt marveled at how Peter and Linda grappled with their ordeal. Supreme Court judge Hassen Mall, an Indian South African, chaired the five-member amnesty committee. Joining him were judge Andrew Wilson, an English-speaking white South African; advocate Chris de Jager, an Afrikaner; and two black South Africans, judge Bernard Ngoepe and Ms. Sisi Khampepe. They sat behind an extended, judicial-looking bench, their backs to a banner that read "Truth: The Road to Reconciliation." Two lawyers represented the applicants: Norman Arendse, a mixed-race South African, and Nona Goso, who had assisted the defense during their trials. The lawyers helped the young men prepare their statements and would field questions from the amnesty committee and lawyer Robin Brink. During the reading of the statements and the cross-examinations, the young men and their lawyers wore headsets so they could hear simultaneous translations into their own languages when necessary.

As Peter and Linda entered the hearing room, they shook hands with the four men's parents. Evelyn Manqina sat behind the Biehls, clad in an Amy Biehl Foundation T-shirt that the Biehls had given her. Linda and Evelyn hugged and held each other's hands as photographers pressed forward. Archbishop Tutu, who was undergoing cancer treatment in New York at the time, later said that the gesture "sent electric shocks down your spine" because it so vividly portrayed reconciliation. The room was crowded with spectators and the press, both black and white. Rolene Miller of Mosaic attended, as did Melanie Jacobs, Amy's former housemate. Other friends and colleagues of Amy came as well. A group of PASO members sat together in one part of the room and gave the PAC salute to their four comrades as they entered the room. Linda had seen Mongezi, Easy, and Vusumzi at their trial, but this was the first time Peter encountered the young men. Both he and Linda hoped to learn what the young men's motivations were for attacking Amy. The young men didn't make eye contact with the Biehls as they took their seats. During their trial, they had denied participating in the attack on Amy. Now they were going to reveal their role in her death in the hope that they would be freed.

In many respects, this case was even more controversial than the PAC's other attacks on civilians, because Amy's murder had not been explicitly ordered by the PAC or its military wing, APLA. It was an unplanned attack by students. Amnesty was not a foregone conclusion. The committee would try to determine the extent to which the attack on Amy was "political." How politicized were the young men? Were they instructed or encouraged to attack white people on August 25, 1993? Why target Amy if she was a political ally? What was unique about that day, given that they hadn't killed whites before? How would killing Amy help PASO meet its objectives? In her opening statement, Nona Goso sought to address some of these fundamental questions. She said that the applicants would demonstrate that they met the conditions for amnesty, because they would fully disclose their actions and show that the offense for which they were convicted—the murder of Amy Biehl—was "associated with a political objective." Whether the amnesty committee would agree was an open question.

Ntobeko Peni, the youngest of the four and the last to be convicted, was the first to testify. He had initially been reluctant to appear before the TRC, believing that the ANC had "sold out" by establishing the commission in the first place. As far as he was concerned, the PAC didn't believe blacks should ever have to explain why whites were attacked. But when he heard about the Biehls' conciliatory attitude, his hostility ebbed. In his affidavit, he talked about hearing militant speakers at the relaunch of PASO at Langa High School, where he had been elected branch chairman. At the meeting, he and other PASO members were instructed to make the townships ungovernable, to target government and company vehicles, and to attack all white people who crossed their path as they were doing so. "One settler, one bullet" was the rallying cry that day. He admitted to stoning vehicles that afternoon and then joining the attack on Amy near the Caltex station in Gugulethu.

"I deeply regret the killing of Amy Biehl and I ask her parents, her relatives, and friends to forgive me," he said. He admitted under questioning that even if he'd heard Amy's fellow passengers identify her as a "comrade," it probably wouldn't have stopped him from participating in the attack, because "At the time we were in very high spirits and the white people were oppressive, we had no mercy on the white people." Later, when asked to reflect on his actions, he said this:

> I feel very sorry and down-hearted especially today realizing the contribution Amy Biehl played in the struggle. When I look closely at what I did I realize that it was bad. I took part in killing someone that we could have used to achieve our own aims. Amy was one of the people who could have, in an international sense, worked for our country. . . . I ask Amy's parents, Amy's friends and relatives, I ask them to forgive me. Just to hear that they have forgiven me would mean a great deal to me. For me it would be starting a new life. I have led an abnormal life under the struggle in South Africa. I do not think I would commit such an act again because right now the situation in South Africa is different. I ask for forgiveness and I am sorry.

Robin Brink, a hostile questioner, asked how the "killing of an unarmed, defenseless woman" would have helped advance the cause of Africans. Peni said such action would pressure the white minority to give in to African demands. Brink then asked, "Mr. Peni, isn't it [true] that on that dreadful afternoon you were involved in a mindless, savage attack on this young woman, and that it was not politically motivated at all?" "Our killing of Amy Biehl had everything to do with politics," Peni responded. In another exchange, chairman Hassen Mall suggested that the phrase "one settler, one bullet" was just a slogan used by the PAC, not a policy. But Peni said that he and his fellow students clearly understood it as an instruction on the day they attacked Amy.

Like his friend Ntobeko, Easy Nofemela had not wanted to appear before the Truth Commission and believed it was a "sell-out." "But then I read in the press that Linda and Peter had said that it was not up to them to forgive; it was up to the people of South Africa to learn to forgive each other. I decided to go and tell our story and show remorse," he said. In his affidavit, Nofemela noted that he was also a PASO organizer, had attended the PASO launch at Langa High School, and had participated in the attack on Amy. He admitted that his statement to police was not forced from him and apologized for giving that impression during the trial. He had been motivated by the militant speeches at the Langa political rally to make the townships ungovernable; the slogan "one settler, one bullet" inspired him (and others) to attack whites that day. He expressed regret for what happened to Amy and apologized for his role in Amy's death. "The deed was committed at the time when we, as PASO members, were highly politically motivated and when we were hostile towards any settler whom we regarded as any white person living in this country," he said.

In his questioning, Brink tried to suggest that the attack was racial, not political. He asked Nofemela if he would've participated in the attack on Amy had he known she was a "comrade." "Yes," Nofemela answered, because "during that time my spirit just says I must kill the whites." Brink later said, "You see what I am going to suggest to you Mr. Nofemela [is] that the attack and brutal murder of Amy Biehl could not have been done with a political objective, it was wanton brutality, like a pack of sharks smelling blood, isn't that the truth?" "No, that's not true, that's not true," Nofemela insisted. "We are not such things." He described how the youths had been further inflamed during a confrontation with police earlier that afternoon, when police shot at them after they had thrown stones at their vehicles. "What happened with the police is that they shot at us. Some of the white people who were passing by also helped the police. That made us to be very emotional, that each and every white person we met we will try and do something to that person." When Nofemela described how killing whites would "get our land back," several PASO members in the audience interjected "Yes!"

Mongezi Manqina looked down as Arendse read his statement aloud. In his affidavit, he admitted tripping Amy as she ran toward the Caltex station, asking for a knife, and then stabbing her to death. Distressed at hearing the details of what her son did, Evelyn suddenly staggered out of the hearing room. Arendse continued reading Manqina's statement. "I was highly politically motivated by the events of that day and by the climate prevailing in the township," he wrote, his language clearly reflecting advice from his legal team. "I have always been inspired by the slogan 'one settler, one bullet.'" He had believed that making the townships ungovernable involved attacking and killing white people. But he said that he regretted what he'd done and that he had "lied during the criminal trial in order to get off." "I apologize sincerely to Amy Biehl's parents, family and friends and I ask their forgiveness."

Brink asked Manqina whether there had been a specific instruction to kill white people that day. He also suggested that the order to make the townships ungovernable merely meant to destroy property, not kill whites. Manqina replied that killing whites was part of the order, because they were "oppressors." Brink then countered, "You had no mercy in your heart that day?" "No," Manqina replied. He believed at the time that killing white people would pressure the government to "respond to our grievances." Like the others, he said that he hadn't known that Amy was there helping black South Africans and he didn't hear anyone say that she was a "comrade." Brink doubted whether the killing of Amy Biehl would have ended the educational dispute at the time or forced the government to return the land to the Africans. He believed the action didn't meet the requirement of "proportionality"—whether their act could reasonably be considered to have helped the perpetrators achieve their goals. Judge Ngoepe asked about Manqina's education to reveal his likely level of political sophistication at the time. When he killed Amy, he was in the equivalent of eighth grade.

The Biehls were transfixed by the proceedings. Journalists searched for signs of visible emotion, but only reported that Linda "blinked rapidly" and Peter "stroked his cheek" as they listened to the young men. Even though they had long known how Amy died, it was still difficult to hear Manqina's testimony about how he stabbed her. As Peter listened to the testimony, he sometimes wondered whether the young men's statements reflected their actual thoughts or what they'd been told to say in order to increase their chances for amnesty. The applicants' statements of regret were virtually identical, suggesting that they were indeed coached by their legal representatives. The first day of the hearing adjourned just before 5 p.m.; the Biehls' presentation was scheduled for the next day.

Day two, July 9, opened with testimony from Vusumzi Ntamo. In his statement, Ntamo said he was a member of the PAC and supported PASO but had only the equivalent of a sixth grade education. Unlike the others, he wasn't in school at the time of the attack, but he had attended the rally at Langa High School with Manqina. He admitted to throwing stones at Amy's head at close range during the attack that claimed her life. He said he had participated in the attack in solidarity with PASO members, believing that he was helping to attack a "settler." He expressed regret for what he did and, like the others, asked Amy's parents, friends, and relatives for forgiveness.

Then it was the Biehls' turn to speak. If they were nervous, they didn't show it. "Because Amy was killed in South Africa, because our lives have now become forever linked to South Africa, we are here to share a little of Amy with you," Linda began. "Amy was a bright, active child." She then described Amy's energetic spirit and her academic interests. While she spoke, Peter showed photos of Amy to the amnesty panel and the young men. The previous day, the young men had avoided direct eye contact with the Biehls, but now they looked intently at Peter and Linda as they brought Amy to life.

Peter looked directly at the young men when he gave his statement. "We come to South Africa as Amy came, in a spirit of committed friendship, and make no mistake about it, extending a hand of friendship in a society which has been systematically polarized for decades is hard work at times," he said. "But Amy was always about friendship, about getting along, about the collective strength of caring individuals and their ability to pull together to make a difference, even to transform corrupt nation states." Later, he read from the letter Amy wrote to the *Cape Times* two months before she died: "'Racism in South Africa has been a painful experience for blacks and whites, and reconciliation may be equally painful. However, the most important vehicle toward reconciliation is open and honest dialogue.'" Peter continued: "Amy would have embraced your Truth and Reconciliation process. We are present this morning to honor it and to offer our sincere friendship. We are all here in a sense to consider and to value a committed human life which was taken without opportunity for dialogue. When this process is over, we must link arms and move forward together."

Peter concluded by affirming his and Linda's unequivocal support for the TRC, noting that, without it, the democratic elections for which Amy worked would not have occurred. He concluded:

> At the same time we say it's your process, not ours. We cannot, therefore, oppose amnesty if it is granted on the merits. In the truest sense, it is for the community of South Africa to forgive its own. . . . Amnesty is clearly not for Linda and Peter Biehl to grant.
>
> You face a challenging and extraordinarily difficult decision. How do you value a committed life? What value do you place on Amy and her legacy in South Africa? How do you exercise responsibility to the community in granting forgiveness? There are clear needs for prisoner rehabilitation, literacy training, education, and job skill training. We, as the Amy Biehl Foundation, are willing to do our part as catalysts for social progress. All anyone need do is ask.
>
> Are you, the community of South Africa, prepared to do your part?

Everyone in the room was spellbound—including the four young men applying for amnesty. Manqina later said that he was "shocked" that Amy's parents didn't oppose amnesty, given the pain involved in losing a child—"a wound that never heals." Peni was equally moved by the Biehls' presentation. When he saw a picture of Amy with Namibian president Sam Nujoma, it opened his eyes to her real contribution. The Biehls' presentation had awakened all four of the young men to Amy's commitment to southern Africa's liberation struggles.

After the applicants and the Biehls testified, Arendse urged the committee to grant amnesty. Although the killing of Amy Biehl was tragic and misguided, he argued, it was committed in the context of a political struggle. The applicants deeply regretted their actions and asked for forgiveness. "Amy Biehl's parents have said so movingly, so eloquently before us this morning that they are prepared to forgive them," he said. "Who are we not to?" In his summary, Brink argued against amnesty, saying the murder was a racist attack committed by a mob and not political. He also argued that the murder did not meet the "proportionality" threshold required for amnesty. "The murder itself was a senseless murder and cannot be said to have been committed with a political objective. It's out of all proportion, on their own evidence," he said.

The amnesty committee engaged in a back-and-forth discussion with both Arendse and Brink, probing their arguments and questioning their assumptions. The nature of this discussion showed that amnesty was not going to be granted automatically, and, if granted, it was going to be the result of careful, deliberate thought. The amnesty committee did not tip its hand about its ultimate decision. Their minds were not made up by any means.

Once the hearing ended, the young men approached the Biehls and shook their hands. They would now return to prison to await the amnesty decision, which could take another year. The Biehls spoke to the media immediately after the hearing ended. Reporters asked them if they believed their daughter's murder might have been politically motivated. "To me it is plausible that young men with these educational backgrounds and these contextual frames of reference could attend a rally and be incited to a high level," Peter replied. He now understood the young men's mindset on the day they killed Amy and admitted that South Africa was "an intensely political place" at the time. He believed that the truth had begun to emerge during the hearings and was encouraged that the young men were "genuinely sorry" for killing Amy, even though remorse wasn't required for amnesty. But he still had concerns about the young men's future conduct if amnesty was ultimately granted. "The chances are that at least two of the killers will become regarded as young lions in the black community and might kill again. That is why we spoke to their mothers—to see if they can control these boys," he said. But he emphasized that he still did not feel angry about Amy's death and believed in forgiveness.

JUST as Amy's death four years earlier had caused South Africans to reexamine their country's prospects, the Biehl amnesty hearings prompted South Africans to take a hard look at the TRC and debate its main principles. Were new truths being revealed that could help the nation heal? Was "restorative justice" preferable to "retributive justice"? What did it take for actions to be considered politically motivated? What violent acts were and were not forgivable? Why weren't more leaders stepping forward before the TRC to take responsibility for the orders they gave or the hateful slogans they popularized? Was the TRC healing or reopening old wounds? Was it ultimately helping or hurting South Africa's future prospects?

In many quarters, the Biehls were portrayed as role models of reconciliation whom the rest of South Africa should emulate. Archbishop Tutu viewed the Biehls as embodying the very spirit of reconciliation that the TRC sought to promote. Other members of the TRC appreciated the Biehls' conciliatory attitude and praised them for not opposing amnesty and recommitting themselves to South Africa's future, just as Amy had. The *Cape Times* agreed: "Only parents who have suffered similar senseless losses—and there have been far too many in South Africa—could imagine the courage and forbearance it took for Peter and Linda Biehl to sit in on the TRC hearing this week and hear firsthand, without apparent bitterness, how PAC youths tried to justify the brutal and merciless killing of their daughter Amy." The paper marveled at how the Biehls shook hands with the mother of one of the killers and hugged senior members of the PAC. "The Biehls personified the reconciliation that is so necessary if the TRC process is to work as intended," the editors wrote. Perhaps British journalist Alec Russell captured the Biehls' impact best. By saying that their daughter would have supported the TRC and by not opposing the amnesty bid, the Biehls reflected "the spirit of President Mandela himself, who has made reconciliation the hallmark of his leadership," he wrote.

Other reactions to the Biehl hearings were less celebratory and reflected concerns about the TRC and South Africa more generally. In the wake of the hearings, some observers demanded that political leaders be held more accountable for their followers' deeds. A number of columnists wondered why the PASO leaders who addressed the rally of August 25, 1993, weren't coming forward for amnesty since they had incited the young people who eventually killed Amy Biehl. The Biehl hearings also renewed criticism of racial hate speech. The *Cape Times* concluded its editorial praising the Biehls by pointing out the deadly impact of the racist slogan "one settler, one bullet." "War talk has undoubtedly contributed to this country's bloodshed . . . and this is the antithesis of reconciliation embodied by the Biehls," it said.

Some South Africans reacted angrily to the conciliatory attitude of Amy's parents. Concerned about rising crime and their future under black majority rule, they decried the amnesty hearings and the possibility that Amy's killers could be pardoned. They worried that granting amnesty would send the wrong signal, that people could commit crimes with impunity and escape accountability.

They agreed with Robin Brink, the lawyer at the hearing who opposed amnesty and viewed the young men as "simply a pack of murderers." As these and other comments show, concerns about South Africa's crime wave translated into an antiamnesty mood among many whites, especially when black perpetrators were involved. Many white South Africans felt under siege, and their rejection of amnesty and the Biehls' conciliatory attitude reflected their perceived vulnerability in the postapartheid nation.

The Biehl hearings also attracted considerable attention in the United States. Many Americans praised the Biehls' generosity of spirit. *Los Angeles Times* columnist Dana Parsons had followed the Biehls' story from the beginning and admired Peter and Linda for traveling to South Africa and preaching not revenge but reconciliation. Few could react with such humanity as the Biehls did in the face of such loss. "As if Amy Biehl didn't give her own life enough meaning," he wrote, "her parents have now gone halfway around the world and added immeasurably to it." The *Christian Science Monitor* praised the Biehls for not opposing the amnesty bid. "Peter and Linda Biehl brought mercy like Shakespeare's 'gentle rain from heaven' to a 'place beneath' that needs all it can get," the paper said. As these and other articles indicate, the Biehls were becoming international models of forgiveness, to be studied, talked about, debated, and admired in the years to come.

But, as in South Africa, there were dissenting voices in the United States. Some American conservatives expressed opposition to the amnesty bid; many even questioned the TRC itself. Others observers—not necessarily conservative—echoed South African concerns that the Biehls were attracting disproportionate attention because of their daughter's death. A caller to National Public Radio asked how Peter and Linda felt about this, given that many more black South African parents lost their children tragically but received no attention. The Biehls welcomed the question, which did not offend them in the least. Amy would have agreed that disproportionate attention to white deaths was wrong, they said, but the fact that she was an American with a fairly high profile made press coverage inevitable. They speculated that the overcoverage of Amy ultimately had a beneficial effect in that it energized the peace movement in South Africa.

The Biehl case was one of many TRC hearings to attract widespread publicity. Others transfixing South Africa included those relating to the Cradock Four, the Trust Feed massacre, the death of Steve Biko, the activities of security policemen such as Craig Williamson and Jeff Benzien, and the role of Winnie Mandela and her notorious "Mandela Football Club." Immediately following the Biehl hearings, the St. James hearings magnified the attention on the PAC and its tactics. Like the four who killed Amy Biehl, the St. James amnesty applicants apologized for the attack, although they explained that it had been part of their fight against continued white minority rule. But, unlike the death of Amy, the St. James attack was officially planned and authorized by APLA. Dawie Ackerman, whose wife was killed at the church, originally planned to oppose the killers' amnesty application. But when the killers expressed remorse and said that conditions in South Africa at the time made them do what they did, Ackerman withdrew his objections. He told the amnesty committee that he held no personal grudge toward the men who killed his wife and that he'd come to realize the extent of the suffering inflicted on black South Africans during apartheid. He said that he forgave the men for the hurt they caused him, but not for the sin they committed. A few others who lost loved ones in the attack or were seriously injured also expressed qualified forgiveness.

Forgiveness, when it came, took different forms at the TRC. Some who lost family members or were injured in attacks by liberation organizations forgave the perpetrators after attending the TRC hearings, listening to the applicants' testimony, and reflecting on the damage done by apartheid. Black South Africans also sometimes forgave those who had inflicted damage on them on behalf of the white minority government or right-wing extremists. Nelson Papuyana, whose son was killed by whites seeking to disrupt the 1994 elections, accepted the killers' plea for forgiveness and comforted them. Babalwa Mhlauli, whose activist father was killed by security police in the Eastern Cape in the 1980s, expressed her willingness to forgive the perpetrators if they stepped forward to admit what they'd done. At the hearing on the 1992 Bisho massacre, the mostly black audience broke into applause once the officers responsible for the shooting admitted what they'd done and apologized. Needless to say, the Biehls weren't the only ones to be magnanimous during the TRC hearings.

But many victims were less forgiving. Roland Palm could not forgive those who sought amnesty for the Heidelberg Tavern attack in which his daughter was killed. Fort Calata's widow rejected the apology of the white policeman who sought amnesty in her husband's murder. The family of slain Black Consciousness leader Steve Biko opposed amnesty for the security police who beat him to death. Some of the mothers of the Gugulethu Seven angrily confronted the black South African policeman who had collaborated with his white colleagues and lured his own people into a death trap. Others who refused to forgive or support amnesty might have been glad to see the perpetrators come forward and admit their deeds, but they believed those perpetrators had to stand trial and be held accountable for their crimes. Others were troubled that relatively few of the perpetrators of apartheid testified and thus never had to account for their actions.

In some hearings, victims and victims' relatives could directly address the perpetrators, creating difficult and emotional scenes. The degree of remorse the applicants expressed varied. One study concluded that most victims and their families opposed amnesty applications filed by their perpetrators and most perpetrators "offered little remorse." Even though the young men involved in the Biehl and St. James attacks apologized, the degree of remorse expressed by PAC supporters varied. During a TRC hearing on armed forces in October 1997, the high-ranking APLA leader Dan Mofokeng refused to apologize for APLA's attacks on "soft targets" (specifically St. James, King William's Town golf club, and Heidelberg Tavern). "The leadership of APLA takes full responsibility for these operations; we do not regret that such operations did take place, and there is nothing to apologize for." He did not specifically address the Biehl murder, which was not explicitly authorized by APLA. APLA's director of operations, Letlapa Mphahlele, was initially much less conciliatory than his foot soldiers who applied for amnesty. He too refused to express regret for attacks on unarmed white civilians and said that APLA had nothing to apologize for. He opposed the establishment of the TRC, believing it was mainly designed to protect white interests. Later, however, Mphahlele publicly reconciled with the mother of one of those killed in the 1993 Heidelberg Tavern attack, which he had authorized.

Immediately following the Biehl hearing, a public debate arose regarding the PAC's actions during the liberation struggle. PAC secretary general Ngila Muendane, who had been among the PAC leaders who met Peter and Linda, reiterated that the killing of Amy Biehl had been a mistake. He said it had occurred during a time of unrest at a place where antiwhite feeling was high. He said that Amy's death had not benefited the liberation struggle and that she had not been a "legitimate, designated, or a priority target." He also admitted that the attacks on the St. James Church and the King William's Town golf club were errors, because APLA operatives mistakenly thought military personnel would be there.

But others in the PAC were still disturbed that the controversial actions of the liberation movements had allegedly received undue attention, as if both they and the apartheid government were equally culpable for past actions. Motsoko Pheko, the deputy president of the PAC, wrote a column in the *Sowetan* criticizing press coverage of the Biehl and St. James amnesty hearings. He argued that the press had made the amnesty applicants seem like criminals, when they were fighting a just war against brutal apartheid repression. Although Pheko admitted that the Biehl and St. James "incidents" were "regrettable," he believed the attacks needed to be seen in the context of the wider struggle against apartheid. It was "immoral to blame the victims of apartheid for the manner in which they responded in self-defense and to liberate themselves," he argued. Pheko continued:

> Those who blame the PAC for the regrettable loss of life which resulted from some operations of its fighters must not forget that more Africans were killed in massacres such as Sharpeville, Langa, Carletonville, Soweto, Sebokeng and Boipatong. The PAC is grateful to the parents of Amy Biehl. They have shown more understanding towards the PAC than the hypocrites who want to pile the sins of apartheid on the PAC and expect the youth of this country to have shown more maturity than the adult perpetrators of the massacres of the African people.

A columnist for the *Star* criticized Pheko for suggesting that because the liberation movement was fighting a just war, all of its actions were justifiable, even if some were "mistakes." Robert Brand believed that even in a just war, there can be unjust actions, and, according to international law, the killing of innocent civilians was unjust and therefore worthy of censure. He argued that the attacks on Biehl and the St. James Church were unjust and criminal, even if the PAC's larger struggle against apartheid was justifiable. Even those who accepted the armed struggle should condemn attacks on innocent civilians, he wrote. "People responsible for atrocities on either side of the apartheid struggle should accept . . . responsibility, and not hide behind concepts such as just war," he continued. "In plain language, they should be able to say: I was wrong, although I believe my cause was just." Once again, reactions to Amy Biehl had become a national conversation that cast South Africa's fault lines into sharp relief.

The hearings had been emotionally draining for the Biehls. Not only had they been the center of media attention, but they had had to confront again the pain of Amy's death, hearing in excruciating detail how she died. But their spirits were bolstered by their foundation, which they believed would continue to grow in the years ahead. They were also heartened by the welcome they received in the country, especially in the townships, where people thanked them for coming to South Africa and contributing to the country's future. Even though many South Africans walked up to them and thanked them for coming, others "think we're probably crazy," Linda admitted. South Africans often asked them "how they were coping," which touched Linda and Peter immensely. "People in South Africa will come right up to you and they'll just take your hand and they'll look at you straight in the eye and they'll say 'thank you—thank you for coming, thank you for returning to our country; thank you for the gift of your daughter,'" Peter said.

Not all of Peter and Linda's activities in Cape Town involved the Truth Commission. The couple attended an event marking Mandela's 79th birthday, at which Peter met the great man for the first time. Linda and Peter also attended a lecture by the Chilean human rights activist Ariel Dorfman. In the question-and-answer session, Peter asked Dorfman to comment on the notion of "closure," about which the Biehls were often asked. Dorfman said that a form of closure is sometimes reached when a perpetrator asks for forgiveness and repents. But he admitted that closure couldn't return a lost loved one and that the TRC itself could not offer closure. "Each person will find his own form of closure," Dorfman said. "Closure is both satisfactory—it's a haven—but closure also means to close, and close is the opposite of life." The Biehls themselves would not strive for closure, for that would mean putting Amy behind them; on the contrary, they found fulfillment by keeping her spirit alive. As Peter would later explain, "We have never sought closure and have no desire to close the book on Amy."

12

Amnesty

ON JULY 28, 1998, a year after the Biehl hearings, the Truth and Reconciliation Commission (TRC) announced its decision: it would grant amnesty to the young men who had killed Amy Biehl. The amnesty committee's decision was unanimous. In its official statement, the committee briefly reviewed the circumstances of Amy's death and the applicants' statements before explaining its decision.

> Although they did not act on the orders or instructions of APLA or [the] PAC on that day, they believed they owed loyalty to the same cause.
> . . . As members of PASO, which was a known political organization of students, they were active supporters of the PAC and subscribed to its political philosophy and its policies. By stoning company delivery vehicles and thereby making it difficult for deliveries into the townships, they were taking part in a political disturbance and contributing towards making their area ungovernable. To that extent, their activities were aimed at supporting the liberation struggle against the State. But Amy Biehl was a private citizen, and the question is why was she killed during this disturbance. Part of the answer may be that her attackers were so aroused and incited, that they lost control of themselves and got caught up in a frenzy of violence. One of the applicants said during his evidence that they all submitted to the slogan of ONE SETTLER, ONE BULLET. To them that meant that every white person was an enemy of the Black people. At that moment to them, Amy Biehl was a representative of the white

community. They believed that by killing civilian whites, APLA was sending a serious political message to the government of the day. By intensifying such activity the political pressure on the government would increase to such an extent that it would demoralize them and compel them to hand over political power to the majority of the people of South Africa. When the conduct of the applicants is viewed in this light, it must be accepted that their crime was related to a political objective.

The committee then quoted from Peter Biehl's statement at the hearings, in which he spoke of the family's respect for the TRC process and their decision not to oppose amnesty "if it was granted on the merits." Finally, the committee found that the applicants had fully disclosed the relevant facts in the case. For these reasons, it concluded that amnesty was justified.

The committee sensed that its decision would be controversial, especially its finding that the murder was politically motivated. Committee member Chris de Jager hinted at his own inner doubts in the addendum he attached to the decision. In it, he wrote that although the PAC hadn't issued an order to murder Amy Biehl—and it was never the PAC's policy to kill foreigners in South Africa—the murder "was associated with a political objective." The question of political motivation had long been the sticking point for many observers. Yes, the youths were supporters of a political organization and had just attended a political rally. But they had not been instructed to kill Amy Biehl. Not only did Biehl not represent the white minority government or the security forces, she was a "comrade," as her fellow passengers had told the mob. Anticipating the controversy to come, the committee issued a press release stating that "the decision was a unanimous one of the five longest-serving members of the Amnesty Committee." No other press release from the committee had been worded this way. But if it hoped to defuse criticism with such a statement, it was bound to be disappointed.

The Biehls' magnanimous statement at the hearings and their decision not to oppose amnesty clearly influenced the amnesty decision. Archbishop Tutu, chairman of the TRC, said as much several years later. He was not on the amnesty committee, but he followed the Biehl case closely. He called Amy's murder "an outrageous atrocity, particularly because it was against someone who was on the side of the crazy bunch of young people. She more than anybody else would've understood their cries." Biehl's parents should have been embittered, "but they were quite extraordinary." As relatives of a victim, the Biehls could say whether they supported amnesty, "and this would count significantly in whether the perpetrators would be granted amnesty." The Biehls' public statements had been generous and understanding toward the young men, and this reflected the spirit of national reconciliation that the TRC wanted to promote. As one scholar of the Truth Commission put it, "granting amnesty to the killers of Amy Biehl was a public relations coup which the TRC could not afford to pass by." Had the Biehls opposed amnesty, the outcome might have been different.

Manqina, Nofemela, Ntamo, and Peni were released from prison on the day the decision was announced. Journalists flocked to Brandvlei Prison, 70 miles (113 kilometers) from Cape Town, to film Manqina's release and get a statement. "I want to say that I am sorry to Amy Biehl's family for what I have caused to their daughter," Manqina told reporters as he left the prison grounds. "I know how much they love their daughter, like any parents who love their sons or daughters." His mother Evelyn was outside the gates to greet him. "As a mother, I am very happy, but on the other side I am not happy," she said. "I feel the pain of Mrs. Biehl. I am not glad because of what my child has done." The other three young men were released from a prison in Malmesbury, near Cape Town.

Peter and Linda were notified of the amnesty decision at 1 a.m. California time on July 28, only a day after they had returned from their latest trip to Cape Town. They had expected that amnesty would be granted and so were relatively prepared when the decision was announced. But as they watched news footage of the young men being welcomed by their families, they couldn't help pondering that Amy wasn't around to receive such a welcome or to return home. The Biehls released a statement to the press that morning: "In the cases of the four amnesty applicants in Amy's murder, we hope they will receive the support necessary to live productive lives in a non-violent atmosphere. In fact, we hope the spirits of Amy and of those like her will be a force in their new lives. . . . Amy was drawn to South Africa as a student and she admired the vision of Nelson Mandela of a 'Rainbow Nation.' It is this vision of forgiveness and reconciliation that we have honored."

The Biehls publicly supported the TRC process because they believed Amy would have done so, but they didn't envision befriending the young men who ended her life. "Are we going to rush across a crowded room and embrace these men? No. No," Peter said. Yet he and Linda hoped they would be able to turn their lives around. "We hope for better results in the lives of Amy's forgiven attackers," the Biehls told supporters of their foundation weeks later. "They have referred to Amy as a struggle 'hero.' We hope they will honor her with their life examples, this second time around." The more people expressed amazement at the Biehls' willingness to forgive, the more comfortable the Biehls felt about it. Peter expressed the couple's sentiments this way: "To us, forgiveness is opening the door to a full and productive life. We can honor Amy, be true to her convictions, and can carry on with her work and ours. Forgiving is liberating. By contrast, it seems to us that hatred consumes tremendous energy—negative energy—and robs people of their productivity. Hatred, in the end, is a totally selfish behavior."

The amnesty decision brought almost as much media attention to the Biehls as Amy's death had five years earlier. Within a half hour of being notified of the decision, their telephone began ringing nonstop as journalists called to get their reaction. The media crush continued all day, only ending when the last camera crew left their house at 7:30 p.m. that night. The Biehls did a live telephone interview with CNN the next morning before catching a flight to New York for an appearance on ABC's *Good Morning, America* on July 30. Unrelenting as it was, Peter and Linda welcomed the press coverage because it gave them the opportunity not only to explain their attitude toward amnesty but to discuss their efforts to continue Amy's work. When journalists inevitably asked if amnesty brought the Biehls closure, they would respond that they weren't seeking closure, because that would mean the end of Amy's legacy.

The amnesty decision made headlines in South Africa and was one of the most highly publicized stories of the entire TRC process. In most of the articles published on the decision, the Biehls' magnanimous response took center stage. In one column, published in both Cape Town (*Cape Argus*) and Johannesburg (*Star*), John Yeld called the Biehls "an inspiration for all South Africans committed to reconciliation." Not only did they refuse to condemn those who killed their daughter, "they expressed a level of understanding and a willingness to reconcile that almost defied belief." Instead of wallowing in grief or anger, they dedicated themselves to their daughter's vision of a better South Africa and set up a foundation to help the very communities that produced their daughter's killers. Despite not being South Africans, the Biehls were "making an extraordinary contribution to our society. South Africans could hardly wish for a better example."

Other South Africans expressed their admiration for the Biehls in the days ahead. Author Sindiwe Magona, who knew Manqina's mother Evelyn, wrote a column for the *New York Times* shortly after the amnesty decision was announced. She noted that all South Africans bore some responsibility for Amy Biehl's death because they had allowed racial hatred to flourish. But "in a remarkable show of compassion," Amy's parents supported the TRC's decision to free her killers and hoped the young men would receive the support they needed to live productive, nonviolent lives. Magona urged South Africans to follow the Biehls' example and move past hatred and violence as they strove to build on "the miracle of 1994." The Biehls' statements strengthened the respect some Gugulethu residents felt toward the family and their foundation. "If [the young men] hadn't been released, we would have faced problems," said Sophia Benge, a Gugulethu resident who ran an after-school program supported by the foundation. "But now, with this sacrifice, there will only be gain. Support for Amy Biehl is everywhere." Benge greatly admired the Biehls for expressing forgiveness and believed that by doing so, they ensured that Amy would symbolize reconciliation rather than racial hatred.

But many South Africans were deeply troubled by the amnesty decision. In fact, judging from the South African press, the Biehl decision was among the TRC's most controversial actions. Some South Africans who had been hostile to the Truth Commission from the start cited the decision as further evidence that the commission was inherently flawed. Other South Africans supported the TRC in general but opposed the Biehl decision—and the amnesties granted to others who killed innocent civilians. The prominent, progressive Afrikaner journalist Rian Malan, author of *My Traitor's Heart,* wrote a column for the London *Sunday Telegraph* in which he cited the Biehl decision as a prime example of the flaws of the TRC. Not only was the commission biased in favor of the liberation movements, he wrote, but it had created more racial tension than it eased. He admitted that the Biehls' effort to promote forgiveness and build bridges with disadvantaged communities "was precisely the spirit of reconciliation that the TRC was hoping to foster, but it left many South Africans shaking their heads." He argued that the Biehls' conciliatory spirit was the exception rather than the rule and that "South Africa's bid to bury its past [was ending] with few truths and little reconciliation."

Discomfort with the Biehl amnesty decision was not restricted to Afrikaners. Rhoda Kadalie was also appalled. Her outspoken criticisms received widespread publicity, partly because she knew Amy, but also because she was a leading public intellectual and a former member of the South African Human Rights Commission (1995–97). While Kadalie didn't oppose the principle of amnesty and believed that some targets could be justified in the liberation struggle, she argued that amnesty should not have been granted to those who killed innocent civilians. "Targeting a military installation is one thing," she said. "Attacking a church, or a bar, or dragging an innocent woman out of her vehicle, that crosses a sacred boundary. The truth commission's decisions have been disturbing and irresponsible."

Other South Africans who knew Amy also expressed reservations. Kader Asmal, a minister in Mandela's government, had known Amy when he was law professor at UWC in the early 1990s. Although he supported the TRC, he was "a bit baffled" by its decision to grant amnesty in the Biehl case. He viewed Amy's murder as "a crude and vulgar" act and not necessarily politically motivated. But he greatly admired Amy's parents, whose "generosity and magnanimity surpasses that of ordinary mortals." Amy's friend Maletsatsi Maceba also found it difficult to accept the amnesty decision, but she believed that Amy would have forgiven the youths who attacked her because she knew the conditions under which they lived. Amy's housemate Melanie Jacobs expressed dismay over the decision, although she had expected it. She told reporters that she hoped the freed young men wouldn't kill again.

A July 1998 poll revealed that approximately two-thirds of South African urban dwellers believed that the TRC's hearings had worsened race relations in the country. According to the same poll, almost 70 percent of whites doubted that the TRC would help South Africans live harmoniously with each other. Some South Africans welcomed the truths the TRC had revealed about past human rights violations, but the commission triggered a divisive, often angry debate about whether justice was served by pardoning the perpetrators of these abuses.

Concerned that recent amnesty decisions were increasing hostility toward the TRC, Archbishop Tutu issued a series of statements to counter the trend. Responding to critics who charged that the commission had worsened race relations, he highlighted the instances of reconciliation that the commission had witnessed. "When you take specific cases like that of Amy Biehl—in whose name the Amy Biehl Foundation was formed to promote reconciliation as a result of the work of the TRC—you see a magnanimity that her parents had displayed in forgiving her killers," he told reporters. He was disappointed too that many white South Africans didn't appreciate the magnanimity shown by many victims of apartheid, who just wanted their pain acknowledged.

Pumla Gobodo-Madikizela, one of Tutu's colleagues on the Truth Commission, felt the same way. Gobodo-Madikizela, a clinical psychologist, was a member of the TRC's human rights violations committee. Once the commission concluded its work, she wrote *A Human Being Died That Night: A South African Story of Forgiveness,* which focused on the notorious security policeman Eugene de Kock, who had systematically murdered antiapartheid activists on behalf of the white minority regime. Gobodo-Madikizela explored whether despite his atrocities, De Kock—and, by extension, other perpetrators of human rights violations—could be forgiven for his actions. Like Archbishop Tutu, she pointed to the Biehls as embodying the spirit of forgiveness: "Stories of forgiveness from the victims of human rights abuses, like that of Amy Biehl's parents, Peter and Linda Biehl, are significant not only because they mark some of the most memorable moments and moral achievements in the life of the TRC hearings, but also, even more important, because they translate the forgiveness model from high-minded homily to actual practice." Gobodo-Madikizela viewed the Biehls as role models, not only for South Africans, but for the wider world. They demonstrated that "it is within the grasp of ordinary people to forgive evil and end the generational cycles of violence."

Tutu's and Gobodo-Madikizela's thinking was reflected in the wording of the TRC's final report, issued in 2003, which highlighted the Biehls' generosity of spirit. "The Amy Biehl incident provided the Commission with an extraordinary example of reconciliation," the report noted. Understandably, the TRC viewed the Biehl case as validating its work. But as the heated public debate surrounding the amnesty decision showed, the reality was more complex. Reactions to the Biehl case highlighted the country's persistent racial divisions as much as they did the potential for racial reconciliation.

One former security policeman based in Port Elizabeth was inspired to seek forgiveness by the Biehls' example. Gideon Nieuwoudt had been implicated in the deaths of several prominent antiapartheid activists, including the Black Consciousness leader Steve Biko (1977). When he heard about the Biehls forgiving the men who killed their daughter, he hoped the family of Siphiwo Mtimkulu, whom he helped kill in 1982, would be equally forgiving. Accompanied by a press crew, Nieuwoudt went to the home of the Mtimkulu family to ask for forgiveness in early August 1998. When he arrived and identified himself, Mtimkulu's son struck him on the head with a vase, fracturing his skull. Mtimkulu's family was not ready to forgive Nieuwoudt for killing their husband and father and believed he had lied about the murder when he appeared before the TRC. "Nieuwoudt said he was disappointed by the course of events," a newspaper later reported. "He had hoped for forgiveness as Amy Biehl's parents had forgiven her murders." Nieuwoudt, it seems, had failed to consider the different contexts of his victim's murder and Amy Biehl's. Siphiwo Mtimkulu was deliberately poisoned, paralyzed, and then killed by foot soldiers of the apartheid regime, which made his murder harder to forgive, at least in the eyes of his family. In 2000 Nieuwoudt was granted amnesty for Siphiwo Mtimkulu's death, although his amnesty application for Steve Biko's death was unsuccessful. He died of cancer five years later at the age of 54.

THE granting of amnesty to Amy's killers was widely reported in the American press. The stories often highlighted the Biehls' response—their extraordinary forgiveness and their full-time commitment to South Africa. Some journalists saw symbolism in the Biehls' story and called the family's reaction "emblematic of a country trying to heal." Others captured the disbelief many felt when they learned about the Biehls' attitude. One reporter suggested that the Biehls had become "an object of curiosity, and at times, downright bafflement" for having not only forgiven their daughter's killers but accepting their release from prison. The Biehls' attitude did indeed amaze many Americans.

Some of the many Americans who admired the Biehls viewed their story from a religious perspective. A reader of the *Los Angeles Times* praised the Biehls, "who, through the miracle of forgiveness, are bringing life from a tragic death." He noted that while the Biehls' attitude wasn't necessarily shaped by "a religious instinct," he wished "that many of the intolerant 'Christians' we see strutting about the country" would emulate the Biehls, who truly embodied the teachings of Jesus. Donald W. Shriver Jr., an emeritus professor of applied Christianity at Union Theological Seminary in New York, praised the Biehls in an article in *Christian Century*. In a country (the United States) where family members of murdered loved ones often called for the death penalty, he wrote, the Biehls took another path: "They responded to the murder of their loved [one] with sensitivity and a concern for the broader social good. . . . The Biehls have put the building of a new just nation above their understandable desire to see their daughter's murderers punished." Their attitude offered hope that South Africa and the larger world could build a better, more peaceful future, he wrote.

But as the nation's newspapers showed, many Americans questioned the Biehl amnesty decision. The *Wall Street Journal* condemned it, writing that "the unprovoked murder of a defenseless woman is always and everywhere wrong," and charging that the release of Biehl's killers set a dangerous precedent for South Africa's legal order. A Los Angeles area resident praised the Biehls for raising a daughter who wanted to help end apartheid but castigated them for forgiving those who killed her. "That they now 'forgive' and 'understand' the racist African thugs who savagely stoned, stabbed, and beat their lovely young daughter to death, solely because she was a white European American, is not commendable," he wrote. "Rather, it is as reprehensible as it is incomprehensible." A contributor to a neo-Nazi website innocuously titled "Free Speech" criticized the Biehls as well. Not only was Amy misguided to work on behalf of black South Africans in the first place, he wrote, but by accepting amnesty for their daughter's killers, her parents showed a blatant disregard for other white women in South Africa, who were allegedly in danger because "these sadistic Black murderers" had been freed. The author made no attempt to disguise his blatantly antiblack, anti-Semitic views in his September 1998 internet post. Although his reaction was relatively unusual in its sheer toxicity, it didn't mark the first time—or the last—that right-wing, white supremacist groups tried to use Amy's story to spread their message of hate.

Legal scholars would also scrutinize the Biehl amnesty decision in years to come. In his study of the TRC published in 2001, law professor Richard A. Wilson closely examined the Biehl case and questioned whether the perpetrators could realistically be labeled "politically motivated." Anurima Bhargava put forth similar arguments in an article published in the *Columbia Law Review* a year later. As these and other writings show, it wasn't just right-wing whites who objected to the decision; there were genuine grounds for debate among those who approached the issue objectively.

Other amnesty decisions triggered heated public debates as well. When the killers of Chris Hani were denied amnesty in 1999, some criticized the amnesty committee for denying that Hani's killers were politically motivated. "Was not Hani—the former military leader of a revolutionary party contending for political power by force of arms—a more 'legitimate target' than the young and idealistic Amy Biehl?" the *Mail & Guardian* asked. Other amnesty decisions generated controversy in cases where civilians had been targeted. The decision to grant amnesty to those who attacked the St. James Church raised an outcry, as some asked how people worshipping at a church could be considered legitimate political targets. Even though the TRC granted amnesty to PAC supporters for the attacks on Amy Biehl, the St. James Church, and the Heidelberg Tavern, its final report called the crimes "heinous" and a violation of international law and the Geneva Conventions. Also controversial were amnesty decisions in favor of whites who had attacked black civilians. Brian Mitchell, the white police officer responsible for the deaths of eleven black civilians, received amnesty, as did two white members of the Afrikaner Resistance Movement who murdered a black motorist. But despite criticisms of specific amnesty decisions, amnesty was far from automatic. Of the 7,127 applications it received, the TRC ultimately granted amnesty in only 1,146 cases.

The Biehls' story became one of several legendary examples of reconciliation to which journalists pointed when discussing the Truth Commission. An air force officer blinded by the 1983 Pretoria bombing publicly shook hands with the ANC operative who organized the attack; Beth Savage forgave the PAC attackers who seriously injured her when they bombed the King William's Town golf club; and some of the mothers of the Gugulethu Seven forgave two of the policemen who murdered their sons. But despite some "striking examples of reconciliation" to which the TRC could point as it completed its work, racial harmony was still a long way off in South Africa. Archbishop Tutu understood this and insisted that reconciliation was a process, not an event. "Reconciliation is not going to be cheap or easy," he wrote in the *Cape Times* on August 4, 1998. "It is a national project requiring the participation of every single South African. . . . The TRC has helped lay the foundation for true reconciliation—it has unearthed a great deal of the truth. The rest is up to each one of us."

13

Mr. and Mrs. Amy Biehl

BY THE late 1990s, the euphoria surrounding South Africa's first democratic election had dissipated. Although the black majority had gained full political rights in the new democracy, social and economic equality was still a distant dream for most of the country's citizens. In an address to the UN General Assembly in 1994, five months after taking office as president, Nelson Mandela acknowledged that South Africa's transformation was incomplete while so many were still mired in poverty. "The success of South Africa's democracy depends on our ability to change the material conditions of our people so that they not only have the vote, but bread and work as well," he said. After Mandela's government took office, foreign investment in South Africa increased modestly, but not at the rate needed to dent the country's high unemployment rate. By the late 1990s, the economy was heading in the wrong direction. GDP growth declined, the value of the rand dropped, unemployment rose, and emigration among professionals increased, leaving South Africa with a shortage of skills needed for a healthy economy. The country's black unemployment rate was staggeringly high—almost 40 percent in the mid-1990s—exacerbating poverty. A 1998 report noted that 61 percent of black South Africans lived below the poverty line.

The antiapartheid struggle may have been over, but the struggle to create a stable new nation had only just begun, as the Biehls knew only too well. Poverty, unemployment, crime, and poor education threatened South Africa's fragile new democracy, and these problems seriously blighted Cape Town's impoverished black townships. During her summer break at Stanford in mid-1998, Solange

Jacobs spent several months back home in Cape Town and painted a sobering picture of life in the city's black townships: "Violence is at a ridiculous high; children are running around the streets with guns; it seems the number of street children has doubled; gangsters are running the townships; schools have become war zones due to gang activity. I went to church in Gugulethu on the first Sunday morning and cried as I watched the beautiful kids who have nothing, and without some kind of miraculous intervention will never have anything."

"Blown away" by the tremendous need, the Biehls began exploring how they could expand their humanitarian work in Cape Town. They envisioned developing a set of programs for township youths that would provide constructive activities to counter boredom and prevent violence. They learned that the typical school day ended in the early afternoon, but because most black parents worked outside the home, youths were left unsupervised and on the streets. Determined to address the root causes of township violence, Peter and Linda began discussing ways they could expand the Amy Biehl Foundation. In an effort to identify new sources of funding, Peter and Linda traveled to Washington, D.C., during the spring of 1997 and spoke to staff members at NDI, the State Department, and the United States Agency for International Development (USAID). In a fortunate twist of fate, Brian Attwood, the head of NDI during Amy's tenure there, had become the director for USAID. Attwood was enthusiastic about the Biehls' expansion proposals and encouraged them to work with the USAID staff in South Africa to iron out the details. In order to receive USAID funding, the Biehls would have to create a South Africa–based organization to carry out the foundation's work. Although Attwood worried that the Biehls lacked social-work experience, the potential symbolic value of having them run an antiviolence program in South Africa attracted him.

Peter and Linda spent months drawing up a proposal. They spoke to a wide range of South Africans about the needs facing Cape Town's black townships, from minister of health Nkosazana Dlamini-Zuma to community leaders and ordinary residents of Gugulethu. Shortly after the TRC hearings in July 1997, Peter discussed the establishment of the Amy Biehl Foundation in South Africa with USAID officials in Cape Town. He and Linda wanted to focus on youths aged 10 to 15 who lived in "historically disadvantaged communities" in and around Cape Town. If they could provide constructive after-school activities for this age group, they reasoned, they could help stem the rising tide of crime and violence that threatened to cripple the next generation. Peter and Linda dove into their fact-finding mission with gusto and submitted a proposal. On September 19, 1997, USAID and the newly formed Amy Biehl Foundation Trust signed an agreement titled "Weaving a Barrier against Violence." USAID awarded the new charitable trust $440,000 for its violence prevention program, with the understanding that funding would last one year and that the trust would continue to raise funds from other sources. While the United States–based Amy Biehl Foundation would continue to exist, it would henceforth serve as a "conduit" for Americans to support the programs of the South African–based trust. The Biehls' commitment to South Africa had just risen to another level.

Peter and Linda realized that, as outsiders, they couldn't change South Africa on their own, but they believed they could contribute to positive change. They set up an office in Rondebosch, a suburb of Cape Town, and hired Sheila Roquitte as the trust's first program director. Roquitte, an American, would take time off from her studies at Princeton's Wilson School of Public and International Affairs to help get the organization started. Peter and Linda also sought professional advice from an American-trained psychologist who grew up in Gugulethu and who held workshops in which township youths discussed what would improve their lives and prospects. They established an advisory board that included Rhoda Kadalie, one of Amy's mentors and a member of South Africa's Human Rights Commission; former ambassador Princeton Lyman, who was now assistant secretary of state for International Organizational Affairs; and other experts in the fields of mental health, substance abuse, and violence prevention. Most important to the Biehls was listening to township dwellers themselves. In late 1997, they frequently visited townships to talk with residents and even spoke with gang members in Manenberg, a notoriously crime-ridden township on the Cape Flats. The next day, Peter and Linda visited Pollsmoor Prison and were appalled to see children in overcrowded cells. These experiences opened the Biehls' eyes to South Africa's problems in ways they hadn't thought about before.

The Biehls chose to fund programs based on the personal relationships they established with township residents, rather than on formal grant proposals submitted by strangers. Their relationships were the product of extensive time spent in the townships meeting, listening, and talking about community needs. "We're very good listeners," Peter told a reporter. "We basically let the community people inspire our programs. We let the community cook it up, and we work with them to develop the logistics and make it happen." He and Linda didn't want to simply "throw money" at the poor; they supported projects that the local people wanted, projects that ideally would create jobs and help the foundation generate its own income. They hoped that their actions would honor Amy's memory. As Linda said, "I know Amy would be thrilled to see what we are doing . . . I can just see her delighted surprise and hear her voice: 'Mom! What in the world are you doing now?'"

Three months after the paperwork was signed, the Amy Biehl Foundation Trust was publicly launched at St. Gabriel's Church in Gugulethu on December 13, 1997. Before the event was planned, Peter and Linda had expected to be at home in the United States, but their plans changed thanks to Secretary of State Madeleine Albright. Albright was in the midst of a seven-nation tour of Africa that month and planned to stop in South Africa to meet with Mandela and his deputy president, Thabo Mbeki. When Albright floated the idea of attending an official launch of the trust, the Biehls quickly packed and flew to Cape Town to welcome her. Joining them at St. Gabriel's for the event were Father Basil van Rensburg, Dullah Omar, Rhoda Kadalie, US ambassador to South Africa James Joseph, South African ambassador to the United States Franklin Sonn, and a host of community leaders and residents. When one speaker criticized the United States for not doing enough to help South Africa, Albright responded, "We are often criticized for not doing enough, but let me remind you that in Amy Biehl we gave you our best. And in her parents, Linda and Peter Biehl, we continue to give our best." After her remarks, she hugged the Biehls and joined them in a joyous rendition of the "Madiba shuffle" as a local dance troupe performed.

The jubilation of the launch soon gave way to reality. Beginning the real work of the trust would not be easy for the Biehls. Peter in particular became frustrated by the time it took to get things done in South Africa. It took approximately three weeks to get a phone line, a fax, and a computer for the trust's new office. In the words of Paul Haupt, one of the Biehls' liaisons at the TRC, Peter was a "corporate American male used to getting things done yesterday." There were other hoops to jump through. When the Biehls tried to bring in musical instruments and athletic equipment to distribute in the townships in 1997, the goods were confiscated by South African customs officials because the Biehls had not filed the necessary paperwork. In early 1998, the Biehls hoped to gain tax-exempt status from the South African government so that large donations to the trust would be tax deductible. To the Biehls' chagrin, approval from the South African Revenue Service came only a year later, after lengthy negotiations and lobbying from some high-profile backers of the trust. Another potential obstacle for the Biehls existed. After generations of apartheid, black South Africans were sometimes suspicious of whites, foreigners, and Americans who claimed to want to "help" them. White-led organizations could face difficulties when they attempted to operate in black townships. Peter and Linda weren't immune to these potential minefields. When they invited Darrell Williams, a mixed-race South African, to manage one of their projects during the early days of the trust, Williams was suspicious at first. "I remember thinking to myself, now what do these white people really want?"

Looking back years later, Linda said that she and Peter "weren't totally naïve" as they launched the trust, but they underestimated the challenges they would face.

The Biehls had some important advantages, of course. Their reputation for understanding South Africa's inequities and their track record of working with local citizens had earned them trust and respect. The forgiveness they demonstrated during the amnesty process further reinforced their positive standing in Gugulethu and in other black townships. In addition, Peter's organizational skills, business experience, and contacts with corporate America would prove immensely helpful. With Peter's managerial skills and Linda's ability to understand local issues, the trust was well positioned to set down roots and gain community support. Another factor in the Biehls' favor was the strengthening US dollar. As the South African rand weakened in the 1990s, American dollars went a long way in South Africa, especially when it came to paying staff salaries.

The trust's programs were extensive and varied. In July 1998, the Biehls began a long-term partnership with the Buthisizwe Training Centre in Philippi township to expand its training programs in sewing, welding, carpentry, and leatherwork for local residents. The trust donated musical instruments to the Themba Music Project, an after-school program that the Biehls believed was not only enjoyable but potentially life changing for young people. After just a few months of operation, the trust also expanded an after-school tutoring program at St. Gabriel's Community Centre and launched programs in special education and youth mentoring. In mid-1998, the trust announced plans to build playing fields in Cape Town's black townships, in cooperation with the departments of education and sport and recreation in the Western Cape. The Biehls planned to unveil approximately 20 more initiatives in the months ahead.

When Peter and Linda surveyed Gugulethu residents about what staples they needed most, bread was at the top of the list. But because black townships lacked large discount grocery stores, bread was available only at local "spaza" shops that charged higher prices. A light went on in Peter's head. He had been hoping to establish a "for-profit enterprise" that would generate revenue to fund the trust's various community projects. He had always wanted to own a bakery and envisioned bread as being the hub of the trust's community work. Why not establish a bakery that would give township residents jobs in baking, selling, and delivering bread? And if businesses could be persuaded to donate resources, the bakery would be able to sell bread for less than the local shops, making it more affordable to township residents. Peter successfully lobbied local companies to donate yeast for the bread, as well as flour and discounted ovens. He hired Darrell Williams, a Harvard-educated Capetonian, to lead what was dubbed the Community Baking

Trust. Williams originally wanted the bakery to be in Gugulethu, but because of the high crime rate there, he and the Biehls chose a site in Parow, about nine miles (15 kilometers) north. The trust provided the startup funds for the bakery, Williams hired the workers, and he and Peter recruited distributors in Gugulethu. Peter left the day-to-day management of the bakery to Williams. When it opened in October 1998, the Parow facility was a modern bakery with new, state-of-the-art equipment that would produce not just thousands of loaves of bread a day, but much-needed jobs.

The Biehls were understandably excited about the opening of the bakery. Some of the bread was sold from distributors' homes in Gugulethu and some was sold at schools. Because the bread was less expensive than that sold at the "spaza" shops, it attracted many buyers. Sales generated income for those who baked and sold it and for the trust itself, which used the profits to fund other community projects, from antiviolence programs in schools to sports and recreation projects. After six months, the bakery was more successful than the Biehls had expected and demand for bread was exceeding supply. In the years ahead, the Biehls would open additional bakeries and distribute "Amy's bread" free in Gugulethu on Amy's birthday. The Community Baking Trust had become one of the Biehls' core programs in South Africa.

Another key program for the trust involved Victor West, the ambulance driver who had arrived in Gugulethu after Amy was killed in 1993. Traumatized by Amy's brutal murder and by speculation that he hadn't arrived at the scene quickly enough, West had sunk into a deep depression in the years since and began drinking and using drugs to ease his pain. After four years of therapy, someone suggested he contact the Biehls. Over dinner in early 1998, Peter and Linda assured him that no one could have saved Amy on the night she was killed and that he shouldn't blame himself for her death. But there was something he could do. They talked about the need for first aid training and equipment in the townships and asked whether Victor would be interested in setting up a first aid course for the trust. Victor agreed to help. In July 1998, he and a colleague launched the Amy Biehl Foundation Trust's First Aid Training Program designed specifically for Gugulethu police officers and community volunteers. It later expanded to include high schools and youth clubs. By December 1998, Victor had trained more than 300 people in first aid and provided first aid kits to trainees and schools, helping people save lives and quite possibly saving his own. Victor stopped using drugs shortly after agreeing to work with the Biehls. Thanks to his efforts, the trust's First Aid Training Program would grow in the years ahead.

The Biehls' youngest daughter Molly helped launch the trust's Youth Reading Role Models Program. After earning her master's degree in sociology at the

University of New Orleans, Molly had settled in San Diego and become director of the city's Family Literacy Foundation. Armed with her professional experience, she adapted her San Diego literacy project for use in Gugulethu. In July 1998, she traveled to South Africa to start a program in which older students would read to younger students under the supervision of trained adult coordinators. She edited her American training manual to fit conditions in South Africa and brought books donated from the United States. By October 1999, more than 400 children at five schools were participating in the Youth Reading Role Models Program; in 2000, five more schools in the Western Cape adopted the program. It would spread to still more schools in the years ahead.

As the trust spread its wings, it recruited student interns from the United States to help in its work. Many of the first interns came from Stanford. The university's Haas Center for Public Service launched its Amy Biehl Fellowship in the summer of 1998, after Center director Timothy Stanton became acquainted with the Biehls and Amy's story. Each summer, two or three undergraduates would be awarded summer internships to work on community development projects sponsored by the trust in Cape Town's black townships. Solange Jacobs was among the first fellows selected. She and another intern organized after-school programs at a primary school in Gugulethu; the third Stanford student wrote a handbook outlining domestic workers' rights. Later interns worked on issues relating to the bakery, AIDS education, business training, music programs, and many others, and they provided the foundation with much-needed staff support. The trust's summer interns would eventually be drawn from many different universities and would become an essential component of the organization.

Peter and Linda's commitment to the Amy Biehl Foundation Trust changed their lives. Setting up an office, meeting with township leaders and residents, establishing and maintaining programs, and coordinating the work of interns completely absorbed them. This wasn't a casual hobby they were engaging in, but a full-time humanitarian mission. Peter and Linda had always liked to travel, but now they were crisscrossing the Atlantic on a regular basis. They were in South Africa more often than the United States. By spending so much time in South Africa and devoting their energy to the causes Amy believed in, Peter and Linda had found a way to keep their daughter's spirit alive. But flying between Los Angeles and Cape Town so frequently would tire even the savviest traveler. "Age is definitely not our friend in this department," Peter and Linda admitted in one of their 1998 newsletters. "There are occasions when we exhaust ourselves. There are times when we come close to exhausting the foundation's financial resources in our desire to push Amy's envelope a bit further."

During a visit to Cape Town in early 2000, Kim was amazed at how well her parents had learned to navigate the maze of streets in Gugulethu. Their cell phones never stopped ringing, and the callers "ranged from township residents to ambassadors, reporters to musicians." At first the Biehls stayed at Cape Town hotels, but they rented an apartment in the city in late 1999 after the frequency of their trips multiplied. By this time, they were traveling alone into the townships, but they kept in close contact with local residents and "if things are a little edgy we don't come in," Linda told a journalist. The Biehls didn't receive an income from their foundation work, and in order to support the family, Peter continued his consulting work for a group of companies in the United States, Mexico, and Japan. But the bulk of the couple's time was devoted to Amy's foundation and trust. Their work was exhausting and exhilarating at the same time. "This is in many ways the richest, busiest, most fulfilling time of our lives," Peter said. He openly admitted that his and Linda's quest to improve life in Cape Town's black townships was a way of holding onto Amy. "Amy's death changed us in ways that are unquantifiable," he told a reporter. "I guess this is really our way of keeping her." Linda agreed. "In all the world," she added, "this is the one place Amy feels most alive to us."

The Biehls' efforts were recognized in South Africa and the wider world. During President Clinton's three-day visit to South Africa in March 1998, US ambassador James Joseph invited the Biehls to attend a private reception in Cape Town for the president, the first lady, and the White House delegation. There USAID director Brian Attwood introduced Peter and Linda to President Clinton, perhaps not realizing that they had met him four and a half years earlier at the White House. The next day, March 27, 1998, President Mandela invited Linda and Peter to the state dinner honoring Clinton at Vergelegen Estate in Somerset West. The Biehls' inclusion in these high-profile events showed the extent to which their expanding humanitarian work was appreciated by leaders on both sides of the Atlantic.

But it wasn't just leaders who applauded the Biehls' efforts; residents of Cape Town's black townships did as well. In August 1998, two Gugulethu residents wrote to the Biehls to say that the skills they had acquired from the trust's programs, such as first aid, conflict management, and crime prevention, would help them "cure the virus that is destroying our community. We have no words to express our sadness for the tragedy that you have experienced, the unfortunate death of your beloved daughter Amy Biehl, but we honestly believe that it was God's will and blessing in disguise that you must come here in South Africa particularly at Gugulethu and help people like us to make our community better. Gugulethu is not short of intelligent people, but it is short of courageous people like you." An assessment conducted by a Stanford MBA student in mid-1999 found that young black South Africans viewed the trust's programs as highly beneficial. Both males and females believed that the programs kept them safe and exposed them to new knowledge and activities that boosted their skills and confidence. Peter and Linda attended countless events at which they could mingle with township residents and see their programs in action. They savored these grassroots occasions and felt honored that those in attendance embraced their efforts. By this time, Peter and Linda had become so familiar to township residents that some called them "Mr. and Mrs. Amy Biehl." Widely recognized all over Cape Town, they were occasionally greeted with this honorary title even in the city center.

As the trust grew, the Biehls began taking visitors into the townships to see its many programs. They were among the relatively few whites who ventured into Gugulethu on a regular basis, even after apartheid ended. The visitors they escorted were often potential donors, representatives of philanthropic organizations, journalists, American academics, or social workers. Peter and Linda would typically give the visitors a feel for the area and show them St. Gabriel's Church, home to one of the trust's afterschool programs; an empty lot where the Biehls hoped to build a sports field; and the schools that were being assisted by the trust. Despite being foreigners, the Biehls were usually more familiar with the townships than most white Capetonians.

The trust began to attract a growing number of volunteers who were attracted to the Biehls' work and wanted to help. The Kendalls of suburban St. Louis increased their involvement in the trust's work, traveling to Cape Town multiple times to observe conditions in black schools and sponsor workshops for black teachers. In 1999, two attorneys from Vancouver contacted the Biehls, traveled to Cape Town, and volunteered to work for the trust for six weeks. During their stay, they worked on behalf of domestic workers and later contributed financially to the trust. In 2000, a couple from Duluth, Minnesota, visited the trust's projects and wondered how they could contribute to South Africa's new democracy. As a result of their visit, they volunteered to work at the trust for the next two years. They were part of a group of volunteers that Peter and Linda dubbed "Amy's Peace Corps," illustrating how people of many different backgrounds sought to continue Amy's work.

As their work in South Africa expanded, the Biehls' activities in the United States focused primarily on fundraising and publicizing their message of reconciliation and community service. The Biehls spent much of their time in the United States on the road, appearing at venues large and small. They spoke at colleges, churches, schools, and organizations across the country, from the United

Nations in New York to the Crystal Cathedral in southern California. They welcomed these opportunities to discuss the work they were doing, and they were warmly received by audiences who admired their capacity to forgive and find goodness from tragedy.

The greatest honor that the Biehls received since Amy's death was their inclusion in Mandela's Congressional Gold Medal ceremony in Washington, D.C. In mid-1998, the US Congress voted to award Mandela the medal, the body's highest civilian honor. Part of the bill read as follows: "Millions of individuals of all races and backgrounds in the United States and around the world followed Nelson Mandela's example and fought for the abolition of apartheid in the Republic of South Africa and in this regard the Congress recognizes Amy Elizabeth Biehl, an American student who lost her life in the struggle to free South Africa from racial oppression, and the spirit of forgiveness and reconciliation displayed by her parents, Peter and Linda Biehl." Mandela, the first African to receive the medal, traveled to Washington with his new wife, Graça Machel, for the award ceremony in late September. Mandela's staff invited the Biehls to a celebratory breakfast at Blair House just prior to the ceremony. Zach was in college and could not attend, but Kim and Molly accompanied their parents to the event. When Mandela strode into the dining room, he immediately recognized Kim and Molly as Amy's sisters and asked that he be photographed with them. "Of course, everyone had been waiting for him, as he was the honored guest," Kim recalled years later. "But he walked straight past the likes of Ted Kennedy and other well-known and important people, straight for us. Molly and I were both shocked."

The award ceremony was held at the Capitol rotunda on September 23. VIPs from Congress and the American antiapartheid movement were there. The Biehls were seated in the front row, facing Mandela and President Clinton. In his remarks, Clinton discussed how Americans could honor Mandela's achievements beyond merely giving him a distinguished award: "If this day is to be more than a day in which we bask in his reflected glory, we should ask ourselves what gift we can really give Nelson Mandela in return for 10,000 long days in jail. How can we truly redeem the life of Amy Biehl? How can we honor all of those who marched and worked with Nelson Mandela who are no longer standing by his side?" Clinton believed that forging a new, closer partnership with Africa was one step; another was to live by Mandela's example and "to tear down every last vestige of apartheid in our own hearts." When Mandela approached the podium to accept the award, he said that he now felt like the heavyweight champion of the world. Mandela then paid tribute to those Americans who helped end apartheid, whether they were government officials or ordinary citizens: "Among those we remember today is young Amy Biehl. She made our aspirations her own and lost her life in the turmoil of our transition as the new South Africa struggled to be born in the dying moments of apartheid. Through her our peoples have also shared the pain of confronting a terrible past as we take the path of reconciliation and healing of our nation." The Biehls felt honored that Amy's contribution was acknowledged in the bill and in the remarks of both Clinton and Mandela. Peter and Linda were moved beyond words, and later told the foundation's friends, "This was—quite possibly—the most humbling experience of our lives."

Later that year, the Biehls were honored at a very different kind of event. At a ceremony at the Crystal Cathedral in Orange County, California, on November 22, 1998, Linda was among three people whom Dr. Robert Schuller presented with a "Scars into Stars" award for "transforming tragedy into victory." Schuller was one of the most famous "televangelists" in the United States and his "Hour of Power" program reached millions of viewers each week. Despite not being evangelical Christians, the Biehls participated in such events because it gave them the opportunity to discuss their work in South Africa and generate new support for the foundation.

As the internet took off and became a forum for communication and personal reflection in the late 1990s and beyond, articles, opinion pieces, and blogs on the Biehls began to proliferate. Christians writing on such platforms often drew on the Biehls' example to underscore biblical precepts of forgiveness. Secular writers and bloggers found the Biehls equally awe inspiring and frequently reflected on the implications of their bigheartedness for the wider world in terms of violence prevention, criminal justice reform, and racial reconciliation. When people marveled at how the Biehls could be so forgiving, they sometimes assumed it came from a religious motivation. But as Linda said, "We're not Bible people. We're ethics people." Peter told a reporter that in their efforts to understand his and Linda's attitude, some couldn't believe it was just a matter of honoring what Amy stood for. "People somehow always want more," he said. "'It can't be that simple,' they say. 'Come on and give it to me straight. What's really going on?' Well, we are that simple. Go away!" Then he burst out laughing.

High-profile television coverage intensified the public's fascination with the Biehls. On January 17, 1999, Peter and Linda appeared on CBS's *60 Minutes*, one of America's most watched and respected news programs. Host Leslie Stahl portrayed the Biehls as seeking to fill the void caused by Amy's death by following in her footsteps and working to improve life in Cape Town's black townships. The segment identified some of the projects the Biehls had started, such as job training, afterschool tutorials, and the bakery. Stahl asked Archbishop Tutu to share his perspective on the Biehls. "The logic would be that the South Africans should be giving some kind of reparation to the Biehls," he said. "They've turned it all upside down . . . It's the victims, in the depth of their own agony and pain, who say, 'The community which produced these murderers—we want to help that community be transfigured.'" Four months later, Oprah Winfrey aired a segment titled "Remembering Amy" on her top-rated daytime talk show. After such high-level publicity, supportive letters and speaking invitations began filling up the Biehls' mailbox even more rapidly.

IN her remarks at the 10th anniversary celebration of the Faith and Politics Institute in Washington, D.C., in 2001, Linda reflected on both the promise and the perils of South Africa's young democracy: "Although South Africa was now free, there was much work left to be done. Violence did not subside, but it was no longer political violence. Poverty and frustration confronted the young men [who killed Amy] when they got out of prison. They were dismayed that although South Africa was 'free,' conditions remained the same, if not worse, on their streets." The future was indeed questionable for Mongezi Manqina, Vusumzi Ntamo, Easy Nofemela, and Ntobeko Peni once they were released from prison in mid-1998. Mongezi was on the run after raping a disabled teenager, and Vusumzi was eventually jailed on an assault charge. Easy and Ntobeko could easily have drifted into a life of crime after their release, because crime was the only steady means of survival for many township dwellers in a country with mass black unemployment. Ntobeko had been particularly scarred by the violence he'd both experienced and perpetrated. After he was released back into Gugulethu, he had difficulty sleeping, forming healthy relationships, and finding steady work. He felt a dark cloud hanging over him and was haunted by his role in Amy's death. Easy experienced some of the same difficulties. In prison, the two had talked about doing something constructive for township youth, and when they were released they formed a youth club in Gugulethu that sponsored group activities such as soccer matches and hikes on Table Mountain. But the dark cloud remained.

Within a year of Easy and Ntobeko's release, Nancy Scheper-Hughes asked to interview them. Scheper-Hughes had been in South Africa when Amy was killed in 1993 and had attended part of the first trial in Cape Town in 1994. She returned to South Africa in May 1999 to explore how years of violence had affected youths who came of age under apartheid. Easy and Ntobeko reluctantly agreed to meet with her in Gugulethu. During their discussion, the two young men spoke of the guilt they felt over Amy's death and wished they could explain themselves to the

Biehls. "I thought that there was one thing that could possibly make me better," Ntobeko said. "I wanted to tell Mr. Biehl that I did not take the death of his daughter lightly. That this thing has weighed heavily on me. And I wanted him to know that he is a hero father to me. I thought to myself, if I could just get that Peter Biehl to listen to me and to forgive me to my face—why, that would be as good as bread."

Peter had just arrived in Cape Town after the birth of his first grandchild, Molly's son Alexander. Scheper-Hughes contacted Peter and told him that Easy and Ntobeko were interested in meeting him. Peter telephoned Linda, who was still in California with Molly, and the two discussed Easy and Ntobeko's request. Although Peter and Linda had accepted amnesty for the young men and hoped they would lead productive lives, they hadn't planned on seeing them again. But when they heard that Easy and Ntobeko were trying to turn their lives around and help their community, the Biehls agreed that a meeting might be worthwhile. "The fact that they wanted to talk to us, and made that happen through an intermediary—that was very pleasing," Peter said later. The next day, Scheper-Hughes took Peter to Easy's house in Gugulethu. Easy, Ntobeko, and a few of their friends waited inside. At first there was an awkward silence. Then Easy and Ntobeko explained their past actions and said they regretted their involvement in Amy's murder, which they said should never have happened. Peter sat expressionless but listened intently. Easy and Ntobeko then told Peter about the youth group they had started and showed him photos of the hikes they took on Table Mountain. As the young men spoke, Peter sensed sincerity in their voices and body language, and the initial tension dissipated. Later that day, Peter told Linda about the encounter over the telephone.

When Linda arrived in Cape Town days later, Peter took her to meet Easy and Ntobeko in Gugulethu. Easy told Linda he was one of seven boys and pointed to a family photo on the wall. Then Linda took out a photo of her new grandson and showed it to Easy and Ntobeko. "Oh, Makhulu," Easy said. Linda asked what that meant, and he said, "Grandmother." He and Ntobeko would call her "Makhulu" from that day forward. The short meeting seemed "very natural and intimate" to Linda, but no one knew where it might lead. "We wanted to meet them because we knew they were helping others," Easy told a journalist, "but we did not want to open up wounds. It turned out the Biehls also wanted to meet us."

Over the next few months, the Biehls got to know Easy and Ntobeko better. It took time for the four to become fully comfortable in each other's presence. Peter sometimes thought about Amy's death when he was with the young men. Because Amy had spoken about the oppression of young black males in South

Africa, Linda had a basic sense of the difficult lives they'd had. She saw them as former child soldiers trying to readjust to civilian life and to contribute constructively to their community. She never viewed Easy and Ntobeko as killers. "They didn't know who they were attacking," she said. "It wasn't personal. They were striking against what they perceived as the oppressor. I never blamed them for the attack." Long suspicious of whites, Easy began to change his views as he got to know the Biehls. "Not until I met Linda and Peter did I understand that white people are human beings too," he said. His distrust melted when he realized that the Biehls understood the problems facing South Africa and that they weren't interested in recrimination, but healing.

Shortly after their initial meetings in May 1999, the Biehls began to support Easy and Ntobeko's youth club. They came to a meeting of the club, were impressed by what they saw, and offered to provide T-shirts to the group and help arrange outings. Later they began to help fund the club. "It's their idea," Linda said. "We had nothing to do with it. They discovered that there was a greater need to help the youth in their community to stop crime and drugs. So they came to us with the idea and we supported it." From the Biehls' perspective, Easy and Ntobeko's efforts to get youths off the streets and into productive activities paralleled the efforts of the trust. Ntobeko was cautiously optimistic about the relationship that he and Easy were building with the Biehls. "We still have to break the ice," he said, "but the more we see of each other the more comfortable we will be. Our conversations are helping me deal with the trauma because it is one thing to be forgiven, but another to forgive yourself."

On July 10, 1999, the Biehls came to the place where Amy died to attend the official launch of the youth club in Gugulethu. A crowd of young township residents watched as Linda placed a rose on the spot where Amy was killed. Peter also laid flowers at the site. According to a black reporter, the youths who witnessed the scene were "humbled by the courage shown by Ms. Biehl's parents." Easy told the crowd, "Out of a bad thing, there can be a good thing . . . Both myself and Mr. Peni have learned a hard lesson the hard way. Now we are committed to educating the youth about important things in life." To those who were there, the event was unforgettable, for it embodied reconciliation in ways that even the leaders of the Truth and Reconciliation Commission could never have imagined. Easy's mother was among those in the crowd. "I am hypnotized," she told a journalist. "I do not know what to say or how to feel . . . I'm happy to see that these people have sincerely forgiven our children. I can see that they are also sorry for what they did."

When the Biehls forged a relationship with Easy and Ntobeko, it led to a whole new round of publicity in South Africa and the United States. Two months after the launch of the youth club, CBS began preparing a follow-up piece on the Biehls for *60 Minutes II* that would be broadcast early the following year. Program host Leslie Stahl was incredulous that the Biehls could befriend the men who killed their daughter. So were many other Americans and South Africans. Linda admitted that some of their friends in the States struggled to understand their new lives and their obsessive commitment to helping black South Africans half-way around the world. "You can see them thinking: 'My God, what do I say to Peter and Linda?'" she said.

The unease extended to the Biehls' children. Kim, Molly, and Zach didn't nec-essarily object to their parents' relationship with Easy and Ntobeko, but they were sometimes troubled that Peter and Linda spent so much time in South Africa. Although they fully supported the mission of the foundation, Kim, Molly, and Zach had their own lives apart from Amy and her legacy. Conscious that they had to attend to their American lives and family, Peter and Linda tried not to "talk too much" about South Africa with their three children or their neighbors in Califor-nia. They knew a balance was needed, but as their South African work expanded, that balance became difficult to maintain.

AS Mandela said in 1999, the last year of his presidency, "The long walk is not yet over. The prize of a better life has yet to be won." On the plus side, his govern-ment had extended electricity, running water, and housing to millions of people. It had also preserved the political freedoms won in 1994. But great and interlocking economic challenges remained, chiefly poverty, unemployment, and crime. South Africa's economic problems continued after Thabo Mbeki became president in 1999. Although some blacks had joined an elite class of government officials and corporate executives, most of their fellow citizens remained poor during the first decade of democracy. Inequality was growing between the small, wealthy elite and the black masses. The country needed economic assistance more than ever.

With this need in mind, USAID announced a new $1.4 million grant to the Amy Biehl Foundation Trust in September 1999. This figure was nearly a threefold increase from the initial grant and would be good through March 2001. Clearly US foreign policy makers saw value in aligning themselves with the Biehls in the interest of promoting ties between the United States and South Africa. The en-larged grant was also a vote of confidence in the Biehls' methods, organization, and impact. Grateful for the new grant, the Biehls enlarged the trust's staff and moved its headquarters to a high-rise office building in central Cape Town within the next year.

One of the initiatives that became a priority for the trust was South Africa's escalating AIDS crisis. The country had one of the most serious AIDS epidemics in the world in the late 1990s and early 2000s. As in the rest of southern Africa, life expectancy was dropping as millions died from AIDS-related diseases each year. A whole generation of AIDS orphans was being created, some of whom would turn to crime in order to survive. Mbeki's government erected barriers to the use of preventive drugs, saying the medications were both overpriced and toxic. Mbeki argued that poverty, not HIV, caused AIDS. His "denialist" stance prevented the country's health services from adequately addressing the crisis, which grew worse and cost countless lives. Between 1999 and 2005, death rates from AIDS in South Africa nearly doubled.

In 2000, the trust launched a new campaign to educate South Africans on AIDS. It printed 350,000 bread wrappers containing information on AIDS prevention and then used the wrappers for bread baked at the trust's own bakery. On August 25, the seventh anniversary of Amy's death, Peter and Linda personally handed out free loaves of "Amy's bread" to Gugulethu residents. In 2001, the Biehls stepped up the trust's AIDS education efforts. In order to raise awareness about the disease, the trust's staff trained more than 50 volunteers to conduct entertaining teaching sessions in bars on how to use condoms and on the ABCs of AIDS (abstinence, be faithful, condomize). Thanks to an agreement between the trust and South Cape beer distributors, patrons who purchased beer in bars and liquor stores would also receive free condoms. The trust hoped to provide more than 100,000 condoms a month to township residents.

The Biehls supported a very different initiative at about the same time. In July 1997, a photographer introduced Peter and Linda to a group of men who called themselves "the hidden golfers of Khayelitsha." Khayelitsha, a vast shantytown of approximately a million residents, was Cape Town's largest black settlement. A hilly area of shacks, windswept sand dunes, and desperate poverty, it was farther from central Cape Town than Gugulethu and, if possible, even less developed. This unlikeliest of places was home to a handful of golf enthusiasts who had learned the game as caddies but, because of apartheid, had been denied opportunities to play. Undeterred, the golfers had roamed around looking for ad hoc places to practice, mostly empty fields and vacant lots. The golfers told the Biehls about the need for a place where young people from disadvantaged areas could learn the game. The spokesman for the group, Vusi Sixhaso, asked if the Biehls would help fund a driving range for the area. Being a golf enthusiast himself, Peter was intrigued. He and Linda believed that sports programs helped prevent violence, and a driving range in Khayelitsha would not only give youths a place to learn the game, but would employ local residents. Soon ambitious plans were under way. As envisioned by the Biehls, the Khayelitsha golf club would become part of the trust's violence prevention program. During the next two years, plans for tee boxes, a clubhouse, and putting greens were drawn up, along with a commitment from the trust to supply clubs and balls. Peter secured a donation from Larry Moriarty, a former professional football player in the States who supported youth sports programs. A local firm designed the clubhouse; a professional golf course designer planned the course; and approximately R1 million was raised to construct the facility. In May 2000, the trust officially launched what it called "The People's Driving Range."

The trust also moved into the construction business. In mid-1999, the Biehls were involved in a joint initiative with the Western Cape Department of Education and an independent construction firm to train black and mixed-race residents of Cape Town for jobs in the building industry. Less than two years later, the trust had its own start-up construction company and was involved in building two schools, a community hall, and housing at Spier, a wine estate near Stellenbosch. The Biehls were clearly interested in expanding the trust beyond the black townships of Cape Town. By mid-2000, the trust also had projects in Strand, a seaside community on False Bay, and George, a regional town 266 miles (428 kilometers) east of Cape Town. A trust bakery began operations in George in late 2000. It would support reading and youth programs in the area's black township and employed 40 people by early 2002. Another bakery was set up in Strand and aimed to operate around the clock and produce 5,000 loaves a day. By this time, the trust managed 30 programs on the Cape Flats and in Strand and George, requiring Linda and Peter to spend approximately 75 percent of their time in South Africa.

Such rapid expansion brought challenges. Because they were Americans and received funding from a US government agency, the Biehls were sometimes perceived as wealthier than they were. "The expectation is that if you're a white American, you're rich," Linda observed. The Biehls realized that their trust was relatively well endowed for the time being, but more people began to ask for funding than the trust had money to give. The Biehls worried that the trust was wrongly perceived as having unlimited financial resources. They received at least five proposals for programs a week, more than they could support. In reality, fundraising was ongoing, hard work. The Biehls didn't just rely on USAID money; they were continually exploring ways to attract new donations so they could sustain and expand the trust's programs. Despite occasional grants from large institutions, most of the trust's supplemental funding came from individual donors.

Even though the Biehls were spending the majority of their time in South Africa by 1999–2000, they still viewed their work in the United States as important. Their extensive experience in South Africa, combined with their many speaking engagements in the United States, led Peter and Linda to view themselves as "bridges" between the two countries. They hoped to "migrate" some of their successful South African programs to the United States. For instance, the Biehls began working with the Red Cross Association to establish a first aid training program for the La Quinta, California area, based on the first aid training that Victor West had developed for the trust in South Africa. The program was launched in 2000. The Biehls expanded their ties to American universities at the same time. Students at US colleges and universities performed crucial work with the trust in Cape Town, and the Biehls embraced their presence, partly because their youthful energy and idealism reminded them of Amy. Between 1998 and 2001, the Biehls gave presentations at many colleges, including Berkeley, Duke, Georgetown, Harvard, Notre Dame, and the universities of Maryland and Massachusetts. By early 2001, about 40 undergraduates and MBA students had worked as interns at the trust.

The political intelligentsia in Washington, D.C., regarded the Biehls almost as unofficial ambassadors to South Africa during this period and solicited their views on a wide range of issues. In early 1999, the Biehls were invited by a professor at Georgetown to speak about conflict resolution. The Biehls also testified before the Congressional Black Caucus and the House International Affairs Committee. At the Congressional Black Caucus hearings in September 2000, the focus was on foreign aid to Africa. In their testimony, the Biehls discussed the trust's work and emphasized the importance of listening to people at the grassroots and learning from them. The trust's programs were succeeding, they believed, "because the people conceive them and partner with us to bring ideas . . . to realities."

On March 28, 2001, USAID announced that it would provide the trust with an additional four years of funding. The Biehls were thrilled, but the growth of the trust meant that their workload became even more frenetic. Every day in Cape Town they hosted visitors or had meetings. One day they would visit project sites; on another they would meet with a South African company to explore possible partnerships; on yet another they would meet with a government official to discuss linkages or host a delegation from the United States. By 2001–2, the Biehls were making about nine trips a year to South Africa. Kim, Molly, and Zach sometimes worried about the heavy work load their parents took on, but Peter and Linda seemed determined to work "incessantly."

Meanwhile, the couple's relationship with Easy and Ntobeko continued to grow. In the months following the launch of their youth club in July 1999, the two young men volunteered to be security guards for the trucks that delivered Amy's bread to Cape Town's black townships. The Biehls viewed the two as sincere and hardworking and intent on turning their lives around. "They want to build something for themselves and are willing to work damn hard for it," Peter said. He eventually hired Easy and Ntobeko to work full-time for the trust. The Biehls began to socialize with Easy and Ntobeko and their girlfriends, taking them out to dinner, going to the movies, and even visiting amusement parks together. The relationship grew to such an extent that Easy and Ntobeko began to regard Peter and Linda as surrogate parents. Ntobeko told a reporter, "I don't know how they found it in their hearts to forgive us for what we did, but I can tell you that it has greatly enriched my life. I will never forget what we did that night, but I will also never forget the kindness they have shown me when they had every reason to hate me." The Biehls found their relationship with Easy and Ntobeko tremendously rewarding. It offered them some of their most fulfilling moments as they dealt with the challenges of running their foundation. They believed that their friendship showed that restorative justice could work. "If it had not been for the Truth and Reconciliation Commission," Peter said, "I would never have met these guys and would never have been able to care." But the friendship didn't happen magically; it took time for a mutual understanding to develop. "If you understand why someone wronged you, then you can accept that person and you can reconcile," Peter continued. "The real effort comes from building the relationship."

The Biehls had not been in touch with Mongezi and Vusumzi, who had committed other crimes, although Mongezi's younger sister was involved in one of the trust's after-school programs. "We've been able to help two of the four men that murdered Amy—a 50 percent success rate using a restorative system of justice, rather than a punitive one," Peter said. "I think that alone speaks for itself." Linda shared her husband's sentiments completely. The Biehls were clearly investing their hopes in Easy and Ntobeko, because, if they succeeded, then Amy's dream of a better South Africa might become a reality.

But Amy's dream was still far from being fulfilled. The new South Africa was an intensely violent society, with among the world's highest rates of rape, assault, and murder. South Africa had always had a comparatively high crime rate—a feature of many countries with vast social inequality—but crime rates had soared since 1994. It didn't take long for crime to hit the trust's projects. In 1999, one of the trust's after-school mentoring programs in Gugulethu was threatened when violence became so severe that parents began to fear for their children's safety. As a consequence, parents started keeping their children home. In October 2000, Ashleigh Murphy, a Northwestern graduate and trust employee, was carjacked as

she visited an after-school program in New Crossroads. Days later, workers at one
of the trust's building projects near Stellenbosch were robbed by four armed men.
The next day, the trust bakery in George was robbed. Crime became even worse
in 2001. Early that year, a guard at the Khayelitsha driving range was shot and
killed, and the trust's bakery in Parow was burned down by arsonists. In July 2001,
a driver for the bakery in George was shot and killed as he was delivering "Amy's
bread," devastating his family and the Biehls in equal measure. A month later,
one of the bakery's drivers was shot and killed in Gugulethu. The Biehls were
in shock. They asked themselves if they could "knowingly place [their] people at
risk" by continuing the bread deliveries in Gugulethu. They decided they could
not. In late August 2001, Peter announced that the trust would stop delivering its
low-cost bread to Gugulethu because of safety concerns. The Biehls couldn't hide
their sadness and frustration. "South Africa's disadvantaged people don't require
an oppressor to rob them of their futures," they wrote. "They are, sadly, capable
of doing it to themselves." The Biehls began negotiating a deal with the grocery
chain Pick n Pay to sell the trust's bread in wealthier suburban areas, but that
would be small consolation. The Gugulethu bread project had been a labor of
love for Peter and one of the trust's core programs.

The limitations of the trust's work had become clear. There was little it
could do to change the socioeconomic structure in South Africa that perpetu-
ated poverty and unemployment, which in turn exacerbated crime. This creeping
realization took a toll on the Biehls' optimism, although they never considered
packing up and leaving South Africa. As the disastrous year of 2001 came to a
close, the Biehls reflected on an experience they had had two years earlier, which
became more meaningful in hindsight. In 1999, they had addressed students at
a high school near Somerset West. After they finished, a student leader told his
peers in the audience, "The Biehls really are black people with white faces and we
thank them for returning to South Africa." After the event ended, the student approached Linda and said, "But, you know, Mrs. Biehl, it's still about the land." The
Biehls remembered that remark for years, because it was "a chilling reminder of
unfinished business here." As significant as the Biehls' efforts were, they couldn't
resolve South Africa's underlying problems.

The mounting challenges the trust faced were stressful for the Biehls. They
noticed that because economic opportunities were so limited, some township
residents would become jealous of those who led the trust's programs and would
refuse to cooperate. Peter and Linda wondered whether such feelings had led to
the fire that destroyed the trust's bakery in Parow or to the collapse of plans to
develop community centers in Philippi and Nyanga. The Biehls also encountered

something they called "a fear of success." They worried that disadvantaged citizens were so unaccustomed to outside help that they developed fears that often manifested themselves "at the very moment when success appears." Such fears could delay or derail projects that were on the verge of being successfully implemented. Peter explained, "The people in South Africa are so unaccustomed to a dream fulfilled, or a promise kept, that suspicion develops. In almost every project, at the eleventh hour, someone will say 'we feel we were not adequately consulted.' It always happens. So we've developed strategies for dealing with it. To combat this you need a peer leader; support must come from the community." An undeniable mood of anxiety plagued the Biehls in late 2001, but these feelings were not permanent and did not derail the foundation. Despite the many challenges the trust faced, the Biehls weren't about to give up. "Amy has committed us to South Africa for life," the Biehls wrote in November 2001. "We are challenged by the magnitude of human need, humbled by our very finite resources and fearful of the safety of our dedicated people. But we won't abandon the people we are here to serve."

Fortunately, positive reactions made their work worthwhile. Several observers accompanying the Biehls to Gugulethu observed how warmly the residents greeted the Biehls, even amid the rising crime of 2000–2001. A seamstress who worked at the Buthisizwe Centre told a journalist how grateful she was that the Amy Biehl Foundation Trust was assisting township residents. "The Biehls came just when we needed them the most," she said. She and her friends had struggled to sell their products before the Biehls lent them assistance. "Losing their daughter like that, I cannot imagine what the pain must feel like. But from that one horrible moment, so much light has come into the world." In his final report, one intern described how impressed he was with the trust's impact in the Cape Town area. "Just at the mention of the name Amy Biehl, heads turn and smiles grow," he wrote. "It is easy to see the impact this organization has had simply by walking through the townships, not to mention the support from local businesses."

Soon there was tangible evidence of Gugulethu's support. Sometime in 1999, township residents erected a memorial to Amy next to the Caltex station where she was fatally attacked. A small cement cross was placed there, beneath a hand-painted banner that read, "Amy Biehl's Last Home: Section 3 Gugs." In mid-2001, some Gugulethu residents tried to have the street on which Amy was killed, NY1, renamed in her honor. Although the municipality and the provincial authorities had yet to agree on the proper procedure for street name changes, the effort showed the extent to which some Gugulethu residents wanted to honor Amy and her legacy.

Equally gratifying was the close friendship that the Biehls developed with Ahmed Kathrada, an icon of South Africa's liberation struggle. Kathrada was one of the Rivonia trialists sentenced to life in prison in 1964 and was among Mandela's closest confidants in prison from the 1960s to the 1980s. The Biehls first met him in mid-1997, when they and the Kendalls were part of a group that visited Robben Island with Kathrada, South African novelist André Brink, and Ariel Dorfman. Kathrada was impressed not only with the Biehls' embrace of reconciliation, but their continued work on behalf of black South Africans. He and the Biehls grew closer in the years ahead. In 1999, the Biehls hosted a birthday party for Kathrada, who was about to turn 70. Three years later, he agreed to be the chief spokesman for the trust's first South African fundraiser. As he announced the plans to the public, he drew a parallel between the Biehls and former Robben Island prisoners like himself. "Robben Island is about reconciliation and forgiveness, looking into our future while not forgetting our past. We shook hands with our former enemies to build a new country." He saw the Biehls as doing the same thing.

Listing all the American honors the Biehls received between 1999 and 2001 would require a book of its own. Perhaps most meaningful to the Biehls was their receiving the Averell Harriman Democracy Award from NDI on November 28, 2001. The award was presented annually to those who "exemplified NDI's commitment to democracy and human rights," a commitment Amy shared during her two years there. Ironically, Amy had helped plan these very NDI award dinners in the early 1990s. Brian Attwood presented the award to the Biehls. In praising their commitment to South Africa in the face of personal loss, he compared their message of reconciliation with Nelson Mandela's. "If Amy is looking down tonight, and some of us know she is," he said, "she is bursting with pride that her parents are receiving this award." Events like these showed that since Amy's death, Peter and Linda had become among the most widely admired humanitarians in the United States.

AFTER celebrating Christmas 2001 and the New Year with their family in the States, it was time for Peter and Linda to resume their work. February 2002 was a busy month for the Biehls in Cape Town. Besides their usual briefings from staff and visits to project sites, they hosted a visit by former ambassador Lyman and members of the Northern California World Affairs Council. They addressed students on board a "Semester at Sea" ship while it docked in the city, which had become a tradition for them. Although Peter started having stomach cramps during their stay, he assumed that he'd picked up a local bug and pressed on.

Even though the previous year had been a stressful one for the Biehls, the trust had made undeniable strides since its beginnings in 1997. In the field of education, it sponsored after-school programs in reading, math, life skills, nutrition, art, drama, music, and sports. In the field of health and safety, it ran AIDS education and peer counseling programs, a condom distribution program, and first aid training. In the field of economic empowerment, it offered jobs skills training, bakeries, and a sewing consortium. In sports and recreation, it supported facilities and coaching for golf, soccer, cricket, and basketball. And its environmental programs included projects on green-space creation and environmental awareness. In Cape Town, Strand, and George, thousands benefited from the trust's programs. By early 2002, the trust had spent approximately $5 million on community development projects. There was another invaluable benefit of the trust—it helped break down racial barriers. As whites and blacks worked together in the office and in the townships, as black youths interacted with white interns and volunteers, trust grew. When asked what benefits the Amy Biehl Foundation Trust offered, one young participant said simply, "You get to know people. We were scared of white people. It has given us confidence."

Upon their return home to southern California, Peter still didn't feel well, so he checked into the Eisenhower Medical Center in Rancho Mirage on March 3, 2002. There he was diagnosed with colon cancer. Despite the grim news, Peter fully expected to recover. But his kidneys failed shortly thereafter and he remained hospitalized. As reality set in, he told Linda, "You go for it. Keep this thing we started going." During surgery to remove a tumor in his colon, he went into shock, his liver failed, and he never recovered. Peter died on Easter Sunday, March 31, 2002, at the age of 59. Linda had lost her husband of 38 years, and Kim, Molly, and Zach had lost their father. The Biehl children believed that South Africa had not only claimed their sister Amy, but their father as well, who had neglected his own health as he devoted all his energy to the foundation. Kim felt particularly bitter. "I was angry at the foundation because he gave everything to it," she said.

After Peter died, the Biehls' fax machine in La Quinta whirred nonstop with letters of condolence, just as it had when Amy died nine years earlier. Once again, the outpouring of support comforted Linda and the family. All hailed Peter's generosity of spirit and his dedication to the poor and downtrodden in South Africa. As the Biehls discussed how they could best celebrate Peter's life, Rev. W. Douglas Tanner, founder of the Faith and Politics Institute, contacted the family and suggested that a memorial service be held at the National Cathedral in Washington, D.C. At first Kim, Molly, and Zach hesitated, wary of the public nature of such an event. But they understood that many leaders in and around Washington had been pillars of support to their parents and the foundation over the years. The service was held on April 26, 2002, on what would have been Amy's 35th birthday. Those who contributed tributes to the memorial program included Madeleine Albright, Brian Attwood, and Georgia congressman John Lewis, an icon of the American civil rights movement. Ambassador James Joseph spoke at the service, as did South African author Sindiwe Magona. Linda and Zach spoke as well. Linda noted that Peter's transition from corporate marketing consultant to coleader of an international humanitarian foundation was something he had never imagined for himself. It was a role that brought him "great frustration but great joy." Despite the "huge" learning curve, Peter found the work energizing, especially forging partnerships with others in a common goal—nation building. His relationship with Easy and Ntobeko had redoubled his faith in restorative justice and gave him great hope for the future.

Now it fell on Linda's shoulders to keep Peter's vision of hope and healing alive. Going forward without his companionship, without his business and managerial acumen, and without him by her side seemed unthinkable, but she was determined to try. Three days after the memorial service, Linda headed back to South Africa once again.

14

Makhulu

SOME PEOPLE wondered whether Linda could keep the foundation going after Peter's death. "I think they were wondering what was going to happen, if I had the strength to go on," Linda said. "I quickly decided I did have the strength to go on." She was determined to keep the spirit of her husband and daughter alive. Because USAID funding would expire in 2005, Linda began to focus on how she could make the foundation sustainable in the long term, especially because so many people were participating in the trust's programs by 2002. Amy still motivated Linda every day. "I think she's kicking me in the rear end," she told a reporter. "She did that when she was alive, and I think she's still doing that. She's still a force. She's challenging me to get up out of the chair and do something. To live life fully. To make a better world in some small way." Rather than sapping her energy, Peter's death renewed Linda's commitment to the foundation and further strengthened her ties to South Africa.

Within days of Linda's return to Cape Town, 400 people gathered on the streets of Gugulethu to pay tribute to Peter. Blacks and whites sang, danced, and waved flags as they marched to St. Gabriel's Church to celebrate Peter's life on May 4, 2002. Easy and Ntobeko joined Linda at the service. They had regarded Peter as a friend and mentor and were shocked by his sudden loss. Their relationship with Linda grew closer in the months ahead. Both men began traveling with her to speaking engagements, moved by her commitment to the children of South Africa and her humanity. They still called her "Makhulu" (Grandmother), a sign of respect for a female elder. Like the Biehl children, Ntobeko suspected that Peter's commitment to the foundation had cost him his health, and he worried about Linda suffering a similar fate. "She works so hard, I try to tell her. If she's not in the foundation full time, it could collapse. That's bad for her health," he said. Linda viewed Easy and Ntobeko as her South African children, and she bought two plots of land for them in Gugulethu on which they could build their own houses one day. She realized that many South Africans had a hard time understanding her relationship with the two young men. But just as they had "adopted" Peter and her, she had adopted them.

The Amy Biehl Foundation Trust held its first annual South African fund-raiser at the Grand West Casino in Cape Town on May 16, 2002. The event, titled "Taste of the Nation," was dedicated to Peter. Linda received a standing ovation as she addressed the guests. "It is a privilege to be part of South Africa and its developing democracy," she said. Easy and Ntobeko attended the evening's festivities, as did government officials, academics, and other friends and supporters of the trust. South African movie producer Anant Singh helped underwrite the event, at which Hugh Masekela performed. Linda was the first person on the dance floor when the music began.

On her return to the United States, Linda made changes in her own life and that of the foundation. She left La Quinta and moved back to Newport Beach, where she shared a condominium with her son Zach. Now 25, Zach was a football coach at Newport Harbor High School, his alma mater, and at Santa Ana College. He had avoided South Africa for years after the family's trip there in October 1993. He didn't resent South Africa, but he wanted to live his own life, separate from South Africa and the foundation. It was hard having his parents travel to South Africa so frequently, but he understood the importance of their work and respected it. Now, with his father gone, his attitude shifted. Because Linda traveled so much, someone was needed to help with the logistics of the foundation, such as fund-raising, coordinating speaking engagements, and communicating with the public. Zach decided it was time for him to "step up" and continue his father's work. By mid-2002, Zach became the American operations manager for the Amy Biehl Foundation. He began to accompany Linda to speaking engagements in southern California and offered his perspectives from the podium as well. In August 2002, he traveled to South Africa for two weeks, where he visited the trust's programs, spoke with staff, ran a youth baseball clinic in George, and spoke at a first aid training graduation ceremony at Pollsmoor Prison. Like his mother, Zach viewed the legacies of Amy and his father as inspirational, not tragic.

In mid-2002, Easy and Ntobeko joined Linda at speaking engagements in the United States for the first time. The pair had never been out of South Africa or on a plane before, and they were eager to share their stories with American audiences.

The trio first spoke at the annual meeting of the American Family Therapists Academy in New York on June 26, 2002. Their panel, titled "A Story of Interracial Reconciliation," was introduced by Sindiwe Magona, the black South African author from Gugulethu who worked in New York. Easy and Ntobeko described their experiences growing up in South Africa under apartheid. The next day the three participated in a program called "Amy's Magic: Living Reconciliation" at the University of Massachusetts–Amherst. Easy and Ntobeko discussed their transformation from political activists to community workers, and Linda spoke about reconciliation. Easy and Ntobeko hoped that their audiences would see them not as killers, but as former child soldiers during a time of political oppression. They wanted to show that they had dedicated themselves to healing and community upliftment. Linda was proud of how the pair helped educate Americans about South Africa. From 2002 onward, Linda, Easy, and Ntobeko would become touring advocates of reconciliation and restorative justice, both in the United States and South Africa.

Linda's work on behalf of the foundation made her feel closer to Amy and Peter, and she felt more energized than ever as she discussed reconciliation at various events in the months after Peter's death. In 2002 and 2003, she traveled to South Africa about once a month and spent approximately six months each year there. While she was in Cape Town, she stayed at a one-bedroom apartment on Queen Victoria Street near Parliament and the public gardens. When she walked the streets of the city, strangers frequently asked her how she could forgive the men who killed her daughter. "When people ask me how I can do this, all I can tell them is that everyone reacts differently," she said. "Coming to South Africa has made it easier to deal with the loss. Here nearly everyone has a story that would make your heart break. Here I've discovered that I am not the only one who has suffered." Many strangers admired her stance and approached her in a friendly manner, but she occasionally encountered people who were hostile. Although Kim, Molly, and Zach hadn't developed the close relationship with Easy and Ntobeko that Linda had, they supported what she was doing. They only insisted that she not drive in South Africa. Although he and his sisters knew about South Africa's high crime rate, Zach wasn't particularly worried about his mother's safety in Cape Town's black townships. "I'm more worried about what white South Africans would do to my mom, not black South Africans," he said.

After Peter's death, the Amy Biehl Foundation Trust continued to focus on education, health and safety, sports and recreation, arts and music, and job training programs. Ntobeko took visitors to the trust on tours of Gugulethu, while Easy ran the organization's after-school sports programs. A staff meeting at the trust's office in Cape Town in July 2002 revealed the organization's dynamism. It brought together white and black South Africans, white and black Americans, and foreigners and South Africans, all of whom were seeking to improve conditions in South Africa's disadvantaged areas. Ashleigh Murphy, an American in her twenties and the organization's local director, ran the meeting, not Linda. One intern who worked on the trust's drama program was developing ways of communicating AIDS awareness to children in an entertaining, dramatic style. Linda encouraged the staff to strengthen its relationship with Artscape, a prominent theater in Cape Town, because such an arrangement could benefit both the trust and the theater. The interns and South African staff members welcomed the idea and exuded an energetic "can-do" spirit. This was not an organization about to collapse because Peter was no longer there. A white South African lawyer attending the meeting as a guest quoted something he had heard Robert F. Kennedy say in Cape Town 36 years earlier: "Each time a man stands up for an ideal, or acts to improve the lot of others, or strikes out against injustice, he sends forth a tiny ripple of hope, and crossing each other from a million different centers of energy and daring those ripples build a current which can sweep down the mightiest walls of oppression and resistance." This statement reflected not only Robert Kennedy's idealism, but the idealism and spirit of the trust's employees and interns.

The news was not all good. The trust's bakery in Strand had to be closed for financial reasons. This was disappointing, especially after the closure of the Parow bakery and the suspension of bread deliveries in Gugulethu. Linda urged the staff not to get discouraged about setbacks and told them that sometimes good things could arise from problems. A case in point was the trust's relationship with the South African supermarket chain Pick n Pay. Not only was Pick n Pay selling "Amy's bread," it would soon sell "Amy's rice" and "Amy's milk" in all of its stores, sending a percentage of profits back to the trust.

A year after Peter died, Linda felt encouraged by the status of the foundation. It was receiving more support from South African partners, both public and private. The staff was growing and becoming more independent. And the US-based foundation had a network of support not only in southern California, but in St. Louis, Seattle, the San Francisco Bay Area, Washington, D.C., New York, Boston, Santa Fe, and Albuquerque. Linda envisioned traveling to South Africa about five times a year, working to create a sustainable organization that would continue to thrive after USAID funding ended in 2005. "I want to take on the role that will not entail micromanaging but will give appropriate direction and support for all the pain and learning that has occurred over the last ten years," she wrote. She was encouraged by the signs of growth in the trust. By mid-2003, the Youth Reading Role Models Program had expanded to 26 schools. That year, dance was among the trust's most popular after-school activities. Three hundred participants performed at festivities marking Human Rights Day (March 21) and Youth Day (June 16). Almost a thousand youths participated in the trust's instrumental music program, which was held at two primary schools and was made possible by donations of musical instruments. The trust's sports program had expanded and offered training in soccer, cricket, rugby, and netball.

As the 10th anniversary of Amy's death approached in 2003, Amy and the Biehls received renewed public attention. Evelyn Mayipheli, a supporter of the trust in George, wrote a traditional African praise poem honoring Amy in preparation for the trust's August fundraiser. Calling Amy "the star of America and South Africa," Mayipheli thanked her for sacrificing her life for the good of South Africans. The blood she shed was like a seed that had blossomed into wonderful programs that enriched the lives of many people. Now the name Amy was unforgettable and hailed throughout the land. Mayipheli's poem did more than just fill a spot on the anniversary program—it showed how some black South Africans had come to regard Amy as a kind of folk hero.

In August 2003, South Africa's *Carte Blanche* television program (modeled on *60 Minutes* in the United States) aired a segment on Linda and the foundation. Saying that Amy's murder 10 years earlier was "imprinted on South Africa's memory," the program's message was that the Biehls had turned tragedy into triumph. The segment was not overly sugar coated, however. It noted that many white South Africans were horrified by the Biehls' conciliatory attitude toward the killers of their daughter. When reflecting on how she and Peter had dedicated their lives to South Africa after Amy's death, Linda seemed at peace. "Amy would have expected us to step up to the plate and . . . come and see," she said. "In retrospect, it was absolutely the best thing we could have done." After the program aired, several South Africans wrote to the trust to express their support. One white South African said, "The images of you working with your daughter's killers were so powerful and I was blown away by the miraculous change in the attitudes of the young activists whose lives have been so positively changed by the active steps you and your late husband took to create the miracle of reconciliation." Letters like this, plus positive coverage in the Afrikaans-language newspaper *Rapport,* showed that many white South Africans greatly admired the Biehls.

Linda continued her tradition of being in South Africa on the anniversary of Amy's death. She was gratified that Amy's legacy had lived on among those who worked on behalf of others and among the many South Africans who had benefited from the trust's programs. But she was especially pleased that Easy and Ntobeko were so integral to the trust's work. "It is their transformation that truly represents the powerful legacy of Amy Biehl. Their transformation is what Amy was working for," Linda wrote. She understood why some people were shocked by her relationship with the two young men and realized that her life had taken an unexpected turn. "If you told me 10 years ago that I would be here doing this now, I would have laughed," she said.

There were some unexpected bumps along the way. A Cape Town advertising agency made two public service announcements for the trust that aired on South African television in mid-2003. Both generated considerable controversy. In one of the spots, a young black boy said, "Hello. My name is Thomas. In seven years' time, we'll meet at a stop street. I'll walk up to your car and put a gun to your head. If you don't get out of the car, I will shoot you." Another ad depicted a young white boy who told viewers that in a few years, he would stab someone who refused to give him money. The ads ended with the line, "With no education, this is a likely future. Educate. Educate. Educate." The director of the ad agency said that he and his staff wanted the ads to shake people up and to show what could happen when children were denied an education. Linda had seen and approved the ads. The trust's media director, Leyla Haidarian, expected that the ads would ruffle some feathers but believed they would remind viewers that current deprivation could have serious consequences. The ads were shown on South Africa's eTV and M-Net, but not on the SABC, whose director objected to the alleged portrayal of black children as future criminals. Some viewers complained that the ads "used scare tactics to solicit financial support"; others asserted that the ads appeared to justify crime and violence. After receiving 23 such complaints, South Africa's Advertising Standards Authority ordered that the ads be banned from the airways. Officials called the ads "chilling" and "shocking" because they allegedly used fear to promote a cause and portrayed street children as potential criminals to be feared. The trust didn't lose money when the ads were pulled because they had been produced and broadcast free of charge. But the attempt to generate support had backfired in this case. A week after the ads were banned, the trust released a statement saying, "In the context of how Amy Biehl was murdered and how her parents responded to the tragedy, this is a story of responding with reconciliation and hard work instead of with anger and a call for retribution." The staff had a point. The ads were indeed jarring, but it seemed that many of the complainants refused to see the connection between poverty, poor education, and crime.

Mongezi Manqina made news at around the time the ads were pulled. A year earlier, shortly after Peter died, Mongezi came to see Linda at the trust's office. He had heard that Easy and Ntobeko worked for the trust and hoped Linda would give him a job as well. Linda hesitated. She felt that Easy and Ntobeko had earned the opportunity to work for the trust because they had contributed to society through their youth club, whereas Mongezi (and Vusumzi Ntamo) had not. Still, she told Mongezi about the First Aid Training Program in prisons, but he never followed up with Victor West. Easy and Ntobeko didn't want Mongezi to work at the trust, having heard that he was on the run for another crime. In the end, Linda did not offer him a job. In early November 2003, Mongezi was found guilty of raping a mentally handicapped teenager who lived in his neighborhood, and he was sent back to prison. Not surprisingly, Mongezi's conviction received significant publicity in South Africa. It gave ammunition to those who opposed amnesty and who believed that amnesty freed criminals. The *Sunday Times* quoted only one critic of the original amnesty decision, but many readers would probably have shared his thoughts. Patrick Laurence, the editor of *Focus,* a journal published by the liberal Helen Suzman Foundation, said, "[Manqina's] conviction of raping a handicapped girl reinforces skepticism of the original decision to grant the youths amnesty. It raises suspicions that he was not really contrite and seems to have thought that the amnesty gave him some sort of immunity from prosecution or license to do whatever he wanted." As Peter had pointed out years earlier, the Biehl case had yielded a 50 percent success rate, high enough for those who supported amnesty, perhaps, but too low for those who opposed it.

IN March 2004, Solomon Makosana became the first black South African director of the Amy Biehl Foundation Trust. An educator for 32 years, he had worked for the trust since 2001 and was now taking over from Ashleigh Murphy, a white American 30 years his junior. He sensed that people viewed the trust as an American organization and hoped it could be transformed into a South African NGO. Victor West was disappointed that he had not been considered for the position, and soon his criticisms of the trust made their way into the press. He told a reporter that he had been passed over "because he was not black enough," a comment that reflected South Africa's ever-present racial sensitivities. Many mixed-race and Indian South Africans justifiably believed that they had been discriminated against in the past because they weren't "white enough." Now, under black majority rule, they believed that they were being denied opportunities because they weren't "black enough." West also wondered why the trust's programs didn't address needs in mixed-race areas. "I'm asked why all programs are in African townships," he said. "Are there no poor people in Coloured areas?" Some wondered why it had taken so long for a South African to be appointed director of the trust. West noted that the trust's board was predominantly white and speculated that Makosana's appointment amounted to tokenism. Although his anger toward the trust eventually dissipated, West's remarks reflected South Africa's racial dynamics. Apartheid had been legally dismantled 10 years earlier, but its legacy of inequality still affected perceptions, attitudes, and conditions in South Africa. Despite its best efforts, the trust was not immune to the racial undercurrents that still bedeviled South African society.

Makosana was soon confronted with the impending loss of USAID funding, which was scheduled to end in 2005. The trust's operation in George was an early casualty of cost-cutting measures. Makosana and Linda believed that the trust's limited resources could best be used in the Cape Town area, and so they reluctantly ended the programs in George in 2004. But another source of revenue soon revealed itself—township tours. Cape Town was bursting with tourists in the early 2000s, and many visitors were interested in visiting Cape Town's historically black areas and interacting with township residents. Cape Town's city government recognized potential visitor interest in "sites of struggle," and they worked with local tour companies to develop township tours as the influx of overseas visitors increased. Township residents also recognized the potential economic benefits of township tours for bed-and-breakfasts, arts and crafts, purveyors of food and drink, and more. Among the regular stops for township tours in the early 2000s was the Amy Biehl memorial in Gugulethu.

Many white South Africans also called the trust's office and asked to be taken into the townships, where most had never been before. Linda encouraged Ntobeko's interest in developing a tourism project for the trust. Many of his early township tours were conducted free of charge and gave visitors an inside look at project sites, such as the Buthisizwe skills center, after-school programs, and the golf driving range in Khayelitsha. Eventually the trust charged for some tours in order to generate revenue. By 2010, the trust hosted at least one township tour a week.

There was more evidence that the Amy Biehl story had become part of South Africa's historical narrative. On June 12, 2004, runners carried the Olympic torch on a 35-mile route past some of Cape Town's important public sites in advance of the summer games in Athens. One torchbearer handed Nelson Mandela the torch on Robben Island; another took it to a school in Gugulethu that had sent a student to work with NASA in the United States; another took it past the site where Amy was killed 11 years earlier. "It's symbolic because Amy's parents, instead of being bitter, came out to South Africa and formed the Amy Biehl Foundation and reconciled with their daughter's killers," one of the run's organizers said. The Biehls' story was also highlighted in an exhibit in Johannesburg in December 2004. As part of events marking Reconciliation Day in South Africa (on December 16), an exhibition on forgiveness was held at the Fort Atrium on Constitution Hill. It featured some of South Africa's most important proponents of forgiveness, such as Archbishop Tutu, Father Michael Lapsley (an antiapartheid cleric whose hands were blown off by a letter bomb), Duma Kumalo (one of the Sharpeville Six who was wrongly imprisoned for murder), and Linda Biehl, who was shown in a photo with Easy and Ntobeko. The *Star* newspaper highlighted the important lessons the exhibit offered and used the Biehls as prime examples of forgiveness. "The Biehls . . . heeded the words of Archbishop Desmond Tutu when he said, 'If you can find it in yourself to forgive then you are no longer chained to the perpetrator. You can move on, and you can even help the perpetrator to become a better person too.'"

These events further raised the profile of the trust, but the looming end of USAID funding still clouded its future. Linda wanted to strengthen the infrastructure of the foundation in the United States so that events and fundraising would grow as USAID funding dried up. Zach became her "right-hand man" and helped arrange a speaking schedule that would take her all over the country. She traveled to St. Louis regularly to speak to groups, showcase the work of the trust, and discuss restorative justice with Easy and Ntobeko. She also developed a growing connection with Seattle, home to the Desmond Tutu Peace Foundation since 2000. There she met with students studying reconciliation in South Africa and participated in programs that brought together South African and American teenagers to discuss human rights. In southern California, Linda regularly spoke at Whittier College, her alma mater. She also helped launch the Amy Biehl International Peace Festival at Soka University in Orange County. At these events and countless others, Linda enjoyed stepping away from the podium and interacting with young people who were interested in community service and restorative justice.

By the mid-2000s, the relationship between Linda and Easy and Ntobeko symbolized for many Americans the kind of work the Amy Biehl Foundation Trust was trying to accomplish in South Africa. The trust's website highlighted the fact that Easy and Ntobeko worked for the organization. They were presented as "a living embodiment of the values" that the trust sought to teach Cape Town youth, such as forgiveness, reconciliation, and tolerance. The two men gave Linda hope for the new South Africa. "They're not perfect, no one is," she said. "Everyone has to work to reconcile, to make communities better. . . . We're getting to know each other. They trust me." Linda admitted that her work with the trust was hard, but her relationship with Easy and Ntobeko was natural and comfortable. In her many interviews with journalists, Linda liked to distinguish between forgiveness and reconciliation. As she explained it, the victim forgives in order to ease the pain and bitterness he or she felt. Reconciliation was a longer process that involved the victim and the perpetrator working together for positive change.

"Forgiveness is a big word," she told a journalist in 2005. "You did something bad to me, I am bigger than that, I am going to forgive you and walk away. I think the bigger word is reconciliation. Reconciliation takes work. Forgiveness is more for yourself. Reconciliation takes two people. If I'd fought against amnesty for these men, they'd never have become productive members of society."

In the years ahead, Linda and Ntobeko spoke about restorative justice at more venues across the United States. They both believed that restorative justice could make a better world. They were a living example of how people once at odds could recognize each other's humanity, work together, and build a better future. At a joint appearance at Marquette University in 2006, a reporter asked Linda to describe how restorative justice benefited society. She replied, "When individuals are at peace with themselves, when individuals are feeling part of their communities, when they don't feel alienated, when they have opportunities, when they can live their lives positively and productively and have hope, our whole society at large will benefit. It's disenfranchised people . . . [who] resort to disturbing the harmony in our society by violent means."

The concept of restorative justice had its fair share of skeptics, particularly in the United States and South Africa. In the United States, the criminal justice system had become noticeably more punitive in the late 20th century, and in South Africa many citizens felt under siege in a society racked by violent crime. Because Linda was such an outspoken advocate of restorative justice, she was sometimes a lightning rod for controversy, just as she and Peter had been in the past. Disdain toward Linda's conciliatory attitude sometimes bubbled up after she received high-profile press coverage. When the *Boston Globe* published an article about her in 2003, "many readers responded angrily. What was wrong with these parents? How could they possibly embrace the killers?" Linda occasionally received hate mail from those who disapproved of her relationship with Easy and Ntobeko. In 2007, the trust decided to remove the guest book from its website because of the hateful comments that appeared. Linda took the diatribes in her stride. She understood that some were mystified or even horrified by her relationship with Easy and Ntobeko, but she didn't try to force people to accept her perspective. "It's a personal issue between victim and perpetrator," she said simply.

Other matters concerned her more than periodic criticism from angry whites. The impending loss of USAID funding presented serious financial challenges to the Amy Biehl Foundation Trust. The USAID grants were not meant as permanent sources of funding, but rather as seed grants to get projects up and running. With the last USAID grant scheduled to end in December 2005, Linda and Makosana were forced to reduce the trust's staff and cut funding for some key programs. One casualty of the downsizing was the Khayelitsha golf driving range. Despite some support from the South African Golf Development Board, the trust didn't have enough money to maintain the infrastructure for the club or hire adequate security. The clubhouse was eventually vandalized and the fairway became littered with garbage, forcing a member of the Khayelitsha golf club to coach youths on soccer fields and open plots of land, just as he did in the 1990s. The trust also ended its First Aid Training Program after a successful seven-year run. Despite the loss of these programs, people were still donating, and so the trust could continue its work in other areas.

The need for community service organizations like the trust was greater than ever. In the early 2000s, South Africa was stable politically, but it still faced daunting social and economic problems. Improving education was among South Africa's most serious challenges. Its struggling school system was failing to equip black students with the skills they needed to get better-paying jobs, emerge from poverty, and move into better homes and neighborhoods. Linda believed that addressing the needs of black youth was one of South Africa's greatest challenges. She also believed that change would only occur in South Africa once black children had the educational opportunities that white children had. With these concerns in mind, she ensured that the trust's educational programs were not only maintained, but expanded. By 2007, the Youth Reading Role Models Program had more than 4,000 participants. In one month alone, the trust held reading workshops at 15 schools, training older students to teach young students to read. One of the trust's main goals was to "supplement the shortcomings of the educational system." Besides helping children improve their reading ability, the trust's programs helped them develop creative skills in art and music, which the formal education system deemphasized. The trust's AIDS peer education program continued as well, ensuring that hundreds of primary school pupils understood issues surrounding the disease. The trust also offered a simple but important economic benefit to its participants: by providing safe havens for youths after school, it enabled their parents to continue working in the afternoon.

As the trust intensified its efforts to supplement South Africa's education system, it faced another setback. Makosana's health started to decline in 2006. In his late fifties by then, Makosana was diabetic and had a heart ailment. As his health deteriorated, he spent less time in the office, leaving the trust without a daily leader. In July, Makosana was hospitalized; he died on August 3, 2006. Linda lamented Makosana's loss and the void it left at the trust.

From Linda's perspective, one of the challenges of the foundation was finding the right people to staff it. She knew that the trust was perceived as a white organization, but she had her eye on Kevin Chaplin, a white South African, as Makosana's replacement. Chaplin headed the First National Bank in the Western Cape and had strong contacts in the business world. He first met the Biehls through the US consulate in Cape Town and became a trustee of the Amy Biehl Foundation Trust after Peter died. Linda believed he had the business background the trust needed, but she realized that appointing a white male to the directorship would bring "complications." She did so anyway. By early 2007, Chaplin made the transition from banking to leading a high-profile nonprofit organization. But even though his background differed sharply from previous directors—idealistic young Americans and Solomon Makosana—he had long admired what the Biehls stood for.

Although some observers grumbled that the trust still lacked a long-term black director, the benefits of appointing Chaplin soon became clear. He was instrumental in stabilizing the trust's finances at a pivotal time. One way he did so was by establishing new connections between the trust and South African businesses and corporations. Among those enlisted to help sponsor the trust's 2008 fundraiser were Appletiser, the Mount Nelson Hotel, Nedbank, Protea Hotels, and Woolworths. In June 2008, the trust partnered with Coca-Cola to launch the Amy Biehl Youth Spirit Awards for South African youths who had distinguished themselves in community service. The Blue Ribbon Bakery now produced "Amy's bread"; the Rosendal Winery produced "Amy's wine"; and the Zama Dance School and the Cape Town City Ballet helped sponsor the trust's dance programs. These partnerships showed how well respected the trust had become since its founding.

Chaplin and his staff also forged new partnerships that extended beyond the business world. Cape Town's city government collaborated with the trust on several sports programs and in new projects in historically mixed-race townships. To bolster the Youth Reading Role Models Program, the trust not only recruited parents as readers but also enlisted high-profile government officials, such as the speaker of Parliament and the minister of education. In order to expand its music programs, the trust partnered with the University of Cape Town's School of Music and the Artscape theatre. The trust also established partnerships with Diocesan College ("Bishops") and the Hugo Lambrechts Music Centre in Parow. Each week, students from township schools visited these institutions for guitar, brass, and stringed instrument lessons. The trust's environmental program worked to improve landscaping in the townships by planting trees, flowers, and vegetable gardens at local schools. This program received assistance from Kirstenbosch Botanical Gardens and the University of the Western Cape, which helped supply trees, flowers, and volunteers. New international links bolstered the trust's sports programs. In August 2008, a women's field hockey club from Northern Ireland held a weeklong academy for girls at the trust's programs in Langa and Manenberg. Later that month, 16 girls from those communities traveled to Northern Ireland for more training.

Generating funds for the trust became important for the long-term sustainability of the organization. Soon, several income-producing projects were in place: Amy Biehl Cultural Township Tours, which were supported and promoted by Cape Town's tourism authority; the sale of greeting cards, "Amy's bread," and other products; the annual fundraiser; the Gugulethu Jazz Festival; the Amy Biehl Fun Run; and recycling initiatives at the trust's office and after-school centers. A Cape Town flower shop began selling "Amy's roses" and donating some of the profits to the trust. Former South African president F. W. de Klerk even agreed to be auctioned off as a lunch date to help raise money for the trust.

The signs of growth and dynamism were undeniable. In 2008, the trust opened another after-school center in Gugulethu that would accommodate 240 children. Sports programs now included soccer, field hockey, diving, cricket, table tennis, swimming, and diving. More participants in the trust's music program signed up for instrumental lessons. A Rondebosch-based church group began teaching guitar to youths in New Crossroads. In April 2008, the children in the trust's guitar, marimba, violin, and brass ensembles performed at a function hosted by Archbishop Tutu. That same month, the trust's art and dance students held an exhibition and performance at Cape Town's Victoria and Alfred Waterfront. Almost three years after USAID funding had ended, the trust was alive and well, thanks to the sustained, behind-the-scenes efforts of its entire staff. Growing support from key constituencies in Cape Town and beyond helped as well.

New and returning visitors from all over the world came to Cape Town to see the trust's programs in action. Americans from many schools and colleges visited, including "Semester at Sea" students, as did those representing the State Department, Congress, and the American Council on Education. As it had from the beginning, the trust benefited from a continual stream of volunteers, both from South Africa and abroad. They stayed for weeks or months, offering valuable help in many areas. A newly minted graduate of UCT's medical school created an AIDS education program for high school youths in Crossroads. Interns—who most often came from the United States, Canada, Germany, Norway, Austria, Holland, and the United Kingdom—helped with fundraising and programs in music, AIDS education, sports, reading, and art. Interns also helped design, launch, and maintain the trust's website. Many interns worked side by side with Easy and Ntobeko, marveling at how the Biehls had not only supported amnesty for them but befriended and hired them. An intern from Wheaton College was particularly impressed with Easy and Ntobeko. "They are two of the most humane, remarkable and compassionate people you will ever meet," he wrote, "and their personal transformations—the way they work in Amy's memory, their commitment to the kids they serve—is precisely the kind of change Amy sought in South Africa."

In the years since Peter's death, Linda's status as an icon of reconciliation had grown. In April 2008, she was named the first Greeley Scholar for Peace at the University of Massachusetts–Lowell. At the inaugural event on the campus, she spoke about the journey she had taken from grief to forgiveness to reconciliation. Ntobeko was there by her side, and he spoke about his "gradual redemption" from militant to prisoner to humanitarian worker. Over the next month, Linda would give numerous talks at the university, participate on panels, and interact with students and faculty.

Then, during her residency in Massachusetts, Linda was notified that she would receive one of South Africa's highest honors. She would be presented with the O. R. Tambo award in bronze, named after the longtime ANC leader who had been Mandela's law partner in the 1950s. The Tambo award was one of South Africa's national orders of merit, bestowed on those who had "contributed to making a better life for current and future generations" in South Africa, particularly in the areas of freedom, nation building, and democracy. The Order of the Companions of O. R. Tambo was given to foreign nationals who had made exemplary contributions to South African life. Linda later learned that her friends Sahm Venter and Ahmed Kathrada had lobbied the award committee on her behalf.

Linda flew to Pretoria to attend the ceremony, held at the Union Buildings on April 22, 2008, a day after her 65th birthday. Those receiving Tambo awards included Ron Dellums, a leading member of the Congressional Black Caucus, and Harry Belafonte, another beacon of America's antiapartheid movement. Linda received her award "for displaying [an] outstanding spirit of forgiveness in the wake of the murder of her daughter and contributing to the promotion of non-racism in post-apartheid South Africa." Linda beamed as President Mbeki placed the award banner around her neck. In the coming years, she would regard the Tambo award as her greatest honor.

Meanwhile, Linda's whirlwind schedule had become exhausting. She was scrambling between speaking engagements all over the United States, working at the trust's office in Cape Town, and spending time with her children and grandchildren back home in California. She still wanted to do more with the trust, but she was determined to scale back her travel to South Africa. Fortunately, Kevin Chaplin's mixture of managerial experience and fundraising success made it possible for her to do so by 2008–9.

The year 2008 marked a decade since Easy and Ntobeko had been released from prison. Both fathers in their mid-30s and key staff members of the Amy Biehl

Foundation Trust, they had become as much a part of the Amy Biehl story as the Biehls themselves. The two were just as committed to working in Amy's name as they had been when the Biehls first hired them. By mid-2007, Ntobeko had been appointed to a managerial position with the trust. Amy's death still haunted him. "Deep down, it's very difficult for me to accept my own actions," he told a journalist. "I felt I had contributed to a new South Africa and that what I did was for political reasons. But when I thought of Amy . . . One has to find peace within in order to live. It's odd, but sometimes people who offer forgiveness are so disappointed when the people they forgive cannot forgive themselves. This foundation has helped me forgive myself." Like Ntobeko, Easy found it difficult to talk about Amy's death. He'd been deeply saddened by Peter's passing but had grown closer to Linda, whose consistent kindness reshaped his views of whites, whom he had distrusted before. He shared Linda's belief in racial reconciliation but believed South Africa still had a long way to go. He was still angered by the racial prejudice he'd encountered. "I will never run away from the fact that the oppression in South Africa was done by white people," he told an interviewer in 2008. "The white man was prepared to kill. I, also, was prepared to kill. But now, I'm working to spread the spirit of Amy." From Linda's perspective, Easy and Ntobeko had come a long way since the 1990s. She was proud of the way they had developed as parents, employees, and responsible members of their community. She was so accustomed to their presence at speaking engagements that she sometimes felt lost when they weren't by her side.

By 2010, Amy was being commemorated in new ways. On August 16, Brigitte Mabandla gave the first annual Amy Biehl Memorial Lecture at the University of the Western Cape. She outlined Amy's efforts to end violence against women and said that Amy's research in the 1990s continued to be relevant in contemporary South Africa. On August 25, the 17th anniversary of Amy's death, a new stone monument in her honor was unveiled next to the Caltex station in Gugulethu. With Easy and Ntobeko nearby, Linda swayed to the beat of the Amy Biehl choir as the ceremony began. US ambassador Donald Gips hailed Amy's commitment to a free South Africa and dedicated the memorial on behalf of the US Fulbright program. The memorial's inscription read:

AMY BIEHL 26 APRIL 1967—25 AUGUST 1993

KILLED IN AN ACT OF POLITICAL VIOLENCE,

AMY WAS A FULBRIGHT SCHOLAR AND A TIRELESS HUMAN RIGHTS ACTIVIST.

THE AMY BIEHL FOUNDATION, FOUNDED IN 1997, TO
DEVELOP & EMPOWER YOUTH IN SOUTH AFRICA THROUGH
EDUCATIONAL & CULTURAL PROGRAMMES.

As a Cape Town headline read days earlier, "The power of the Biehl family's forgiveness is still inspirational."

Although Linda could never have imagined it on the day Amy died, many observers now regarded her as a living embodiment of Mandela's and Tutu's values.
The two leaders had striven to heal the wounds of the past and to promote forgiveness, without which there could be no future in South Africa. The Biehls had
embraced this cause, and in turn, Mandela and Tutu had embraced them. More
evidence that the Biehls had become part of South Africa's pantheon of reconciliation was to follow. Jonathan Jansen, rector of the University of the Free State (UFS)
and one of South Africa's leading public intellectuals, published a weekly column
on South Africa's "Times Live" website. In 2008, just before he came to UFS, a
group of white students was filmed crudely harassing black workers on the campus,
sparking widespread outrage. Instead of heeding calls to prosecute the offending
students, Jansen sought to rehabilitate them, triggering a heated, nationwide debate
that brought South Africa's racial tensions to a boiling point. In an October 2009
column, Jansen wrote that although the road to reconciliation was a difficult path
filled with obstacles, it was preferable to retribution and recrimination, which would
only deepen racial tensions as South Africans tried to build a stable new nation. The
choice was to forge ahead along the path set out by Mandela, Tutu, the Biehls, and
the black mothers who forgave the police for killing their sons, or go down the path
taken by Rwanda and the Middle East, where the reservoirs of hate were so deep
that the future seemed irredeemably violent and unstable. Jansen chose the path
taken by Mandela, Tutu, the Biehls, and the black mothers. He wrote,

> Reconciliation is complex. There are no predetermined rules. Legal
> prescription cannot mend hearts. Political injunction cannot force
> change. There is no cookbook recipe in the daily and difficult pursuit of
> being human.
>
> Sometimes the perpetrator is beaten up by his victims on making
> the approach. Sometimes the approach made by the victims in search
> of peace receives no response. Often, the perpetrator stands fast in
> denial, doing irreparable harm to others and himself. When, in rare
> circumstances, the perpetrator and victim together meet to acknowledge
> pain inflicted and received, something magical happens.
>
> What we do know is that a failure to reconcile at crucial moments in
> history can destroy a nation. We can build such deep divides in anger that
> it might take generations to overcome, or never.

Linda Biehl could not have said it better herself.

39 US Secretary of State Madeleine Albright joins Peter and Linda at the official launch of the Amy Biehl Foundation Trust in Gugulethu, December 13, 1997. (Reuters)

40 Nelson Mandela with Linda and Peter in Washington, D.C., on the morning of Mandela's Congressional Gold Medal ceremony, September 23, 1998. (Biehl family)

41 Molly (*left*) and Kim (*right*) with Nelson Mandela, September 23, 1998. (Biehl family)

42 Peter and Linda with Archbishop Tutu, c. late 1990s. (Biehl family)

43 Linda and Peter being interviewed about "Amy's bread" in Gugulethu, c. late
    1990s. (Biehl family)

44 (*left*) A banner put up by Gugulethu residents marking the spot where Amy was killed, 2001. (Steven Gish)

45 (*below*) Linda with participants in the Amy Biehl Foundation's music program, c. early 2000s. (Biehl family)

46 Linda with Easy Nofemela (*left*) and Ntobeko Peni (*right*) at a workshop on reconciliation in St. Louis, 2008. (Larry Kendall)

47 South African president Thabo Mbeki presenting Linda with a Tambo award in Pretoria, April 22, 2008. (Biehl family)

48 (*above*) Linda with children in the Amy Biehl Foundation's after-school ballet program at the University of Cape Town, 2009. (Biehl family)

49 (*left*) The Amy Biehl Memorial in Gugulethu, dedicated in 2010. (NKansahrexford/ Wikimedia commons)

The Amy Biehl Foundation in action (2010)

50 Arts & crafts program.
    (Larry Kendall)

51 Arts & crafts program.
    (Larry Kendall)

52 Trombone lesson. (Larry Kendall)

53 Practicing the violin. (Larry Kendall)

54　An after-school academic program. (Larry Kendall)

55　Working on laptop computers. (Larry Kendall)

56   Mastering new skills. (Larry Kendall)

57 Learning the basics of soccer. (Larry Kendall)

58 Linda with Ntobeko Peni's daughter Avile on the 20th
anniversary of Amy's death, August 25, 2013. (Steven Gish)

59 Linda and Easy Nofemela at a ceremony in Gugulethu marking the 20th
    anniversary of Amy's death, August 25, 2013. (Ana Venegas/*Orange County
    Register*)

15

The Legacy Lives On

EVER SINCE the events of August 25, 1993, Amy Biehl and her parents had captured the attention of people all over the world. Fascination with their story gained momentum as the focus shifted from Amy to her parents' unique gestures of forgiveness and reconciliation. A wide range of observers—journalists, novelists, filmmakers, educators, theologians, psychologists, and others—sought to tell the family's story in new ways and bring it to new audiences. Amy was long gone, but her legacy acquired a life of its own.

The first book based on Amy's story was the work of a black South African from Cape Town. Sindiwe Magona had previously written autobiographical works and short stories and was working for the United Nations in New York when Amy died. She had been a domestic worker during the apartheid era, struggling to raise her children while working for a white family, and had lived in the very area of Gugulethu where Amy was killed. When she traveled to South Africa to vote in the April 1994 election, she learned that her childhood friend Evelyn Manqina was the mother of one of Amy's killers. While grieving for the Biehl family, Magona also empathized with Evelyn, who had suffered under apartheid and struggled to raise a family during a life of hardship and dislocation. Magona realized that one of the killers could easily have been her own son. "The urge to explain the inexplicable to the Biehls would not leave me," she said later. "If only they could see what [Evelyn] had gone through . . . understand what her life had been . . . they might better understand how a senseless, cruel, evil thing could happen."

Magona's "urge to explain the inexplicable" resulted in the novel *Mother to Mother,* published in South Africa in 1998 and in the United States a year later. Her book took the form of a letter from the mother of the killer to Mrs. Biehl, explaining how apartheid oppression scarred many black South Africans and ultimately "bred the violent mob that killed Amy." The novel doesn't excuse Amy's murder but dramatizes the social context that contributed to the crime. Although Magona feared that Peter and Linda would hate the book, the Biehls loved *Mother to Mother.* Linda said the book helped her better understand the conditions facing black families under apartheid. "That was the whole point of my book," Magona said. "My Pulitzer Prize!"

A decade after its initial publication, *Mother to Mother* was turned into a play. A well-known South African actress, Thembi Mtshali-Jones, found the novel powerful and urged the director of the Baxter Theatre in Cape Town to read it. He was equally impressed, and the two persuaded Magona to adapt her novel for the stage in 2009. The one-woman play starring Mtshali-Jones as the mother premiered at the Baxter on September 16, 2009, and won significant press attention and positive reviews. Between 2011 and 2013, Mtshali-Jones performed the play in North Carolina and Bermuda and then back in South Africa at the National Arts Festival in Grahamstown, Johannesburg's Market Theatre, and the Baxter again. A reviewer in Johannesburg found the play "disturbingly relevant" because it raised important questions about where responsibility for violence lay: with society, parents, politicians, or just the perpetrators.

An American journalist wrote the first nonfiction book on the Biehls' story. Justine van der Leun became interested in Amy Biehl after marrying a South African. During an extended stay in Cape Town beginning in 2011, she wanted to escape the mostly white suburbs and venture into the townships to see conditions facing black South Africans. But her in-laws advised her to be careful, "otherwise you might end up like Amy Biehl." That remark piqued her curiosity and inspired her to learn more about Biehl. In doing her research, she befriended Easy Nofemela, who talked to her at length about growing up in Cape Town's black townships during the apartheid era. In her book *We Are Not Such Things* (2016), Van der Leun writes about Amy's death, the trial of her killers, and the reconciliation process, largely from the perspective of Gugulethu residents. She interweaves conflicting memories about what happened the day Amy was killed with vignettes of life in contemporary South Africa.

Other authors, while not writing directly about the Biehls, were nonetheless intrigued by the family's story and wrote works of fiction that closely mirrored the Biehls' experiences. In her young adult novel *Many Stones* (2000), American novelist Carolyn Coman tells the story of a teenage girl and her estranged father who travel to South Africa a year after older sister Laura was brutally killed near the Cape Town school where she was volunteering. The story is set against the backdrop of the Truth and Reconciliation Commission. The girl and her father wonder if black South Africans can forgive those who tortured and murdered their loved ones, just as they wonder if they can forgive those who killed Laura. The Indian author Shashi Tharoor was working at the UN in New York when he read about Amy Biehl's death. The main character in his book *Riot* (2001) is an idealistic American student in her mid-20s who had come to India to work on behalf of women's health programs. After 10 months abroad, she was killed by a rioting mob just before she was to return to the United States. The fictional quotations from the young woman's parents and professors are virtually identical to those uttered after Amy's death. Amanda Ward, a Texas-based author, had been interested in South Africa for years and was captivated by Peter and Linda's willingness to forgive their daughter's killers. In her novel *Forgive Me* (2007), Ward tells the story of an American reporter who goes to South Africa to cover the trial of black youths who beat a young American student to death. Ward "explores the ideas of truth and forgiveness" in ways that would be familiar to those who followed the Biehls and the TRC in general.

The Biehls' story also proved irresistible for filmmakers. In *Long Night's Journey into Day* (2000), Americans Frances Reid and Deborah Hoffman told the story of the Truth and Reconciliation Commission by focusing on four cases: Amy Biehl, the Cradock Four, the Magoo's Bar bombing, and the Gugulethu Seven. In the segment on Amy, Peter and Linda are shown making their statement at the amnesty hearings and visiting Evelyn Manqina for the first time. Other scenes show the four young men under questioning at the hearings and Mongezi reflecting on his actions after his release. The film was designed to present the complexities of forgiveness and reconciliation, not to suggest that the TRC offered easy answers. The film premiered at the Sundance Film Festival in Park City, Utah, in January 2000, where it won the Grand Jury Prize for documentary film. Linda and Peter attended the premiere at Sundance and found the film powerful and honest. After its debut, Reid and Hoffman took the documentary to film festivals and events in Berlin, New York, California, Cape Town, and elsewhere. It received an unusual amount of publicity for a documentary, most of it positive. Audiences found the film emotionally powerful, as perpetrators sought to explain their role in atrocities, while victims and their families considered whether or not to forgive. *Long Night's Journey into Day* was nominated for an Academy Award for Best Documentary in 2001.

Other filmmakers were eager to dramatize the Biehls' story for the big screen. Various studios, producers, writers, and actors expressed interest for years, but the final product seemed elusive. The high-profile American actress Reese Witherspoon even wanted to portray Amy at one point. In mid-1995, South African film producer Anant Singh contacted the Biehls to express his interest in doing a film on Amy. Singh had produced *Cry, the Beloved Country, Sarafina,* and many other South African–themed movies. In late 1995, Peter and Linda signed a contract granting Singh the film rights for Amy's story. But the Biehls had problems with the script produced by the first screenwriter assigned to the project. They were troubled by its fictional elements and by its dark ending, which didn't seem to offer hope for the future. At the same time, the Biehls began to have second thoughts about the proposed film. While they trusted Anant Singh and believed he could produce a movie that would be true to Amy, they didn't want a film that would create hostility toward the trust. These were valid concerns. A movie with big-name Hollywood stars and a focus on Amy might be profitable in the United States, but it would certainly be controversial in South Africa. It would seem inauthentic without a South African cast and would elevate Amy's role and death above the countless others who fought and died in the antiapartheid struggle. Furthermore, the Biehls' children didn't want a film because it would inevitably fictionalize Amy. Getting the approval of Kim, Molly, and Zach was important to Peter and Linda, because they knew that the children were sometimes uncomfortable with the amount of time their parents spent in South Africa. Peter and Linda didn't want to pursue a project that would magnify this discomfort. During the next decade and a half, the movie project drifted between studios and screenwriters without materializing. As time passed, it seemed unlikely that "The Amy Biehl Story" would ever hit the big screen.

In 2013, the movie project began to move forward again. Johanna Baldwin, a New York–based author, wrote a new screenplay that dramatized Amy's story and the Biehls' reconciliation with Easy and Ntobeko. Three years later, the well-known African American actor Tyler Perry announced that he would coproduce a film based on Baldwin's script. The film, to be titled *The Year of the Great Storm,* would be directed by Karzan Kader, a young Kurdish filmmaker who had won a student Oscar for a short film in 2011. Tyler Perry Studios and a consortium of other producers began casting the movie in 2016 and hoped to begin filming shortly thereafter.

As the movie industry was seeking to produce a film about the Biehls, two American educators in New Mexico began envisioning a physical monument to Amy. In 1999, Tony Monfiletto and Tom Siegel discussed developing a charter high school for at-risk youths in Albuquerque. They hoped to establish a school that would combine scholarship with community service, and they wanted to name it after a young American who could inspire other young people. Once they learned more about Amy Biehl, they realized that she would be an ideal namesake. "Amy was a budding scholar who had the desire and intellect to change the world around her," Monfiletto wrote. "That was what we wanted for our students." As a charter school, the new school would be run more independently than typical establishments. All students would be required to engage in community service and take at least two college courses in order to graduate. As they discussed their proposed school, Monfiletto and Siegel asked the Biehls if they would agree to have a school named after Amy. Even though the two men didn't know a great deal about Amy initially, Peter and Linda gave them their blessing.

The Biehls attended the grand opening of Amy Biehl High School on July 28, 2000. In 2006, the school moved to the old post office building in downtown Albuquerque, putting students closer to Albuquerque's community service organizations, the main city library, and museums. By 2009, 98 percent of the school's graduates had gone on to college, a notable achievement for an inner-city school with a nonwhite majority student population. When the Amy Biehl High School Foundation purchased the school building in 2015, Linda was there to help celebrate the occasion. By then, New Mexicans had named another new school after Amy: the Amy Biehl Community School at Rancho Viejo, which opened its doors in Santa Fe on August 23, 2010, and served students from kindergarten to sixth grade.

Another of the Biehls' most visible legacies can be found in academia—in the field of forgiveness studies. As more and more authors began publishing in this new field, they repeatedly referred to the Biehls to show how forgiveness could help individuals, groups, and societies heal from past conflicts or traumas. Forgiveness studies began to attract attention in the late 1990s and gained momentum especially after the terrorist attacks of September 11, 2001. As authors pondered how the world could address violence and break the cycles of hatred between people, groups, and nations, they frequently turned to the Biehls as examples. One branch of the discipline focused on truth commissions, which had been established in dozens of countries throughout the world in the late 20th century. A related branch of forgiveness studies focused on the benefits of "restorative justice" versus "retributive justice." A third branch explored the links between spirituality and forgiveness. Yet another focused on how forgiveness benefited individuals psychologically and medically. The Biehls featured prominently in all of these subfields.

Forgiveness was not just relevant to geopolitical or legal studies, of course; it was central to the world's major religions as well. Growing numbers of Christians in particular drew inspiration from the Biehls' example as the years passed. Self-help books and articles also attracted a widespread readership, and in the years after Amy's death they too began to refer to the Biehls as role models of forgiveness. Even Desmond Tutu joined the legion of self-help authors. He and his daughter Rev. Mpho Tutu collaborated to write *The Book of Forgiving: The Fourfold Path for Healing Ourselves and Our World* (2014). Not surprisingly, the Tutus drew on the Biehls multiple times as role models of forgiveness. As a *New York Times* columnist observed, forgiveness had become a "mainstream tool of holistic healing, conflict resolution, and self-help." Writings on forgiveness were appearing everywhere, and in those writings the Biehls' story was a staple. The family was even mentioned in a McGraw-Hill psychology textbook, *Interpersonal Conflict* (2001).

The Biehls had also become part of South Africa's national consciousness. In Cape Town in mid-2008, city officials were still soliciting recommendations for renaming some of the area's streets. Some suggested that NY1 in Gugulethu be renamed in honor of Steve Biko, but ANC officials in Cape Town (who weren't in power at the local level) said that people in Gugulethu wanted it named after Amy Biehl. By 2013, proposals for renaming Gugulethu's streets had moved forward. A public panel recommended that NY1 be named Steve Biko Drive and NY147 be named after Amy Biehl. Seven months after the proposal was accepted, a group of residents on NY147 protested the decision. One resident was even photographed painting over the new name on a street sign. Opponents of the renaming didn't object to Amy Biehl herself but feared being associated with her murder. Others felt that the old name was part of the community's heritage and shouldn't be taken away. By 2014, the street was known by both its old and new names, NY147 / Amy Biehl Street.

On August 25, 2013, Linda, then 70, marked the 20th anniversary of Amy's death in Gugulethu, along with about 40 friends and supporters. The morning's events began with a service at St. Columba's Anglican Church, a block away from the memorial site where Amy had been killed. Linda led the procession to the memorial, holding a sign from 1993 reading "Amy, a comrade" in one hand and the small hand of Ntobeko's 3-year-old daughter in the other. Easy and Ntobeko were there, along with Nancy Scheper-Hughes, the anthropologist who had arranged their first meeting with the Biehls 14 years earlier. As the crowd gathered at the stone monument next to the Caltex station, children from the Amy Biehl Foundation Trust began playing the marimba. Linda told the onlookers that Amy had a gift for bringing diverse people together, just like the crowd that morning. Twenty years after her death, her legacy was "about the lives that have been touched and changed."

Hidden from the occasion that day were the tensions that had developed between Linda and Kevin Chaplin, the director of the Amy Biehl Foundation Trust. Their differences of opinion over the trust's mission statement and future direction strained their working relationship and prompted Linda to reassess her own future. "I think it is good if they are changing missions and visions," Linda said, "but maybe it is time for me to let go and move on." She even came to believe that the trust's name should be changed to signify its South Africanization and the end of her family's formal involvement.

Linda began traveling to South Africa less frequently, mindful that she should pass the reins of the trust to South Africans. But she was not ready to pull away entirely. By August 2013, Easy was the trust's township tour coordinator, while Ntobeko continued as the organization's program manager. The two men still felt close to Linda. "When I see Makhulu, I remember I'm still doing the right thing," Easy said. "I'm walking the right path. When I see Makhulu, I feel free." Linda was immensely proud that he and Ntobeko had worked to improve life in their community since their release from prison. In 2015, the trust was still growing. It opened a new skills training center in Athlone, furnished with a computer lab, an arts and crafts area, and a test kitchen. The children of Cape Town's black townships needed the safe havens the trust provided more than ever. The organization served approximately 2,000 young people in those townships, providing after-school programs, free meals, tutoring, crafts, music lessons, and AIDS education. It also provided rides into the more affluent suburbs so that township children could participate in karate, surfing, and ballet. The Biehl family's legacy continued to be recognized in South Africa. Marianne Thamm, for whom Amy did some research in 1993, publicly thanked the Biehls in 2015 for providing such an important example to South Africa, which still needed their message. She wrote, "[Amy's] story and the subsequent brave journey undertaken by Amy's parents and those who took her life continue to inspire and serve as an example of what can be accomplished even in the face of great tragedy, when anger and rage do not drive human interaction."

While Linda reevaluated her role in South Africa, her work in the United States kept her as busy as ever. In April 2014, she joined South African human rights advocate Albie Sachs at a program on "Peacebuilding" at the University of Massachusetts–Lowell. Later that month, she traveled to St. Louis where she, Ntobeko, and an ex-warder from Mandela's last prison spoke about "Nelson

Mandela's Legacy of Reconciliation." She and Ntobeko also spoke at events at the National Underground Railroad Freedom Center in Cincinnati and at Whittier College and Long Beach, California. As long as there were still audiences interested in hearing about reconciliation and restorative justice, Linda would answer the call.

Because she and her family had invested so much time and emotion into the foundation, Linda found it hard to conceive of stepping away from it. In a way, the foundation had become another child of Linda's, her "baby." But she believed that her future was rooted in the United States with her American children and grandchildren, and that it was time to say goodbye to the Amy Biehl Foundation Trust in South Africa. In late 2016, the trust announced that it would henceforth be known as the "Amy Foundation SA." Linda would still maintain a connection to Cape Town, a place of dear friends, unforgettable experiences, and good memories. Her reluctance to abandon the foundation mirrored her reluctance to part with her second daughter. As of 2017, she still had the box containing Amy's ashes.

Acknowledgments

This book had a long gestation. It never would have been completed without the unfailing cooperation of the Biehl family. Linda Biehl offered help and encouragement over many years, spoke with me at length in South Africa and the United States on numerous occasions, and gave me unrestricted access to the family's vast collection of papers and photographs. While she and her children were always ready to help, they never tried to control what I wrote or how I wrote it. Kim, Molly, and Zach were equally ready to lend a hand, answering questions, unearthing file boxes, and sending photos. I cannot thank them enough for their cooperation. If they ever grew tired of my repeated requests for information, they never showed it. My only regret is that I never met Peter Biehl, who died just as I began this project.

I am grateful to many others in the United States, South Africa, and beyond. After our 2005 interview, Scott Greenwood-Meinert responded to my stream of follow-up questions promptly and thoughtfully. Others who went out of their way to assist me in California include David Abernethy, one of Amy's professors at Stanford; Karen Fung, Stanford's Africana librarian; Bruce Thompson, Amy's humanities instructor; and Rick Schavone, Stanford's diving coach. In Washington, D.C., Margaret Collard entrusted me with her scrapbook on Amy and Gina Bjornland helped me with photographs long after our initial interview. Amy's friends Carole Sams Hoemeke in Georgia and Anna Wang in Switzerland provided me with unique sources from their own archives, for which I am grateful. I also received much-needed assistance from Suzanne Abel at Stanford's Haas Center for Public Service, Daniel Hartwig at the Stanford University Archives, Dana Simmons at the Clinton Presidential Library, and Jonathan Wilks at Amy Biehl High School in Albuquerque, New Mexico.

In South Africa, Christopher Saunders at the University of Cape Town encouraged me from the moment I began this project and offered sage advice as it developed. I have been grateful for his counsel for many years. Thanks also go to

Greg Cuthbertson at the University of South Africa and, in Cape Town, Mohamed Adhikari at UCT, Sandra Shell and her staff at UCT's African Studies Library, the staff at the South African National Library, Gerald Friedman, and Sandra Liebenberg. At the Amy Biehl Foundation in Cape Town, Easy Nofemela and Ntobeko Peni offered me important perspectives on Gugulethu, youth politics, and South Africa's turbulent 1990s.

One of the joys of this project was conducting interviews, and I thank those who spoke with me over the years and offered their perspectives. They are listed in the bibliography.

Grants from the Research Council and the Department of History at Auburn University at Montgomery enabled me to make multiple research trips to Cape Town and California. I am grateful for this generous support from my home institution.

As my manuscript took shape, several scholars read drafts of my work and offered helpful suggestions, including Jonathan Jansen at the University of the Free State and Stanford University, Peter Limb at Michigan State University, and an anonymous reader in South Africa. I am particularly indebted to Robert Edgar at Howard University for his close reading of my manuscript and for providing detailed comments. It was also an honor to work with Russell Martin, who helped me condense my first draft into the more streamlined final version. And as always, Cathy Quillin was an excellent proofreader.

For granting permission to reproduce text, I thank the Stanford University Archives, Stanford's Graduate School of Business, and Taylor & Francis publishers. Those who helped me identify photographs and secure the necessary permissions include Michele Cardon, *Orange County Register;* Walaa Elsiddig, *People;* Justin Frable, Thomson Reuters; Alan George, Stanford Athletics; Willem Jordaan, *Die Burger;* Clive Kirkwood, University of Cape Town; Ian Landsberg, Independent Media, Ltd.; Sue Lisk, Agence France Presse; and Matthew Lutts, Associated Press. Larry Kendall was unusually helpful in providing DVDs and photographs relevant to the story; he also illuminated me on the long-standing partnership between his family and the Biehls. Louise Gubb, Mike Hutchings, and Sasa Kralj graciously allowed me to use their photographs. I'm grateful to Brian Balsley for designing the maps.

Gillian Berchowitz expressed interest in my project while it was under way, welcomed me as it crossed the finish line, and guided me through the publication process. I thank Gill and her excellent team at Ohio University Press for helping bring this book to life.

The warm hospitality of friends sustained me during the extended periods of research and writing. In Cape Town, Hanni van den Heever, Michele Le Roux, and Ron and Bernie September deserve special mention for their kindness; in the Johannesburg area, heartfelt thanks go to Ranji Hansrajh and Keneilwe Molotsi. I've been fortunate to have Kyle Horch as a friend as I shuttled back and forth between London and Cape Town for research. In the United States, Gail Bohles, Elizabeth Fairweather, Patrick Furlong, Stanley Hansrajh, and Tom Holien encouraged me along the way. In my home base of Montgomery, I'm grateful to Jan Bulman, Judith Cantey, and Michael Fitzsimmons, whose friendship I treasure.

Finally, I thank Bobbie and Marv Gish for their unwavering love and support. They were there from the beginning.

Notes

CHAPTER 1: COMPLETE DETERMINATION

7   "You want to raise your children": Linda Biehl, author interview, July 17, 2006.

8   "The children were curious": Ibid.

8   "extra-challenging—highly motivated": Linda Biehl, remarks at the 10th anniversary celebration of the Faith & Politics Institute, Washington, D.C., October 24, 2001. (Biehl family papers, hereafter referred to as BFP)

8   "Even in the womb": "A Daughter's Dream Lives at the Scene of Her Death," *Washington Post,* February 18, 2001.

8   "Amy was very much a tomboy": Linda Biehl interview, July 17, 2006.

8   "Amy was completely determined": "Inside the Struggle: The Amy Biehl Story," *Turning Point,* ABC News, April 20, 1994.

9   "human energy in its purest form": "Family, Friends Mourn Biehl," *San Jose Mercury News,* September 4, 1993.

9   she was "hell on wheels": Phil Taylor, "'Hell on Wheels,'" *Stanford* 22, no. 1 (March 1994): 26–31.

9   "Amy always kind of ran the family": Kim Biehl, author interview, June 3, 2005.

10   "There is nothing wrong": Amy Biehl, journal entry, November 15, 1983. (BFP)

10   "driven, demanding, and difficult": Zach Biehl, author interview, June 1, 2005.

10   "It is far more fun": Amy Biehl, journal entry, September 13, 1983. (BFP)

10   "My problem": Amy Biehl, journal entry, December 13, 1983. (BFP)

10   During a particularly hard: Amy Biehl, journal entry, c. 1981–82. (BFP)

11   "Amy was my beacon": Molly Biehl, author interview, July 16, 2006.

11   "consistently the happiest": John Petring to the Biehls, August 28, 1993. (BFP)

11   "Whatever she did": Zach Biehl interview.

12   "When you raise your kids": Linda Biehl interview, July 17, 2006.

12   "I love diving": Amy Biehl, journal entry, undated. (BFP)

12   "There is a high": Linda Biehl interview, July 17, 2006.

12   "I would often hear": Molly Biehl interview.

12   "I kind of am addicted to exercise": Amy Biehl, journal entry, October 3, 1983. (BFP)

13   "a fullness of life, a vitality": Rev. John Huffman, remarks at Amy Biehl's memorial service, Newport Beach, September 3, 1993.

13   "What stood out": Richard Schavone, email to the author, January 10, 2010.

13–14 Schavone was known as "a yeller": Scott Greenwood-Meinert, author interview, June 8, 2005.

14   "I remember the big smile": Bruce Thompson, email to the author, October 5, 2009.

14   [The class] had a large share of black students: Kennell Jackson to Linda Biehl, August 1, 2003. (BFP)

15   she was the most outspoken person in her class: author's personal observation, Fall 1987.

16   she and Katie would sometimes get up: Katie Bolich, author interview, March 15, 2007.

16   "actually forced us to go out": Greenwood-Meinert interview.

16   she had improved "tremendously": Schavone email.

16   she had a "depth and a discipline": Bolich interview.

16   "Amy knew she wasn't the best diver": Greenwood-Meinert interview.

17   "Such a project requires": *Stanford University Bulletin: Courses and Degrees, 1989–1990,* 471.

17   "Amy definitely had in mind": Kennell Jackson, remarks at Amy Biehl's memorial service in Newport Beach, September 3, 1993.

17   if he responded too briefly: Ibid.

17   "Africans look for people": Amy Biehl, "Chester Crocker and the Negotiations for Namibian Independence: The Role of the Individual in Recent American Foreign Policy," honors thesis, Stanford University, May 1989, 91.

18   "She felt sorry for herself": Greenwood-Meinert interview.

18   "She reconstituted": "The Slaying of Amy Biehl: Remembering," *San Jose Mercury News,* August 27, 1993.

20   "So far, this trip has been very good": Amy Biehl to Scott Meinert, August 1, 1989. (BFP)

20   "She told me about a conversation": Scott Greenwood-Meinert, email to the author, June 22, 2010.

21   "I guess what I want to express": Amy Biehl, journal entry, c. September 1989. The ellipsis points are Amy's. (BFP)

CHAPTER 2: TO WASHINGTON AND BEYOND

22   Amy was ready to "dive in": Margaret Jones Collard, author interview, January 29, 2010.

22   a "pretty fringy" area: Ibid.

23   "It reminds me so much": Amy Biehl to Christine Jolls, January 8, 1990. (BFP)

23   Amy "was very interested in getting to know people": Collard interview.

23   "[Amy] wasn't necessarily interested": Ibid.

23   She was very pretty: Gina (Giere) Bjornlund, author interview, January 29, 2010.

24   "Well, Mom, the crack dealers": Peter Taylor, "An Honorary African," *Sunday Times Magazine* (London), March 27, 1994, 59.

24   "We're watching out for her": Scott Greenwood-Meinert, author interview, June 8, 2005.

24   "She always told me": "Woman Would Not Condemn Her Killers, Family Says," *Orange County Register,* August 26, 1993.

25   "It was all these young . . . kids": Bjornlund interview.

25 Gina found Amy "fun, super enthusiastic": Ibid.

26 "It's hard to put into words": "She Was 'Light in All Our Lives,'" *OCR*, August 27, 1993.

26 "People would regularly underestimate": Collard interview.

26 "She was very bright": Patricia Keefer, author interview, January 30, 2010.

26 "When you went to work": Ibid.

26 "She was brilliant": Ibid.

26 "[Amy] came in really wide-eyed": Bjornlund interview.

27 In her two years at the Institute: Amy Biehl, passport, issued May 3, 1989. (BFP)

27 "Namibia wasn't just one more": Keefer interview.

27–28 "The funny thing": Amy Biehl to Scott Meinert, c. March 1991. (BFP)

28 "Amy was impressed": J. Brian Atwood, remarks at NDI's 14th annual Averell Harriman Award ceremony, November 28, 2001.

29 "The weather in Lusaka": Amy Biehl to Margaret Jones, September 29, 1991.

29 "As a young woman in Washington": Amy Biehl, statement of proposed study, Fulbright application, c. Fall 1991. (BFP)

30 "The scenario of chaos": Amy Biehl, "Briefing Paper: South Africa," October 1991, 44. (BFP)

31 "It's an interesting time": Amy Biehl to Margaret Jones, c. October 1991.

31 "This is really what Cape Town looks like": Amy Biehl to Scott Meinert, October 30, 1991. (BFP)

31 "a traveling road show": Mary Hill to the Biehl family, September 2, 1993. (BFP)

31 The things I will remember: Amy Biehl, journal entry, c. October–November 1991. (BFP)

32 "a long-distance reverberation": David Ottaway, "At a Namibian Hunting Lodge, Lessons in Democracy," *Washington Post*, January 22, 1992.

32 "After you have acquired a constitution": Ibid.

32 "young and eager": J. Brian Atwood remarks.

33 I think that Nelson Mandela is uniquely qualified to lead: Amy Biehl to Zach Biehl, May 10, 1992. (BFP)

35 "She interacted at a pretty young age": Lionel Johnson, author interview, February 1, 2010.

35 "Amy did a lot to set up": Keefer interview.

35 she enjoyed being in Addis Ababa: Amy Biehl to Margaret Jones, c. September 1992.

36 Amy . . . began to push NDI to "do something about Malawi": Taylor, "An Honorary African."

36 she was "the only American I trusted": Marilyn Lewis, "Death in an Angry Land," *San Jose Mercury News,* October 10, 1993.

36 He put Amy in touch: Aleke Banda to Peter and Linda Biehl, September 5, 1993. (BFP)

36 "Amy proved to be an important ally": Tim Johnston to the Biehls, August 27, 1993. (BFP)

36 Amy's interests had shifted: Collard interview; Lewis, "Death in an Angry Land."

37 Her friend and coworker Gina: Bjornlund interview.

37 "I would like to initiate a discussion": Amy Biehl to NDI staff, August 12, 1992. (BFP)

37 NDI needed to "make gender equality an institutional priority": Ibid.

37   she drafted a statement: Amy Biehl, draft text for gender section, c. August 1992. (BFP)

37   The program was directly inspired: "Kenyan Women Plan to Broaden Political Role," *NDI Reports,* Summer/Fall 1993.

38   a tribute to Amy's "commitment and energy": Johnson interview.

38   "African people from grassroots societies": Amy Biehl, "Challenges and Lessons of Democratization in Africa," *Liberal Times,* no. 1 (July 1992), 5. (BFP)

38   "The most significant changes": Ibid.

38   On a continent where population: Ibid., 6. (BFP)

39   "She regaled me with all these stories": "Amy Biehl, '89 Grad, Fulbright Scholar, Killed in South Africa," *Campus Report,* Stanford University, September 8, 1993.

39   "She was so driven": Collard interview.

CHAPTER 3: INTO SOUTH AFRICA

40   "black South Africans" constituted about 76 percent: The population statistics in this paragraph are taken from South African Institute of Race Relations, *Race Relations Survey 1993/94* (Johannesburg: SAIRR, 1994), 84.

41   "I come here because of my deep interest": Quoted in *Robert Kennedy in South Africa* (Johannesburg: Rand Daily Mail, 1966), 7.

41   "Negroes in America fight": Quoted in Steven D. Gish, *Alfred B. Xuma: African, American, South African* (New York: New York University Press, 2000), 147.

43   the white minority government: Steven Mufson, *Fighting Years: Black Resistance and the Struggle for a New South Africa* (Boston: Beacon Press, 1990), 311.

45   between 70,000 and 80,000: Anthony Sampson, *Mandela: The Authorized Biography* (New York: Vintage Books, 1999), 456; Allister Sparks, *Tomorrow Is Another Country: The Inside Story of South Africa's Negotiated Revolution* (Sandton: Struik, 1994), 149.

45   "Although there are no guarantees": Amy Biehl, "Project Idea: Women in South Africa's Democratic Transition," c. Fall 1991. (BFP)

45   "but we would never have tried to stop her": Linda Biehl, author interview, July 17, 2006.

45   "Don't cry, Mom": Ibid.

46   "one of the least segregated cities": John Western, *Outcast Cape Town,* 2nd ed. (Berkeley: University of California Press, 1996), xvi.

47   "determined not to live within a white prison": "Amy Biehl, '89 Grad, Fulbright Scholar, Killed in South Africa," *Campus Report,* Stanford University, September 8, 1993.

47   the two "agreed to keep out of each other's way": Melanie Jacobs to the Biehls, August 27, 1993. (BFP)

48   intentionally getting a "crappy car": Scott Greenwood-Meinert, author interview, June 8, 2005.

48   "Our Land Needs Peace": "Two Held for Death of US Student," *Argus,* August 26, 1993; "Two Arrested for Fatal Attack on O.C. Woman," *OCR,* August 27, 1993.

48   "university of the left": UWC's vice-chancellor Jakes Gerwel coined this phrase in the late 1980s.

48   "absolutely committed": Centre for Development Studies, UWC, "Facing the Challenges of the 1990s," November 1989. (BFP)

49   he was not generally fond: Randi Erentzen to Linda and Peter Biehl, August 27, 1993. (BFP)

49   She was impressed with Amy's command: "Gentle Amy Loved by All," *Weekend Argus*, August 28/29, 1993.

50   Brigitte "seems to have a lot for me to do": Amy Biehl to Miruni Soosaipillai, October 20, 1992, quoted in Miruni Soosaipillai, "Dear Amy . . . My Unstoppable Friend, Slain in South Africa," *NYT*, September 5, 1993.

50   The men at the seminar: Amy Biehl to Dullah Omar, November 6, 1992. (BFP)

50   She wanted to stay: Greenwood-Meinert interview.

51   "the proverbial pushy American": "She Was 'Light in All Our Lives,'" *OCR*, August 27, 1993.

51   Amy described her housemates as "very cool": Amy Biehl to Miruni Soosaipillai, October 20, 1992, quoted in Soosaipillai, "Dear Amy."

51   Linda Biehl later learned: Linda Biehl interview, July 17, 2006.

51   "She wouldn't clean up": Peter Taylor, "An Honorary African," *Sunday Times Magazine* (London), March 27, 1994, 60.

52   The Jacobses had "very little money": Amy Biehl to Charles Batts, December 5, 1992. (BFP)

52   Amy would sometimes help: Rhoda Kadalie, author interview, June 7, 2004; Melanie Jacobs to the Biehls, August 27, 1993. (BFP)

52   Amy was the partner Melanie needed: Linda Biehl interview, July 17, 2006.

52   Amy was becoming Solange's "dad": "The Slaying of Amy Biehl: Remembering," *San Jose Mercury News*, August 27, 1993.

52   "Amy quickly became part": Solange Jacobs-Randolph, author interview, June 2, 2005.

52   "She didn't have much": Ibid.

52   "I remember snapping at her": Melanie Jacobs to the Biehls, August 27, 1993. (BFP)

52   she "just told them that she had a great big boyfriend": Marilyn Lewis, "Death in an Angry Land," *San Jose Mercury News*, October 10, 1993.

52   "We went into a shop": Ibid.

52–53   "I'm so glad not to be living": Amy Biehl to Charles Batts, December 5, 1992. (BFP)

53   "Quick, athletic, it fit Amy's style completely": Mary Speur, "The Energy That Will Not Die," unpublished typescript, c. 1993. (BFP)

53   Gregory Williams, nicknamed "Bucks": Gregory Williams, author interview, July 14, 2004.

53   "You should see the looks": Amy Biehl to Miruni Soosaipillai, November 20, 1992, quoted in Soosaipillai, "Dear Amy."

53   "Take care of yourself": Yetem Nicodimos to Amy Biehl, October 20, 1992. (BFP)

54   Another friend: Ashley Sparks to Amy Biehl, December 6, 1992. (BFP)

54   Finnegan called such attempts "crossing the line": William Finnegan, *Crossing the Line: A Year in the Land of Apartheid* (New York: Harper & Row, 1986).

54   Amy "wouldn't accept": "Amy's Murder an Ironic Tragedy," *Daily Dispatch*, August 28, 1993.

54   even the vagrants in Mowbray: Rhoda Kadalie, author interview, June 7, 2004.

54   racial tension in Cape Town seemed milder: Lewis, "Death in an Angry Land."

54   The many photographs Amy took: Amy's photos are currently held by the Biehl family.

55   "one of those people": Kim Christensen, "Sorrow in Black and White," *OCR*, November 21, 1993.

55   Amy made a particularly strong impression: Maletsatsi Maceba, author interview, July 20, 2004.

55   Amy believed Maletsatsi had a bright future: Amy Biehl to Miruni Soosaipillai, June 10, 1993, quoted in Soosaipillai, "Dear Amy"; Maletsatsi Maceba to Linda and Peter Biehl, August 30, 1993. (BFP)

55   Amy's natural outspokenness: Lewis, "Death in an Angry Land."

56   "She related to me": Maceba interview.

56   "teach me one word in Xhosa": Ibid.

56   Amy joined discussions: Sandra Liebenberg, author interview, July 1, 2004.

56   Amy took notes and photos: Amy Biehl, Report of the Women's Coalition-Western Cape Workshop, November 21, 1992; Amy Biehl, Workshop on a Women's Charter, November 21, 1992. (BFP)

57   As the political scientist: Hannah Britton, *Women in the South African Parliament: From Resistance to Governance* (Urbana: University of Illinois Press, 2005), 40.

57   "I did my best": Amy Biehl to Dullah Omar, December 14, 1992. (BFP)

58   "Towards a Women's Package": Amy Biehl to Dullah Omar and Brigitte Mabandla, December 10, 1992. (BFP)

58   she didn't want to be perceived: Kadalie interview; Greenwood-Meinert interview.

58   Amy was developing: Kader Asmal, author interview, June 7, 2004.

58   her "spirit, warmth, and commitment": Lehn Benjamin to Peter and Linda Biehl, August 26, 1993. (BFP)

58   When he arrived at the airport: Greenwood-Meinert interview.

59   They left Cape Town on January 2: Amy Biehl, notes on itinerary for Scott's visit, December 1992 (BFP); Amy Biehl's receipts, 1992–93 (BFP); Greenwood- Meinert interview.

59   Scott remembered: Greenwood-Meinert interview.

59   "a real political education": Amy Biehl to Becky Slipe, March 8, 1993. (BFP)

CHAPTER 4: YEAR OF THE GREAT STORM

60   3,706 people would lose their lives: South African Institute of Race Relations, *Race Relations Survey 1993/94* (Johannesburg: South African Institute of Race Relations, 1994), 27.

61   their organization regarded "every black man as an enemy": Ibid., 654.

62   APLA declared 1993 the "Year of the Great Storm": Thabisi Hoeane, "The State of the Pan-Africanist Congress in a Democratic South Africa," in *State of the Nation 2008,* ed. P. Kagwanja and K. Kondlo (Cape Town: HSRC Press, 2009), 68.

62   "the PAC would fight to the bitter end": "PAC Slams Power Sharing and Warns ANC on Making Deals," *Argus,* February 15, 1993.

62   the *Weekly Mail* newspaper reported a growing divide: "White Victims, More Than One Target," *Weekly Mail,* March 26 to April 1, 1993.

63   "I wish also to caution": Heribert Adam and Kogila Moodley, *The Negotiated Revolution: Society and Politics in Post-Apartheid South Africa* (Johannesburg: Jonathan Ball, 1993), 229n30.

63   "[It's] clear that South Africa is caught": Amy Biehl, ideas for paper on violence, January 1993. (BFP)

64   she would also "observe and play": Amy Biehl, conceptual framework for research, c. January 1993. (BFP)

64   "Rhoda did an outstanding job": Amy Biehl to Dullah Omar, February 1, 1993. (BFP)

64   when she tried to befriend Amy: Rhoda Kadalie, author interview, June 7, 2004.

64   In the short space of time: Rhoda Kadalie, reminiscences on Amy Biehl, Friends of Amy Biehl website, friendsofamybiehl.com/kadalie.php.

65   "the same people": Amy Biehl to Dullah Omar, February 1, 1993. (BFP)

65   because of her "sensitivity": Amy Biehl to Gill Garb, February 2, 1993. (BFP)

65   "Brigitte thinks": Amy Biehl to Dullah Omar, March 1, 1993. (BFP)

65   "She thought as an American": "The Slaying of Amy Biehl: Remembering," *San Jose Mercury News,* August 27, 1993.

65   "She understood that solutions": Stephen Stedman, letter to the editor, *Washington Times,* September 14, 1993.

65   "She seemed to believe": Peter Taylor, "An Honorary African," *Sunday Times Magazine* (London), March 27, 1994.

66   "When the music started": Amy Biehl to Patty Delgado, February 9, 1993. (BFP)

66   "By the way, I met Nelson Mandela": Amy Biehl to Kennell Jackson, March 10, 1993. (BFP)

66   it wasn't "meeting enough": Amy Biehl to Dullah Omar, March 1, 1993. (BFP)

67   Amy called the bill: Amy Biehl to Patty Delgado, February 9, 1993. (BFP)

67   "I know that this type of thing": Amy Biehl to Dullah Omar, February 5, 1993. (BFP)

67   "The right to free practice of religion": Amy Biehl, preliminary thoughts on government's bill of rights proposal, February 5, 1993. (BFP)

68   "I hope you don't think": Amy Biehl to Dullah Omar, February 5, 1993. (BFP)

68   "Minister Coetsee began": Amy Biehl, report on national conference, March 8, 1993. (BFP)

68   Amy wrote a poem: Amy Biehl, handwritten poem in unlabeled notebook, c. March–April 1993. (BFP)

69   "Upon the completion of a Ph.D.": Amy Biehl, statement for Javits Fellowship, March 10, 1993. (BFP)

69   Amy was "hurt and incredulous": Marilyn Lewis, "Death in an Angry Land," *San Jose Mercury News,* October 10, 1993.

70   "All of the boys were in love": Anna Wang, author interview, January 14, 2010.

70   "She would talk for 20 minutes": Taylor, "An Honorary African."

70   "some of my best friends are communists": Ibid.

70   Hani was the second-most-popular: William-Mervin Gumede, "Hamba Kahle— Comrade Hani," *Student Voice,* University of the Western Cape, April 19, 1993.

70   Hani stood up for the "poor, oppressed, and dispossessed": Ibid.

70   "a crucial link between the leadership": Stephen Stedman, preface to *South Africa: The Political Economy of Transformation* (Boulder, CO: Lynne Rienner, 1994), viii.

70   "A white man, full of prejudice": Allister Sparks, *Tomorrow Is Another Country: The Inside Story of South Africa's Negotiated Revolution* (Sandton: Struik, 1994), 189.

71   "No more peace, no more peace!": "An Anger That Couldn't Be Controlled," *Weekly Mail,* April 16–22, 1993.

71   "You can't kill a leader": Ibid.

71   "Kill the Boer!": "On the Brink," display at the Apartheid Museum, Johannesburg, 2004.

71   she was "heartbroken": "Inside the Struggle: The Amy Biehl Story," *Turning Point*, ABC News, April 20, 1994.

71   Scott soon realized: Scott Greenwood-Meinert, email to the author, June 22, 2010.

71   "My God, who cares about me?": "Inside the Struggle," *Turning Point*.

71   "I was very worried": "Violence—American," Sapa-AP wire report, August 26, 1993.

71   Amy understood the hatred: Scott Greenwood-Meinert, author interview, June 8, 2005.

72   Rev. Frank Retief . . . felt the rising tension: Frank Retief, *Tragedy to Triumph: A Christian Response to Trials and Suffering* (Milton Keynes, UK: Word Publishing, 1994), 14–16.

72   "Hani's murder not only angered": Sipho Pityana, "The Masses Are Getting Restive," *Weekly Mail*, May 21–27, 1993.

73   Sabelo Phama . . . called for the armed struggle: "APLA's Warlord Speaks Out," *Weekend Argus*, June 26/27, 1993.

73   According to a poll: "'10 % Support for Attacks on Whites,'" *Cape Times*, July 1, 1993.

73   "We were aware of the risks": Wang interview.

73   "She has always said": Anna Wang to the Biehls, August 26, 1993. (BFP)

73   Others close to Amy agreed: Stephen Stedman, author interview, March 12, 2007; Linda Biehl, author interview, July 17, 2006.

74   "you've done more in your 26 years": Molly Biehl to Amy Biehl, April 8, 1993. (BFP)

74   "Well, dear child": Gill Noero to Amy Biehl, May 11, 1993. (BFP)

74   "The differences among South African women": Amy Biehl, "Structures for Women in Political Decision-Making," Community Law Centre, University of the Western Cape, c. May 1993. (BFP)

75   She drew on Amy's report: Brigitte Mabandla, "Choices for South African Women," *Agenda*, no. 20 (1994): 22–29.

75   "in order to promote the full citizenship": Amy Biehl, letter of invitation to custom and religion conference, April 16, 1993. (BFP)

75   The conference, "Custom and Religion": *Custom and Religion in a Non-Racial, Non-Sexist South Africa: Report of the International Seminar of the Community Law Centre at the University of the Western Cape, 14–16 May 1993* (Bellville: Community Law Centre, UWC, 1994).

76   Her summary was also published: Amy Biehl, "Custom and Religion in a Non-Racial, Non-Sexist South Africa," *Women against Fundamentalism*, no. 5 (1994): 51–53.

76   "I'm supposed to go to an ANC": Amy Biehl to Scott Meinert, May 21, 1993. (BFP)

76   "She is in her element": Amy Biehl to Scott Meinert, c. May 22 or 23, 1993. (BFP)

77   "I hope I don't die!": Amy Biehl to Scott Meinert, May 21, 1993. (BFP)

77   "I pledge myself with integrity": Pledge, National Peace Accord and 1993 Comrades Marathon for Peace, May 31, 1993. (BFP)

78   As a white follower of Sandile: Amy Biehl to Colin Howell, June 21, 1993. (BFP)

79   Stedman offered to include Amy's essay: Amy Biehl, "Dislodging the Boulder: South African Women and the Democratic Transition," in *South Africa: The Political Economy of Transformation*, ed. Stephen Stedman (Boulder: Lynne Rienner, 1994), 85–107.

79   "The security situation": Ibid., 103.

80   "Although the ANC has made": Ibid., 104.

80   She was once accused: Kadalie interview.

80   "As a white middle class": Rhoda Kadalie, reminiscences on Amy Biehl, Friends of Amy Biehl website, friendsofamybiehl.com/kadalie.php.

80   "In the last few phone calls": Taylor, "An Honorary African."

80   I would caution ambitious student researchers: Amy Biehl, final report for Fulbright grant, c. August 1993. (BFP)

81   Peter and Linda donated: Linda Biehl interview, July 17, 2006.

81   "So, while I am having these amazing experiences": Amy Biehl to Scott Meinert, c. May 22 or 23, 1993. (BFP)

81   Her friend was "becoming a fixture": Becky Slipe, journal, June–July 1993. (BFP)

81   One night she accompanied Amy: Ibid.

82   She and Scott seem to glow: Photos in the possession of the Biehl family and Maletsatsi Maceba.

CHAPTER 5: GUGULETHU

95   "We prized personal details": Rhoda Kadalie, reminiscences of Amy Biehl, Friends of Amy Biehl website, friendsofamybiehl.com/kadalie.php.

95   "A year is a *very* long time": Amy Biehl to Scott Meinert, c. July 26, 27, or 28, 1993. (BFP)

95   "feeling fine about heading": Ibid.

95   "things should wind up": Ibid.

96   his organization didn't make a distinction: "Church Arrest Places Spotlight on APLA," *Weekend Argus,* July 31/August 1, 1993.

96   "Did you hear about the church bombing?": Amy Biehl to Scott Meinert, c. July 26, 27, or 28, 1993. (BFP)

96   "Aren't you glad I don't go to church?": Linda Biehl, author interview, July 17, 2006.

96   "Amy was appalled": Stedman, preface to *South Africa: The Political Economy of Transformation* (Boulder, CO: Lynne Rienner, 1994), ix.

96   She pondered how South Africa: Amy Biehl, handwritten notes, July–August 1993. (BFP)

97   "There is still a lot": Marianne Thamm, "Storming the House," *Femina,* August 1993.

97   she'd be coming home: Amy Biehl to Molly Biehl and Margaret Jones, August 13, 1993; Amy Biehl to Carole Hoemeke, August 13, 1993.

98   "an urgent plea for assistance": Amy Biehl to Larry Diamond, August 5, 1993. (BFP)

98   it was unprecedented: Peter Dennis Bathory to Peter and Linda Biehl, September 24, 1993. (BFP)

98   "The contacts, materials": Amy Biehl, final Fulbright report, c. August 1993. (BFP)

98   She ended her report: Ibid.

99   The results of an opinion: "Black, White Relationship 'Worse,'" *Cape Times,* July 16, 1993.

99   more people died in political violence: South African Institute of Race Relations, *Race Relations Survey 1993/94* (Johannesburg: SAIRR, 1994), 653.

99   Archbishop Tutu called for international peacekeepers: "SA Death Toll Close to Highest Ever," *South*, August 7–11, 1993.

99   Between 5 and 8 percent: "Violence Born of Injustice," *South*, August 14–18, 1993.

100   what many commentators called "a lost generation": Nancy Scheper-Hughes and Carolyn Sargent, introduction to *Small Wars: The Cultural Politics of Childhood*, ed. N. Scheper- Hughes and C. Sargent (Berkeley: University of California Press, 1998), 25.

100   The Western Cape was probably the PAC's strongest region: L. Mphahlele, *Child of This Soil: My Life as a Freedom Fighter* (Cape Town: Kwela Books, 2002), 173.

101   some blacks jokingly called it "Gugulabo": Sindiwe Magona, *Mother to Mother* (Boston: Beacon Press, 1998), 27.

101   Gugulethu had the highest per capita: Mamphela Ramphele, *Across Boundaries: The Journey of a South African Woman Leader* (New York: Feminist Press, 1999), 159.

101   "when the violent repression": Ibid., 169.

101   "Warning. Proclaimed Non-European Township": Historical exhibit, Sivuyile Tourism Centre, Gugulethu, 2004.

102   A government official speculated: SAIRR, *Race Relations Survey, 1993/94*, 81.

102   Mamphele Ramphele conducted a major study: Mamphela Ramphele, *Steering by the Stars: Being Young in South Africa* (Cape Town: Tafelberg, 2002).

103   "I was shocked and angry": "Hope Springs from Sleeping with the Enemy," *Sydney Morning Herald*, September 11, 1993.

104   tear gas was his "daily breakfast, lunch, and supper": Easy Nofemela, author interview, June 30, 2005.

104   "Something was inspiring me inside": Easy Nofemela, author interview, June 22, 2007.

104   "I wanted serve, suffer, and sacrifice": Nofemela interview, June 30, 2005.

104   "I thought this was where I belong": Ibid.

105   "How do you fight apartheid?": Ibid.

105   South Africa "was taken by the barrel": Ibid.

105   "maximum damage to the enemy": Ibid.

106   "How do we stop the violence?": Ibid.

106   "Our parents earned peanuts": Ntobeko Peni, author interview, June 19, 2007.

106   "The PAC called a spade a spade": Ibid.

106   "the oppressed can't negotiate": Ntobeko Peni, author interview, July 25, 2002.

107   "There was no reason to negotiate": Peni interview, June 19, 2007.

107   "the hate that hate produced": "The Hate That Hate Produced," Mike Wallace and Louis Lomax, producers, WNTA-TV, July 13–17, 1959.

107   "an outcome of 300 years": Sindiwe Magona, author interview, July 14, 2004.

107   "Die, settler!": Nancy Scheper-Hughes, "Violence and the Politics of Remorse," in *Subjectivity: Ethnographic Investigations*, ed. João Biehl, Byron Good, and Arthur Kleinman (Berkeley: University of California Press, 2007), 228n1.

107   "This is ridiculous": "Violent Racism at March," *South*, August 14–18, 1993.

107   "One settler down!": Ibid.

107   "The Cape squatter camps": R. W. Johnson, "American Victim Symbolises South Africa's Bitter Tragedy," *Times*, August 27, 1993.

108   "We can turn the whole": "Pupil Violence Rocks Townships," *Argus*, August 24, 1993.

108   a white healthcare worker . . . was attacked: "Mob Tries to Steal Rings on Health Worker's Hand," *Argus*, August 24, 1993.

108   a group of visitors: Frances Nye to Linda and Peter Biehl, October 9, 1993. (BFP)

109   she "refused to stop driving her black friends home": "2 Arrested in American's Death," *Times-Picayune* (New Orleans), August 27, 1993.

109   "she'd dismiss me": "Inside the Struggle: The Amy Biehl Story," *Turning Point*, ABC News, April 20, 1994.

109   "She was intellectually aware": Larry Diamond, author interview, March 14, 2007.

109   "We knew there were risks": Anna Wang, author interview, January 14, 2010.

109   [Amy] may not have been completely fearless: Anna Wang, unpublished essay, c. 1993.

110   Omar, who held Amy's hand: Peter Taylor, "An Honorary African," *Sunday Times Magazine* (London), March 27, 1994.

110   "She was particularly alive": Anna Wang, unpublished essay, c. 1993.

110   "Your advice and common sense": Elmarie Nelson to Amy Biehl, August 20, 1993. (BFP)

111   "'My stay here was too good'": "Amy Biehl Had Premonition," *OCR*, August 28, 1993.

111   "Whether that was a premonition": Ibid.

111   "She said she would come back": "The Slaying of Amy Biehl: Remembering," *San Jose Mercury News*, August 27, 1993.

111   Amy spoke to Greg Williams: Greg Williams, author interview, July 14, 2004.

111   Amy and Rhoda spoke at length: Rhoda Kadalie, author interview, June 7, 2004.

111   "I find it so difficult to leave": Taylor, "An Honorary African."

111   "Now that she was about to go back": "Mourners Told of Amy's Premonition," *Daily News* (Durban), August 27, 1993.

111   Rhoda told Amy that she'd heard reports: Rhoda Kadalie, reminiscences of Amy Biehl, Friends of Amy Biehl website, friendsofamybiehl.com/kadalie.php.

111   "the vitriol had picked up": Scott Greenwood-Meinert, author interview, June 8, 2005.

111   Evaron Orange asked Amy: Evaron Orange, author interview, June 17, 2004.

112   That morning had been quiet: Maletsatsi Maceba, author interview, July 20, 2004.

112   she was "generous to a fault": Kadalie interview.

112   "He knew he had been there so long": Keith Richburg, *Out of America: A Black Man Confronts Africa* (New York: Basic Books, 1997), 46.

112   "Yes, I'll drive safely": "Gentle Amy Loved by All," *Weekend Argus*, August 28/29, 1993.

113   Simpiwe Mfengu . . . and Wanda Mathebula: Testimony of Easy Nofemela, TRC transcript, July 8, 1997.

113   "One settler, one bullet!": Testimony of Ntobeko Peni, TRC transcript, July 8, 1997.

114   "a student died at Nyanga Junction": Iris Films, *Long Night's Journey into Day*, 2000.

114   "What happened with the police": Easy Nofemela, TRC transcript, July 8, 1997.

115   Amy was excited at the prospect: Orange interview, and Maceba interview.

115   Amy drove onto NY1 in Gugulethu: Cape High Court, State versus Ntobeko Peni, summary of essential facts, 1995, and Cape High Court, Judgment, State versus Mongezi Manqina, Mzikona Nofemela, and Vusumzi Ntamo, case # SS 136/93, October 24, 1994.

115 "Here comes a settler!": "Two Arrested for Fatal Attack on O.C. Woman," *OCR*, August 27, 1993.

115 "Drive! Drive!": Marilyn Lewis, "Death in an Angry Land," *San Jose Mercury News*, October 10, 1993; Taylor, "An Honorary African."

115 someone reached in: Cape High Court, trial transcript, case # SS 136/93, November 22, 1993.

115 the youths were not interested: Ibid.

116 the woman deserved to die "because she is a settler": "South African Mob Stones and Kills O.C. Woman," *OCR*, August 26, 1993.

116 "You must go": Lewis, "Death in an Angry Land."

116 eyewitness accounts suggest otherwise: "Black Teenagers Stone, Stab White Fulbright Scholar," *Washington Times*, August 27, 1993; Lewis, "Death in an Angry Land"; Taylor, "An Honorary African"; Cape High Court, Judgment, State versus Manqina et al., case # SS 136/93, October 24, 1994; Cape High Court, transcripts, records, and evidence, Ntobeko Peni trial, case # SS 18/95, May 1995; testimony of Mongezi Manqina, TRC transcript, July 8, 1997; Orange interview.

116 "Please help me": Anna Wang to the Biehls, August 26, 1993 (BFP); Cape High Court, Judgment, State versus Manqina et al., case # SS 136/93, October 24, 1994.

116 Mongezi got a knife from someone: Testimony of Manqina, TRC transcript, July 8, 1997.

116 "How can you stop us?": "American Woman Killed in S. Africa," *Washington Times*, August 27, 1993; "'Help my,' het student vir oulaas gefluister," *Die Burger*, August 27, 1993.

116 when "impromptu mob justice" takes hold: Barry Bearak, "Constant Fear and Mob Rule in South Africa Slum," *NYT*, June 30, 2009.

116 Many of those who witnessed: "Black Teenagers Stone"; Cape High Court, Judgment, State versus Manqina et al., case # SS 136/93, October 24, 1994.

117 Amy somehow managed to stand up: "Two Arrested for Fatal Attack on O.C. Woman"; Lewis, "Death in an Angry Land"; Cape High Court, trial transcript, case # SS 136/93, November 22, 1993; Taylor, "An Honorary African"; Cape High Court, Judgment, State versus Manqina et al., case # SS 136/93, October 24, 1994; Orange interview.

117 Rhodes radioed for an ambulance: Cape High Court, trial transcript, case # SS 136/93, November 22, 1993.

117 Evaron thought about putting her back: Orange interview.

117 Amy had been stabbed: Cape High Court, Judgment, State versus Manqina et al., case # SS 136/93, October 24, 1994; official death certificate, Department of Justice and coroner's description of injuries to Amy Biehl from Cape High Court, transcripts, records, and evidence, Ntobeko Peni trial, case # SS 18/95, May 1995.

117 He placed a sheet over Amy's head: Victor West, author interview, July 13, 2004.

CHAPTER 6: "COMRADES COME IN ALL COLORS"

118 "They were distraught": Randi Erentzen to Linda and Peter Biehl, August 27, 1993. (BFP)

118 "The world came crashing down": Solange Jacobs-Randolph, author interview, June 2, 2005.

118 "Is she dead?": Molly Biehl, author interview, July 16, 2006.

119 "It was the only way": Iris Films, *Long Night's Journey into Day*, 2000.

119   "I think I fell to the floor": Kim Biehl, author interview, June 3, 2005.

119   "Mom, are you sitting down?": Ibid.

119   "He told me she'd hung in": Scott Greenwood-Meinert, author interview, June 8, 2005.

119   "I hope she did some good": Princeton Lyman, *Partner to History: The U.S. Role in South Africa's Transition to Democracy* (Washington, D.C.: United States Institute of Peace Press, 2002), 154.

119   "Lord, forgive them": Linda Biehl, author interview, July 17, 2006.

119   "The low point was looking at the faces": Ibid.

119   Linda felt "hollow and empty": Ibid.

120   "From day one my parents weren't angry": Zach Biehl, author interview, June 1, 2005.

120   "I am deeply and personally saddened": Coretta Scott King to Peter and Linda Biehl, August 27, 1993. (BFP)

120   "We sensed that Amy was part of history": Linda Biehl interview, July 17, 2006.

121   "We were so surrounded": "Instant Celebrities Are Sometimes Seared by Media Spotlight," *LA Times*, February 16, 1994.

121   "We made the decision": "She Was 'Light in All Our Lives,'" *OCR*, August 27, 1993.

121   "[Amy] was a very humanitarian person": "Race Hate Cited in S. Africa Slaying," *San Francisco Examiner*, August 26, 1993.

121   I don't have any anger: "'My Daughter's Legacy Was to Reach Out to Everyone,'" *Argus*, August 27, 1993.

122   "As parents who have lost": Linda Biehl, *Today Show*, NBC, August 27, 1993.

122   "We're at peace with Amy": Peter Biehl, *Evening News*, CBS, August 27, 1993.

123   "condemned across the political spectrum": SABC Television news, August 26, 1993.

123   "Murdered Girl Had Packed for Home": *Cape Times*, August 26, 1993.

123   "Amy's Agony": *Argus*, August 26, 1993.

123   "Gentle Amy Loved by All": *Weekend Argus*, August 28, 1993.

124   Amy had been "absolutely dedicated": "Mob Kills U.S. Woman Student," *Citizen*, August 26, 1993.

124   "Your beloved Amy": Dullah Omar to Peter and Linda Biehl, August 25, 1993. (BFP)

124   "She would have said they learned to hate": "Two Arrested in Fatal Attack on O.C. Woman," *OCR*, August 27, 1993.

124   "She was truly part of us": "Inside the Struggle: The Amy Biehl Story," *Turning Point*, ABC News, April 20, 1994.

124   "She was one of the liveliest": "Mob Kills U.S. Woman Student."

124   "She was in and out of the townships": "Two Arrested in SA Killing of 'Beautiful American,'" *Independent*, August 27, 1993.

125   "We want to thank all": "Amy Devoted to SA—Mum," *Daily Dispatch*, August 27, 1993.

125   Other signs read "Comrades come in all colours": "How American 'Sister' Died in a Township," *NYT*, August 27, 1993; "Slain Student's Efforts to Heal South Africa Recalled," *LA Times*, August 27, 1993; "'Help my,' het student vir oulaas gefluister," *Die Burger*, August 27, 1993.

125   more than one participant sensed hostility: Nancy Scheper-Hughes, "Who's the Killer? Popular Justice and Human Rights in a South African Squatter Camp," in *Violence in War and Peace*, ed. Scheper-Hughes and P. Bourgois (Malden, MA: Blackwell, 2004), 254; Rhoda Kadalie, author interview, June 7, 2004.

125 "When we were abroad fighting for freedom": "'She Had a Premonition She Was Going to Die,'" *Argus*, August 27, 1993.

126 "We are deeply concerned and shocked": *Evening News*, CBS, August 27, 1993.

126 "This incident can only be described as racism": Reuters wire report, August 26, 1993.

126 "We regard the killing of Amy": "Killing Condemned by ANC," *Argus*, August 26, 1993.

126 Yengeni conceded that Operation Barcelona should be condemned: "Comrades Asked to Explain by ANC," *Argus*, August 26, 1993.

127 He insisted that the PAC was not involved: "Campaign Halted: 'Unproductive Banditry'—ANC," *Cape Times*, August 27, 1993.

127 PAC officials also sent an official letter: PAC, "The Armed Struggle," submission to the Truth and Reconciliation Commission, August 20, 1996, 9–10; Lyman, *Partner to History*, 155.

127 "How many blacks have been killed": Mgwebi Mtuze, author interview, July 7, 2004.

127 An article in the *Times* of London: "The Tragedy of Amy: How a Dream Died in a Black Township," *Times*, August 29, 1993.

127 "They [the ANC] must not use Amy Biehl's death": "Focus: Death in South Africa," *OCR*, August 27, 1993.

127 "claiming it was the product": "PAC and ANC in Row over Student Death," *Guardian*, August 27, 1993.

127 the influential *Star* newspaper: "The Right Thing," *Star*, August 28, 1993.

127–28 neglecting "its core constituency—blacks": Mondli waka Makhanya, "Mandela Should Quit Pandering to White Fears," *Weekly Mail & Guardian*, October 1–7, 1993.

128 A lead editorial in the *Natal Mercury*: "An Evil Killing," *Natal Mercury*, August 27, 1993.

128 Residents of Cape Town: "ANC 'Sanctimonious' about Girl's Murder," *Cape Times*, August 28, 1993.

128 it was "curious" that the ANC was blaming the PAC: "Focus: Death in South Africa."

128 Township dwellers rarely went to the police: "Tragedy Touches a Nerve," *Sunday Times*, August 29, 1993.

128 "We are not surprised": "Sad Farewell for Slain Amy," *Citizen*, August 27, 1993.

129 As the *Weekly Mail & Guardian* pointed out: "The PAC's Double Speak . . . To Kill or not to Kill Whites," *Weekly Mail & Guardian*, September 3–9, 1993.

129 Patricia de Lille later conceded: Lyman, *Partner to History*, 158.

129 "We deplore and are deeply grieved": Albertina Sisulu, message of condolence to the Biehl family, August 31, 1993. (BFP)

129–30 "The killing of Amy in daylight": Centre for Adult and Continuing Education, UWC, untitled statement on Amy's Biehl's death, c. 26 August 1993. (BFP)

130 "If it should transpire": "Violence—AZAPO," Sapa wire report, August 26, 1993.

130 AZAPO's publicity secretary: Ibid.

130 Besides deploring Amy's "senseless and brutal killing": NADEL, untitled statement on Amy Biehl's death, August 26, 1993.

130 Law and Order Ministry spokesman: "More Attacks Possible—Paso," *Star*, August 27, 1993.

130   "the constitutional crisis": "Stop the Petty Politics—and Talk," *Pretoria News,* August 30, 1993.

130   "It is particularly tragic": Harry Schwarz to Peter and Linda Biehl, August 26, 1993. (BFP)

131   "The shocking death of 26-year-old Amy": "Tragedy Touches a Nerve," *Sunday Times,* August 29, 1993.

132   "[Amy's] death has touched": Michael Millsap to Peter and Linda Biehl, August 29, 1993. (BFP)

132   "I have one great fear": Alan Paton, *Cry, the Beloved Country* (New York: Charles Scribner's Sons, 1948), 276.

132   Kadalie described her friend's killers as "young monsters": Quoted in Scheper-Hughes, "Who's the Killer?" 254.

132   "South African political leaders": Ibid.

132   One American reporter believed: Neil McMahon, "American Woman Killed in S. Africa," *Washington Times,* August 27, 1993.

132   Karin Chubb . . . felt the despair: Karin Chubb, author interview, July 22, 2002.

133   "the fabric of our society is disintegrating": A.S.F. (All Structures Forum), UWC, to C.D.S. (Centre for Development Studies), UWC, August 26, 1993. (BFP)

133   "Amy Biehl's death doesn't fall": Keith Richburg, *Out of America,* 208–9.

133   "blind racial hatred," "unbridled bloodlust," and "frustrated and irresolute mob": "'n Blinde moordlus," *Die Burger,* August 27, 1993.

133   "among conservative elements": Alec Russell, "S Africa Mob Kills Election Aide from US," *Daily Telegraph,* August 26, 1993.

134   "We've warned in the past": "South Africa: Racism Knows No Colour Bar in South Africa," Reuters wire report, September 8, 1993.

134   "They [blacks] are like that": Marilyn Lewis, "Death in an Angry Land," *San Jose Mercury News,* October 10, 1993.

134   Some of the people most upset: Stanley Hansrajh, author interview, June 6, 2005.

134   "The attacks exposed decades": Liz Sly, "Black Rage Pops Liberal Cape Town's Delusions," *Chicago Tribune,* October 4, 1993.

134   "Cape Town has lost its innocence": Ibid.

134   South African officials became increasingly concerned: "Decrease in Visitors Expected," *Cape Times,* August 28, 1993; "Violence Threatens to Kill Off Tourism," *Weekend Argus,* August 28/29, 1993; "Student Died Trying to Overcome Racism," *Albuquerque Journal,* August 28, 1993.

135   In 1993, about 8,100 South Africans emigrated: SAIRR, *Race Relations Survey 1994/95* (Johannesburg: SAIRR, 1995), 16–17.

135   "one of the catalysts prompting them to leave": Gail and Anthony Mosse to Peter and Linda Biehl, March 23, 1994. (BFP)

135   In 1992, 382 South Africans immigrated: Bronwen Reid, "No Place Like Home," *Time* (international edition), March 21, 1994.

135   "Oh my God! Don't the students know": Jonathan Jansen, author interview, July 7, 2004.

135   "I am sure every sane and decent South African": Freeman Bukashe, "Little Pride in Guguletu," *Star,* September 3, 1993.

135   "unfortunate racial stereotypes": "Comment," *Sowetan,* August 27, 1993.

135   "confirm their worst racist prejudices": Ibid.

135   "How many blacks have been killed?": Iris Films, *Long Night's Journey into Day*, 2000.

136   Themba Mbane, a young supporter of PASO: Sly, "Black Rage Pops Liberal Cape Town's Delusions."

136   "If I have to kill white people": "Guguletu 'Unsafe for Whites,'" *South*, September 3–7, 1993.

136   "People are very angry": "Student Died Trying to Overcome Racism."

136   "Some whites are standing with us": "Township Women Honour Amy in Prayers for Peace," *Argus*, August 27, 1993.

137   "Oh Lord, we call upon you": Ibid.

137   the church placed an ad in the *Weekend Argus:* "In Celebration of the Life of Amy Biehl," August 28, 1993.

137   Cape Town journalist Anthony Heard: "Service Held for Slain Student in S. Africa," *LA Times*, August 30, 1993.

137   "She showed her courage": "S. Africans Mourn Slain O.C. Woman as a Friend," *OCR*, August 30, 1993.

138   "May Amy's death inspire us": Amanda Botha, untitled condolences, *Women's Bulletin*, UWC 1, no. 4, September 1993, 5.

138   Amy's death was "an indictment": Sindiwe Magona, author interview, July 14, 2004.

138   Amy's death became synonymous with "no more bloodshed": Lewis, "Death in an Angry Land."

138   the *Cape Times* wrote that racist sloganeering: "Shameful," *Cape Times*, August 27, 1993.

139   "It would be a fitting tribute": "Cycle of Violence (1)," *Argus*, August 27, 1993.

139   how dangerous "blood curdling" slogans could be: "Tutu Slates 'Dangerous Slogans,'" *Argus*, August 27, 1993.

139   Mokaba's slogan "Kill the farmer, kill the Boer": "Moord op student nie deel van ANC- stryd—Sexwale," *Die Burger*, August 27, 1993.

139   the struggle for democracy: "More Attacks Possible—Paso," *Star*, August 27, 1993.

139   "We know that South Africa needs": "No-Go Areas," *South*, September 3–7, 1993.

140   He called whites "our brothers and our sisters": "South Africa: Mandela Appeals for Racial Tolerance from Blacks," Reuters wire story, September 12, 1993.

140   "It is not military action": "We Need the Whites: Blacks Must Not Drive Them Out, Mandela Tells Biko Rally," *Daily Mail*, September 13, 1993.

140   "This is not the time for panic": "Mandela Calls on Whites to Join in Burying the Past," *Times*, September 15, 1993.

140   As blacks and whites expressed: Jerry Eckert to the Biehls, August 30, 1993. (BFP)

140   "bring a new understanding to the meaning of 'umlungu'": Barbara Gettleman to the Biehls, August 28, 1993. (BFP)

141   "our comrades from outside": "End 'No-Go' Myth," *Argus*, August 31, 1993.

141   "drawn the people of the Cape": "Peace!" *Cape Times*, September 2, 1993.

141   "All over South Africa, millions of office workers": Peter Wade, "Peter's Intermittent Newsletter," September 9, 1993. (Kennell Jackson papers, Stanford University)

141   "senseless violence to prevent the advent": "Prayers Won't Pacify South Africa," *NYT*, September 4, 1993.

141   both of which "openly derided" the occasion: Ibid.; "Peace Comes to S Africa—For a Day," *Sydney Morning Herald*, September 4, 1993.

142 to "assert the fundamental principle": "Guguletu 'Unsafe for Whites,'" *South*, September 3–7, 1993.

142 "We must reaffirm": "Marchers' Feat for Harmony," *Sunday Times Cape Metro*, September 5, 1993.

142 the "meaningful, forgiving and deep-rooted Christian way": Luthando Adams to Peter and Linda Biehl and family, August 29, 1993. (BFP)

CHAPTER 7: THE AMY PHENOMENON

144 Amy's death "brought home to many Americans": Ben Macintyre, "American Victim Symbolises South Africa's Bitter Tragedy," *Times* (London), August 27, 1993.

145 "No one I know personifies better": Chester Crocker to Peter and Linda Biehl, August 30, 1993. (BFP)

145 effective, "on the ground" work: Becky Slipe to the Biehls, October 1, 1993. (BFP)

145 "How sad that one who saw injustice": Ginger Steyer to Peter and Linda Biehl, August 29, 1993. (BFP)

145 "I was so crushed": Kennell Jackson to Helen Stark Tompkins, November 17, 1993. (Kennell Jackson papers, Stanford University)

145 Larry Diamond . . . felt a mixture of "shock, horror, outrage": Larry Diamond to Linda Biehl, August 25, 1993. (BFP)

145 "As you reflect with justifiable pride": David Abernethy to Peter and Linda Biehl, August 28, 1993. (BFP)

145 For Lionel Johnson, Amy's loss was "a very personal blow": Lionel Johnson, author interview, February 1, 2010.

146 "her life's work and her beliefs": Brian Attwood to Peter and Linda Biehl, August 31, 1993. (BFP)

146 "As a black man from Harlem in NY": Ken Baker to the Biehls, August 27, 1993. (BFP)

147 "Slain Student Remembered for Idealism": "Slain Student Remembered for Idealism," *San Francisco Chronicle*, August 27, 1993.

148 "Amy's valiant effort and supreme contribution": Coretta Scott King to Peter and Linda Biehl, August 27, 1993. (BFP)

148 "a heroic and altruistic volunteer": Raymond Levitt to the Biehls, August 26, 1993. (BFP)

148 "Your daughter represented the best": John Brademas and Carl Gershman to Peter and Linda Biehl, September 1, 1993. (BFP)

148 "I don't think that Amy Biehl would want": Christine Keener, "Death in South Africa Mustn't Kill Hope," *NYT*, September 7, 1993.

149 "This pretty girl was killed by apartheid": Richard Hamer, "Death in South Africa," *LA Times*, September 3, 1993.

150 "All Americans must begin to hold themselves more accountable": Robert Wozniak, "Racial Violence," *Star Tribune* (MN), September 4, 1993.

150 "Your encouraging words": Mary Hill to the Biehls, September 2, 1993. (BFP)

150 "A USA citizen has no business": E. Mendoza to the Biehls, September 17, 1993. (BFP)

151 "You see? You can't help these people": Sue Hutchison, "Amy Biehl's Death Needs Perspective," *San Jose Mercury News*, September 3, 1993.

151 Amy would have been "safe at home": Margot Silk Forrest, "Biehl Story Was Wrong to Call the U.S. 'Safe,'" *San Jose Mercury News*, September 3, 1993.

151   some of these Americans: Bill Keller, "How American 'Sister' Died in a Township," *NYT*, August 27, 1993.

151   recommended that the State Department: American consulate, Johannesburg, to Secretary of State, September 7, 1993, NSC cables, [Biehl], OA/ID 505000, Clinton Presidential Records, William Clinton Presidential Library.

152   his program had stopped: "Township People Back Drive for Peace," *Argus*, August 31, 1993.

152   a story published in the *Orange County Register*: "S. Africa Expects U.S. Companies to Trickle Back," *OCR*, September 26, 1993.

152   the press coverage was unlike anything: Jerry Eckert to the Biehls, August 30, 1993. (BFP)

153   "A hundred blacks die every day": "The Death That Won't Go Away," *Daily News* (Durban), May 1, 1994.

153   One such incident occurred: Benedict Carton and Leslie Bank, "Forgetting Apartheid: History, Culture and the Body of a Nun," *Africa* 86, no. 3 (August 2016): 472–503.

154   "People stoned anything that symbolized the state": Raymond Whitaker, "Soweto: The Day That Changed a Nation's History," *Independent*, June 16, 2006.

154   Kader Asmal described Amy as "a very attractive blond": John Carlin, "Two Arrested in SA Killing of 'Beautiful American,'" *Independent*, August 27, 1993.

155   "she had the glowing, healthy looks": Meg Voorhes to Peter and Linda Biehl, August 26, 1993. (BFP)

155   Some of Amy's friends: Miruni Soosaipillai, author interview, March 14, 2007.

155   superior to that of "our oppressors": "Amy Built for Freedom and Died for It, Mourners Told," *Argus*, August 31, 1993.

155   "It's painful to say, I'm sorry": Ibid.

155   "I was probably angrier": Solange Jacobs-Randolph, author interview, June 2, 2005.

156   "I've had my life taken away from me": Ron Arias et al., "Legacy of Love," *People*, September 20, 1993.

156   "If they can make you hate": Marilyn Lewis, "Death in an Angry Land," *San Jose Mercury News*, October 10, 1993.

156   "Amy was my little sister": videotape recording, Amy Biehl memorial service, September 3, 1993. (BFP)

156   "What words could I say to my sister": Ibid.

156   "Unfortunately, our flag bearer has fallen": Ibid.

156   "I was going to ask Amy to marry me today": Ibid.

157   "We are so proud of our daughter": "Hosannas for Slain Activist Memorial," *LA Times*, September 4, 1993.

157   "Let us rejoice in friendship": Biehl family, "To our friends in Santa Fe," September 1, 1993. (BFP)

157   "Each time I read from the newspapers": A. V. Hlekani to Peter and Linda Biehl, c. September 1993. (BFP)

157   Maybe it's because I knew: Ilze Olckers to the Biehls, September 3, 1993. (BFP)

158   "such Americans embrace the African National Congress": R. W. Johnson, "American Victim Symbolizes South Africa's Bitter Tragedy," *Times*, August 27, 1993.

159   "the kind of attitude that gets nice Americans into trouble": Simon Barber, "Murder Is Murder, and One Is No Less Evil Than Another," *Business Day*, August 31, 1993.

159   "It is pathetic that Simon Barber": Larry Diamond, "Bitterness Tarnishes Memory," *Cape Times*, September 12, 1993.

159   Samuel Francis . . . launched an even harsher: Samuel Francis, "The Tiger and the Murdered Lady," *Washington Times*, September 3, 1993.

159   Stedman . . . called Francis' column "a vile missive of hate": Stephen Stedman, "What Amy Tried to Do for South Africa," *Washington Times*, September 14, 1993.

160   Two more of Amy's admirers: Joseph Duffey, "What Amy Tried to Do for South Africa," *Washington Times*, September 14, 1993; Karen Clark, "Misguided Attack," *Washington Times*, September 26, 1993. See also Robert Faelan, "The High Price of Living in an Alice-in-Wonderland World," *Washington Times*, October 15, 1993.

160   Angered that the young American: Clive Keegan, author interview, June 10, 2004.

160   "I invited the family": "Biehl Family Invited to S. Africa," *OCR*, September 14, 1993.

161   "The people that she touched": Ibid.

161   "deal with our many": Linda Biehl to Melanie Jacobs, c. September 1993. (BFP)

161   "We are confident that Amy's": Arias, "Legacy of Love," *People*, September 20, 1993.

161   "Amy was not fearless": Stephen Stedman, "Stedman's Remarks at Biehl Memorial Service: 'Amy Was the Bravest Soul I've Ever Known,'" *Campus Report*, Stanford University, October 13, 1993.

161   "How did a person so small": "Tears, Smiles at Biehl Memorial," *Stanford Daily*, October 8, 1993.

CHAPTER 8: "WELCOME TO THE STRUGGLE, FAMILY"

165   "Perhaps you might consider this": Lisa Soloway to Peter and Linda Biehl, August 30, 1993. (BFP)

166   "It is fair to say that Amy's friends": The Biehls to Amy's friends and colleagues at the University of the Western Cape, September 12, 1993. (BFP)

166   "to participate in a few": Peter Biehl to David Halsted, September 19, 1993. (BFP)

166   Molly expressed similar concerns: Molly Biehl to Linda, Peter, Kim, and Zach Biehl, October 6, 1993. (BFP)

166   Halsted sympathized: David Halsted to Peter and Linda Biehl, September 23, 1993. (BFP)

166   He wrote the Biehls: Dullah Omar to Linda and Peter Biehl, September 23, 1993. (BFP)

166   Although the Biehls: Linda Biehl to Dullah Omar, September 28, 1993. (BFP)

167   "We are trying to maintain": Ibid.

167   Peter feared for the family's safety: Molly Biehl, author interview, July 16, 2006.

167   "resented by black South Africans": Molly Biehl to Linda, Peter, Kim, and Zach Biehl, October 6, 1993. (BFP)

167   officials from the US State Department: Linda Biehl, author interview, July 17, 2006.

167   the ANC also provided an armed guard: Molly Biehl interview.

167   Peter told a journalist: "The Biehls Arrive in South Africa," *OCR*, October 10, 1993.

167   "Amy is no longer": Ibid.

167   "We are here in peace": Ibid.

168   United Nations observers in South Africa: "Family of Slain Woman Calls for Peace," *LA Times,* October 11, 1993.

168   "It's hard to imagine a place": Kim Christensen, "Sorrow in Black and White," *OCR,* November 21, 1993.

168   "Since the struggle began in our country": "Inside the Struggle: The Amy Biehl Story," *Turning Point,* ABC News, April 20, 1994.

168   "a hundred times worse": Christensen, "Sorrow in Black and White."

168   they were uncomfortable: Ibid.

168   "I tell them we were broken-hearted": "Rest in Peace, Amy," *OCR,* October 11, 1993.

169   "Our coming here was to say": "Amy's Family Visits Place She Died," *Argus,* October 11, 1993.

169   They had no personal interest: "Rest in Peace, Amy"; "Family Coming to Terms with Amy Biehl's Death," *Sunday Times,* October 17, 1993; Christensen, "Sorrow in Black and White."

169   "Rest in peace, Amy": "Inside the Struggle," *Turning Point.*

170   the *Cape Times* published: "Heartbroken" and "Biehl Family at Killing Site," *Cape Times,* October 11, 1993.

170   In a prominent editorial: "Atoning for Amy," *Cape Times,* October 12, 1993.

170   the sadness and pain: "Biehl Family Sees the Sights," *OCR,* October 12, 1993.

170   ceremony in their honor: "Inside the Struggle," *Turning Point.*

170   the family wasn't prepared: Zach Biehl, author interview, June 1, 2005.

170   "UWC still hurts after the loss": "Biehl Family's Sad Visit to Campus," *On Campus* (University of the Western Cape), October 15–21, 1993.

170   "What you see here today": "South Africans Offer Biehls Cheers, Tears," *OCR,* October 13, 1993.

171   "Take a message to Amy as you pray": "Friends and Family Unite to Honour Slain Student Amy," *Argus,* October 13, 1993.

171   "Amy was no more and no less than one of you": "South Africans Offer Biehls Cheers, Tears."

171   the young people of South Africa could "really shape [the country]": "Biehl Family's Sad Visit to Campus."

171   a man yelled "One settler, one bullet!": Christensen, "Sorrow in Black and White."

171   "I was not going to let": Ibid.

171   "All these [singers and poets]": Ibid.

172   "I felt terrible as we jumped": Ibid.

172   "It's just ironic that": Ibid.

172   Linda realized that if nothing: "Inside the Struggle," *Turning Point.*

172   Telite urged the PAC to "stop appearing on television": "PAC to Talk, But Also Vows to Continue Its Armed Struggle," *Argus,* October 14, 1993.

172   the Biehls praised the choice: "Biehl's Family Praises Choice of South Africans for Prize," *OCR,* October 16, 1993.

173   "to express our solidarity": "US Victim Honoured," *Sunday Times,* October 17, 1993.

173   "You do Amy a great honor": "'We Are Committed to SA,' Says Amy's Dad," *Weekend Argus,* October 16/17, 1993.

173 The Biehls were there "to show their solidarity": "Courageous Pilgrims of Peace," *Weekly Mail & Guardian,* October 22–28, 1993.

173 "You're part of the ANC": Scott Greenwood-Meinert, author interview, June 8, 2005.

174 "they've experienced the violence": Molly Biehl, author interview, July 16, 2006.

174 "It's just like meeting": "Families of Biehl, Hani Meet," *Cape Times,* October 18, 1993.

174 she was "in awe" of her daughter: "Inside the Struggle," *Turning Point.*

174 "I have pretty much hated": Christensen, "Sorrow in Black and White."

175 "Everybody was celebrating": Greenwood-Meinert interview.

175 South Africa's future "depends mightily on the efforts of those like the Biehls": "Clarity Out of Tragedy," *LA Times,* October 13, 1993.

175 "I don't think we are going": "Biehls Head Home from South Africa," *OCR,* October 17, 1993.

175 "I have never felt any anger": Ibid.

175 Peter had said that those accused: Ibid.

175 "They killed Amy": "Amy Biehl's Killers Should Not Hang Says Boyfriend," AP, October 14, 1993; published under headline "Boyfriend Says Biehl Killers Shouldn't Die," *Stanford Daily,* October 15, 1993.

CHAPTER 9: TIME OF TRIALS

176 In the eyes of one perceptive journalist: Amy Waldman, "Amy Biehl Is Dead," *Voice* 39, no. 9 (March 1, 1994): 25.

176 "Settler, settler, war, war": "South Africa: PAC Youths Chant 'War, War' at South African Court," Reuters, September 13, 1993; "'War, War' Chants at Amy Biehl Hearing," *Argus,* September 13, 1993; "Amy Biehl's Family to Visit City," *Argus,* September 14, 1993.

177 "Every settler deserves a bullet!": "Second American Is Stabbed in S. Africa," *LA Times,* October 10, 1993.

177 "the Cape's most senior jurist": Waldman, "Amy Biehl Is Dead," 21.

177 the crime "did nothing to advance": Ibid., 22.

177 Tutu wondered how Poswa: Ibid.

177 "In every sense, they are children": Nancy Scheper-Hughes, "Who's the Killer? Popular Justice and Human Rights in a South African Squatter Camp," *Social Justice* 22, no. 3 (Fall 1995): 143–65.

178 "One settler, one bullet!" and "Every settler deserves a bullet!": "Three Blacks Off Hook in Killing," *Washington Times,* November 23, 1993; Peter Taylor, "An Honorary African," *Sunday Times Magazine* (London), March 27, 1994, 56–61.

179 "Never have I wept more": Vesta Smith, letter to the editor, *Argus,* December 7, 1993.

179 "Anyone who talks to the police": "S. African Trial over Slain O.C. Scholar Falling Apart," *LA Times,* December 11, 1993.

179 Judge Friedman believed: "News in Biehl Case Termed No Surprise," *LA Times,* November 24, 1993; "Second Delay in Biehl Trial," *Cape Times,* November 24, 1993.

180 "occasionally sucked his thumb": Scheper-Hughes, "Who's the Killer?"

180 she would "end up the same as Amy": Taylor, "An Honorary African," 61.

180 "I feel intimidated": "Life of Witness Is Threatened in Amy Case," *Weekend Argus,* November 27/28, 1993.

180   "the crowd in the public gallery": Ibid.

180   "We were shocked by what happened": "'Amy's Killers 'Just Thugs,'" *Weekend Argus*, November 27/28, 1993.

180   "I'm not testifying": Ibid.

180   "Judge Friedman, revolted by their outburst": Scheper-Hughes, "Who's the Killer?"

181   "Jeers at Amy agony": "Jeers at Amy Agony," *Argus*, November 25, 1993.

181   "The clerk to the court": "Laughter in Murder Court Chills S Africa," *Times*, November 28, 1993.

181   "Kill the settler!": "Witnesses Testify Biehl's Attackers Ignored Pleas," *San Diego Union Tribune*, November 26, 1993.

181   "Most [of the black youths attending the trial]": Waldman, "Amy Biehl Is Dead," 24.

181   "Were these young militants children at all": Nancy Scheper-Hughes and Carolyn Sargent, introduction to *Small Wars: The Cultural Politics of Childhood*, ed. N. Scheper-Hughes and C. Sargent (Berkeley: University of California Press, 1998), 25.

182   "Our parents, they are cowards for the Boer": Bill Keller, "A Brutalized Young Generation Turns Its Rage against Whites," *NYT*, December 7, 1993.

182   "I understand it": "Three Suspects Freed in Biehl Case," *OCR*, November 23, 1993.

182   Peter wondered whether arrangements: Peter Biehl to Kyra Eberle, November 27, 1993; Peter Biehl to Dullah Omar, November 27, 1993; Princeton Lyman to Peter Biehl, January 4, 1994. (BFP)

182   State Department officials worked: "Maletsatsi Maceba," *Amy Biehl Foundation Newsletter* 1, no. 2 (c. March 1995).

183   "he was proud to have killed": Gerald Friedman, Judgment, Amy Biehl trial, October 24, 1994 (#SS 136/93); "Biehl Killing Confessions Read in Court," *LA Times*, September 1, 1994.

183   "police had used force": "One Has to Look at the Future," *U.S. News & World Report*, December 20, 1993.

183   "trial within the trial": "S. African Trial over Slain O.C. Scholar Falling Apart."

184   the trial seemed to be unraveling: Ibid.

184   "It's a horrible incident": "Murder Trial Awash with Anger" *Boca Raton News*, January 5, 1994.

184   "Symptoms of a growing contempt": "Amnesty and the Law," *Argus*, December 6, 1993.

184   "I also thought that some respect and dignity": Paul Taylor, "The Trials of Linda Biehl," *Washington Post*, March 7, 1994.

184   he responded cautiously: Princeton Lyman to Peter Biehl, January 4, 1994. (BFP)

185   "The latest massacre": "Four Die in Terror Gun Attack on Cape Whites," *Daily Telegraph*, January 1, 1994.

185   "We have failed in our political education": Waldman, "Amy Biehl Is Dead," 23.

185   They stayed with the family of Paul Welsh: Linda Biehl, author interview, June 3, 2009; Molly Biehl, author interview, July 16, 2006.

185   "We've seen things": "Biehl's Mother, Sister Taunted," *OCR*, February 2, 1994.

185   Linda sensed that she and her daughter: Linda Biehl, author interview, July 17, 2006.

186   "I'm sure hundreds of people saw": Waldman, "Amy Biehl Is Dead," 24.

186   "Was he smiling at me": "Victim's Sister Gets a Grin from Suspect," *Times-Picayune* (New Orleans), February 1, 1994; "Accused Grins at Biehl Sister in Courtroom," *Cape Times*, February 1, 1994.

186   a young black man shouted "settler, settler": "Victim's Sister Gets a Grin from Suspect."

186   "We really know very little": "Biehl's Mother 'Picks Up the Torch,'" *OCR*, February 6, 1994.

186   "I know that not long ago they were shiny-eyed children": Catherine Eden, "A Mother's Journey," *Fair Lady*, May 4, 1994, 92–93.

186   "Hey, guys, she was there for you": Kimberly Jardine, "Trial of Tears," *Orange Coast*, August 1994, 59.

186   "One settler, one bullet!": "Biehl's Mother, Sister Taunted."

186   "I am quite entitled to attend the trial": "Hostile Mob Heckles Biehls," *Cape Times*, February 4, 1994.

186–87 "I can't be hurt more": "Blacks at S. Africa Court Harass Mom of Slain American Woman," *Chicago Tribune*, February 2, 1994.

187   "We are not going to give in": "The Amy Biehl Case," *Sunday Times*, February 6, 1994.

187   "There was a five-year-old": Eden, "A Mother's Journey," 92.

187   "Anger and bitterness": Taylor, "The Trials of Linda Biehl."

187   the trial had been "an ordeal": Ahmed Gora Ebrahim to Peter and Linda Biehl, February 8, 1994. (BFP)

187   Linda's inscription read: "PAC Sorry for Taunts at Biehl Trial," *Cape Times*, February 14, 1994.

187   Linda sat next to ANC elder: Linda Biehl, author interview, June 3, 2009.

187   to light a "flame of freedom and reconciliation": "Mandela Comforts Slain Student's Kin," *San Jose Mercury News*, February 3, 1994.

187   "We were really devastated": "Inside the Struggle: The Amy Biehl Story," *Turning Point*, ABC News, April 20, 1994.

187   "Well, [Amy] loved you": Ibid.

188   "The death of Amy Biehl gave us a pain": "Biehl's Mother 'Picks Up the Torch.'"

188   she took Linda and Molly: "Hostile Mob Heckles Biehls."

188   "Because the ANC and Nelson Mandela": Jardine, "Trial of Tears," 54.

188   Nofemela had been examined "at the time of his confession": Waldman, "Amy Biehl Is Dead," 24.

188   "She would have been ecstatic": "South Africa's Joy Spreads to O.C.," *OCR*, May 3, 1994.

188   a PAC official discussed his party's: "Pan Africanist Congress Probes Election Failure," *Green Left Weekly* (Australia), no. 159, September 14, 1994.

188–89 South Africa had truly become "another country": Allister Sparks, *Tomorrow Is Another Country: The Inside Story of South Africa's Negotiated Revolution* (Sandton: Struik, 1994).

189   "Many persons worked": Princeton Lyman to Linda Biehl, June 10, 1994. (BFP)

189   some of whom reportedly taunted whites: "$70 Bail Set for 3 in U.S. Student's Killing," *NYT*, May 24, 1994.

189   "If they would have gotten more physical evidence": Jardine, "Trial of Tears," 55.

189   The prosecution wondered "whether to proceed with a weak case": Princeton Lyman to Linda Biehl, June 10, 1994. (BFP)

190   "Amy was still an important person": "Biehls Revisit Radically Different S. Africa," *LA Times*, August 14, 1994.

190   "I think there will be some accountability": "Biehl Killing Confessions Read in Court," *LA Times*, September 1, 1994.

190–91   the testimony against them was "inconsistent": "S. Africa Trial in Killing of U.S. Student Ends," *LA Times*, October 13, 1994.

191   Friedman ended up writing a 120-page judgment: "In the Supreme Court of South Africa (Cape of Good Hope Provincial Division), case no. SS 136/93, in the matter between the State versus Mongesi [sic] Manqina, Mzikhona Nofemela, Vusumsi [sic] Samuel Ntamo, October 24, 1994."

191   "The state has proved": "Three Guilty of Killing Amy Biehl," *OCR*, October 26, 1994.

191   "It's closure on the one hand": "3 S. Africans Guilty in U.S. Activist's Death," *San Francisco Examiner*, October 25, 1994.

191   Linda admitted that she would've been "crushed": "Verdicts Bring Biehl Family Sense of Relief," *LA Times*, October 26, 1994.

191   "I wouldn't like to think it's just a verdict": Ibid.

191   "we can understand what they've been going through": "3 Guilty of Killing U.S. Student," *Chicago Tribune*, October 26, 1994.

191   "I am very worried about Amy Biehl's mother": Untitled wire story, AP, October 25, 1994; "3 Convicted of Murdering Biehl in South Africa," *Campus Report*, Stanford University, October 26, 1994.

191   "I certainly appreciate her beautiful thoughts": Untitled wire story, AP, October 25, 1994; "3 S. Africans Convicted of Murder in U.S. Student's Death," *Star Tribune*, October 26, 1994.

191   the defendants' supporters in the gallery "erupted": "3 South Africans Guilty in Slaying of Amy Biehl," *LA Times*, October 26, 1994.

191   "This was a racist killing": "State Asks for Death for Biehl's Killers," *Argus*, October 26, 1994.

192   his three clients had been "swept up": "3 S. Africans Guilty in U.S. Activist's Death."

192   "The court needs to look at the youth": "State Asks for Death for Biehl's Killers."

192   hoped the sentence would be "as rehabilitative as possible": "3 S. Africans Guilty in U.S. Activist's Death."

192   "There has to be accountability": "Murder Verdict in Biehl Trial," *San Jose Mercury News*, October 26, 1994.

192   "turn these people around": "18-year Sentences for Amy Biehl's Killers," *Business Day*, October 27, 1994.

192   Friedman said the murder "was cold-blooded": "Biehl Killers Sentenced to 18 Years in Prison," Reuters wire story, October 27, 1994.

192   the young men "had been caught up in a spiral of violence": "Biehl Killers Given 18 Years," *Cape Times*, October 27, 1994.

192   "One settler, one bullet!": "Biehl's Killers Spared Death, Given 18 Years," *LA Times*, October 27, 1994.

192   "Any sentence cannot bring Amy back": Ibid.

192   "I just don't think more death": "Amy's Mother Sees Hope for Her Murderers," *Cape Times*, October 27, 1994.

193   "[Their daughter's] gone": "Biehl's Killers Spared Death, Given 18 Years."

193   Americans, especially Californians: Gerald Friedman, author interview, June 22, 2004.

193   held the Biehls up as role models: "Justice for a Friend of Democracy," *LA Times,* October 27, 1994; Joal Ryan, "A Family Shows Civility in the Face of Trying Times," *Advocate* (Newark, OH), November 15, 1994.

193   Judge Friedman had described the crime: Mark Hill to Peter and Linda Biehl, November 14, 1994. (BFP)

193   "I do not think they should be": "Dateline Africa," *OCR,* November 9, 1994.

193   "When I saw the three accused": "Amy Biehl's Killers Go on Hunger Strike Protest," *LA Times,* November 9, 1994.

194   Judge Friedman said that Amy's murder: Friedman interview.

194   Constitutional Court abolished: "South Africa's Supreme Court Abolishes Death Penalty," *NYT,* June 7, 1995.

194   Amy had educated them: "Amy Biehl's Family Moves Ahead after 4th Conviction," *OCR,* June 7, 1995.

194   "It has been a tragedy": "Three Found Guilty of Murdering Biehl," *Business Day,* October 26, 1994.

CHAPTER 10: LAYING A NEW FOUNDATION

205   "We didn't set out to do it": Linda Biehl, author interview, July 18, 2006.

205   "the political empowerment of women": "Amy Biehl Memorial Fund Established at NDI," *NDI Reports,* Summer/Fall 1993, 3.

206   the president summoned them: Linda Biehl, email to the author, June 24, 2015.

207   "the realization of a great dream": Bill Clinton, remarks on the signing of the South African Democratic Transition Support Act of 1993, November 23, 1993, *Public Papers of the Presidents of the United States: William J. Clinton, 1993: Book II.*

207   "I want to especially recognize the presence here": Ibid. See also White House diary entry 1211, November 23, 1993, electronic daily diary, [Biehl] [11.23/1993] OA/ID 150000, Clinton Presidential Records, William Clinton Presidential Library.

207   "Your daughter is part of South African history now": "Biehl's Mother 'Picks Up the Torch,'" *OCR,* February 6, 1994.

207   "go on with [their] lives": Linda Biehl interview, July 18, 2006.

207   "We all formed the foundation": Molly Biehl, author interview, July 16, 2006.

207   "Parents die in peace": "Memorial to Two Who Died Aiding Others," *Long Beach Press Telegram,* May 30, 1994.

207   the Amy Biehl Foundation was officially created: Peter Biehl and Rolene Miller, "The New Math of Grassroots Community Work," *Reflections* 2, no. 4 (Fall 1996).

208   "When someone dies very young": "Biehl's Mother 'Picks Up the Torch.'"

208   "another angry mob needing to kill": Linda Biehl, "A Birthday," March 17, 1994. (BFP)

208   "If we pray, hope, invest": Ibid.

208   "'I said, yes, give it to them'": "Biehl's Cause Lives On," *San Jose Mercury News,* October 23, 1994.

208   "ascribed to a democratic ethos": Patricia Keefer, author interview, January 30, 2010.

208   "While her murder was horrific": Gregory Branch and Claudia Pryor, "Race Plays a Decisive Role in News Content," *Neiman Reports* 55, no. 1 (Spring 2001): 65–68.

209   "My students and I": Charles Beach to Peter and Linda Biehl, July 18, 1994. (BFP)

209 "Viewers who couldn't have cared": Don Kladstrup to the Biehls, January 2, 1995. (BFP)

210 ABC received the Alfred I. DuPont "Gold Baton": "ABC News Garners Top DuPont-Columbia Nod," *Daily Variety*, January 27, 1995.

210 "As you celebrate the election": President Bill Clinton to Molly Biehl, April 28, 1994, 9403146[1], OA/ID 193, NSC Records Management, Clinton Presidential Records, William Clinton Presidential Library.

210 "training and education programs": Biehl family, invitation to memorial concert, April 1994. (BFP)

211 "My entire management life": Peter Biehl, "My Professional Journey," c. 1997. (BFP)

211 Helping her bond with this new country: Linda Biehl to Sahm Venter, August 10 and 11, 1994; Sahm Venter to Linda Biehl, August 11, 1994. (BFP)

211 Many of the donors were "not big money people": "Foundation to Continue Work of Amy Biehl," *LA Times* (Orange County edition), March 19, 1995.

212 "You don't have to be a huge foundation": Ibid.

212 the foundation managed: Peter Biehl, Amy Biehl Foundation financial statement, October 1995; Peter Biehl, Foundation activity highlights since February 1994, c. 1997. (BFP)

212 "The generosity with which you and the rest": Dullah Omar to Peter and Linda Biehl, August 31, 1995. (BFP)

212 Omar might be willing to "facilitate some quiet reconciliation sessions": Peter Biehl to Dullah Omar, January 24, 1995. (BFP)

212 he was also a "point man for the Mandela government's mission": *Amy Biehl Foundation Newsletter* 1, no. 3 (c. July 1995).

212–23 they could work on the foundation: "'At Least Her Life and Death Were Purposeful,'" *Desert Sun*, September 7, 1996.

213 the couple's first "exploratory, fact-finding" trip: P. Biehl and Miller, "The New Math of Grassroots Community Work."

213 the Biehls sought to "identify the need": Everett Harper, "The Amy Biehl Foundation Trust," case number SI-01, Graduate School of Business, Stanford University, October 2000, 6.

213 Mosaic was a "training, service, and healing center for women": P. Biehl and Miller, "The New Math of Grassroots Community Work."

214 Moloi suggested that all: Alosi Moloi, "Commentary," *Reflections* 2, no. 4 (Fall 1996).

214 Peebles-Wilkins called Peter's use of such terms "paternalistic and patronizing": Wilma Peebles-Wilkins, "Commentary," *Reflections* 2, no. 4 (Fall 1996).

214 Kenneth Lutterman . . . supported the efforts: Kenneth Lutterman, "Commentary," *Reflections* 2, no. 4 (Fall 1996).

214 Ruthann Rountree . . . refrained from commenting: Ruthann Rountree, "Commentary," *Reflections* 2, no. 4 (Fall 1996).

214 Peter seemed to take the critiques in his stride: *Amy Biehl Foundation Newsletter* 3, no. 1 (c. early 1997).

215 "I was the first project": Solange Jacobs-Randolph, author interview, June 2, 2005.

215 the foundation's support of Mosaic: "Amy's Legacy," *LA Times*, August 25, 1996.

215 "You have much of [President Mandela's] traits": Jeremy Ractliffe to Linda Biehl, October 14, 1996. (BFP)

215 "We are quite certain that Amy would not wish": Peter and Linda Biehl to Jeremy (Ractliffe), November 12, 1996. (BFP)

216 a connection between the Biehls and the Kendalls: Larry and Judy Kendall, "Biehl-Kendall Relationship/History," July 3, 2015.

216 "The students were shown": *Amy Biehl Foundation Newsletter* 3, no. 1 (c. early 1997).

216 they expanded their involvement: Larry and Judy Kendall, "Biehl-Kendall Relationship/History."

216 "When I watched the movie": "Letters of Inspiration," *Hillsborough Beacon* (NJ), May 9, 1996.

217 "It took an enormous amount of courage": Ibid.

217 "I thought this is really an amazing thing": "Hillsboro Kids to Dance for S. African Foundation," *Courier-News* (NJ), May 8, 1996.

CHAPTER 11: THE TRUTH AND RECONCILIATION COMMISSION

218 thereby establishing the Truth and Reconciliation Commission (TRC): The literature on the Truth and Reconciliation Commission is vast. Useful works include Alex Boraine, *A Country Unmasked* (Cape Town: Oxford University Press, 2000); Audrey R. Chapman and Hugo van der Merwe, eds., *Truth and Reconciliation in South Africa: Did the TRC Deliver?* (Philadelphia: University of Pennsylvania Press, 2008); Lyn S. Graybill, *Truth and Reconciliation in South Africa: Miracle or Model?* (Boulder, CO: Lynne Rienner Publishers, 2002); Wilmot James and Linda van de Vijver, *After the TRC: Reflections on Truth and Reconciliation in South Africa* (Athens: Ohio University Press, 2001); Antjie Krog, *Country of My Skull* (Johannesburg: Random House, 1998); Jeremy Sarkin, *Carrots and Sticks: The TRC and the South African Amnesty Process* (Antwerp: Intersentia, 2004); Desmond Tutu, *No Future without Forgiveness* (New York: Doubleday, 1999); Charles Villa-Vicencio and Erik Doxtader, eds., *The Provocations of Amnesty: Memory, Justice and Impunity* (Trenton, NJ: Africa World Press, 2003); Richard A. Wilson, *The Politics of Truth and Reconciliation in South Africa: Legitimizing the Post-Apartheid State* (New York: Cambridge University Press, 2001).

219 "to forgive rather than demand retribution": Tutu, *No Future without Forgiveness*, 31.

219 the "devastating but also exhilarating work": Ibid., 69.

220 "We are charged to unearth the truth": Ibid., 114.

220 "I think there has to be some sentence here": "Murder Verdict in Biehl Trial," *San Jose Mercury News*, October 26, 1994.

220 On the Amy Biehl issue: *Truth and Reconciliation Commission Report*, vol. 6, 412–13.

221 "We know people on this commission": "S. African Group Urges Amnesty in Biehl Slaying," *LA Times* (Orange County edition), August 21, 1996.

221 "We don't feel it was a political crime": "Give Biehl Killers Amnesty, South African Militants Urge," *OCR*, August 21, 1996.

221 they wanted to "support the process": Linda Biehl, author interview, July 18, 2006.

221 "Our feeling is [that]": "Biehls Won't Oppose Amnesty Plea," *LA Times*, April 30, 1997.

221 "whether they have any feelings about what the young men did": "Amy's Killer to Seek Amnesty," *Cape Times*, April 28, 1997.

222 "Amy was completely devoted": Peter Biehl to Robin Brink, May 4, 1997. (BFP)

222   "speak from your heart": Linda Biehl, Facebook post, Amy Biehl Foundation USA, July 8, 2016, www.facebook.com/usaabf/.

222   "One of the reasons we want to participate": "In Honor of a Daughter's Memory," *Houston Chronicle*, May 11, 1997.

222   "That's going to be a little difficult": "Biehls Won't Oppose Amnesty Plea."

222   "Amy would have wanted": "In Honor of a Daughter's Memory," *Houston Chronicle*, May 11, 1997.

222   "it was a logical consequence": Ibid.

223   "it was the right thing to do": Scott Greenwood-Meinert, author interview, June 8, 2005.

223   the men should "serve out the remainder of their sentences": Scott Meinert, statement to the Truth and Reconciliation Commission, c. July 1997. (BFP)

223   a "committed life": *Talk of the Nation*, NPR, July 30, 1997.

223   the Biehls lost their daughter "for no reason": Iris Films, *Long Night's Journey into Day*, 2000.

223   "I looked at her and wondered": "In the Steps of a Slain Scholar," *St. Louis Post-Dispatch*, September 9, 1997.

224   "It's the beginning of a new life": "Biehls Meet Mother of Daughter's Killer," *LA Times* (Orange County edition), June 29, 1997.

224   "This is what it's all about": Ibid.

224   "It's liberating to forgive": Ibid.

224   "not of our own choosing": "Biehl a Victim of Struggle," *Sowetan*, July 9, 1997.

224   "We were really humbled": "PAC Leaders 'Humbled' by Parents' Attitude," *Cape Times*, July 9, 1997; "Victim's Parents Declined to Fight S. Africa Amnesty," *USA Today*, July 10, 1997.

225   the hearings scheduled for Cape Town would "revive memories": "Testing Time for the TRC," *Cape Times*, July 7, 1997.

225   "Like the killing itself": "Biehl's Parents Bring Killers to Tears at Hearing," *LA Times* (Orange County edition), July 10, 1997.

225   Haupt marveled at how Peter and Linda: Paul Haupt, author interview, July 21, 2004.

226   the gesture "sent electric shocks down your spine": Michael Henderson, *Forgiveness: Breaking the Chain of Hate* (Portland, OR: Arnica Publishing, 2003), 174.

226   the murder of Amy Biehl—was "associated with a political objective": TRC transcript, July 8, 1997.

226   the ANC had "sold out": Ntobeko Peni, author interview, July 25, 2002.

227   "I deeply regret the killing of Amy Biehl": TRC transcript, July 8, 1997.

227   "At the time we were in very high spirits": Ibid.

227   I feel very sorry and down-hearted: Ibid.

227   Brink . . . asked how "the killing of an unarmed": Ibid.

227   "Mr. Peni, isn't it [true]": Ibid.

227   "Our killing of Amy Biehl": Ibid.

227   "But then I read in the press": Marianne Thamm, "Amy Biehl and Her Killers," *Daily Maverick*, July 28, 2015.

228   "The deed was committed at the time": TRC transcript, July 8, 1997.

228   "during that time my spirit just says": Ibid.

228 "You see what I am going to suggest to you": Ibid.

228 "No, that's not true": Ibid.

228 "What happened with the police": Ibid.

228 several PASO members in the audience interjected "Yes!": "Past Flashes by in Death of a Golden Girl," *Mail & Guardian*, July 11–17, 1997.

228 "I was highly politically motivated": TRC transcript, July 8, 1997.

228 "You had no mercy in your heart that day?": Ibid.

229 Linda "blinked rapidly" and Peter "stroked his cheek": "Killer Tells How He Struck the Fatal Knife Blow," *Cape Argus*, July 9, 1997.

229 he sometimes wondered whether the young men's statements: Peter Biehl, *Talk of the Nation*, NPR, July 30, 1997.

229 He expressed regret for what he did: TRC transcript, July 9, 1997.

229 "Because Amy was killed": Iris Films, *Long Night's Journey into Day*.

229 "We come to South Africa as Amy came": TRC transcript, July 9, 1997.

230 At the same time we say it's your process: Ibid.

230 Manqina later said: Iris Films, *Long Night's Journey into Day*.

231 "Amy Biehl's parents have said so movingly": TRC transcript, July 9, 1997.

231 "The murder itself was a senseless murder": Ibid.

231 "To me it is plausible": "Where Are the Politicians Who Incited the Biehl Killers?" *Cape Times*, July 15, 1997.

231 South Africa was "an intensely political place": "Biehls Believe Their Daughter's Killers Are 'Genuinely Sorry,'" *Cape Times*, July 10, 1997.

231 "The chances are that at least two": "Forgiveness That Stunned South Africa," *Sunday Times Magazine* (London), July 13, 1997.

231 the Biehl amnesty hearings prompted: Steven Gish, "From Admiration to Anger: Reactions to the Amy Biehl Amnesty Decision," in *Healing South African Wounds*, ed. Gilles Teulié and Mélanie Joseph-Vilain (Montpellier: Presses universitaires de la Méditerranée, 2009), 233–49.

232 "Only parents who have suffered": "Humbled by the Biehls' Attitude," *Cape Times*, July 10, 1997.

232 the Biehls reflected "the spirit of President Mandela himself": Alec Russell, "Amy's Killers Test Limits of South African Forgiveness," *Sunday Telegraph*, July 13, 1997.

232 "War talk has undoubtedly contributed": "Humbled by the Biehls' Attitude."

233 "simply a pack of murderers": "Forgiveness That Stunned South Africa."

233 "As if Amy Biehl didn't give her own life": Dana Parsons, "The Biehls Add Meaning to an Already Significant Life," *LA Times*, July 11, 1997.

233 "Peter and Linda Biehl brought mercy": "Gentle Rain in South Africa," *Christian Science Monitor*, July 11, 1997.

233 A caller to National Public Radio: *Talk of the Nation*, NPR, July 30, 1997.

234 he held no personal grudge: *Truth and Reconciliation Report*, vol. 6, 399.

234 few of the perpetrators of apartheid: Robert Edgar, personal communication with the author, March 2017.

235 One study concluded that most victims: Ron Krabill, "Review of *Long Night's Journey into Day*," *Safundi* 3, no. 2 (2001), cited in Graybill, *Truth and Reconciliation in South Africa*, 53.

235 "The leadership of APLA takes full responsibility": Quoted in Graybill, *Truth and Reconciliation in South Africa,* 47.

235 He too refused to express regret: *Truth and Reconciliation Report,* vol. 6, 392, 403.

235 Later, however, Mphahlele publicly reconciled: Marina Cantacuzino, *The Forgiveness Project: Stories for a Vengeful Age* (London: Jessica Kingsley Publishers, 2015), 54–58.

235 she had not been a "legitimate, designated, or a priority target": "PAC Admits to Blunders," *Sowetan,* July 22, 1997.

235–36 It was "immoral to blame the victims of apartheid": Motsoko Pheko, "PAC Defends APLA," *Sowetan,* July 24, 1997.

236 "People responsible for atrocities": Robert Brand, "A Just War, but Criminal Actions," *Star,* July 28, 1997.

236 others "think we're probably crazy": *Talk of the Nation,* NPR, July 30, 1997.

236 "People in South Africa will come": Ibid.

237 "Each person will find": *Amy Biehl Foundation Newsletter* 3, no. 2 (c. August 1997).

237 "We have never sought": Henderson, *Forgiveness: Breaking the Chain of Hate,* 175.

CHAPTER 12: AMNESTY

238 Although they did not act on the orders: TRC amnesty committee, Biehl amnesty decision, July 28, 1998, www.justice.gov.za/trc/decisions/1998/980728_ntamo%20penietc.htm.

239 "if it was granted on the merits": Ibid.

239 the murder "was associated with a political objective": C. de Jager, addendum to the Biehl amnesty decision, Ibid.

239 the youths were supporters of a political organization: Technically, only Nofemela, Manqina, and Peni were members of PASO; Ntamo supported PASO's goals and activities, although he was not a formal member of the organization.

239 "The decision was a unanimous one": Quoted in Jeremy Sarkin, *Carrots and Sticks: The TRC and the South African Amnesty Process* (Antwerp: Intersentia, 2004), 223.

239 He called Amy's murder "an outrageous atrocity": Desmond Tutu, author interview, April 29, 2003.

239 "and this would count significantly": Tutu interview.

240 "granting amnesty to the killers of Amy Biehl": Richard A. Wilson, *The Politics of Truth and Reconciliation in South Africa: Legitimizing the Post-Apartheid State* (New York: Cambridge University Press, 2001), 92.

240 "I want to say that I am sorry": "S. Africa Frees 4 Killers of Southland Student," *LA Times,* July 29, 1998.

240 "As a mother, I am very happy": "Four Get Amnesty in Amy Biehl Death," AP, July 28, 1998, www.nytimes.com/aponline/i/AP-South-Africa-Biehl.html.

240 they couldn't help: ABF, "July 28, 1998," *Amy Biehl Foundation Newsletter* 4, no. 2 (late 1998).

240 "In the cases of the four amnesty applicants": Quoted in "S. Africa Panel Pardons Killers of U.S. Student," CNN.com, July 28, 1998.

240 "Are we going to rush": "Biehls Not Surprised by Killers' Release," *OCR,* July 29, 1998.

240 "We hope for better results": ABF, "July 28, 1998."

240   "To us, forgiveness is opening the door": Peter and Linda Biehl, "The Story of Linda and Peter Biehl: Private Loss and Public Forgiveness," *Reflections: A Journal for the Helping Professions* 4, no. 4 (Fall 1998): 20–21.

241   John Yeld called the Biehls "an inspiration for all South Africans": John Yeld, "From Amy's Brutal Death, Legacy of Hope," *Cape Argus*, July 29, 1998; Yeld, "Biehls Set an Example to All in SA," *Star*, July 30, 1998.

241   "in a remarkable show of compassion": Sindiwe Magona, "South Africa's Curse," *NYT*, August 4, 1998.

242   "If [the young men] hadn't been released": "Biehl's Living Legacy Gets Boost from Killers' Release," *LA Times*, July 30, 1998.

242   many South Africans were deeply troubled: Steven Gish, "From Admiration to Anger: Reactions to the Amy Biehl Amnesty Decision," in *Healing South African Wounds*, ed. Gilles Teulié and Mélanie Joseph-Vilain (Montpellier: Presses universitaires de la Méditerranée, 2009), 233–49.

242   "was precisely the spirit": Rian Malan, "South Africa's Bid to Bury Its Past Ends with Few Truths and Little Reconciliation," *Sunday Telegraph*, August 2, 1998.

242   "Targeting a military installation": "Amnesty for Biehl's Killers Draws Support and Anger," *Business Day*, July 29, 1998.

242   he was "a bit baffled": Kader Asmal, author interview, June 7, 2004.

243   Maletsatsi Maceba also found it: Maletsatsi Maceba, author interview, July 20, 2004.

243   Melanie Jacobs expressed dismay: "Amy's Flatmate 'Not Happy' As Killers Freed," *Cape Times*, July 29, 1998.

243   A July 1998 poll: "Most Believe Truth Body Harmed Race Relations," *Business Day*, July 27, 1998; "S. Africa Frees 4 Killers of Southland Student."

243   "When you take specific cases": "Healing Our Wounds," *Sowetan*, July 31, 1998.

243   He was disappointed too: Desmond Tutu, "The TRC Has Helped Lay a Firm Foundation for True Reconciliation," *Cape Times*, August 4, 1998.

243   "Stories of forgiveness": Pumla Gobodo-Madikizela, *A Human Being Died That Night: A South African Story of Forgiveness* (Boston: Houghton Mifflin, 2003), 118.

244   "it is within the grasp": Gobodo-Madikizela, *A Human Being Died That Night*, 118.

244   "The Amy Biehl incident provided the Commission": *Truth and Reconciliation Commission of South Africa Report*, vol. 6 (Cape Town: TRC, 2003), 413.

244   "Nieuwoudt said he was disappointed": "No Forgiveness for Nieuwoudt," *Business Day*, August 5, 1998.

244   "emblematic of a country trying to heal": Elizabeth Wilberg, "Release Another 'Step along the Way,'" *Desert Sun*, c. July 29, 1998.

244   the Biehls had become "an object of curiosity": Carol Masciola, "For Biehls, Vengeance Decried," *OCR*, November 22, 1998.

245   A reader of the *Los Angeles Times* praised the Biehls: Robert Goyette, "Amy Biehl," *LA Times*, August 5, 1998.

245   "They responded to the murder of their loved [one]": Donald Shriver Jr., "Looking beyond Murder," *Christian Century* 115, no. 23 (August 26, 1998): 772–73.

245   "the unprovoked murder of a defenseless woman": "Respect for the Law," *Wall Street Journal*, August 3, 1998.

245   "That they now 'forgive' and 'understand'": Brian Donner, "Amy Biehl," *LA Times*, August 5, 1998.

245 "these sadistic Black murderers": William Pierce, "The Lesson of Amy Biehl," *Free Speech* 4, no. 9 (September 1998), https://nationalsatanist.wordpress. com/2016/06/18/the-lesson-of-amy-biehl/.

245–46 Richard A. Wilson closely examined the Biehl case: Wilson, *Politics of Truth and Reconciliation*, 91–92.

246 Anurima Bhargava put forth similar arguments: Anurima Bhargava, "Defining Political Crimes: A Case Study of the South African Truth and Reconciliation Commission," *Columbia Law Review* 102, no. 5 (June 2002): 1304–39.

246 "Was not Hani—the former military leader": "Making a Mockery of Democracy," *Mail & Guardian*, April 9–15, 1999.

246 its final report called the crimes "heinous": *TRC Report*, vol. 6, 715–16.

246 Of the 7,127 applications: Michael Morris, *Every Step of the Way: The Journey to Freedom in South Africa* (Cape Town: Human Sciences Research Council, 2004), 288.

246 despite some "striking examples of reconciliation": Greta Steyn, "South African Home Truths Fail to Heal a New Nation's Divide," *Financial Times*, July 31, 1998.

246 "Reconciliation is not going to be cheap": Tutu, "The TRC Has Helped Lay a Firm Foundation for True Reconciliation."

CHAPTER 13: MR. AND MRS. AMY BIEHL

247 "The success of South Africa's democracy": Leonard Thompson, *A History of South Africa*, 4th ed. (New Haven: Yale University Press, 2014), 280.

247 A 1998 report noted: Ibid., 283.

248 "Violence is at a ridiculous high": "Suggested Quotations from 1998 Amy Biehl Fellows," Haas Center for Public Service, Stanford, c. 1998.

248 "Blown away" by the tremendous need: Paul Haupt, author interview, July 21, 2004.

248 "historically disadvantaged": Program for official launch, Amy Biehl Foundation Trust, December 13, 1997. (BFP)

248 "Weaving a Barrier against Violence": Everett Harper, "The Amy Biehl Foundation Trust," Graduate School of Business, Stanford University, case number SI-01, October 2000.

249 it would henceforth serve: Amy Biehl Foundation, annual report, 1998. (BFP)

249 These experiences opened the Biehls' eyes: Linda Biehl, author interview, July 17, 2006.

249 "We're very good listeners": "For the Biehls, Vengeance Decried," *OCR*, November 22, 1998.

249 He and Linda didn't want to simply "throw money": "Peter Biehl, Symbol of Forgiveness, Dies," *OCR*, April 2, 2002.

250 "We are often criticized for not doing enough": "Albright Honours the Memory of Amy Biehl," *Cape Times*, December 15, 1997.

250 Peter was a "corporate American male": Haupt interview.

250 the goods were confiscated: "Customs Snag Biehls' Gifts," *Cape Times*, November 24, 1997.

250 White-led organizations could face difficulties: Mamphela Ramphele, *Steering by the Stars: Being Young in South Africa* (Cape Town: Tafelberg, 2002), 130–38.

250 "I remember thinking to myself": Jon Jeter, "A Daughter's Dream Lives at Scene of Her Death," *Washington Post*, February 18, 2001.

251 He had always wanted to own a bakery: "Parents Speak about Legacy of Daughter Who Died in South Africa," *Massachusetts Daily Collegian,* November 8, 2001.

252 "Amy's bread": *Amy Biehl Foundation Newsletter* 6, no. 1 (June 2000).

252 West had sunk into a deep depression: Victor West, author interview, July 13, 2004.

252 Peter and Linda assured: "For the Biehls, Vengeance Decried."

252 Molly helped launch the Trust's Youth: *Amy Biehl Foundation Newsletter* 6, no. 2 (November 2000); Jane McFann, "The Legacy of Amy Biehl," *Reading Today* 19, no. 5 (April/May 2002).

253 "Age is definitely not our friend": *Amy Biehl Foundation Newsletter* 4, no. 1 (April 1998).

254 the callers "ranged from township residents to ambassadors": *Amy Biehl Foundation Newsletter* 6, no. 1 (June 2000).

254 "if things are a little edgy": "Determined to Make a Difference," *Cape Times,* October 25, 1999.

254 "This is in many ways the richest": Michael Henderson, "In Family's Forgiveness, a Renewed Thanksgiving," *Oregonian,* November 25, 1999.

254 "Amy's death changed us": Jeter, "A Daughter's Dream."

254 "I guess this is really our way": Ibid.

254 US ambassador James Joseph: *Amy Biehl Foundation Newsletter* 4, no. 1 (April 1998).

254 Brian Attwood introduced Peter and Linda: Brian Attwood, remarks at NDI award dinner, November 28, 2001. (BFP)

254 Mandela invited Linda and Peter: *Amy Biehl Foundation Newsletter* 4, no. 1 (April 1998).

254 "cure the virus that is destroying our community": Mandla Majola and Monene Duze to Peter and Linda Biehl, August 17, 1998. (BFP)

254–55 An assessment conducted by a Stanford MBA student: Harper, "The Amy Biehl Foundation Trust," October 2000.

255 "Mr. and Mrs. Amy Biehl": "For the Biehls, Vengeance Decried"; "Forgiveness Elevated to Leading Role," *OCR,* March 29, 2000; *Amy Biehl Foundation Newsletter* 6, no. 1 (June 2000); Linda Biehl, author interviews, June 8, 2004, and July 18, 2006.

255 "Amy's Peace Corps": *Amy Biehl Foundation Newsletter* 6, no. 2 (November 2000).

256 "Millions of individuals of all races": To Present a Congressional Gold Medal to Nelson Rolihlahla Mandela, Pub. L. No. 105-215 (1998).

256 "Of course, everyone had been waiting": Kim Biehl, in *Our Madiba: Stories and Reflections from Those Who Met Nelson Mandela,* ed. Melanie Verwoerd (Cape Town: Tafelberg, 2014), 52.

256 "If this day is to be more": "Remarks by President Clinton and President Nelson Mandela at Presentation of Congressional Gold Medal to President Nelson Mandela," The White House, Office of the Press Secretary, September 23, 1998.

256–57 "Among those we remember today": Ibid.

257 "the most humbling experience of our lives": *Amy Biehl Foundation Newsletter* 4, no. 2 (December 1998).

257 "Scars into Stars" award: Ibid.

257 "We're not Bible people": Simon Fanshawe, "Amy Biehl's Passion for Human Rights Led Her to Some of the Most Dangerous Parts of the World . . . ," *Daily Telegraph Magazine,* July 28, 2001.

257 "People somehow always want more": Ibid.

258   "The logic would be": "Amy's Story," *60 Minutes*, CBS, January 17, 1999.

258   "Although South Africa was now free": Linda Biehl, remarks at the 10th anniversary celebration of the Faith and Politics Institute, October 24, 2001. (BFP)

258   He felt a dark cloud: Nancy Scheper-Hughes, "After the War Is Over," *Peace Review* 12, no. 3 (September 2000); "Violence and the Politics of Remorse," 221–23.

258   the two had talked: Gavin du Venage, "Cycle of Forgiveness Completes Itself in South African Shantytown," *San Francisco Chronicle,* October 28, 2001.

259   "I thought that there was one thing": Scheper-Hughes, "After the War Is Over."

259   Peter telephoned Linda: Scheper-Hughes, "Violence and the Politics of Remorse," in *Subjectivity: Ethnographic Investigations,* ed. João Biehl, Byron Good, and Arthur Kleinman (Berkeley: University of California Press, 2007), 221–23; Linda Biehl, author interview, July 18, 2006; Linda Biehl, email to the author, January 21, 2016.

259   "The fact that they wanted to talk to us": "Amy's Story," *CBS News.com*, February 28, 2000, www.cbsnews.com/stories/2000/02/2860II/printable165933.shtml.

259   Peter sat expressionless: Nancy Scheper-Hughes, "Dangerous and Endangered Youth: Social Structures and Determinants of Violence," in *Inclusion and Exclusion in the Global Arena,* ed. Max Kirsch (New York: Routledge, 2006), 314.

259   "Oh, Makhulu," Easy said: Linda Biehl, remarks at the 10th anniversary celebration of the Faith and Politics Institute, October 24, 2001 (BFP); Linda Biehl, email to the author, January 21, 2016.

259   The short meeting seemed "very natural and intimate": Linda Biehl, remarks at the 10th anniversary celebration of the Faith and Politics Institute.

259   "We wanted to meet them": "Killers Ask Victim's Parents for Aid," *Sunday Times Metro,* June 27, 1999.

259   Peter sometimes thought about Amy's death: CBS, "Amy's Story."

260   "They didn't know who": Linda Biehl, author interview, July 17, 2006.

260   "Not until I met Linda and Peter": Marina Cantacuzino, *The Forgiveness Project: Stories for a Vengeful Age* (London: Jessica Kingsley Publishers, 2015), 134–35.

260   "It's their idea," Linda said: "Biehls Fund PAC Killers," *Cape Times,* June 22, 1999.

260   "We still have to break the ice": "Killers Ask Victim's Parents for Aid."

260   "humbled by the courage shown": "Six Years Later, Amy's Legacy Lives on in Guguletu," *Cape Argus,* July 12, 1999.

260   "Out of a bad thing": Ibid.

260   "I am hypnotized": Ibid.

261   "You can see them thinking": Jeter, "A Daughter's Dream."

261   The unease extended: Renee Tawa, "Life after Death," *LA Times,* August 1, 1998.

261   Peter and Linda tried: Ibid.

261   "The long walk is not yet over": Thompson, *A History of South Africa,* 287.

262   death rates from AIDS in South Africa: Ibid., 309.

262   "the hidden golfers of Khayelitsha": *Amy Biehl Foundation Newsletter* 3, no. 2 (August 1997; "The Hidden Golfers of South Africa," *CNN.SI.com*, November 12, 1997, sportsillustrated.cnn.com/features/1997/weekly/971117/gp1117/e.html.

262   The spokesman for the group, Vusi Sixhaso: "Feeling at Home on the Range" and "A Legacy of Loving the Game," *Cape Times,* October 25, 1999.

263   "The Peoples' Driving Range": Amy Biehl Foundation Trust, information sheet on the Khayelitsha Golf Driving Range, c. March 2003.

263   "The expectation is that": Linda Biehl, author interview, July 18, 2006.

263   most of the Trust's supplemental funding: Peter Biehl, Pax Christi Justice Grant application, c. January 2001. (BFP)

264   led Peter and Linda to view: *Amy Biehl Foundation Newsletter* 6, no. 4 (November 2001).

264   They hoped to "migrate" some: *Talk of the Nation*, NPR, December 26, 2001.

264   "because the people conceive them": Linda and Peter Biehl, comments at meeting of Congressional Black Caucus, September 15, 2000. (BFP)

264   Peter and Linda seemed determined: Molly Biehl Corbin, comments in *Amy Biehl Foundation Newsletter* 7, no. 1 (December 2002).

265   "They want to build something": du Venage, "Cycle of Forgiveness Completes Itself."

265   "I don't know how they found it": Jeter, "A Daughter's Dream."

265   "If it had not been for the Truth": Fanshawe, "Amy Biehl's Passion for Human Rights."

265   "We've been able to help two of the four men": "Talk Proposes Positive Way of Dealing with Criminals," *Elm Student Newspaper*, April 13, 2001, elm.washcoll.edu/past/072/25/72_25tal.php.

266   They asked themselves if they could "knowingly place": *Amy Biehl Foundation Newsletter* 6, no. 4, November 2001.

266   "South Africa's disadvantaged people": Ibid.

266   "The Biehls really are black people": Ibid.

267   "a fear of success": "Whittier Scholars Retreat Combines Theory and Practice," *Communiqué*, Whittier College, October 3, 2001.

267   "at the very moment when success appears": *Amy Biehl Foundation Newsletter* 6, no. 4 (November 2001).

267   "The people in South Africa are so unaccustomed": "Whittier Scholars Retreat Combines Theory and Practice."

267   "Amy has committed us to South Africa for life": *Amy Biehl Foundation Newsletter* 6, no. 4 (November 2001).

267   "The Biehls came just when we needed": Jeter, "A Daughter's Dream."

267   "Just at the mention": Warren Acuncius to Ashleigh Murphy, January 3, 2002. (BFP)

267   some Gugulethu residents tried: "Gugulethu Bid to Keep Biehl Memory Alive," *Cape Argus*, May 14, 2001.

268   "Robben Island is about reconciliation": "Masekela Headlines Fund-Raising Show," *Cape Times*, March 28, 2002.

268   to those who "exemplified NDI's commitment to democracy": NDI, "The W. Averell Harriman Democracy Award: 2001," www.ndi.org/support/harriman/2001/2001award_pf.asp.

268   "If Amy is looking down tonight": Brian Attwood, remarks at NDI award dinner, November 28, 2001. (BFP)

268   Peter started having stomach cramps: "Peter Biehl, 59; Forgave Killers of Daughter," *LA Times*, April 2, 2002.

269   the trust had spent approximately $5 million: Sandy Banks, "Out of Tragedy, a Legacy of Forgiveness," *LA Times*, April 9, 2002.

269   "You get to know people": *Amy Biehl Foundation Newsletter* 6, no. 3 (May 2001).

269   "You go for it": "Peter Biehl, 59; Forgave Killers of Daughter."

269   The Biehl children believed: Deepa Bharath, "Freed by Compassion," *OCR*, November 24, 2013.

269 "I was angry at the foundation": Kim Biehl, author interview, June 3, 2005.

269 At first Kim, Molly, and Zach hesitated: *Amy Biehl Foundation Newsletter* 7, no. 1 (December 2002).

270 "great frustration": Linda Biehl, remarks at memorial service, April 26, 2002. (BFP)

CHAPTER 14: MAKHULU

271 "I think they were wondering": "Toward 'a Better World,'" *OCR*, November 22, 2002.

271 "I think she's kicking me": Ibid.

272 "She works so hard": "Why Do They Forgive Us?" *Boston Globe*, April 23, 2003.

272 But just as they had "adopted" Peter and her: Linda Biehl, author interview, June 8, 2004.

272 "It is a privilege to be part of South Africa": "Fundraiser Has Guests Swinging to a Jazzy Beat," *Cape Argus*, May 17, 2002.

272 he wanted to live his own life: *Amy Biehl Foundation Newsletter* 7, no. 3 (August 2003).

272 it was time for him to "step up": *Amy Biehl Foundation Newsletter* 7, no. 2 (June 2003).

272 Zach viewed the legacies of Amy: *Amy Biehl Foundation Newsletter* 7, no. 3 (August 2003).

273 Their panel, titled "A Story of Interracial Reconciliation": Program, American Family Therapy Academy annual meeting, June 2002. (BFP)

273 a program called "Amy's Magic: Living Reconciliation": "Martyrdom's Extraordinary Legacy," *U Mass Mag online*, Fall 2002, www.umassmag.com/Fall-2002/Martyrdom_s_ extraordinary_legacy-336.html.

273 "When people ask me how I can do this": Maureen Harrington, "A Mother Forgives Her Daughter's Killers," *People*, July 21, 2003.

273 They only insisted that she not drive: Linda Biehl interview, June 8, 2004.

273 "I'm more worried about what white": Zach Biehl, author interview, June 1, 2005.

274 A white South African lawyer: author's notes, Amy Biehl Foundation Trust staff meeting, July 16, 2002.

274 "Each time a man stands up for an ideal": Robert F. Kennedy, Day of Affirmation speech, University of Cape Town, June 6, 1966, reproduced in *Robert Kennedy in South Africa* (Johannesburg: Rand Daily Mail, 1966), 11.

274 the trust's relationship with the South African supermarket chain: *Amy Biehl Foundation Newsletter* 7, no. 1 (December 2002).

274 "I want to take on the role": Linda Biehl to Carlos [no last name given], c. May 2003. (BFP)

275 Calling Amy "the star of America and South Africa": Dianne Webber to Linda Biehl, April 29, 2003. (BFP)

275 Amy's murder 10 years earlier was "imprinted": Carte Blanche transcript, M-Net, August 10, 2003, beta.mnet.co.za/carteblanche/Article.aspx?Id=2293#.

275 "Amy would have expected": Ibid.

275 "The images of you working with your daughter's killers": Katherine Reardon to Linda Biehl, August 10, 2003. (BFP)

275 the Afrikaans-language newspaper *Rapport*: Hanlie Retief, "Ná die pyn, soveel hoop," *Rapport*, November 2, 2003.

275 "It is their transformation": *Amy Biehl Foundation Newsletter* 7, no. 3 (August 2003).

276   "If you told me 10": Harrington, "A Mother Forgives."

276   "Hello. My name is Thomas.": "Ads Cause the SABC to Wince," *Business Day*, August 29, 2003.

276   he and his staff wanted the ads: Ibid.

276   Leyla Haidarian, expected: "'Insensitive' TV Advert Withdrawn," *Sunday Tribune*, November 2, 2003.

276   the ads "used scare tactics to solicit financial support": "'Chilling' Amy Biehl Adverts Ordered Off the Air," *Cape Argus*, October 31, 2003.

276   Officials called the ads "chilling" and "shocking": Ibid.

276   "In the context of how Amy Biehl was murdered": "Biehl Ads 'Insensitive,'" *Financial Mail*, November 7, 2003.

276   He had heard that Easy and Ntobeko: Ntobeko Peni, author interview, July 25, 2002; Linda Biehl, author interviews, June 8, 2004, and July 18, 2006; Zach Biehl interview; Linda Biehl, email to the author, January 21, 2016.

277   Mongezi was found guilty: Retief, "Ná die pyn, soveel hoop"; "Biehl Killer Guilty of Raping a Disabled Woman," *Pretoria News*, November 5, 2003; "Amy Biehl's Murderer Strikes Again," *Sunday Times*, November 9, 2003.

277   "[Manqina's] conviction of raping": "Amy Biehl's Murderer Strikes Again."

277   He sensed that people viewed : Solomon Makosana, author interview, June 21, 2004.

277   he had been passed over "because he was not black enough": "Biehl Trust Fracas over Black Manager Post," *Asia Africa Intelligence Wire*, October 21, 2005.

277   "I'm asked why all programs are": Victor West, author interview, July 13, 2004.

278   potential visitor interest in "sites of struggle": "Township Tours Get Thumbs-Up from MEC," *Cape Argus*, December 14, 2005.

278   Many of his early township tours: author's notes during township tour led by Ntobeko Peni, July 25, 2002.

278   "It's symbolic because Amy's parents": "Running for Glory," *Cape Argus*, June 11, 2004.

278   The Biehls' story was also highlighted: "The F-Word That Brings Only Joy," *Star*, December 17, 2004.

279   "The Biehls . . . heeded the words of Archbishop Desmond Tutu": "We Need the F Word," *Star*, December 17, 2004.

279   Zach became her "right-hand man": "Where Are They Today," *Today Show*, NBC, February 11, 2004.

279   Linda enjoyed stepping away: "Mother, Daughter's Killer Visit West," *Belleville News-Democrat*, September 28, 2007.

279   "a living embodiment of the values": "About the Foundation," Amy Biehl Foundation Trust website, c. 2008, www.amybiehl.co.za.

279   "They're not perfect, no one is": Linda Biehl interview, July 18, 2006.

279   the victim forgives in order to ease the pain: Linda Biehl, "Making Change," *Greater Good* 1, no. 2 (Fall 2004): 12.

280   "Forgiveness is a big word": Lavern de Vries, "A Friendship Carved out of Tragedy," *Drum*, May 5, 2005.

280   "When individuals are at peace": "Mother of Slain Human-Rights Worker Finds Healing in Forgiveness," *Milwaukee Journal Sentinel*, November 15, 2006.

280   she was sometimes a lightning rod: Brian Johnson to "Dear Sir," July 25, 2003 (BFP); "Linda Biehl dans met moordenaar van haar dogter," *Afrikaner*, November 24, 2005.

280   "many readers responded angrily": Bella English, "Forgive-You-Nots," *Boston Globe,* October 27, 2009, www.boston.com/lifestyle/articles/2009/10/27 /forgiveness_is_easier_said_than_done?mode=IF.

280   Linda occasionally received hate mail: Unknown correspondent, handwritten notes to Linda Biehl on pages of magazine, August 2003. (BFP)

280   "It's a personal issue between": Linda Biehl, author interview, July 17, 2006.

281   the Youth Reading Role Models Program had more than 4,000 participants: ABFT brochure, 2007.

281   "supplement the shortcomings": "About the Foundation," ABFT website.

281   it enabled their parents to continue working: Linda Biehl interview, July 18, 2006.

282   appointing a white male to the directorship would bring "complications": Ibid.

283   F. W. de Klerk even agreed: Linda Biehl, author interview, December 15, 2009.

283   "They are two of the most humane": Aaron Bos-Lun, "Bos-Lun Learns Safety Should Always Be a Priority," *Wheaton Wire,* September 23, 2009, media. thewheatonwire.com/media/storage/paper1134/news/2009/09/23/Commentary /BosLun.Learns.Safety.Should.Always.Be.A.Priority-3779987.shtml.

284   he spoke about his "gradual redemption": "Greeley Scholar Talks of 'New Vision for Peace,'" *UMass Online,* April 2008, www.uml.edu/Media /eNewspring_1_148036_148036.html.

284   "contributed to making a better life": "Statement on the Unveiling of Names of Recipients of the National Orders by the Director-General in the Presidency and Chancellor of Orders, Reverend Frank Chikane," South African government information, April 17, 2008, www.info.gov.za/speeches/2008/ 08041717151001.htm.

284   Sahm Venter and Ahmed Kathrada had lobbied: Linda Biehl, author interview, June 3, 2009.

284   Linda received her award "for displaying [an] outstanding spirit of forgiveness": Program, award ceremony for national orders, Pretoria, April 22, 2008. (BFP)

284   she would regard the Tambo award: Biographical information on Linda Biehl, Millikan High School event flyer, September 24, 2015, www.facebook.com/usaabf.

285   "Deep down, it's very difficult for me": "Working in Their Victim's Name," *LA Times,* October 21, 2008.

285   "the oppression in South Africa was done by white people": Ibid.

285   She was proud of the way: Linda Biehl interview, June 3, 2009.

285   she sometimes felt lost when they weren't by her side: "Guest Lecturer Biehl Tells Complicated Story," University of Alaska–Fairbanks, September 21, 2009, snras. blogspot.com/2009/09/guest-lecturer-biehl-tells-complicated.html.

285   She outlined Amy's efforts: "Mabandla Hails Slain Student Activist Amy Biehl," SABC, August 17, 2010, www.sabcnews.com.

285   Donald Gips hailed Amy's commitment: "Memorial to Amy Biehl Unveiled," News 24, August 26, 2010, www.news24.com/SouthAfrica/News/Memorial-to-Amy-Biehl -unveiled-20100825.

286   As a Cape Town headline read days earlier: "The Power of the Biehl Family's Forgiveness Is Still Inspirational," *Cape Times,* August 16, 2010.

286   Reconciliation is complex: Jonathan Jansen, "At the Crossroads Once More," *Times Live,* October 28, 2009, www.timeslive.co.za/opinion/columnists /article171000ece?service=print.

CHAPTER 15: THE LEGACY LIVES ON

299   "The urge to explain the inexplicable": "Sindiwe Magona Discusses Why She Wrote *Mother to Mother,*" Beacon Press press release, c. September 1999.

300   published in South Africa in 1998: Sindiwe Magona, *Mother to Mother* (Cape Town: David Philip, 1998).

300   "bred the violent mob that killed Amy": "Sindiwe Magona Discusses Why She Wrote *Mother to Mother.*"

300   Magona feared that Peter and Linda: Sindiwe Magona, author interview, July 14, 2004.

300   the Biehls loved *Mother to Mother:* Ibid.; *Amy Biehl Foundation Newsletter* 4, no. 2 (December 1998).

300   "That was the whole point": Magona interview.

300   Thembi Mtshali-Jones, found the novel powerful: "Killer's Mother Speaks Out," *Times* (SA), September 5, 2009, www.thetimes.co.za/PrintArticle.aspx?ID=1060668.

300   A reviewer . . . found the play "disturbingly relevant": Lesley Stones, "On the Stage: Mother to Mother," *Business Day Live,* May 28, 2013, www.bdlive.co.za/life/entertainment/2013/05/28/on-the-stage-mother-to- mother?service=print.

300   "otherwise you might end up like Amy Biehl": Justine van der Leun, conversation with the author, August 25, 2013; van der Leun, "Portrait of a Township: Former Militants on the Post-Apartheid Struggle," *Harper's Magazine,* March 2014.

300   In her book: Justine van der Leun, *We Are Not Such Things* (New York: Spiegel & Grau, 2016).

300   In her young adult novel: Carolyn Coman, *Many Stones* (New York: Puffin, 2000).

301   the Indian author: Shashi Tharoor, "A Departure, Fictionally," *Hindu,* September 16, 2001, www.hindu.com/2001/09/16/stories/13160675.htm.

301   his book: Shashi Tharoor, *Riot* (New York: Arcade Publishing, 2001).

301   Amanda Ward . . . had been interested in South Africa for years: "A Taste of South Africa at Jabberwocky," *Newburyport Current,* February 28, 2008, www.wickedlocal.com/Newburyport/new/x774170336.

301   In her novel: Amanda Eyre Ward, *Forgive Me* (New York: Random House, 2007).

301   Ward "explores the ideas of truth": "Stoning Murder Inspires Author," *New Canaan Advertiser* (CT), July 5, 2007.

301   The film was designed to present: Bruce Newman, "A Bold Initiative for Reconciliation," *San Jose Mercury News,* August 18, 2000.

301   Linda and Peter . . . found the film powerful: "Forgiveness Elevated to Leading Role," *OCR,* March 29, 2000.

301   Audiences found the film emotionally powerful: B. Ruby Rich, "Watching as a Country Remembers Its Nightmares," *NYT,* March 26, 2000.

302   The Biehls began to have second thoughts: Peter and Linda Biehl to Anant Singh, February 10, 2001. (BFP)

302   the Biehls' children didn't want a film: Linda Biehl, author interview, July 18, 2006.

302   Getting the approval of Kim, Molly, and Zach: Peter and Linda Biehl to Anant Singh, February 10, 2001. (BFP)

302   Tyler Perry announced that he would: Silas Leznick, "The Year of the Great Storm: Tyler Perry to Produce Apartheid Drama," *ComingSoon.net,* March 9, 2016, www.comingsoon.net/movies/news/664685-year-of-the-great-storm.

303   "Amy was a budding scholar": Tony Monfiletto, "Toward a New Downtown High School," *Albuquerque Tribune,* c. Fall 2002.

303   Peter and Linda gave them their blessing: Linda Biehl interview, July 18, 2006.

303   98 percent of the school's graduates: Amy Biehl High School information sheet, 2009.

303   The Biehls featured prominently: Examples include Martha Minow, *Breaking the Cycles of Hatred: Memory, Law and Repair* (Princeton, NJ: Princeton University Press, 2002), 26; Donald W. Shriver, "Where and When in Political Life Is Justice Served by Forgiveness," in *Burying the Past: Making Peace and Doing Justice after Civil Conflict,* ed. Nigel Biggar (Washington, D.C.: Georgetown University Press, 2003), 25–43; Tamara Sonn, "The Power of Dialogue: Redefining 'Us,'" in *After Terror: Promoting Dialogue among Civilizations,* ed. Akbar Ahmed and Brian Forst (Malden, MA: Polity Press, 2005), 131–37; John and Valerie Braithwaite, "Shame, Shame Management and Regulation," in *Shame Management through Reintegration,* ed. Eliza Ahmed, Nathan Harris, and John and Valerie Braithwaite (Cambridge: Cambridge University Press, 2001), 3–69; Theodore L. Dorpat, *Crimes of Punishment: America's Culture of Violence* (New York: Algora Publishing, 2007), 252–53; Richard H. Bell, *Rethinking Justice: Restoring Our Humanity* (Lanham, MD: Lexington Books, 2007), 103–5.

304   Christians in particular drew inspiration: Examples include David Augsburger, *The New Freedom of Forgiveness,* 3rd ed. (Chicago: Moody Press, 2000), 35–36; Kurt Senske, *Personal Values: God's Game Plan for Life* (Minneapolis: Augsburg Books, 2004), 43–44; Ray S. Anderson, *The Shape of Practical Theology: Empowering Ministry with Theological Praxis* (Downers Grove, IL: InterVarsity Press, 2001), 291; Ray S. Anderson, *Judas and Jesus: Amazing Grace for the Wounded Soul* (Eugene, OR: Cascade Books, 2005), 23–31.

304   they too began to refer: Examples include Patrick Harbula, *The Magic of the Soul: Applying Spiritual Power to Daily Living* (Thousand Oaks, CA: Peak Publications, 2003), 192; Meredith Jordan, *Standing Still: Hearing the Call to a Spirit-Centered Life* (Biddeford, ME: Rogers McKay Publishing, 2006), 236; Gregg Easterbrook, "Forgiveness May Be Beneficial to Good Health," *Research News & Opportunities in Science and Theology,* May 2002, 5–6; Mariah Burton Nelson, *The Unburdened Heart: Five Keys to Forgiveness and Freedom* (New York: Harper San Francisco, 2000), 7, 45–47, 170, 191; Caroline Hsu, "Forgive," *U.S. News & World Report,* January 3, 2005, 86; Spike Gillespie, *Pissed Off: Finding Forgiveness on the Other Side of the Finger* (Emeryville, CA: Seal Press, 2006), 223–24; Sonja Lyubomirsky, *The How of Happiness: A Scientific Approach to Getting the Life You Want* (New York: Penguin, 2008), 169–70.

304   the Tutus drew on the Biehls: Desmond M. Tutu and Mpho A. Tutu, *The Book of Forgiving: The Fourfold Path for Healing Ourselves and Our World* (New York: HarperOne, 2014), 54, 148–50, 184–85, 209, 228.

304   forgiveness had become a "mainstream tool of holistic healing": Dean E. Murphy, "Beyond Justice: The Eternal Struggle to Forgive," *NYT,* May 26, 2002.

304   The family was even mentioned: Gary W. Hawk, "Transcending Transgression: Forgiveness and Reconciliation," in *Interpersonal Conflict,* ed. William W. Wilmot and Joyce L. Hocker, 6th ed. (New York: McGraw Hill, 2001), 293–317.

304   both its old and new names, NY147 / Amy Biehl Street: "Plug Not Pulled on Renaming," *Cape Argus,* 5 May 2008; "Call for Consultation on Street Renaming," *Sowetan Live,* December 15, 2011, www.sowetanlive.co.za/news/2011/12/15 /call-for-consultation-on- street-renaming?; "Zapiro, Makeba, Biehl among Gugs Street Names," *IOL News,* August 15, 2013, www.iol.za/news/politics /zapiro-makeba-biehl-among-gugs-street-names-1.1562833#.Ug4k4ZLOm8B; "Residents' Road Rage over New Street Name," *Die Burger,* March 21, 2014, m24argo2.naspers.com/argief/berigte/dieburger/2014/03/21/3/

mcmrejectstreets_29_0461544202.html; "Talking Streets March: Street Community Building in Gugs," *Open Streets Cape Town*, April 4, 2014, openstreets.org.za/news /talking-streets-march-street-community-building-gugs.

305   her legacy was "about the lives that have been touched": Deepa Bharath, "Amy Biehl Legacy: Reconciliation That Spans Generations," *OCR*, August 25, 2013.

305   the tensions that had developed: Deepa Bharath, "Freed by Compassion: Charitable Foundation Benefits Poverty-Stricken Black Township, Brings Healing to Biehl Family and Amy's Killers," *OCR*, November 25, 2013, www.ocregister.com/articles /amy-538413-foundation-biehl.html.

305   "I think it is good if they": Ryland Fisher, "Interview: Linda Biehl's Memories of Amy," *Daily Maverick*, August 23, 2013, https://www.dailymaverick.co.za /article/2013-08-23-interview-linda-biehls-memories-of-amy/.

305   "When I see Makhulu": Bharath, "Freed by Compassion."

305   "[Amy's] story and the subsequent brave journey": Marianne Thamm, "Amy Biehl and Her Killers' Gift to South Africa—The Enduring Power of Restorative Justice," *Daily Maverick*, July 29, 2015, https://www.dailymaverick.co.za/article/2015-07-29 -amy-biehl-and-her-killers-gift-to-south-africa-the-enduring-power-of-restorative -justice/#.WbwHlHaGPIU.

306   the foundation had become another: Bharath, "Freed by Compassion."

Bibliography

ARCHIVES

Amy Biehl Papers. Stanford University. Stanford, California.

Biehl Family Papers. Costa Mesa and Newport Beach, California. (BFP)

Cape High Court. Trial transcript, records, and judgment. Case # SS 136/93 and # SS 18/95, 1993–95. Cape Town.

Clinton Presidential Records. William Clinton Presidential Library. Little Rock, Arkansas.

Kennell Jackson Papers. Stanford University. Stanford, California.

Pan Africanist Congress (United Nations mission). University of Fort Hare archives. Electronic records. Alice, South Africa.

BOOKS AND ARTICLES

Adam, Heribert, and Kogila Moodley. *The Negotiated Revolution: Society and Politics in Post-Apartheid South Africa.* Johannesburg: Jonathan Ball, 1993.

Adin, Kwame. "The NPP Must Prepare for War!—Rejoinder." *Ghana Web,* June 22, 2007. https://www.ghanaweb.com/GhanaHomePage/features/artikel.php?ID=125809.

African National Congress Women's League–Western Cape. Press statement on the murder of Amy Biehl, August 26, 1993. www.anc.org.za/ancdocs/pr/1993/pr0826b.html (site discontinued).

Ahmed, Akbar, and Brian Forst. *After Terror: Promoting Dialogue among Civilizations.* Malden, MA: Polity Press, 2005.

Amy Biehl High School. "The Legacy of Amy Elizabeth Biehl: A Brave Soul's Spirit Lives On." c.2004.

"Amy's Story." *CBS News.com,* February 28, 2000. https://www.cbsnews.com/news/amys-story/

Anderson, Ray S. *The Shape of Practical Theology: Empowering Ministry with Theological Praxis.* Downers Grove, IL: InterVarsity Press, 2001.

———. *Judas and Jesus: Amazing Grace for the Wounded Soul.* Eugene, OR: Cascade Books, 2005.

Arias, Ron, Barbara Whitaker, and Jamie Reno. "Legacy of Love." *People,* September 20, 1993, 52–53.

Augsburger, David. *The New Freedom of Forgiveness.* 3rd ed. Chicago: Moody Press, 2000.

Bay, Tom, and David Macpherson. *Change Your Attitude: Creating Success One Thought at a Time.* Franklin Lakes, NJ: Career Press, 1998.

Beacon Press. "Sindiwe Magona Discusses Why She Wrote *Mother to Mother.*" Press release, c. September 1999.

Bell, Richard H. *Rethinking Justice: Restoring Our Humanity.* Lanham, MD: Lexington Books, 2007.

Berger, Iris. *South Africa in World History.* New York: Oxford University Press, 2009.

Bhargava, Anurima. "Defining Political Crimes: A Case Study of the South African Truth and Reconciliation Commission." *Columbia Law Review* 102, no. 5 (June 2002): 1304–39.

Bickford-Smith, Vivian, Elizabeth van Heyningen, and Nigel Worden. *Cape Town in the Twentieth Century: An Illustrated Social History.* Cape Town: David Philip, 1999.

Biehl, Amy. "Chester Crocker and the Negotiations for Namibian Independence: The Role of the Individual in Recent American Foreign Policy." Honors thesis for program in International Relations, Stanford University, May 1989.

———. "Challenges and Lessons of Democratization in Africa." *Liberal Times* 1 (July 1992): 5-6.

———. *Structures for Women in Political Decision-Making.* Bellville, Western Cape: Gender Project, Community Law Centre, University of the Western Cape, 1993.

———. "Custom and Religion in a Non-racial, Non-sexist South Africa." *Women against Fundamentalism* 5 (1994): 51–53.

———. "Dislodging the Boulder: South African Women and the Democratic Transformation." In *South Africa: The Political Economy of Transformation,* edited by Stephen J. Stedman, 85–107. Boulder, CO: Lynne Rienner, 1994.

Biehl, Linda. "Making Change." *Greater Good* 1, no. 2 (Fall 2004): 12.

Biehl, Molly. *You've Got This!* [np]: Laptop Lifestyle, 2017.

Biehl, Peter, and Linda Biehl. "The Story of Linda and Peter Biehl: Private Loss and Public Forgiveness." *Reflections* 4, no. 4 (Fall 1998): 11–22.

Biehl, Peter, and Rolene Miller. "The New Math of Grassroots Community Work." *Reflections* 2, no. 4 (Fall 1996): 21–28.

Biggar, Nigel, ed. *Burying the Past: Making Peace and Doing Justice after Civil Conflict.* Washington, D.C.: Georgetown University Press, 2003.

Boraine, Alex. "Adrift between Shadow and Reality." *Democracy in Action,* May 31, 1993.

———. *A Country Unmasked: Inside South Africa's Truth and Reconciliation Commission.* Oxford: Oxford University Press, 2000.

Braithwaite, John, and Valerie Braithwaite. "Shame, Shame Management and Regulation." In *Shame Management through Reintegration,* edited by Eliza Ahmed, Nathan Harris, John Braithwaite, and Valerie Brathwaite, 3–69. Cambridge, UK: Cambridge University Press, 2001.

Branch, Gregory, and Claudia Pryor. "Race Plays a Decisive Role in News Content." *Neiman Reports* 55, no. 1 (Spring 2001): 65–68.

Britton, Hannah E. *Women in the South African Parliament: From Resistance to Governance.* Urbana: University of Illinois Press, 2005.

Brodie, Nechama. "Chasing Amy." *Fair Lady,* April 11, 2001, 54–56.

Brown, Tracey L. *The Life and Times of Ron Brown: A Memoir by His Daughter.* New York: William Morrow, 1998.

Bryson, Donna. *It's a Black/White Thing.* Cape Town: Tafelberg, 2014.

Campbell, Carol, et al. *Great South Africans: The Great Debate.* Johannesburg: Penguin, 2004.

Cantacuzino, Marina. *The Forgiveness Project: Stories for a Vengeful Age.* London: Jessica Kingsley, 2015.

Carton, Benedict, and Leslie Bank. "Forgetting Apartheid: History, Culture and the Body of a Nun." *Africa* 86, no. 3 (August 2016): 472–503.

Cassidy, Michael. *A Witness for Ever: The Dawning of Democracy in South Africa: Stories behind the Story.* London: Hodder & Stoughton, 1995.

Chalandon, Sorj. "Amy, l'Africaine blanche." *Libération,* November 14, 1993.

Chubb, Karin, and Lutz van Dijk. *Between Anger and Hope: South Africa's Youth and the Truth and Reconciliation Commission.* Johannesburg: Wits University Press, 2001.

Coetzee, Carol. "Tears for My Sunshine Child." *You,* July 24, 1997, 16–18.

Coman, Carolyn. *Many Stones.* New York: Puffin, 2000.

Community Law Centre. *Custom and Religion in a Non-racial, Non-sexist South Africa: Report of the International Seminar of the Community Law Centre at the University of the Western Cape, 14–16 May 1993.* Bellville: UWC, 1994.

Crocker, Chester A. *High Noon in Southern Africa: Making Peace in a Rough Neighborhood.* New York: W. W. Norton, 1992.

Damon, Dan. "Who Counts as a Political Prisoner." *New Statesman* 127, no. 4400 (August 28, 1998): 26–33.

Debates of Parliament—South Africa. Hansard, 1993–94. Columns 12305–13792.

De Vries, Lavern. "A Friendship Carved Out of Tragedy." *Drum,* May 5, 2005, 18–19.

Dikeni, Sandile. *Soul Fire: Writing the Transition.* Pietermaritzburg: University of Natal Press, 2002.

Dorpat, Theodore L. *Crimes of Punishment: America's Culture of Violence.* New York: Algora, 2007.

Easterbrook, Gregg. "Forgiveness May Be Beneficial to Good Health." *Research News & Opportunities in Science and Theology,* May 2002, 5–6.

Eden, Catherine. "A Mother's Journey." *Fair Lady,* May 4, 1994, 90–96.

———. "I Forgive My Daughter's Killers." *Marie Claire,* March 1998, 93–97.

Ellis, George F. R. "Afterword: Exploring the Unique Role of Forgiveness." In *Forgiveness and Reconciliation: Religion, Public Policy, and Conflict Transformation,* edited by Raymond G. Helmick, S.J. and Rodney L. Petersen, 395–410. Philadelphia: Templeton Foundation Press, 2002.

Elster, Jon. *Closing the Books: Transitional Justice in Historical Perspective.* New York: Cambridge University Press, 2004.

Englund, Per, and Mlamli Figlan. *The Beautiful Struggle.* rsta, Sweden: Dokument Förkagm, 2006.

Fanshawe, Simon. "Amy Biehl's Passion for Human Rights Led Her to Some of the Most Dangerous Parts of the World . . . ." *Daily Telegraph Magazine,* July 28, 2001.

Field, Sean, Renate Meyer, and Felicity Swandon, eds. *Imagining the City: Memories and Cultures in Cape Town.* Cape Town: HSRC Press, 2007.

Finnegan, William. *Crossing the Line: A Year in the Land of Apartheid.* New York: Harper & Row, 1986.

Fleming, Mike, Jr. "Tyler Perry, Doug Liman Lead Charge to Mount Apartheid Murder Tale 'The Year of the Great Storm.'" *Deadline Hollywood,* March 9, 2016. deadline.com/2016/03/tyler-perry-doug-Liman-apartheid-murder-tale-the-year-of-the-great-storm-karzan-kader-johanna-Baldwin-1201717128.

Foster, Dan, Paul Haupt, and Marésa de Beer. *The Theatre of Violence: Narratives of Protagonists in the South African Conflict.* Cape Town: HSRC Press, 2005.

Fritts, Rev. Roger, and Rev. Kathie Davis Thomas. "The Meaning of the Cross." April 4, 1999. www.cedarlane.org/99serms/s990404-b.html (site discontinued).

"From Murder Comes Reconciliation, Hope." CNN.com, December 9, 2004. www.cnn.com /2004/WORLD/africa/12/09/Biehl/index.html.

Frumkin, Peter. *Strategic Giving: The Art and Science of Philanthropy.* Chicago: University of Chicago Press, 2006.

Gerhart, Gail. *Black Power in South Africa: The Evolution of an Ideology.* Berkeley: University of California Press, 1978.

Gillespie, Spike. *Pissed Off: Finding Forgiveness on the Other Side of the Finger.* Emeryville, CA: Seal Press, 2006.

Gish, Steven. *Alfred B. Xuma: African, American, South African.* New York: New York University Press, 2000.

———. *Desmond Tutu: A Biography.* Westport, CT: Greenwood, 2004.

———. "Reacting to Amy Biehl: Perspectives from South Africa and the United States." In *South Africa and the United States Compared: The Best of Safundi, 2003–2004,* edited by Andrew Offenburger, Christopher Saunders, and Christopher Lee, 151–61. Phoenix: Safundi Publications, 2005.

———. "From Admiration to Anger: Reactions to the Amy Biehl Amnesty Decision." In *Healing South African Wounds,* edited by Gilles Teulié and Mélanie Joseph-Vilain, 233–49. Montpellier: Presses universitaires de la Méditerranée, 2009.

———. "Amy Biehl and the ANC: A Scholar-Activist in South Africa." *African Historical Review* 45, no. 1 (June 2013): 1–21.

Gobodo-Madikizela, Pumla. *A Human Being Died That Night: A South African Story of Forgiveness.* Boston: Houghton Mifflin, 2003.

Gordon, Bart. "A Tribute to Amy Biehl." *Congressional Record,* vol. 139, part 15, 103rd Congress, 1st session, September 14, 1993, 21156–57.

Gordon, Fiona. "Profound Play Tells Amy Biehl's Story." *Artslink.co.za,* September 29, 2009. http://www.artlink.co.za/news_article.htm?contentID=8624.

Graybill, Lyn S. *Truth and Reconciliation in South Africa: Miracle or Model?* Boulder, CO: Lynne Rienner, 2002.

Green, Pippa. *Choice, Not Fate: The Life and Times of Trevor Manuel.* Johannesburg: Penguin, 2008.

Greer, Colin. "Without Mercy, There Is No Healing, Without Forgiveness, There Is No Future." *Parade,* January 11, 1998, 4–6.

"Guest Lecturer Biehl Tells Complicated Story." University of Alaska–Fairbanks, September 21, 2009. http://snrenews.blogspot.com/2009/09/guest-lecturer-biehl-tells-complicated. html.

"Hang Our Heads in Shame!" *APDUSA Views* 49 (October 1993): 4–10.

Harber, Anton, and Barbara Ludman, eds. *Weekly Mail & Guardian A–Z of South African Politics: The Essential Handbook, 1994.* Johannesburg: Penguin, 1994.

Harbula, Patrick J. *The Magic of the Soul: Applying Spiritual Power to Daily Living.* Thousand Oaks, CA: Peak, 2003.

Harper, Everett. "The Amy Biehl Foundation Trust." Case number SI-01, Graduate School of Business, Stanford University, October 2000.

Harrington, Maureen. "A Mother Forgives Her Daughter's Killers." *People,* July 21, 2003, 123–24.

Hawk, Gary W. "Transcending Transgression: Forgiveness and Reconciliation." In *Interpersonal Conflict,* 6th ed., edited by William W. Wilmot and Joyce L. Hocker, 293–317. New York: McGraw Hill, 2001.

Henderson, Michael. *Forgiveness: Breaking the Chain of Hate.* 2nd revised ed. Portland, OR: Arnica, 2003.

Henry, Zane. "House of Pain." Tonight, September 29, 2009. https://www.pressreader.com /south-africa/cape-argus/20090929/282187942067533.

Hoeane, Thabisi. "The State of the Pan-Africanist Congress in a Democratic South Africa." In *State of the Nation: South Africa 2008,* edited by Peter Kagwanja and Kwandiwe Kondlo, 58–83. Cape Town: HSRC Press, 2009.

James, Wilmot, and Linda van de Vijver, eds. *After the TRC: Reflections on Truth and Reconciliation in South Africa.* Athens: Ohio University Press, 2001.

Jansen, Jonathan. "At the Crossroads Once More." *Times Live,* October 28, 2009. www.timeslive .co.za/opinion/columnists/article171000ece?service=print.

Jardine, Kimberly. "Trial of Tears." *Orange Coast,* August 1994, 51–59.

Johnson, Krista, and Sean Jacobs, eds. *Encyclopedia of South Africa.* Boulder, CO: Lynne Rienner, 2011.

Jordan, Meredith. *Standing Still: Hearing the Call to a Spirit-Centered Life.* Biddeford, ME: Rogers McKay, 2006.

Joseph, James. Media conference statement at the signing of an agreement between USAID and the Amy Biehl Foundation, September 29, 1999. www.sn.apc.org/usaidsa/speech18.html.

Kadalie, Rhoda. Reminiscences of Amy Biehl. Friends of Amy Biehl website. friendsofamybiehl.com/kadalie.php (site discontinued).

Kadalie, Rhoda, and Amy Biehl. "Women's Voices Will Be Heard at Last." *Weekly Mail,* April 30 to May 6, 1993.

Kalinga, Owen J. M., and Cynthia A. Crosby. *Historical Dictionary of Malawi.* 3rd ed. Lanham, MD: The Scarecrow Press, 2001.

Karsten, Chris. *Bad Kids: South African Youngsters Who Rob and Kill.* Cape Town and Pretoria: Human & Rousseau, 2007.

Kendall, Larry, and Judy Kendall. "Biehl–Kendall Relationship/History." Unpublished paper, July 3, 2015.

"Killers of Amy Biehl Say Her Murder Was 'Political Expression.'" *The Reagan Information Interchange,* July 9, 1997. www.reagan.com/HotTopics.main/document-7.9.1997.html.

Kingwill, Helena. "Weaving a Barrier against Violence." *Initiatives of Change,* June 1, 2001. http://www.iofcafrica.org/en/weaving-barrier-against-violence.

Krabill, Ron. "Review of *Long Night's Journey into Day.*" *Safundi* 3, no. 2 (2001). http://www .tandfonline.com/doi/abs/10.1080/17533170101002210.

Kraft, Robert. *Violent Accounts: Understanding the Psychology of Perpetrators through South Africa's Truth and Reconciliation Commission.* New York: New York University Press, 2014.

Leznick, Silas. "The Year of the Great Storm: Tyler Perry to Produce Apartheid Drama." *ComingSoon.net,* March 9, 2016. www.comingsoon.net/movies/news/664685-year-of -the-great-storm.

Lloyd, Rosemary. "To Forgive Is Human." First Parish in Lincoln, November 10, 2002. Accessed August 26, 2003. www.firstparishinlincoln.org/Sermons/RL21110A.HTM.

Lutterman, Kenneth. "Commentary." *Reflections* 2, no. 4 (Fall 1996): 36–37.

Lyman, Princeton. *Partner to History: The U.S. Role in South Africa's Transition to Democracy.* Washington, D.C.: United States Institute of Peace Press, 2002.

Lyubomirsky, Sonja. *The How of Happiness: A Scientific Approach to Getting the Life You Want.* New York: Penguin, 2008.

Mabandla, Brigitte. "Choices for South African Women." *Agenda* 20 (1994): 22–29.

Mabandla, Brigitte, and Amy Biehl. "'God-Given' Oppression Upheld by Tradition." *Democracy in Action* 7, no. 4 (July 15, 1993): 22–23.

Mager, Anne. *Gender and the Making of a South African Bantustan: A Social History of the Ciskei, 1945–1959.* Portsmouth, NH: Heinemann, 1999.

Magona, Sindiwe. *Mother to Mother.* Boston: Beacon Press, 1998.

Marks, Susan Collin. *Watching the Wind: Conflict Resolution during South Africa's Transition to Democracy.* Washington, D.C.: United States Institute of Peace Press, 2000.

Martin, Carol Lynn. *Namibia: The Parliament and Democracy Symposium, Windhoek, 18–20 March 1991.* Windhoek: New Namibia Books, 1991.

"Martyrdom's Extraordinary Legacy." *U Mass Mag online,* Fall 2002. Accessed July 26, 2006. www.umassmag.com/Fall_2002/Martyrdom_s_extraordinary_legacy-336.html.

Mattes, Bob. "Where Did It Go?" *Work in Progress* 92 (September 1993): 19–20.

McDonnell, Sharon. "Killer Queries for Articles: How to Write a Pitch That Sells in Record Time." In *The Writer's Handbook 2005*, edited by Abbe Elfrieda, 39–45. Waukesha, WI: Kalmbach Publishing, 2004.

McFann, Jane. "The Legacy of Amy Biehl." *Reading Today* 19, no. 5 (April/May 2002): 22.

Meiring, Piet. *Chronicle of the Truth Commission.* Vanderbijlpark: Carpe Diem Books, 1999.

———. "Reconciliation in South Africa: Women's Voices at the Truth and Reconciliation Commission." In *Fullness of Life for All: Challenges for Mission in Early 21st Century,* edited by Inus Daneel, Charles van Engen, and Hendrik Vroom, 201–16. New York: Rodopi, 2003.

Meyer, Stephan. "We Would Write Very Dull Books If We Just Wrote about Ourselves." In *Selves in Question: Interviews on Southern African Auto/biography,* edited by Judith Lütge Coullie, Stephan Meyer, Thengani Ngwenya, and Thomas Olver, 219–30. Honolulu: University of Hawaii Press, 2006.

Mgxashe, Mxolisi. *Are You with Us? The Story of a PAC Activist.* Houghton: Mafube Publishing, 2006.

Mijares, Sharon, Aliaa Rafea, Rachel Falik, and Jenny Eda Schipper. *The Root of All Evil: An Exposition of Prejudice, Fundamentalism and Gender Imbalance.* Charlottesville, VA: Imprint Academic, 2007.

Minow, Martha. *Breaking the Cycles of Hatred: Memory, Law, and Repair.* Princeton, NJ: Princeton University Press, 2002.

Moloi, Alosi. "Commentary." *Reflections* 2, no. 4 (Fall 1996): 29–31.

Morris, Michael. *Every Step of the Way: The Journey to Freedom in South Africa.* Cape Town: HSRC Press, 2004.

Mphahlele, Letlapa. *Child of This Soil: My Life as a Freedom Fighter.* Cape Town: Kwela Books, 2002.

Mufson, Steven. *Fighting Years: Black Resistance and the Struggle for a New South Africa.* Boston: Beacon Press, 1990.

National Association of Democratic Lawyers. Untitled statement on Amy Biehl's death, August 26, 1993.

National Democratic Institute for International Affairs. *The October 31, 1991 National Elections in Zambia.* Washington, D.C.: NDI, 1992.

———. "Kenyan Women Plan to Broaden Political Role." *NDI Reports,* Summer/Fall 1993.

———. "The W. Averell Harriman Democracy Award: 2001." https://www.ndi.org/sites/default/files/2001award_pf.asp_.pdf

Nelson, Mariah Burton. *The Unburdened Heart: Five Keys to Forgiveness and Freedom.* New York: HarperSanFrancisco, 2000.

Nujoma, Sam. *Where Others Wavered: The Autobiography of Sam Nujoma*. London: Panaf Books, 2001.

Nyatsumba, Kaizer. "Military Might or Mighty Mouse?" *Barometer* 5, no. 6 (October 1993): 3–5.

O'Malley, Padraig, and Carol Lynn Martin. *Uneven Paths: Advancing Democracy in Southern Africa*. Windhoek: New Namibia Books, 1993.

Ottaway, David. *Chained Together: Mandela, De Klerk, and the Struggle to Remake South Africa*. New York: Times Books, 1993.

Pan Africanist Congress of Azania. "The Armed Struggle." Submission to the Truth and Reconciliation Commission, August 20, 1996.

"Pan Africanist Congress Probes Election Failure." *Green Left Weekly* (Australia), no. 159, September 14, 1994.

Paton, Alan. *Cry, the Beloved Country*. New York: Charles Scribner's Sons, 1948.

Peebles-Wilkins, Wilma. "Commentary." *Reflections* 2, no. 4 (Fall 1996): 34–35.

Pierce, William. "The Lesson of Amy Biehl." *Free Speech* 4, no. 9 (September 1998). https://nationalsatanist.wordpress.com/2016/06/18/the-lesson-of-amy-biehl/.

"Political Punchlines." *RSA Policy Review* 6, no. 9 (October 1993): 44.

Ramphele, Mamphela. *Across Boundaries: The Journey of a South African Woman Leader*. New York: The Feminist Press, 1999.

———. *Steering by the Stars: Being Young in South Africa*. Cape Town: Tafelberg, 2002.

Reid, Bronwen. "No Place Like Home." *Time* (international edition), March 21, 1994.

Retief, Frank. *Tragedy to Triumph: A Christian Response to Trials and Suffering*. Milton Keynes, UK: Word Publishing, 1994.

Richburg, Keith. *Out of America: A Black Man Confronts Africa*. New York: Basic Books, 1997.

Robert Kennedy in South Africa. Johannesburg: Rand Daily Mail, 1966.

Rogers, Patrick, Kathy Chenault, Jamie Reno, and Nina A. Biddle. "Remembering Amy." *People*, September 8, 1997, 73–74.

Rountree, Ruthann. "Commentary." *Reflections* 2, no. 4 (Fall 1996): 38–39.

"S. Africa Panel Pardons Killers of U.S. Student." *CNN.com*, July 28, 1998.

Saint Gabriel the Archangel Silver Jubilee, 1966–1991. Cape Town: Saint Gabriel Church, c. 1991.

Sampson, Anthony. *Mandela: The Authorized Biography*. New York: Vintage Books, 1999.

Sarkin, Jeremy. *Carrots and Sticks: The TRC and the South African Amnesty Process*. Antwerp: Intersentia, 2004.

Saunders, Christopher, and Nicholas Southey. *A Dictionary of South African History*. Cape Town: David Philip, 1998.

Scheper-Hughes, Nancy. "Who's the Killer? Popular Justice and Human Rights in a South African Squatter Camp." *Social Justice* 22, no. 3 (Fall 1995): 143–65.

———. "Sacred Wounds: Making Sense of Violence." *Theatre Symposium* (Southeastern Theatre Conference and the University of Alabama Press) 7 (1999): 7–30.

———. "After the War Is Over." *Peace Review* 12, no. 3 (September 2000): 423–29.

———. "Dangerous and Endangered Youths: Social Structures and Determinants of Violence." In *Inclusion and Exclusion in the Global Arena*, edited by Max Kirsch, 287–317. New York: Routledge, 2006.

———. "Violence and the Politics of Remorse." In *Subjectivity: Ethnographic Investigations*, edited by João Biehl, Byron Good, and Arthur Kleinman, 179–233. Berkeley: University of California Press, 2007.

Scheper-Hughes, Nancy, and Carolyn Sargent. Introduction to *Small Wars: The Cultural Politics of Childhood,* edited by Nancy Scheper-Hughes and Carolyn Sargent, 1–33. Berkeley: University of California Press, 1998.

Schuller, Robert H. *Turning Hurts into Halos.* Nashville: Thomas Nelson Publishers, 1999.

Senske, Kurt. *Personal Values: God's Game Plan for Life.* Minneapolis: Augsburg Books, 2004.

Shriver, Donald W. "Where and When in Political Life Is Justice Served by Forgiveness?" In *Burying the Past: Making Peace and Doing Justice after Civil Conflict,* edited by Nigel Biggar, 25–43. Washington, D.C.: Georgetown University Press, 2003.

Shriver, Donald, Jr. "Looking beyond Murder." *Christian Century* 115, no. 23 (August 26, 1998): 772–73.

Sonn, Tamara. "The Power of Dialogue: Redefining 'Us.'" In *After Terror: Promoting Dialogue among Civilizations,* edited by Akbar Ahmed and Brian Forst, 131–37. Malden, MA: Polity Press, 2005.

South African Democracy Education Trust. "The Soweto Uprising." In *The Road to Democracy in South Africa.* Vol. 2 (1970–80). http://www.sadet.co.za/docs/RTD/vol2/Volume%20 2%20-%20chapter%207.pdf .

South African History Online. "The Interim South African Constitution, 1993." www.sahistory .org.za/article/interim-south-african-constitution-1993.

South African Institute of Race Relations. *Race Relations Survey 1993/94.* Johannesburg: SAIRR, 1994.

———. *Race Relations Survey 1994/95.* Johannesburg: SAIRR, 1995.

South African Press Association. "Daughter Appeals to Witnesses to Edelstein Killing." July 23, 1996. www.justice.gov.za/trc/media/1996/9607/s960723b.htm.

Sparks, Allister. *Tomorrow Is Another Country: The Inside Story of South Africa's Negotiated Revolution.* Sandton: Struik, 1994.

Stanford University Bulletin: Courses and Degrees, 1989–1990. Stanford, CA: Stanford University, 1989.

"Statement on the Unveiling of Names of Recipients of the National Orders by the Director-General in the Presidency and Chancellor of Orders, Reverend Frank Chikane." South African government information, April 17, 2008. http://www.dirco.gov.za/docs/2008 /ordo418.html.

Stedman, Stephen, ed. *South Africa: The Political Economy of Transformation.* Boulder, CO: Lynne Rienner, 1994.

Steiner, Henry J., Philip Alston, and Ryan Goodman. *International Human Rights in Context: Law, Politics, Morals: Text and Materials.* 3rd ed. New York: Oxford University Press, 2008.

Straker, Gill. *Faces in the Revolution: The Psychological Effects of Violence on Township Youth in South Africa.* Athens: Ohio University Press, 1992.

Tapper, Andrea. "Die Mutter und die Mörder." *Chrismon,* November 2002, 38–43.

Taylor, Peter. "An Honorary African." *Sunday Times Magazine* (London), March 27, 1994.

Taylor, Phil. "'Hell on Wheels,'" *Stanford* 22, no. 1 (March 1994): 26–31.

Thamm, Marianne. "Storming the House." *Femina,* August 1993, 44, 46.

Tharoor, Shashi. *Riot.* New York: Arcade, 2001.

"The Hidden Golfers of South Africa." CNN.SI.com, November 12, 1997. Accessed April 18, 2001. sportsillustrated.cnn.com/features/1997/weekly/971117/gp1117/e.html.

Theroux, Paul. *Dark Star Safari: Overland from Cairo to Cape Town.* Boston: Houghton Mifflin, 2003.

Thomas, Cornelius. *Tangling the Lion's Tale: Donald Card, from Apartheid Era Cop to Crusader for Justice.* East London, SA: Donald Card, 2007.

Thompson, Leonard, and Lynn Berat. *A History of South Africa.* 4th ed. New Haven: Yale University Press, 2014.

To Present a Congressional Gold Medal to Nelson Rolihlahla Mandela. Pub. L. No. 105-215. 1998.

Truth and Reconciliation Commission. *Truth and Reconciliation Commission of South Africa Report.* Vols. 2 and 3. New York: Grove's Dictionaries, 1999.

———. *Truth and Reconciliation Commission of South Africa Report.* Vol. 6. Cape Town: TRC, 2003.

Truth and Reconciliation Commission Amnesty Committee. Biehl amnesty decision, July 28, 1998. www.justice.gov.za/trc/decisions/1998/980728_ntamo%20penietc.htm.

Tutu, Desmond. *No Future without Forgiveness.* New York: Doubleday, 1999.

Tutu, Desmond, and Mpho Tutu. *The Book of Forgiving: The Fourfold Path for Healing Ourselves and Our World.* New York: HarperOne, 2014.

"United States' Policy toward the Transition in South Africa: Hearing before the Subcommittee on Africa of the Committee on Foreign Affairs." House of Representatives, 103rd Congress, 1st session, September 30, 1993. Washington, D.C.: U.S. Government Printing Office, 1994.

van der Leun, Justine. "Portrait of a Township: Former Militants on the Post-Apartheid Struggle." *Harper's Magazine* 328, no. 1966 (March 2014): 52 + 8 pp.

———. *We Are Not Such Things: The Murder of a Young American, a South African Township, and the Search for Truth and Reconciliation.* New York: Spiegel & Grau, 2016.

Van Schalkwyk, Rex. *One Miracle Is Not Enough.* Sandown, SA: Bellweather, 1998.

Verwoerd, Melanie. *Our Madiba: Stories and Reflections from Those Who Met Nelson Mandela.* Cape Town: Tafelberg, 2014

Waldman, Amy. "Amy Biehl Is Dead." *Voice* 39, no. 9 (March 1, 1994): 21–25.

Ward, Amanda Eyre. *Forgive Me.* New York: Random House, 2007.

Warner, Anne P. "From Freedom-Fighting to Forgiveness: How Time and Politics Shaped the Afterlife Narrative of the Amy Biehl Story." Honors thesis for Department of History, Stanford University, May 2012.

Western, John. *Outcast Cape Town.* 2nd ed. Berkeley: University of California Press, 1996.

Wilson, Richard A. *The Politics of Truth and Reconciliation in South Africa: Legitimizing the Post-apartheid State.* New York: Cambridge University Press, 2001.

Winge, Kevin. *Never Give Up: Vignettes from Sub-Saharan Africa in the Age of AIDS.* Minneapolis: Syren Book Co., 2006.

Wisner, Geoff. *A Basket of Leaves: 99 Books That Capture the Spirit of Africa.* Auckland Park, SA: Jacana, 2007.

Woods, Donald. *Rainbow Nation Revisited: South Africa's Decade of Democracy.* London: André Deutsch, 2000.

Xayiya, Sobantu. "'Wrong to Focus on Whites.'" *Democracy in Action* 7, no. 6 (October 15, 1993): 18–19.

FILMS, TELEVISION, AND RADIO

Amy Biehl's memorial service. Videotape recording, September 3, 1993.

"Amy's Story." *60 Minutes.* CBS. January 17, 1999.

Archbishop Tutu with Bill Moyers. Princeton, NJ: Films for the Humanities and Sciences, 1999.

"Carte Blanche." M-Net. August 10, 2003. beta.mnet.co.za/carteblanche/Article.aspx?Id=2293#.

CBS Evening News. CBS. August 27, 1993.

C-Span broadcast honoring Nelson Mandela. December 5, 2013.

The Guguletu Seven. Lindy Wilson, producer and director. 2001.

"The Hate That Hate Produced." Mike Wallace and Louis Lomax, producers. WNTA-TV, July 13–17, 1959.

"Inside the Struggle: The Amy Biehl Story." *Turning Point.* ABC News, April 20, 1994, and August 7, 1997.

KTXL-40 News. Sacramento. August 26, 1993.

Long Night's Journey into Day: South Africa's Search for Truth and Reconciliation. Iris Films. Frances Reid and Deborah Hoffman, directors. 2000.

"Mabandla Hails Slain Student Activist Amy Biehl." SABC. August 17, 2010. www.sabcnews.com.

"Memorial to Amy Biehl Unveiled." News 24. August 26, 2010. www.news24.com/SouthAfrica /News/Memorial-to-Amy-Biehl-unveiled-20100825.

National Democratic Convention. August 16, 2000. https://www.c-span.org/video?158823-2 /democratic-national-convention-day-3-evening.

SABC Television news. August 26, 1993.

Talk of the Nation. National Public Radio. July 30, 1997, and December 26, 2001.

"Test of Time—The Story of Amy Biehl." BBC 2. Andrea Gauld, producer and director. c.1999–2001.

Today Show. NBC. August 27, 1993, and February 11, 2004.

HISTORICAL EXHIBITS

Amy Biehl High School. Albuquerque, New Mexico, 2009.

Apartheid Museum. Johannesburg, 2004.

Sivuyile Tourism Centre. Gugulethu, 2004.

INTERVIEWS

Abernethy, David. Stanford, CA, March 14, 2007.

Asmal, Kader. Cape Town, June 7, 2004.

Biehl, Kim. San Diego, June 3, 2005.

Biehl, Linda. Cape Town, July 15, 2002; Cape Town, June 8, 2004; Newport Beach, CA, July 17–18, 2006; Cape Town, May 31, 2007; Newport Beach, June 3, 2009; Costa Mesa, CA, December 15, 2009.

Biehl, Molly. San Marcos, CA, July 16, 2006.

Biehl, Zach. Newport Beach, CA, June 1, 2005.

Bjornlund, Gina (Giere). Washington, D.C., January 29, 2010.

Bollich, Katie. Burlingame, CA, March 15, 2007.

Boraine, Alex. Cape Town, June 20, 2007 (telephone).

Chubb, Karin. Çape Town, July 22, 2002.

Collard, Margaret Jones. Washington, D.C., January 29, 2010.

Diamond, Larry. Stanford, CA, March 14, 2007.

Friedman, Gerald. Kommetjie, Western Cape, June 22, 2004.

Greenwood-Meinert, Scott. Fresno, CA, June 8, 2005.

Hansrajh, Stanley. Oak Park, CA, June 6, 2005.

Haupt, Paul. Cape Town, July 21, 2004.

Hoemeke, Carole Sams. Suwanee, GA, October 10, 2009.

Jacobs-Randolph, Solange. San Diego, June 2, 2005.

Jansen, Jonathan. Pretoria, July 7, 2004.

Johnson, Lionel. Washington, D.C., February 1, 2010.

Kadalie, Rhoda. Cape Town, June 7, 2004.

Keefer, Patricia. Washington, D.C., January 30, 2010.

Keegan, Clive. Cape Town, June 10, 2004.

Liebenberg, Sandra. Cape Town, July 1, 2004.

Maceba, Maletsatsi. Cape Town, July 20, 2004.

Magona, Sindiwe. Cape Town, July 14, 2004.

Makosana, Solomon. Cape Town, June 21, 2004.

McFaul, Michael. Stanford, CA, March 13, 2007.

Mngqibisa, Cinga. Cape Town, July 15, 2004.

Molotsi, Keneilwe. Johannesburg, July 10, 2004.

Mtuze, Mgwebi. Pretoria, July 7, 2004.

Nofemela, Easy. Cape Town, June 30, 2005 and June 22, 2007.

Orange, Evaron. Cape Town, June 17, 2004.

Peni, Ntobeko. Cape Town, July 25, 2002, and July 20, 2007.

Samoff, Joel. Stanford, CA, March 13, 2007.

Skweyiya, Zola. London, May 21, 2013.

Soosaipillai, Miruni. Redwood City, CA, March 14, 2007.

Stedman, Stephen. Stanford, CA, March 12, 2007.

Tutu, Desmond. Jacksonville, FL, April 29, 2003.

Wang, Anna. Geneva, Switzerland, January 14, 2010 (Skype).

West, Victor. Cape Town, July 13, 2004.

Williams, Greg. Cape Town, July 14, 2004.

TRANSCRIPTS

Congressional Record. Bart Gordon. "A Tribute to Amy Biehl." September 14, 1993. Vol. 139, part 15, 21156–57.

Public Papers of the Presidents of the United States: William J. Clinton, 1993: Book II. Bill Clinton. Remarks on the signing of the South African Democratic Transition Support Act of 1993. November 23, 1993.

The White House. Office of the Press Secretary. "Remarks by President Clinton and President Nelson Mandela at Presentation of Congressional Gold Medal to President Nelson Mandela." September 23, 1998. https://clinton4.nara.gov/textonly/WH/New/html/19980923-977.html.

Truth and Reconciliation Commission. Amnesty hearings for Mongesi (sic) Manqina, Easy Nofemela, Vusumzi Ntamo, and Ntobeko Peni. Cape Town. July 8–9, 1997. http://www.justice.gov.za/trc/amntrans/capetown/capetown_biehl01.htm and http://www.justice.gov.za/trc/amntrans/capetown/capetown_biehl02.htm .

U.S. Department of State. Daily press briefing. August 26, 1993. dosfan.lib.uic.edu/ERC
/briefing/daily_briefings/1993/9308/930826db.html.

WEBSITES

Amy Biehl Foundation Trust. www.amybiehl.co.za and www.facebook.com/pages/Amy-Biehl
-Foundation-Trust (no longer active).

Amy Biehl Foundation—USA. www.amybiehl.org and www.facebook.com/usaabf.

Amy Foundation SA. amyfoundation.co.za and www.facebook.com/AmyBiehlFoundation/SA.

Friends of Amy Biehl. friendsofamybiehl.com (no longer active).

Index